TRANSCULTURAL CHILD DEVELOPMENT

PSYCHOLOGICAL ASSESSMENT AND TREATMENT

**GLORIA JOHNSON-POWELL
AND JOE YAMAMOTO**
EDITORS

GAIL E. WYATT AND WILLIAM ARROYO
ASSOCIATE EDITORS

JOHN WILEY & SONS, INC.

New York • Chichester • Weinheim • Brisbane • Singapore • Toronto

Library of Congress Cataloging-in-Publication Data:

Transcultural child development : psychological
   assessment and treatment / editors Gloria Johnson-Powell and Joe
   Yamamoto ; associate editors Gail E. Wyatt and William Arroyo.
      p.   cm.
   Includes bibliographical references and index.
   ISBN 0-471-17479-3 (alk. paper)
    1. Children of minorities—Mental health—United States.
  2. Psychiatry, Transcultural. 3. Child psychiatry. 4. Child
development—Cross-cultural studies. I. Johnson-Powell, Gloria.
II. Yamamoto, Joe.
RJ507.M54T7 1997
618.92'89—dc21   97-8358

Printed in the United States of America

10 9 8 7 6 5 4 3 2 1

Contributors

William Arroyo, M.D. (Associate
    Editor)
Director, Child and Adolescent
    Psychiatric Clinic
University of Southern
    California
Los Angeles, California

Sonia Bell, M.A.
Graduate School of Education
University of Pennsylvania
Philadelphia, Pennsylvania

Mayka Bouafuely-Kersey
Senior Human Service
    Associate
Department of Psychiatry
University of Minnesota
Minneapolis, Minnesota

Janet M. Camacho, M.S., M.P.H.,
    C.P.N.P.
Honolulu, Hawaii

Ian Canino, M.D.
Clinical Professor
Department of Psychiatry
College of Physicians and
    Surgeons
Columbia University
New York, New York

Davido Dupree, Ph.D.
Graduate School of Education
University of Pennsylvania
Philadelphia, Pennsylvania

Michelle M. Ferrari, M.D.
South Texas Veterans Health
  Care System
Audie L. Murphy Memorial
  Veterans Hospital Division
Department of Psychiatry
San Antonio, Texas

Andrea Guillory, Ph.D.
Assistant Professor,
  Maternal and Child Health
School of Public Health
University of Hawaii at Manoa
Honolulu, Hawaii

Carol Titcomb Hartley, M.D.
Private Pediatrician
Honolulu, Hawaii

Cheng Her, B.S.
Department of Psychiatry
University of Minnesota
Minneapolis, Minnesota

Gloria Johnson-Powell, M.D. Sc.D.
  (Editor)
Professor of Child Psychiatry,
  Harvard Medical School
Senior Advisor on Community
  and Social Policy Research,
  Judge Baker Children's
  Center
Boston, Massachusetts

Luke I. Kim, M.D., Ph.D.
Clinical Professor of Psychiatry
School of Medicine
University of California at Davis
Sacramento, California

Wun Jung Kim, M.D., M.P.H.
Associate Professor and
  Director of Child and
  Adolescent Psychiatry
  Residency Training
Medical College of Ohio at
  Toledo
Toledo, Ohio

Eleanor Lavretsky, M.D., Ph.D.
Gateways Hospital and Mental
  Health Centers
Los Angeles, California

Ann Yu Lung, M.A.
Graduate Student Researcher in
  Clinical Psychology
National Research Center on
  Asian American Mental
  Health
University of California Los
  Angeles
Los Angeles, California

Donald Meland, M.D.
Gateways Hospital and Mental
  Health Centers
Los Angeles, California

Kazutaka Nukariya, M.D.
South Texas Veterans Health
  Care System
Audie L. Murphy Memorial
  Veterans Hospital Division
Department of Psychiatry
San Antonio, Texas

Daniel Plotkin, M.D., M.P.H.
Medical Director
Gateways Hospital and Mental
  Health Center
Los Angeles, California

Veena Kittane Ranganath
Drew/UCLA Medical School
Los Angeles, California

Vijayalakshmi Mandayam Ranganath, M.D.
Assistant Professor, Charles R. Drew Associate Clinical Professor, UCLA Medical School Director, Residency Training, King/Drew Medical Center
Los Angeles, California

Harold Richman, Ph.D.
Center Director and Hermon Dunlap-Smith Professor
Chapin Hall Center for Children
University of Chicago
Chicago, Illinois

David S. Rue, M.D.
Staff Psychiatrist
The Cleveland Clinic Foundation
Cleveland, Ohio

Rolando A. Santos, Ph.D.
Professor, Department of Educational Foundations
School of Education
California State University at Los Angeles
Los Angeles, California

Walid Shekim, M.D.
Clinical Professor of Psychiatry
Department of Psychiatry
Center for The Health Sciences
University of California Los Angeles
Los Angeles, California

J. Arturo Silva, M.D.
South Texas Veterans Health Care System
Audie L. Murphy Memorial Veterans Hospital Division
San Antonio, Texas

Margaret Beale Spencer, Ph.D.
Board of Overseers and Professor of Education
Graduate School of Education
University of Pennsylvania
Philadelphia, Pennsylvania

Stanley Sue, Ph.D.
Professor of Psychology and Director, National Research Center on Asian American Mental Health
UCLA Department of Psychology
Los Angeles, California

Juliette Tuakli-Williams, M.D., M.P.H.
Chestnut Hill, Massachusetts

Faye Untalan, D.S.W., M.P.H.
Associate Professor, Maternal and Child Health
School of Public Health
University of Hawaii at Manoa
Honolulu, Hawaii

Joe Westermeyer, M.D., Ph.D.
Chief, Psychiatry Service
VA Medical Center
Minneapolis, Minnesota

Gail Wyatt, Ph.D. (Associate Editor)
Professor of Medical Psychology
Neuropsychiatric Institute
Department of Psychiatry and Biobehavioral Science
UCLA Center for Health Sciences
Los Angeles, California

Joe Yamamoto, M.D. (Editor)
Professor of Psychiatry
Neuropsychiatric Institute
Department of Psychiatry and Behavioral Sciences
UCLA Center for Health Sciences
Los Angeles, California

Luis H. Zayas, Ph.D.
Associate Professor
Graduate School of Social Service
Fordham University
New York, New York

Foreword

THIS IS A BIG book, with a big title, and an even bigger mission. This is a book for mental health professionals who need an understanding of individual development and treatment issues for children of different backgrounds. It provides an essential beginning appreciation of the developmental themes and contexts for a broad array of ethnic, racial, and cultural groups in this country. This includes not only established minorities but also the newer immigrant groups, and their often stark confrontation with the push and pull of the old and the new. It is impossible to think of understanding a minority child's development and experience or understanding the treatment of these children without the information these chapters provide.

Rich as these chapters are, and hard as it is to imagine providing culturally sensitive or culturally appropriate treatment for a child or family without the information provided here, it is even harder to imagine reading this book and not being inspired to learn more, to deepen one's understanding, and to sharpen one's clinical impressions into generalizable knowledge. Each chapter has some unfinished business, some tantalizing leads, some possible hypotheses that, if followed, promise greater understanding of the expected developmental pathways and family and social contexts for the children under discussion. Without shining yet more light on these pathways, culturally sensitive, appropriate treatment will be more goal than reality. This book is an invitation to learn and a challenge to learn more.

But this book has major significance beyond its function as a reference work for mental health professionals concerned about the functioning and treatment of children from different cultural groups. This is also a book for ministers, schoolteachers, scoutmasters, clinic administrators, physicians, social workers, librarians, and others whose level of understanding can affect the experiences of individual children in navigating a complex environment and whose level of sensitivity can guide the functioning of the institutions that make up that environment.

Reading these chapters together for common themes, rather than individually for differentiating characteristics, one is struck by the critical importance of the community contexts within which minority children develop. These contextual influences on the development of minority children and their families are strong, and similarly significant, across cultural groups. The power of community customs—those of specific cultural communities and also those of the broader community to which they belong—appears in almost every chapter. Such customs can intensify intergenerational conflicts, or they can mediate them; they can exacerbate the task of living in or between two cultures, or they can ease it.

The institutional context within which minority children develop is also especially important. Reading these chapters together, one is sharply reminded of the often decisive roles of schools, health care institutions, and government bureaucracies in the lives of minority children and families and of the power of these institutions to ease or complicate successful development. There are also accounts in these chapters of the roles that other institutions such as churches, clubs, scouts, and sport leagues can play in providing a nurturing and enabling context for development.

There is yet one more meaning to this book. The Contents is a lesson in contemporary American society, an exercise in defining inclusion and a challenge to go from word to deed. In this era, children represent a diminishing proportion of our country's population, and an increasing percentage of children in that diminishing proportion are minority children. These are the children who will shortly share responsibility for the conduct and success of our social, economic, and political institutions. It is therefore deeply in our collective interest that *every* child develop to contribute to our democracy, whose strength is the coming together of many cultures in common enterprise. We are challenged today by demography, by self-interest, and by the elemental notions of fairness and decency to renew that special strength. I can think of no better way to address that challenge than to read this book for its instruction in normal differences and for the implications of that instruction for the functioning of our communities, our institutions, and our democracy.

HAROLD RICHMAN

Chapin Hall Center for Children
University of Chicago
Chicago, Illinois

Preface

WITH THE RAPIDLY INCREASING diversity of the population of the United States, children and families with different cultural, ethnic, and linguistic backgrounds from every corner of the earth can be found in our schools and in our health and human service systems. In 1983, with the publication of *The Psychosocial Development of Minority Group Children*, we attempted to address the needs of this population of children who were invisible in our systems of care, particularly in child psychiatry (Powell, Yamamoto, Romero, & Morales, 1983).

Although transcultural psychiatry has emerged as an important area of research in adult psychiatry, it has not permeated child psychiatry, nor has much attention been paid to the cultural context of the development of children despite such studies in the anthropological literature. The assessment and treatment of culturally and linguistically diverse children has rarely been addressed in child mental health training or service programs.

With the update of the *Diagnostic and Statistical Manual of Mental Disorders (DSM-IV)*, the National Institute of Mental Health convened a special task force to examine the cultural appropriateness of the diagnostic categories for *DSM-IV*, and the publication of its findings is a significant contribution to transcultural psychiatry (Mezzich, Kleinman, Fabrega, & Parron, 1996). However, the application of transcultural psychiatry for children still lags behind that for adults because of the lack of research on the cultural influences in developmental psychopathology.

This volume is designed to provide a bridge between culture and the psychiatric diagnosis of children and adolescents based on four basic premises. First, culture is the context or environment in which various kinds of behavior are developed and expressed. Second, both the context and the content of learning from birth through childhood and adolescence are distinctly cultural. Third, the child's early experiences as a member of an ethnic/racial or cultural group are significant in shaping behavior, organizing and expressing emotions, and discovering ways to meet social and emotional needs. The fourth premise is that information about each racial/ethnic or cultural group is necessary to provide culturally relevant assessment and treatment. Clinicians or service providers cannot rely on the stereotypes of racial/ethnic or cultural groups, but must have knowledge about the social and cultural contexts in which different groups of children grow and learn, recognizing that differences are not deficits. Because of the increased diversity of children in our service systems, mental health professionals need to know specific cultural norms and behaviors—the ways in which different cultural groups think, perceive, and experience the world, and the unique ways of help-seeking behavior that are culturally determined.

This book presents varied ethnic/racial or cultural groups, their histories, beliefs, and cultural patterns of behavior, as well as the stressors in their lives and their ways of expressing the absence of well-being and psychiatric illness. Because research on psychiatric disorders is lacking for some cultural groups and more available for others, some chapters focus more on cultural beliefs and less on psychiatric symptoms whereas others provide both perspectives. With better understanding of culture and behavior for each group, the assessment and treatment process will be more culturally sensitive and appropriate.

Acknowledgments

Funds for editorial assistance and review of manuscripts for this book were provided by a 2-year grant from the van Ameringen Foundation, Inc., in New York City. Although the views and interpretations expressed are those of the editors and contributing authors and are not necessarily those of the van Ameringen Foundation, Inc., the publication of the book would not have been possible without its generous commitment to programs addressing mental health services for disadvantaged and underserved populations in America.

We would also like to acknowledge Sofia I. Albino, Melanie Wilson Williams, Jennie Munoz-Lewis, Rodney N. Powell, and Deborah Harrison Gulfield who helped in the preparation and coordination of the manuscripts. Additionally, we are grateful for the ongoing support of the Judge Baker Children's Center and The Behavioral HealthCare Network of Massachusetts, Inc., during the preparation of this manuscript.

GLORIA JOHNSON-POWELL
JOE YAMAMOTO

Dedication

Lives of great men all remind us we can make our lives sublime.
Longfellow

This book is dedicated to an extraordinary human being, a wise mentor, and a generous friend, Dr. Louis Jolyon West. I first met Dr. West during my third year of a 5-year psychiatric training program at the Neuropsychiatric Institute at the UCLA Center for Health Sciences. He was friendly, approachable, and willing to provide guidance and counseling to an aspiring academician. I was in the throes of my national study on school desegregation, which was graciously and generously supported by many faculty members, including Dr. West. I was too young, then, to appreciate who he really was. I knew simply that he was a friend of Dr. Chester Pierce, another mentor of mine, and that was sufficient for me. Youth, indeed, is wasted on the young.

Dr. West was, in fact, an agent of change, and there was great controversy about his recommendations for the Department of Psychiatry and for the Neuropsychiatric Institute. These changes were to make the Department of Psychiatry and Biobehavioral Sciences one of the most outstanding departments in the country.

I left and wandered about the world, and returned to UCLA to join the faculty in 1974. It was at that time that Dr. West began his travels to South Africa to testify on behalf of Black South African prisoners regarding brainwashing (West, 1985), and I began to recognize his compassion and professional stature. We would have long talks about Africa—South Africa, in particular. At that juncture in my life, I already had spent four years in Africa, in Ethiopia, Tanganyika, Uganda, and then again to Tanzania, formerly Tanganyika. I had also traveled throughout South Africa where I was considered to be "an honorary White" because I was the wife of an official U.S. government employee. I had witnessed the days of "Uhuru" in Tanganyika and Kenya, the reign of terror in Uganda, and had become acquainted with the various liberation movements throughout Africa. It was gratifying for me to share my opinions and observations of the struggle for freedom in South Africa including the instrumental effect of the U.S. Civil Rights movement of the 1960s on the efforts toward independence throughout Africa.

Dr. West shared with me his experiences with the sit-ins in Oklahoma, and I shared with him my activities with the student sit-ins and freedom rides during my years in medical school. He also talked at length about the South African prisoners and the preparation for his trip to South Africa for the trials. How truly wonderful to find someone who could understand how I perceived myself and how my experiences had shaped my goals for a career in psychiatry, particularly my interest in the psychosocial development of minority group children. Slowly I began to understand his expansive personality and his fervent belief in humanistic approaches for resolving inhumanity throughout the world.

Dr. Pierce had shared with me his connections to Dr. West, and when I met Dr. Yamamoto, another mentor of mine, I learned that his path in life had also crossed Dr. West's. From both of them, I learned of his tireless clinical and community service dedicated to helping people "with unwavering courage and insistence on equality for all" (Pierce, 1992). Dr. West's career before coming to the Neuropsychiatric Institute had been luminary not only because of the positions he had, but also because of his commitment to his views about social equality and the curtailing of interpersonal and intergroup violence, based on his studies of the Tarahumara Indians (West, Paredes, & Snow, 1969).

Dr. West has always been a leader, a visionary, and an idealist. It was he who articulated that psychiatry needed to have a biopsychosociocultural focus and particularly an emphasis on culture and ethnicity. "His life," writes Dr. Yamamoto, his medical school classmate, "has followed a rapid-rising trajectory and a fulfillment of his medical student daydreams of becoming the chairperson of the best department of psychiatry in America" (Yamamoto, 1992, p. 97).

And so I came to know Dr. Louis Jolyon West as the chairperson of a dynamic department of psychiatry, a teacher, a mentor, and a dear friend. To know him is to respect and admire him for his courage and kindness, to experience a constant and endearing friend, and to love him for all he has given to me and to so many other people.

GLORIA JOHNSON-POWELL

References

MEZZICH, J. E., KLEINMAN, A., FABREGA, H., & PARRON, D. L. (Eds.). (1996). *Culture and psychiatric diagnosis: A DSM-IV perspective.* Washington, DC: American Psychiatric Association Press.

PIERCE, C. M. (1992). Contemporary psychiatry: Racial perspectives on the past and future. In A. Kales, C. M. Pierce, & M. Greenblatt (Eds.), *The mosaic of contemporary psychiatry in perspective.* New York: Springer-Verlag.

POWELL, G. J., YAMAMOTO, J., ROMERO, A., & MORALES, A. (Eds.). (1983). *The psychosocial development of minority group children.* New York: Brunner/Mazel.

WEST, L. J., PAREDES, A., & SNOW, C. C. (1969, May). *Sanity in the Sierra Madre: The Tarahumera Indians.* Paper presented at the 122nd annual meeting, American Psychiatric Association, Miami Beach, FL.

WEST, L. J. (1985). Effects of isolation on the evidence of detainees. In A. B. Bell & R. D. A. Mackie (Eds.), *Detention and security legislation in South Africa* (pp. 69–80). Durbin, South Africa: University of Natal.

YAMAMOTO, J. (1992). Psychohistorical view of transcultural psychiatry. In A. Kales, C. M. Pierce, & M. Greenblatt (Eds.), *The mosaic of contemporary psychiatry in perspective.* New York: Springer-Verlag.

Contents

PART III

CULTURE AND ASSESSMENT

PART I

CULTURE AND CHILD DEVELOPMENT

CHAPTER 1

A Portrait of America's Children: Social, Cultural, and Historical Context

GLORIA JOHNSON-POWELL

I am not made for one corner of the world. The whole world is my native land. . . .

Anonymous

The Creation of the American Mosaic

BETWEEN 1820 AND 1980, more than 49 million immigrants came to the United States, making it the most culturally diverse country in the modern world (Conk, 1985). Sowell (1981) observed, "The sheer magnitude of American ethnic communities makes them autonomous cultures with lives of their own" (p. 3). These culturally diverse communities constitute the mosaic of American society, which includes people from almost everywhere in the world:

> The mixture of diversity runs through American history as through American society today. No ethnic group has been wholly unique, and yet no two are completely alike. Each group has its own geographic distribution pattern, reflecting conditions when they arrived on American soil and the evolution of the industries and regions to which they became attached. (Sowell, 1981, p. 4)

The history of how and why the United States became such a large ethnically, culturally, and linguistically diverse nation is the history of a changing world—and very often the history of people's inhumanity toward one another. The context in which American children today live and learn is largely determined by the history of immigration to this country as well as by the history of the indigenous people—immigrants, migrants, minorities, slaves, and refugees who are part of the American mosaic. Because the context in which a child lives is so important in understanding the developmental process, this chapter will present a brief overview of the history of immigration, the legislation that influenced immigration patterns, and the ethnic/racial demographic patterns that have emerged.

According to the 1995 census, between 1960 and 1990, 11.5 million persons immigrated to the United States (U.S. Department of Health and Human Services [DHHS], 1996). Unlike the previous waves of massive immigration between 1890 and 1920, these new immigrants were not primarily men alone, in search of work; they came with families. The percentage of children and youth in the United States who are foreign-born has been increasing steadily over the past several decades from 1.2% in 1970 to 3.7% in 1990 with the percentage of foreign-born highest for older children. In 1990, children under the age of 5 represented 1.5% or 1 out of every 15 foreign-born youth.

The percentage of foreign-born youth differs depending on racial and ethnic background. In 1980, 40% of Asian, 14% of Hispanic, and less than 2% of White, African American, and Native American children and youth were foreign-born (U.S. DHHS, 1996). By 1990, the percentage of foreign-born Hispanic or Latino children increased to 32.2% and that for foreign-born Asian children decreased to 33.2%. By 1990, 3.7% of all U.S. children 19 years and under were foreign-born with 6.5% between 15 and 19 years old, 4.3% between 10 and 14 years old, 1.4% between 5 and 9 years old, and 1.5% under 5 years old. These data included legal and illegal immigrants, but do not indicate the birth rates of the new immigrants who have settled permanently in the United States.

Data on immigration, population change, and family environment of children under 18 years old for 1990 showed the following percentages of immigrant children (U.S. DHHS, 1996):

69.1%	White, non-Hispanic
14.7	Black, non-Hispanic
1.0	American Indian, Eskimo, and other
3.1	Asian and Pacific Islander
12.1	Hispanic of any race

The Asian and Pacific Islander children and youth had the following composition:

7.0%	Pacific Islanders
9.4	Vietnamese
12.0	Koreans
11.1	Asian Indians
7.7	Japanese
18.6	Filipinos
18.8	Chinese
15.4	Other Asians

Among the Hispanic children of any race, the following composition was noted:

3.3%	South Americans
4.9	Central Americans
2.2	Dominican Republicans
2.6	Cubans
12.2	Puerto Ricans
66.7	Mexicans
8.1	Unidentified

Mexico is the country of origin for the largest foreign-born immigrant group in the United States, representing 21.7% of the total. Other groups of foreign-born are from the Philippines, Canada, Cuba, Germany, United Kingdom, Italy, Korea, Vietnam,

China, and El Salvador to name some of the many countries of origin. However, 45.7% of foreign-born come from countries other than those mentioned here, increasing an already diverse immigrant population (U.S. DHHS, 1996).

THE NATIVE MINORITIES AND THE NEW IMMIGRANTS

The changes in the immigration patterns over the past three decades have altered ethnicity in the United States, especially in large cities. In the early 1960s, almost two-thirds of all U.S. immigrants entered from Europe (45%) and Canada (12%) (Maldonado & Moore, 1985). A decade later, however, the majority of new arrivals or "new immigrants" (post-1965 Immigration Act) were arriving from Asia and Latin America with less than one-third coming from Europe and Canada. This shift in the origin of immigrants as well as their tendency to arrive with families has contributed to an even greater cultural diversity in urban America than the immigrations from Central, Southern, and Eastern Europe between 1890 and 1920. These new immigrant families represent a changing pattern of immigration that expands the role of transcultural psychiatry and the particular significance and timeliness of transcultural child psychiatry, as discussed by Yamamoto, Silva, Ferrari, and Nukariya (Chapter 2). Mental health professionals and service providers cannot be concerned with just "one corner of the world" because the whole world is now part of our native land.

The Immigration Act of 1965 restructured the U.S. immigration laws and highlighted family unification as the major goal, repealed the historic preference for Northern and Western European nations, discontinued the exclusion of Asians, and allowed entry based on occupational skills and refugee status (Wong, 1985). The limit imposed on immigration from the Western Hemisphere (120,000 per year) and the increase of immigration from the Eastern Hemisphere (170,000 per year), with no nation allowed more than 20,000, saw "the browning" of America (Conk, 1985).

Although the National Origins Acts of 1924 ended the historic American immigration policy, it did not end the migration of unskilled workers to large cities (Conk, 1985). From 1920 to 1970, 15 million (300,000 per year) African Americans migrated to industrial urban centers. Between 1940 and 1970, the numbers of Puerto Ricans in the U.S. mainland increased from 70,000 to 1.4 million, the vast majority of whom became urban dwellers. Meanwhile, the migration of Mexicans, which had increased steadily since the early part of the century, continued first as the migratory agricultural labor for farms of the Southwest and, by 1940, as the unskilled labor force in large industrial cities. Additionally, the Civil Rights movement of the 1960s rekindled the struggle of Native Americans and Asian Americans, who became part of the emerging voice of the minority population. These groups along with those pre-1965 immigrants are viewed as the "old minorities" (Powell, Yamamoto, Romero, & Morales, 1983).

Although the 1965 immigration legislation, which was signed by President Lyndon Johnson in front of the Statue of Liberty, ostensibly repudiated racial and ethnic discrimination, preference was given to those with professional occupations and skills (Wong, 1985). Hence, the new immigrants in contrast to many of the old minorities tend to have higher levels of educational attainment as well as personal and financial resources that help them flourish in their new country; this is particularly true of sophisticated Asians and Africans. Maldonado and Moore (1985) have astutely noted:

> Although most of the social research on race and ethnic issues has focused on Black-White relations, it may not be accurate to assume that the paradigm of that research will provide the kind of information and insight into the social and economic experience of the newest arrivals. (p. 15)

Nowhere has the clash of cultures been more obvious and destructive than during the Los Angeles uprising of 1992, which became symbolic of the needs of the native minorities and the strivings of the new immigrants as well as the lack of knowledge each group had about the other. African Americans did not understand the cultural values of the newer immigrated Korean Americans and vice versa. The ethnocentrism of each group resulted in animosity and conflicts.

The children of the most recent influx of immigrants represent a generation far different from any this country has known before (Fernandez & Velez, 1985; Garcia, 1985; Lieberson & Waters, 1990; Portes, 1996). They are largely non-White and come from the world's developing nations. Portes (1996) provides a poignant picture of these children, who, like the children of the old minorities, experience discrimination in the labor market, struggle with complex problems of racial and ethnic relations in multicultural urban neighborhoods, and attend troubled inner-city schools (Portes, 1995). Children of the old minorities and of the new immigrants face an economy that no longer provides the manufacturing jobs that helped previous immigrants sustain themselves and their families (Maldonado & Moore, 1985; Portes, 1995, 1996). This is the social, economic, cultural, and political context in which America's children live and learn and the context in which mental health professionals and other human services providers are challenged to provide a system of care for culturally and linguistically diverse children and their families.

CHILDREN OF ASIAN IMMIGRANTS AND
PACIFIC ISLANDERS

The Asian American population is now more than 7 million, double the population in 1980 (Chan, 1992b). It is expected that by the year 2000 the Asian American population will have grown to nearly 10 million people (U.S. DHHS, 1996). The increase in the Asian American population, the most rapidly growing ethnic/racial group in America, has been attributed to the 1965 Immigration and Naturalization Act Amendments and the withdrawal of the United States from Vietnam in 1975. Asian refugees and immigrants make up half of all admissions to the United States, more than any other racial/ethnic group in the world (U.S. DHHS, 1996). The Asian American population is very diverse. Its heterogeneity is due to ethnic, sociocultural, and linguistic differences; the geographic origins in Asia (see Table 1–1); differences in political and economics circumstances in their homeland; time of arrival; and the factors that influence their adaptation to the United States (Barringer, Gardner, & Levin, 1995; Chan, 1992b). Although Asian Americans have been hailed as the "Model Minority," the new Asian immigrants still may find themselves viewed as "enigmatic, mysterious strangers" and may be victimized by hate crimes as the "new yellow peril" (Chan, 1992a, 1992b; Takaki, 1989).

Chan (1992b) notes that understanding the histories of the Asian immigrant population is important in the delivery of human services. For services to be effective, children and their families must be viewed within an ecological context, which means that the clinician or provider needs specific knowledge of traditional beliefs, values, and practices, especially those pertaining to family, religion, childbearing, education, health, mental health, and disability. Additionally, language characteristics, communication styles, and cultural orientations and behaviors have been shown to relate to service utilization (Chan, 1992b; Yu & Sue, Chapter 11).

The chapters in this book include several Pacific Islander and Asian American groups: the Hmong, Chinese Americans, Asian Indians, Korean Americans, Filipino Americans, Hawaiians, and Micronesians. Although this is not an exhaustive or

TABLE 1–1
Geographic Origins of Asian Americans

East Asia	Southeast Asia	South Asia
China	Indonesia Singapore Cambodia	India
Japan	Malaysia Laos Philippines	Pakistan
Korea	Vietnam Myanmar (Burma) Thailand	Sri Lanka

comprehensive inclusion of all the Pacific Islander and Asian American groups, it nonetheless provides a view of unique customs, traditions, values, beliefs, and family systems based on political and religious foundations that are thousands of years old.

Although there are many similarities, there are also unique differences among the groups. Asian Indians and Filipinos are generally proficient in English; recent Chinese, Korean, and Southeast Asian immigrants such as the Hmong are not (Chan, 1992a, 1992b). Significant growth is expected among Southeast Asian immigrants because the birth rate for Southeast Asian women between 14 and 40 years of age is almost double the average national birth rate in the United States (Chan, 1992b). On the other hand, the Japanese American population is shrinking because of the significant number of outgroup marriages (Yamamoto & Kubota, 1983).

Because Asian immigration to the United States is expected to remain high as families with infants and young children increase in number, and because Asian Americans represent diverse cultural backgrounds, the access to services will present a challenge as their service needs increase. Chapters 8 and 15 give a picture of Hawaiian and Micronesian children with considerable information about their cultural and social circumstances. Chapter 7 provides similar data about Filipino children, and Chapter 6 focuses on Asian Indians.

CHILDREN OF CHINESE IMMIGRANTS

Yu and Sue (Chapter 11) give a brief demographic update and note that Chinese Americans originate from many different areas dominated by China (i.e., Hong Kong, Taiwan, and numerous Southeast Asian countries). Chinese were the first of the early Asian immigrants. They left the Canton province of Guangdong in the late 1840s attracted by the discovery of gold in California (Chan, 1992b). The Chinese Exclusion Act of 1882 was enacted to address "The Chinese Problem," and by 1922 all Asian immigration was banned. In 1943, when China became an American ally, the Chinese Exclusion Act was repealed. Before the Act was repealed, however, Chinese immigrants faced institutional racism, continuous humiliation, and racial violence as well as loss of property, livelihood, and sometimes lives. Chinatowns were created to organize urban and rural communities built on service industries. Despite the repeal of the Chinese Exclusion Act in 1943, for almost twenty years, only 105 Chinese were permitted to enter the United States and half of them had to be professionals. The Immigration and Naturalization Act of 1965 allowed 22,000 immigrants from each country in the Eastern Hemisphere, but family members were not included in that quota (Wong, 1985).

Thus, the second wave of Asian immigrants began after 1965, and within 15 years Chinese Americans surpassed Japanese Americans as the largest Asian American population (Chan, 1992b). At the same time, nearly two-thirds of all Asian Americans in 1980 were foreign-born. The second wave of Chinese immigrants are considered to be the most highly skilled immigrant group that has ever entered the United States (Takaki, 1989). They are settlers, not sojourners, and they bring their families. The "new Chinese immigrants" speak Mandarin as well as Cantonese, originate primarily from urban areas, and reside primarily in California and New York. Most of these immigrants were initially refugees from the People's Republic of China and usually came to the United States from a second point of departure (e.g., Taiwan or Hong Kong). In 1979, China normalized relations with the United States and was given its own quota. Consequently, there were major increases in immigration as family members tried to unite with their relatives in the United States.

The third wave of Chinese immigration gained momentum between 1978 and 1980 when the ethnic Chinese in Southeast Asia began to face discrimination by the new Communist regime. These "boat people" who escaped in boats, many of which were not seaworthy, came as refugees to the United States in large numbers. The plight of other Southeast Asian immigrants is noted by Westermeyer, Bouafuely-Kersey, and Her (Chapter 9), and will be discussed in greater detail in that chapter. On July 1, 1997, Britain's 99-year lease on the territory that extends from Kowloon to the Chinese borders expired and Hong Kong became a Special Administrative Region of China (Barringer, Gardner, &

Levin, 1995). Large numbers of Hong Kong immigrants already have settled in the Canadian provinces of Ontario and British Columbia where they have accelerated the development of urban and suburban Chinatowns. However, bipolar Chinese American communities have emerged consisting of, on the one hand, an entrepreneurial well-educated professional middle class and, on the other hand, a group of low-wage laborers and service workers. Except for Southeast Asian refugees, the Chinese have the highest number of persons living below the poverty level of all the Asian American groups (Chan, 1992b).

CHILDREN OF KOREAN IMMIGRANTS

Koreans have immigrated to America in three waves. Between 1903 and 1905, approximately 7,000 Koreans immigrated to Hawaii to work on sugar plantations, because of a decline in Chinese and Japanese workers. The first wave also came to escape the Japanese imperial government as well as the poverty, famine, and drought in Korea (Chan, 1992b; Yu & Kim, 1983). Additionally, between 1910 and 1924 about 1,000 "picture brides" who responded to newspaper advertisements, and another 900 Korean students, intellectuals, and political exiles were denied U.S. citizenship and became a small and isolated group widely dispersed without a country. Such communities were organized around the Nationalist Korean Movement, which sought to end Japanese rule in Korea. Between 1945 and 1964, the second wave of Korean immigrants were Korean War brides of American servicemen and war orphans less than 4 years of age. At this time, three-fourths of all Korean immigrants were young women and children who were dependents of American citizens. They dispersed around the country, assimilated, and became known as the "hidden minority" (Chan, 1992b; Yu & Kim, 1983).

A new wave of Korean immigration began after 1965, and the Korean population grew rapidly; by 1976 Korean immigration was exceeding 30,000 annually. Overurbanization, an oversupply of highly educated people, human rights issues, and the desire for greater opportunities are some of the reasons that have promoted Korean immigration since 1976 (Chan, 1992b; Kim,

1987). Most Korean immigrants have settled in Los Angeles, New York City, and Chicago and are widely dispersed particularly in suburban areas.

Although most recent Korean immigrants are well educated, overcome the language difficulties, adjust to American social customs, embark on new financial ventures, and disperse themselves throughout society, some are unable to do so and turn to self-employment or self-owned businesses located primarily in African American and Latino communities (Portes, 1996). Many Korean immigrants face not only family stresses and generational conflicts, but also interethnic strife. Yu and Kim (1983) and Kim, Kim, and Rue (Chapter 10) discuss the immigrant parent-child conflicts that may arise because of communication problems when children are mainly English-speaking. There are continuous acculturation clashes, and the lack of availability of parents who work long hours results in unsupervised children. Chan (1992b) notes that these problems are particularly germane for the generation of school-age children whose parents were not born in the United States. These Koreans lose their original language skills and do not acquire a positive identity with Korean or American culture. Such conflicts are inimical to family stability.

CHILDREN OF HISPANIC OR LATINO IMMIGRANTS

The term *Hispanic* is used by the U.S. Census Bureau to designate a population within the United States whose first language is Spanish and/or come from areas of the world that formerly were dominated by Spanish settlers or were under the rule of Spain. *Latino* is another term often heard. Depending on the geographic region of the United States, either word may be used to refer to this Spanish-speaking group of Americans, many of whom come from Mexico, Central America, South America, Puerto Rico, Cuba, and other islands in the Caribbean, as well as those who come from Brazil and speak Portuguese, and are always referred to as Latino and Latinas. The Hispanic population includes people who are White, those who are of African ancestry, and those who are descendants of Native Americans or are of mixed racial ancestry. Mexican Americans are the largest group and Puerto Ricans are the second largest (see Chapters 3 and 14). Central and South Americans make up 11.5% of all Hispanics; Cubans make up 5.3%; and those from Spain make up 8.1% (Zuniga, 1992).

No matter what term is used (Latino, Hispanic, or Spanish-speaking), this population is diverse in many ways. Although this book includes chapters on Puerto Rican, Mexican American, and Central American children, a discussion of Cuban immigrant children later in this chapter as well as immigrants from the Dominican Republic, Belize, and other countries in the Caribbean and South America are also part of the American mosaic. Many populations discussed in this chapter (e.g., Mexican American, Puerto Rican) are referred to as "immigrants from North America"; immigrants from Canada, who also often belong to diverse racial/ethnic groups, are included. The actual dispute as to how to label those immigrants whose ancestors came from the Iberian Peninsula to the New World speaks to the incredible diversity among the Latino/Hispanic population.

CHILDREN OF MEXICAN IMMIGRANTS

The history of immigration from Mexico includes not only three great waves of people moving into the United States, but also two massive deportation periods between them (Wong, 1985). The first wave began in the early 20th century when Mexican immigrants came to work on the railroad as construction workers, watchmen, or laborers. Shortly thereafter, jobs opened up for them in agriculture and mining. Although some seasonal migratory labor went north to the Rocky Mountains or northern California, most Mexican immigrants settled near the borders of Mexico. During the 1930s, less than 10% of Mexican workers had migrated to the factories in more urban settings; contrary to their more populated urban communities today, early Mexican immigrants lived in rural areas. Whether working on American farms or in factories, the early immigrants were poor by American standards, but prosperous by Mexican standards. Although many intended to stay only temporarily until they could accumulate money, some of these workers never returned to Mexico. In the Southwest, which had the heaviest concentration of Mexican immigrants, they were viewed with disdain and mandated by law to segregated facilities, especially in Texas (Sowell, 1981). However, the 1924 immigration laws that stemmed the tide of immigration from most European countries also decreased the flow of Mexican migration.

The depression of the 1930s brought the first wave to a halt with large-scale deportation. Then during World War II, with labor shortages on the farms, Mexican immigrant contract workers were brought into the country on an emergency basis. In 1945, there were about 50,000 Mexican contract laborers and by 1950 there were 400,000; the program was ended in 1964 (Bean & Tienda, 1990; Lieberson & Waters, 1990).

The urbanization of Mexican immigrants was expanded by jobs in industry that in turn increased the immigration from 2,000 people in 1940 to 10,000 by 1952. In 1956, more than 65,000 Mexican immigrants entered the United States, equal to about one-fourth of all immigrants from the rest of the world (Bean & Tienda, 1990). By 1947, there were mass deportations; in 1950, 500,000 Mexican immigrants were expelled; and in 1951 more than one million were forced to leave (Bean & Tienda, 1990; Lieberson & Waters, 1990; Sowell, 1981).

The third wave of immigration which began in 1959 has led to a diverse population of Mexican Americans due to changes in the immigration laws that allowed families to enter. Over time, economic, political, and social changes in Mexico itself have affected the diversity of Mexican immigrants coming to the United States; more urbanized immigrants have arrived in the third wave than in the earlier ones. Generations differ greatly, and significant differences between native-born Mexican Americans and Mexican immigrants also exist. Zuniga (1992) noted that many Mexican Americans in the United States are not immigrants, have lived in this country for many generations, and can trace their ancestry to the 1700s.

Mexico's economic instability and political problems have been a major impetus for immigration to the United States, both legal and illegal. In 1985, the Simpson-Mazzoli Immigration Act was proposed to stop undocumented immigration, but the bill did not pass because of the economic threat to vested interest groups. Illegal immigration has been a major issue among Mexican Americans because of the shared border between Mexico and the United States (Vega, Hough, & Romero, 1983). However, illegal immigration has also been a difficult issue for other ethnic groups. The effects of illegal entry on immigrant children are discussed later in this chapter. Chapters 4 and 14 by Arroyo explore the specific and unique impact of illegal immigration on Mexican American children and children from Central America.

PUERTO RICAN CHILDREN

Puerto Rico has been part of the United States since the late 19th century and Puerto Ricans are born American citizens. The United States acquired Puerto Rico in 1898, at the end of the Spanish-American war, and Puerto Ricans have had legal citizenship since 1917. Yet, for many of them, mainland society seems foreign. Zuniga (1992) describes the culture shock experienced by Puerto Ricans when the first wave of migration began, and the creation of the barrios. Official statistics mark the massive movements of migration, but in the case of Puerto Ricans, no accurate records reflect the number of people that come to the U.S. mainland, or the number who return to the island (Bean & Tienda, 1990). Such frequent movement between Puerto Rico and the mainland may explain the difficulty in acculturation Puerto Ricans have experienced, not unlike that of French Canadians who returned frequently to Canada in the earlier period of their immigration. Nonetheless, by 1970, there were more Puerto Ricans in New York City than there were in San Juan and about half as many Puerto Ricans in Puerto Rico as there were in the United States (Sowell, 1981). Puerto Ricans represent a multiracial and multiethnic background consisting of European or Spanish settlers, Native American, and African ancestry. According to Sowell, however, the traditions of African slaves disappeared more rapidly in Puerto Rico than in other Caribbean islands.

Substantial migration from Puerto Rico began in the 1930s, but it increased significantly after World War II (Portes, 1996; Sowell, 1981; Zuniga, 1992). Puerto Ricans have settled primarily in New York, but also elsewhere along the Eastern seaboard in Massachusetts, New Jersey, Pennsylvania, and Connecticut. Puerto Ricans also migrated west to Chicago and San Francisco following the usual pattern of settling where there were established Puerto Rican communities. Puerto Ricans have the highest poverty rate among Hispanics and are the second largest Hispanic group (Bean & Tienda, 1990; Zuniga, 1992). Although language differences have complicated the education of Puerto Ricans in U.S. mainland schools, the language problems of Puerto Ricans are similar to those encountered by Italian Americans who also had persistent back-and-forth migrations to their country of origin (Sowell, 1981). Canino and Zayas (Chapter 3) discuss the issue of bilingualism and the differences among Puerto Ricans of different generations as well as the different rates of acculturation. Second-generation Puerto Ricans had significant upward mobility in the 1970s, but the Puerto Rican population as a whole is very young, and consequently many challenges exist in providing health and human services that are linguistically and culturally competent (Canino & Zayas, Chapter 3; U.S. DHHS, 1996).

AFRICAN AMERICAN CHILDREN OR AMERICAN CHILDREN OF AFRICAN ANCESTRY

The very term *African American* connotes the diversity of the American population with African ancestry who were brought to the New World populated by Native Americans and European settlers. The African slave trade to the Western Hemisphere included many African tribal groups, primarily from West Africa. In addition to their diverse African origins, slaves were sent to many countries in the New World (e.g., the United States, Caribbean Islands, South America), and some were emancipated long before the American Civil War. African Americans also include a multiethnic group of people with some European or Native American ancestry. The regional diversity among African

Americans is another factor to be aware of; New England African Americans may be very different from those who come from Louisiana and those from Louisiana will have some distinct differences from African Americans of Texas.

Another important aspect of this mix affects persons of African ancestry whose slave ancestors landed in the Caribbean Islands, which were colonized by the English, the French, and the Spanish. Consequently, a subgroup of African Americans called West Indians come from the former English colonies (Jamaica, Barbados, Trinidad, the Bahamas, St. Kitts, and Nevis) or from the U.S. Virgin Islands (St. Thomas, St. Croix, or St. Johns) and speak English. Although some mores and customs of the West Indians are similar to those of African Americans who have lived on the U.S. mainland since the slave trade began in the 1600s, many others are distinct and indigenous to the islands. Additionally, there are French-speaking African Americans, primarily from Haiti; Spanish-speaking African Americans, from former Spanish colonies in the Caribbean, Central America, and South America; and those who speak Portuguese and come primarily from the former Portuguese colony of Cape Verde, off the west coast of Africa. Most Cape Verdeans in the United States live on the East Coast, particularly in Massachusetts.

Finally, some members of the African American population are new immigrants, who have come from Africa since the ratification of the 1965 Immigration and Naturalization Act. These African Americans, unlike African Americans with slave ancestry, came of their own volition. They tend to be well educated and come with technical and professional skills. The majority are from West Africa, primarily English speakers, and come for economic or political reasons. Others come from East Africa (Ethiopia, Somalia, Uganda, Kenya) or from South Africa to seek educational opportunities or to escape economic hardships and political turmoil.

Most African immigrants settle in the Northeast, but the patterns of settlement are dependent on where others from their country, tribal group, or village have settled. Because of the well-known African Studies Program at the University of California, a diverse population of Africans live in the Los Angeles area. Providence, Rhode Island, is thought to have the largest concentration of Liberians, although there are many Liberian immigrants in Boston and Washington, DC. Chapter 13 on Nigerian children, by Tuakli-Williams, illustrates how these new immigrants retain their cultural beliefs in their new homelands and why. Their worldview, like that of other immigrants from the Eastern Hemisphere, is different from the view of Western Europeans or North Americans as well as from that of West Indians and U.S. African Americans. It is important for clinicians to understand these differences and not assume that because African immigrants are Black, they consider themselves to be African Americans. Most will identify themselves as "African" or use the name of the country of origin; for example, "Nigerian" (usually) or "Nigerian American" (rarely).

U.S.-born African Americans with a slave ancestry are a biological and cultural by-product unique to the Western Hemisphere (Powell, 1973; Sowell, 1981). After more than 200 years of slavery, the descendants of the original slaves lost their ancestral language and culture and were no longer direct descendants of any culture or country in Africa. The slave communities created their own norms and mores, after blending their diverse cultural tribal beliefs with the beliefs of their White masters (Sowell, 1981).

Much before 1860, African Americans migrated out of the rural South and through the early decades of the 20th century increased their numbers dramatically. The migration of 800,000 African Americans out of the South to industrial centers in the Northeast and Midwest was far greater in numbers than the migration of the Irish to the United States (Sowell, 1981). As many scholars have noted, this migration in the 1900s is significant in modern history because it meant a second uprooting within two generations of a group of people with slave ancestry (Gutman, 1976).

In almost every part of the world, there has been a history of slavery. However, slavery had a distinct and unique history in America because, for the first time in human memory, it produced such great controversy. The American Revolution and the ideals on which it was fought caused slavery in a free society to become a continuous and contentious moral issue (Myrdal,

1944; Powell, 1973), whereas moral justification for slavery had never been necessary in other slave societies (Myrdal, 1944). These historic data may explain, in part, why racism toward African Americans has persisted for so long in a nation born out of the quest for freedom but with a tainted past.

In 1985, The National Research Council and its Commission on Behavioral and Social Sciences and Education initiated a study on the changing status of Black Americans since 1940 (James & Williams, 1989). The final report in 1989, *A Common Destiny: Blacks and American Society* reiterates the theme of "two societies, one black, one white—separate and unequal" noted earlier by Charles S. Johnson (1930) in *The Negro in American Civilization*, by Gunnar Myrdal (1944) in *An American Dilemma*, and again by Kerner (1968) in the *Report of the Advisory Commission on Civil Disorders*. After five years of deliberation, the Committee on the Status of Black Americans of the National Research Council stated in their report:

> These findings suggest that a considerable amount of remaining black-white inequality is due to continuing discriminatory treatment of blacks. The clearest evidence is in housing; discrimination against blacks seeking housing has been conclusively demonstrated. In employment and public accommodations, discrimination, although greatly reduced is still a problem. (James & Williams, 1989, p. 13)

The Committee on the Status of Black Americans also noted five major events that occurred between 1940 and 1985 that transformed race relations in the United States:

1. The South-North and rural-urban migration of African Americans that occurred over a period of 30 years.
2. The Civil Rights movement of the 1960s: "Perhaps more than any single event, this revolution produced important changes in the nation's political and educational institutions" (James & Williams, 1989, p. 36).

3. The growth of the U.S. economy during World War II and for 25 more years.
4. The decrease of economic growth and the end of 30 years of African American migration during the 1970s resulting in slower improvements in the status of African Americans.
5. Rapid changes in family compositions that created two groups of African Americans (i.e., families with female heads-of-households, who are overwhelmingly poor, and families headed by two adults, largely middle income).

The Committee on the Status of Black Americans concluded by stating that "the changing status of blacks affects the lives of all Americans" and that "the social position of black people is an indication of the functioning of American institutions" (p. 38).

Chapter 12 by Dupree, Bell, and Spencer, on the ecology of African American child development, is all the more important and salient given the 1989 report *A Common Destiny* (James & Williams, 1989). Dupree and colleagues note that the communities in which African American children grow up are not monolithic. They refute the notion of "a culture of poverty" and examine the validity of Spencer's Phenomenological Variant of the Ecological Systems Theory, which is a unique method of examining the social context in which African American children live and perceive their experiences, as well as the ways in which the context and their perceptions of their experiences influence their coping strategies. In examining the ecology of African American child development, the authors explode the sometimes ethnocentric White middle-class perspective of normalcy versus pathology and describe the context as well as the social support networks created for that context. Drawing on a repertoire of child development research, Dupree, Bell, and Spencer describe normative and nonnormative behavior of African American children in their social context. Although Chapter 12 does not describe psychopathology in terms of psychiatric diagnoses, it goes beyond psychiatric nomenclature and the issues of psychopathology to consider the development of African American children, their stressors, and their coping styles.

The Special Needs of Children of Illegal Immigrants and Refugees

Since 1965, the United States has admitted immigrants from all over the world, but as Conk (1985) pointed out, "a new pariah" group replaced the Irish, Italian, Chinese, Japanese, Koreans, and the East European Jews of previous decades—undocumented immigrants or "illegal aliens" became part of the public debate. Although immigrants from all over the world make up some percentage of the illegal or undocumented immigrants, the focus of the debate has been the immigrant tide from Latin America and, to some extent, from Asia. Immigrants from Latin America and Asia soared in numbers by 1970. In 1980, 125,000 boat people arrived from Cuba and by the mid-1980s, 6 million illegal immigrants were estimated to be living in the United States.

During President Carter's term in office, the debate about immigration reform included those who sought immigration restrictions, others who advocated for amnesty for illegal immigrants, and many who demanded an extension of the *bracero program* which allowed a certain number of Mexicans to enter the United States for specific reasons. The Simpson-Mazzoli immigration proposal surfaced during the Reagan years and was defeated (Conk, 1985; Wong, 1985) by certain political and economic interest groups. Nonetheless, the debate continued with a California proposition against immigration in 1996. Children who live under the stigma of being considered "illegal aliens," with its resulting discrimination, have yet another assault against their sense of self added to the emotional trauma of being displaced and the sequelae of that process. Included among the undocumented immigrants are displaced people or refugees who do not obtain the proper visas to live in the United States because of political controversy (e.g., Haitians, Cubans). Thus, how and why immigrant children arrive in the United States may well provide pertinent information about the adjustment process that will ensue.

In 1991, the U.S. Office of Refugee Resettlement reported that 1,551,870 refugees were admitted to the United States between 1975 and 1991 (Marsella, Bornemann, Ekblad, & Orley, 1994). Of that total, about 66% came from Asia, 17% from the former Soviet Union, 7% from Eastern Europe, 5% from the Near East and South Asia, 3% from Latin America, 2% from Africa, and 0.4% from other places in the world. More often than not, refugees are from developing countries undergoing social upheaval because of war, internal political strife, and natural disasters. Most of the world's refugees are not found in the United States, but in Central America, Southeast Asia, the Middle East, and Africa. Turmoil in Eastern Europe (i.e., Yugoslavia, the former Soviet Union, Romania), has occasioned a resurgence of displaced persons or refugees throughout the European continent. Although refugees or displaced persons and "other uprooted people in flight from a threatening environment" became the concern for humanitarian efforts, migrants and workers who become illegal immigrants encounter disdain and generate political and economic threats (Marsella et al., 1994). In 1991, 11,000 refugees who were fortunate to be admitted to the United States, while more than 216,000 remained on lists.

The legal complexities of different definitions of refugees are beyond the scope of this chapter. However, the United Nations High Commission on Refugees included the following groups as refugees:

1. People covered by the 1951 International Convention on Refugees.
2. People covered by the organization for African Unity Convention.
3. People who are forced to leave and/or prevented from returning home because of man-made disasters.
4. People who are forced to leave and prevented from returning home due to natural disasters or extreme poverty.

5. People who are internally displaced.
6. People who are stateless.
7. People who seek refugee status due to item 1 or 2, but who were considered ineligible for those two categories (Marsella et al., 1994).

Although these seven categories may not always be considered acceptable for refugee status within the United States, they nonetheless provide insight about the experiences of refugees and immigrants prior to coming to the United States as well as the reasons many come without legal immigrant status and often by life-threatening means.

Between 2 and 6 million illegal immigrants or undocumented aliens are living in the United States (Hernandez, 1985). Those who are considered to be undocumented, or without legal visas or expired visas, are a small percentage of those who enter and leave the country during a given period. Equally important in understanding illegal immigrants are the following variables described by Hernandez (1985): (a) the actual and perceived demand for and difficulty of entry; (b) the "chance" evasion of detection; (c) the sponsoring relatives and recruiters to the United States; (d) receiving patterns in urban American society (e.g., labor markets and socioeconomic relations with legally admitted immigrants and the native population); (e) return economic ventures and the significance of remittance to the United States; (f) the political issues the United States has with the country of origin.

Whether perceived to be voluntary or involuntary, human migration is an exceedingly complex act and has many implications for the receiving communities as well as for the individuals themselves. Marsella and his colleagues (1994) have noted the psychological and emotional scars associated with the refugee experience: anxiety, fear, paranoia and suspicion, grief, guilt, despair, hopelessness, withdrawal, depression, somatization, substance abuse and alcoholism, posttraumatic stress disorders, anger, and hostility. Many refugees have difficulty in their workplace and family, and experience marital adjustment problems as well as many tensions in their efforts to acculturate and assimilate into the mainstream. The enormous and lifelong psychological and emotional costs exacted on refugees have been documented by studies of the Holocaust survivors as well as studies of the survivors of other man-made and natural disasters (Freud, 1967; Ressler, Boothby, & Steinbock, 1988; Rigamer, 1986; Wolf, 1945).

Although the psychological consequences for children due to displacement and their process of adaptation to another sociocultural context have been noted previously by many scholars, never before in history have so many forcibly uprooted people experienced the additional trauma of direct violence (Boothby, 1994). As witnessed by the civil war in Rwanda, the majority of people affected by wars are the very poor and often live in rural villages and small towns. The events that make war and political conflict uniquely stressful for children, noting "the interactive effects of loss of family and community and the devastating experiences of severe trauma and deprivation" (Boothby, 1994).

Studies on the effects of political conflict on children in Lebanon, Ireland, South Africa, and Latin America report that (a) war-related trauma are often diverse and multiple, (b) such trauma can occur repeatedly, and (c) children are also participants in political violence (Boothby, 1988, 1992, 1994; Gibson, 1989; Kinzie, Sack, Angell, Manson, & Rath, 1986; Punamaki & Suleiman, 1990). For example, a Lebanese child may well experience five to six types of traumatic events during his or her lifetime including bombardment, the witnessing of violent acts, and bereavement. Black South African children have been witness to "the murder of community leaders, gasoline bombings of their homes and schools, [and] widespread displacement of antiapartheid leaders" as well as exile, unrest, detention, and assault (Straker, 1987).

Although many children learn to survive in these and similar circumstances, their survival is not without cost, as noted in Northern Ireland (McWhirter, 1983), in Palestine (Punamaki & Suleiman, 1990), and in Bosnia. Arroyo (Chapter 4) notes the tragedies of war, violence, loss, and fear experienced by many children from Central America; Westermeyer and his colleagues (Chapter 9) pay particular attention to the plight of

Hmong children and families and the consequences of displacement and acculturation; and Shekim (Chapter 5) writes
about the diversity of the Middle East and the stresses and problems of children who experience lifelong political conflicts, wars,
displacement, and violence. Such children should be viewed as
suffering from a continuous stress syndrome.

One may wonder how children who have lived in refugee
camps without physical safety and with other unmet social and
psychological needs can remain unscathed (Kinzie et al., 1986;
Le, 1983). The same question can be posed for children who have
participated in the violence. Boothby (1994) has noted the cost
of survival for children in Mozambique who were taken from
their villages and taught to be combatants and kill. In El
Salvador and elsewhere in Central America, where political violence has existed for more than three decades, civilian involvement and increased militarization of the public have become
institutionalized. There are many accounts from around the
world of children under 15 years old who are participants
in liberation or guerrilla groups or conscripted into armies
(Boothby, 1988, 1994; Garbarino, Kosteling, & Dubrow, 1991).

The exact number of refugee children arriving in this
country who have lived in refugee camps or who have participated in the conflicts is not known, but is part of the cultural,
social, and diagnostic process that should not be overlooked.
However, the developmental consequences of refugee children
must be viewed in the context of their circumstances because
the conditions vary considerably. Additionally, past research
may lack the multifactorial conceptual models to apply to
today's conflicts. Nonetheless, there are some guideposts for
the assessment of such children. The child who experiences an
acute stress reaction to a sudden stressful event may show
acute anxiety, which dissipates after a few days. When such
experiences are accompanied by loss of family members, especially parents, there may be more psychological turmoil and
disturbances that may continue to exist. Being with family
members and familiar people may modify the child's fear and
anxiety. Continuous and persistent violence and conflict
may cause a continuous reexperiencing of the trauma and

decreased responsiveness, withdrawal from the environment, and fear of dying or disaster (Garmezy, 1982). There may be even more diverse and age-related symptoms depending on the cultural context in which it occurs.

Many scholars have noted the changes in personality, behavior, and moral development in refugee children, particularly those who have been exposed to extreme violence, deprivation, impoverishment, and human abuse. Kenzie et al. (1986) have written about the emotional disturbances of Cambodian children and the posttraumatic symptoms that emerged after leaving Cambodia. However, Coles (1986) has posed questions about the impact on moral development and the role of the stress involved in political conflicts, particularly when the conflict is concerned with ethnic/racial/religious beliefs or national identity. In such cases, the conflict or struggle may become a rite of passage. In Northern Ireland, strong family ties and religious beliefs have protected the social and moral development of children participating in the conflict (McWhirter, 1983). The findings from South Africa indicate that the majority of children can still make the distinction between violence for justice and equality and unjust, inhumane violence (Chikane, 1986; Gibson, 1989; Straker, 1987). For Palestinian children, it has been found that their participation in the political conflict and hardships resulted in active cognitive coping styles (Punamaki & Suleiman, 1990). Although the children's strong belief in the antioccupation movement provided a psychological counterforce to the violence they witnessed and experienced, the hardships they endured had negative mental health consequences. Punamaki and Suleiman (1990) concluded that effective cognitive coping and "courageous" emotional stamina may also put children in danger. As a consequence of participation, many children were detained, their schools were closed, their homes destroyed, and their friends and relatives killed.

Likewise, Boothby's (1994) observations in Mozambique of children who participated in the violence were that the children experienced remorse and recurrent anxiety connected to memories of violent, traumatic events. The strategies implemented in

Mozambique may well inform American clinicians and policy-makers about successful rehabilitation processes to serve as models for intervention in America's inner cities.

Sadly, thousands of children in Eastern Europe, Africa, the Middle East, Southeast Asia, and Central America are still being killed and injured; such are the consequences of war. Those children who become refugees living in camps exist "amidst pain and peril," danger, and adversities, trying to make sense of their daily environments and suffering profound changes in their personalities, socialization skills, and moral development (Marsella et al., 1994). Many such children enter American society burdened with such experiences although there are no data on the exact numbers. The ravages of political conflict are currently visible in Haiti, Eastern and Central Africa, the Near East, and China. Understanding such experiences and the cultural context as well as the child's perception of those experiences is crucial in healing the hurt child.

Conclusion

Significant changes in family pattern, which can be attributed to major changes in American society during the past six decades, have altered the lives of children and their well-being. Such trends include lower marriage rates and a delayed onset of marriage, higher divorce rates, lower birth rates, earlier and increased sexual activity among adolescents, a higher proportion of births to unmarried mothers, higher percentages of children living in female-headed families, a higher proportion of women working outside the home, and a higher percentage of children living in poverty (James & Williams, 1989; Johnson-Powell, 1992; U.S. DHHS, 1996).

The United States is now in the midst of large population increases associated with major shifts toward a population composed of more elderly and more likely to be non-White or to belong to a Hispanic minority group. Thus, the experience of American children in the coming decades will increasingly be the experience of culturally diverse minority children in a society where children constitute a decreasing proportion of the dependent population and the elderly are increasing more rapidly than the birth rate.

Although the proportion of the population of adults between 18 and 64 years of age fluctuated between 55% and 63% between 1900 and 1990, this is expected to decrease to about 56% between 2030 and 2050 (U.S. DHHS, 1996). On the other hand, except for 20 years of the baby boomers, the number of children have declined in proportion to the population and are projected to continue the decline in numbers for 60 years. Demographers have predicted that children under age 18 and adults 65 years and older will be the primary population dependent on a workforce of adults 18 to 64 years of age. In 1900, the dependent child population was 91% of the population; by 2050, children will be 53% of the population (U.S. DHHS, 1996). Thus, the number of working-age adults 18 to 64 will be decreasing with an elderly population increasing. However, the minority population is expected to continue its growth for 50 years, with large numbers of children and smaller numbers of elderly.

By 2030, only 50% of the children under age 18 will be White, 59% of adults 18 to 64, and 73% of the elderly. Thus, in the 21st century, children are more likely than the elderly to be minority group members, and the elderly will be more dependent on minority group working adults for their economic support. The implications for the health and human services as well as education and training provided to today's children and those in future decades are enormous if we are to achieve financial security for all our citizens. Cultural diversity will be the portrait of America's children, and these children must be helped to become part of the mainstream.

The chapters in this book focus on several major themes:

1. Culture provides the context or environment in which various behaviors develop and are expressed.
2. Behavior is learned in a social context.
3. The absence of well-being is expressed differently among different cultures.

4. Psychiatric symptoms are a reflection of culturally learned behavior.

The chapters reflect the different psychosocial and cultural factors that must be included in the assessment and treatment of culturally different children and families. Part of that assessment must be a cultural assessment that will entail basic knowledge about the ethnic/racial group (i.e., religion, language, country of origin, history of the immigration process, and the reception in the host country). The acculturation and assimilation process of family members as well as the perception of the sociocultural context by the child himself will become crucial to the assessment.

Each chapter provides cultural data about the ethnic/racial group discussed and presents the help-seeking behavior as well as patterns of adaptation that children from these diverse backgrounds present. In multicultural settings like Hawaii and Los Angeles, however, it may be difficult to distinguish when inherited cultural tendencies may be affected by the influences of other cultural groups or by the total society. The clinician must remember, then, that detectable differences in values and emphasis within the family and larger groupings may have significant formative influence on the maturing child.

References

BARRINGER, H., GARDNER, R. W., & LEVIN, M. J. (1995). *Asians and Pacific Islanders in the United States.* New York: Russell-Sage Foundation.

BEAN, F. D., & TIENDA, M. (1990). *The Hispanic population of the United States.* New York: Russell-Sage Foundation.

BOOTHBY, N. (1988). *Without moral restraint: Children in the midst of war. Social health review: Special report.* Washington, DC: U.S. Committee for Refugees.

BOOTHBY, N. (1992). Displaced children: Psychological theory and practice from the field. *Journal of Refugee Studies, 5*(2), 106–122.

BOOTHBY, N. (1994). Trauma and violence among refugee children. In A. J. Marsella, T. Bornemann, S. Ekblad, & J. Orley (Eds.), *Amidst pain and peril: The mental health of the world's refugees.* Washington, DC: American Psychological Association.

CHAN, S. (1992a). Families with Filipino roots. In E. W. Lynch & M. J. Hanson (Eds.), *Developing cross-cultural competence: A guide for working with young children and their families.* Baltimore: Brookes.

CHAN, S. (1992b). Families with Asian roots. In E. W. Lynch & M. J. Hanson (Eds.), *Developing cross-cultural competence: A guide for working with young children and their families.* Baltimore: Brookes.

CHIKANE, F. (1986). Children in turmoil: The effects of unrest on township children. In S. Burnam & P. Reynolds (Eds.), *Growing up in a divided society.* New York: Raven Press.

COLES, R. (1986). *The political life of children.* Boston: Houghton Mifflin.

CONK, M. (1985). Immigration reform and immigration history: Why Simpson-Mazzoli did not pass. In L. Maldonado & J. Moore (Eds.), *Urban ethnicity in the United States.* Beverly Hills, CA: Sage.

FERNANDEZ, R. R., & VELEZ, W. (1985). Race, color, and language in the changing public schools. In L. Maldonaldo & J. Moore (Eds.), *Urban ethnicity in the United States.* Beverly Hills, CA: Sage.

FREUD, A. (1967). Comments on trauma. In S. Furst (Ed.), *Psychic trauma.* New York: Basic Books.

GARBARINO, J., KOSTELNG, K., & DUBROW, N. (1991). *No place to be a child: Growing up in a war zone.* Lexington, MA: Lexington Books.

GARCIA, P. (1985). Immigration issues in urban ecology: The case of Los Angeles. In L. Maldonado & J. Moore (Eds.), *Urban ethnicity in the United States.* Beverly Hills, CA: Sage.

GARMEZY, N. (1982). Stressors of childhood. In N. Garmezy & M. Rutter (Eds.), *Stress, coping and development in children.* New York: McGraw-Hill.

GIBSON, K. (1989). Children in political violence. *Social Science and Medicine, 28,* 659.

GUTMAN, H. G. (1976). *The Black family in slavery and freedom, 1750–1925.* New York: Vintage/Random House.

HERNANDEZ, J. (1985). A research strategy for new immigrants. In L. Maldonado & J. Moore (Eds.), *Urban ethnicity in the United States.* Beverly Hills, CA: Sage.

JAMES, G. D., & WILLIAMS, R. M. (Eds.). (1989). *A common destiny: Blacks in American society.* Washington, DC: National Academy Press.

JOHNSON-POWELL, G. (1992). Adolescents in poverty. In S. B. Friedman, M. Fisher, & K. Schonberg (Eds.), *Comprehensive adolescent health care.* St. Louis, MO: Quality Medical.

KIM, I. (1987). Korea and East Asia: Preimmigration factors and U.S. immigration policy. In J. T. Fawcett & B. V. Carino (Eds.), *Pacific bridges: The new immigration from Asia and the Pacific Islands.* New York: Center for Migration Studies.

KINZIE, D., SACK, W., ANGELL, R., MANSON, S., & RATH, B. (1986). The psychic effects of massive trauma on Cambodian children. *Journal of the American Academy of Child Psychiatry, 25,* 370.

LE, D. D. (1983). Mental health and Vietnamese children. In G. J. Powell, J. Yamamoto, A. Romero, & A. Morales (Eds.), *The psychosocial development of minority group children.* New York: Brunner/Mazel.

LIEBERSON, S., & WATERS, M. C. (1990). *From many strands: Ethnic and racial groups in contemporary America.* New York: Russell-Sage Foundation.

MALDONADO, L., & MOORE, J. (1985). Introduction. In L. Maldonado & J. Moore (Eds.), *Urban ethnicity in the United States.* Beverly Hills, CA: Sage.

MARSELLA, A. J., BORNEMANN, T., EKBLAD, S., & ORLEY, J. (1994). Introduction. In A. J. Marsella, A. J. Bornemann, S. Ekblad, & J. Orley (Eds.), *Amidst peril and pain: The mental health of the world's refugees.* Washington, DC: American Psychological Association.

MCWHIRTER, L. (1983). Growing up in Northern Ireland: From aggression to trouble. In A. Goldstein & M. Segall (Eds.), *Aggression in global perspectives* (pp. 75–92). Elmsford, NY: Pergamon Press.

MOORE, J., & PINDERGHUGHES, R. (Eds.). (1993). *In the barrios: Latinos and the underclass debate.* New York: Russell-Sage Foundation.

MYRDAL, G. (1944). *An American dilemma: The negro problem and modern democracy* (2 vols.). New York: Harper and Brothers.

NATIONAL ADVISORY COMMITTEE ON CIVIL DISORDERS. (1968). *Report of the National Advisory Committee on Civil Disorders.* New York: Bantam Books.

PORTES, A. (Ed.). (1995). *Economic sociology of immigration: Essays on network, ethnicity, and entrepreneurship.* New York: Russell-Sage Foundation.

PORTES, A. (Ed.). (1996). *The new second generation.* New York: Russell-Sage Foundation.

POWELL, G. J. (1973). *Black Monday's children: The effects of school desegregation on southern school children.* Englewood Cliffs, NJ: Prentice-Hall.

POWELL, G. J., YAMAMOTO, J., ROMERO, A., & MORALES, A. (Eds.). (1983). *The psychosocial development of minority group children.* New York: Brunner/Mazel.

PUNAMAKI, R., & SULEIMAN, R. (1990). Predictors and effectiveness of coping with political violence among Palestinian children. *British Journal of Social Psychology, 29,* 67–77.

QUARLES, B. (1996). *The negro in the making of America* (3rd ed.). New York: Simon and Schuster.

RESSLER, E., BOOTHBY, N., & STEINBOCK, D. (1988). *Unaccompanied children: Care and protection in wars, natural disasters and mass population movements.* New York: Oxford University Press.

RIGAMER, E. (1986). Psychological management of children in a natural crisis. *Journal of the American Academy of Child Psychiatry, 25,* 364.

SOWELL, T. (1981). *Ethnic America: A history.* New York: Basic Books.

STRAKER, G. (1987). The continuous traumatic stress syndrome: The single therapeutic interview. *Psychology and Sociology, 8,* 48.

TAKAKI, R. (1989). *Strangers from a different shore: A history of Asian Americans.* Boston: Little, Brown.

U.S. DEPARTMENT OF HEALTH AND HUMAN SERVICES. (1996). *Trends in the well-being of America's children and youth: 1996.* Washington, DC: General Accounting Office.

VEGA, W. A., HOUGH, R. L., & ROMERO, A. (1983). Family life patterns of Mexican Americans. In G. J. Powell, J. Yamamoto, A. Romero, & A. Morales (Eds.), *The psychosocial development of minority group children.* New York: Brunner/Mazel.

WOLF, K. (1945). Evacuation of children in war time. *Psychoanalytic Study of the Child, 1,* 389.

WONG, M. G. (1985). Post-1965 immigrants: Demographic and socioeconomic profile. In J. Maldonado & J. Moore (Eds.), *Urban ethnicity in the United States.* Beverly Hills, CA: Sage.

YAMAMOTO, J., & KUBOTA, M. (1983). The Japanese-American family. In G. J. Powell, J. Yamamoto, A. Romero, & A. Morales (Eds.), *The psychosocial development of minority group children.* New York: Brunner/Mazel.

YU, K. H., & KIM, L. I. C. (1983). The growth and development of Korean American children. In G. J. Powell, J. Yamamoto, A. Romero, & A. Morales (Eds.), *The psychosocial development of minority group children.* New York: Brunner/Mazel.

ZUNIGA, M. E. (1992). Families with Latino roots. In E. W. Lynch & M. J. Hanson (Eds.), *Developing cross-cultural competencies: A guide for working with young children and their families.* Baltimore: Brookes.

CHAPTER 2

Culture and Psychopathology

JOE YAMAMOTO, J. ARTURO SILVA,
MICHELLE FERRARI, and KAZUTAKA NUKARIYA

The Interplay of Culture and Psychopathology

THE TERM *CULTURE* REFERS to social reality. It can be defined as a complex collection of components that a group of people share to help them adapt to their social and physical world. Griffith and Gonzalez (1994) defined culture as ". . . shared patterns of belief, feeling, and knowledge that ultimately guide everyone's conduct and definition of reality. Culture refers to a multiplicity of elements that define human life, such as social relationships, religion, technology and economics" (p. 1379). LeVine (1984) placed some emphasis in meaning and communication when he conceptualized culture ". . . as a shared organization of ideas that includes the intellectual, moral and aesthetics standards prevalent in a community and the meanings of communicative actions" (p. 66).

Culture not only affects adaptive and normative behaviors but also finds expression in disease states including psychopathological disorders. Although psychiatric disorders have biological components that are applicable to human beings in general, symptom formation and its associated meaning may be influenced by culture because the latter affects the intrinsic meaning that can be ascribed to a given symptom or symptom complex (Kirmayer, Young, & Robbins, 1994).

Perhaps the most significant indication that culture can affect the way in which illness is recognized can be gleaned from the rates of psychopathology found across different cultures and racial groups. A study by Stanley Sue on psychiatric epidemiology among Chinese Americans in Los Angeles showed that, in general, the Chinese tend to have lower rates of psychopathology (Yamamoto, 1995). In California, the results of the Los Angeles Epidemiologic Catchment Area research study show that non-Hispanic Whites have a much higher rate of drug abuse and dependence than Mexican Americans (Karno et al., 1987). Moreover, drug abuse and dependence also appear to be more strongly associated with a higher level of acculturation to the United States (Burnam, Hough, Karno, Escobar, & Telles, 1987).

The reasons for these epidemiological differences may be found in personality variables and social conditions, both of which may be affected by culture. In the area of personality assessment, Tan (1989) states, "Asian Americans have been found to have greater feelings of isolation, loneliness, and anxiety . . . lower self-restraint, and passivity" (p. 63). These findings, however, should be considered tentative because appropriate questions can be raised about the general reliability of the studies, which were mostly carried out on small samples of college students. In addition, the personality inventories used in these studies have limited validity for assessing cross-cultural personality differences and may increase the risk that cultural minorities will appear to exhibit greater psychopathology than is objectively true. Alternatively, behavioral instruments that have not been standardized in a given culture may fail to detect actual mental disorders.

In evaluating the normal personality development of Asians, cultural values such as filial piety, modesty, and respect for authority may be inappropriately evaluated from a Western perspective as related to negative personality factors such as "introversion, self-abasement, and lack of self-confidence" (Tan, 1989).

Culture may also influence expression including the way some cultural groups experience distress and psychiatric symptoms. Among the Mexican Americans of Los Angeles, women with low levels of acculturation to mainstream society who met *DSM-III* criteria for major depression-dysthymia were more likely to somatize than non-Hispanic White women with similar psychopathology (Escobar, Burnam, Karno, Forsyth, & Golding, 1987).

Transcultural Child Mental Health

More than 10 years have passed since the first edition of *The Psychosocial Development of Minority Children* was published (Powell, Yamamoto, Morales, & Romero, 1983). Since then, we have seen a great expansion of our knowledge of children from the point of view of both general clinical and transcultural child mental health. Furthermore, U.S. society has become increasingly more ethnically and culturally diversified, a trend that is expected to grow well into the next century (McRae, 1994). This growth in diversification is accompanied by the increasing complexity of society in areas such as education, marriage, work, medicine, and law at a pace unprecedented in our country's history. This is bringing about many changes that affect the very nature of the family, norms of child development, and the implementation of approaches to child rearing. Social change always creates many stressors perhaps more likely to be noted in economically depressed, politically disadvantaged, or otherwise socially disenfranchised sectors of the population. This consideration is especially germane to cultural and ethnic minorities, which traditionally have not enjoyed many advantages that are available to members of mainstream U.S. society. As a result, families from minority cultural backgrounds, including their children, have had to face multiple stressors leading to adjustment problems and even serious psychopathology. At the same time, different cultures have evolved an impressive array of strategies to deal with adversity, a testimony to humanity and its ability to define itself as the maker of culture.

The science of transcultural child mental health, therefore, focuses not only on child and adolescent psychopathology from a cultural viewpoint, but also on the many ways that culture can facilitate optimal child development in the family and society in which the child happens to be raised. We will briefly discuss both normal and psychopathological aspects of the child from a cultural context.

Culture, Development, and Personality

Human psychological development has traditionally been understood as an organismic process in which the interacting psychic and biological structures of the person unfold across personal time in a more or less orderly sequence of stages. The psychology of Sigmund Freud represents this tradition. He saw this developmental process as biologically based and therefore inevitable. The psychological pitfalls, then, related to incomplete resolution of the tasks associated with each stage. He believed that this psychological development was wholly shaped by the microenvironment of the family context in which a person was raised (Freud, 1966).

Other theoreticians, such as Erik Erikson (1950), John Bowlby (1973), and Erich Fromm (1970), realized that many social influences, above and beyond the impact of the family, served as necessary integrative influences of the developing child. This broader approach revolutionized the view that mental health professionals and other social scientists took of human development by placing greater emphasis on social and cultural factors. And, as previously mentioned, social and ecological factors tend to be intrinsically related to cultural infrastructures. The introduction of cultural concepts in this area has facilitated our conceptualization of development as a function of both the biology of the organism and the child's psychosociocultural environment.

Even Piagetian concepts of cognitive development, which have traditionally been thought to be universal and, by inference, biological constants in humans, have been criticized because they fail to take adequate account of formal task performance in nonliterate cultures (Dasen, 1975). New evidence suggests that psychological development among children is a function of universal cognitive and emotional stages as well as symbolic systems that are themselves dependent in an orderly fashion on both ecological and psychosociocultural variables. Thus, in China, there is greater emphasis on teaching drawing than is usual in Canadian schools. Because Chinese children are actively encouraged by their teachers to draw the human figure, they outperform their Canadian counterparts in this skill. However, in perspective drawing, which neither culture stresses—presumably leaving its development to the vicissitudes of human nature—no differences are noted between the cultures (Okamoto, Case, Bleiker, & Henderson, 1996).

Of great relevance to child mental health is the development of moral values. Such positive values are also culturally mediated and the differences among cultures represent a relative emphasis in polar concepts such as individualism versus familism. In the United States, there is more emphasis on independence and individualism, whereas in Asia, the emphasis is on interdependence, not only in relation to integrating the family and the kinship clans but also in responding to the community. Religious and philosophical differences occur when professionals compare Asian and U.S. society. The teachings of Confucius emphasize loyalty between lord and subordinates; intimacy between father and son; propriety between husband and wife; order between elder and junior; and trust between friends. This philosophy emphasizes principles of harmony, filial piety, and modesty as well as the interconnectedness of the past, present, and future. The past is symbolically represented and paid homage to by the tradition of ancestor worship. In Asia, the past is relatively more important than in the United States, and personal time is conceptualized more as a continuum with the present and future.

Among Americans, tolerance of differences is exemplified in the diverse clothing worn by children in public schools. In the Orient, the expectation of similarity is visually reinforced by the use of uniforms for schoolchildren from kindergarten through university. There is also a tendency for children to be more modest and less verbally expressive than in the United States (Okamoto et al., 1996).

In the United States, there is a strong emphasis on self-fulfillment and self-development; in Asia, self-fulfillment and self-development are expressed through interpersonal relationships that define and enhance a social group reflecting the emphasis on harmony in Confucian teachings. In the United States, the emphasis is on individual achievement; in Asia, there is greater emphasis on group achievement. As Asian children grow up, they become especially aware of the family group, followed by the school group, and then the work group in adulthood. Very early in the life cycle, children learn to be particularly sensitive to how their thoughts and actions influence the group. The relentless search for newness and change in the United States is exemplified by products that are "new and improved." In Asia, newness and change often remain in a context of tradition.

Because an individual's personality is a function not only of the biology within the organism and family dynamics but also of the social world, including its culture and ecology, the relation between culture and personality can be difficult to discern. The substantial biological and social variability that results within human groups makes deciphering the "national character" or personality of a cultural group a problematic undertaking (Erchak, 1992). Therefore, researchers can best study the extent to which culture influences personality development by using a life-span and ecological perspective that takes into account the effect of culture in relation to biological, psychological, and social interacting factors that affect a group in a given historical moment (Silva & Liederman, 1986). Mental health professionals who understand human personality development and psychopathology in ever-changing physical and psychosocial environments are less likely to accept category fallacies (Lewis-Fernandez & Kleinman, 1994). This approach is especially important in early personality development, when children and adolescents undergo significant biological, psychological, and social transitions with multiple links to the cultural infrastructure. A study by Domino (1992) found that Chinese children who completed the social values task, compared with their American counterparts, engaged in more responses involving equality and group enhancement, whereas American children endorsed more individualist and competitive responses. These results are consistent with the often-mentioned hypothesis that Chinese personality development and culture promote group consciousness and solidarity (Matthews & Matthews, 1983). These findings are tempered by the fact that these 10- to 12-year-old children lived in urban centers during 1990. Other Chinese children, like children from rural settings and those who are raised in other time periods, may show different personality traits suggesting that personality development within a culture may be sensitive to different ecologies, stressors, and historical periods.

Knowledge about both culture and mental health within a biopsychosociocultural framework is likely to deepen professionals' understanding of coping mechanisms, mental disorders, and child development. Complex phenomena frequently associated with psychopathology, such as violence, can be best understood as a function of several levels of behavioral organization spanning society down to the individual person. Griffith and Gonzalez (1994) are well aware of this when they state, "In the inner cities, the cultural milieu often includes poverty, chronic exposure to crime, street and domestic violence, and substance abuse, as well as a predominance of young, undersupported single mothers who are heads of households" (p. 1381). A biopsychosociocultural approach to child mental health also facilitates potential solutions to problems such as poverty and violence. Griffith and Gonzalez cite the work of Comer on how the extended family may counteract these disadvantages. Comer showed that professionals can enhance the school's role in the development of children through systematic planning the work (Haynes & Comer, 1990).

Language and Its Relevance to Psychopathology

Language, like culture, may be an important consideration in understanding mental disorders although it is psychological and institutional prejudice, not language-based phenomena that may predispose some to such disorders. Bilingualism is perhaps the best example of the interaction of language and psychopathology. Although it is estimated that about half of the world's population is bilingual, this language versatility has often been singled out as hindering the development of children's full cognitive potential. Research during the past three decades has done much to dispel this belief, but misconceptions about bilingualism still persist. Nevertheless, bilingualism may stigmatize cultural and ethnic minorities in the United States and elsewhere. They suffer from unemployment, poor housing, and poor educational opportunities and face poor prospects for socioeconomic improvement; the larger society then blames bilingualism for this disadvantaged status. Bilingual children who grow up in these circumstances suffer from a pervasive form of social disenfranchisement that often results in low self-esteem, apathy, and oppositional behaviors along with increased risks for depression, substance abuse, stress disorders, and shame about their culture and native language. Ironically, bilingualism may prove advantageous if the bilingual person has an adequate education and lives in a psychologically and economically secure environment (Hoffman, 1991).

Although a given language in and of itself does not predispose to maladaptive behaviors or mental illness, it may serve as a vehicle of maladaptive marginalization. For example, gang members often develop their own terminology to assert their independence, express their apathy, and demonstrate aggressive opposition to societal norms. Among Mexican American adolescents, the *Pachuco argot*, a Spanish-English language variant, often signals membership in a social group that provides acceptance, a semblance of protection, and a code of aggressiveness along with a psychodynamic of oppositional behavior toward norms of both the Hispanic and mainstream communities (Barker, 1975a). Mental health workers may benefit from understanding not only the cultural links but political, socioeconomic, and educational parameters that influence language in minority children and adolescents. Furthermore, either the indigenous or the mainstream language may be used depending on the stressors and psychosocial challenges in different social situations. Therefore, optimal therapy oftentimes can be carried out only when the therapist understands the psychological vehicle that a given language or dialect represents (Barker, 1975b).

Culturally Mediated Stressors and Psychopathology

We live in a multicultural system in which people, to varying degrees, experience culture because all of us belong to a given culture and other cultural systems influence us in many ways. Because the United States is becoming an increasingly complex culture (McRae, 1994), people are likely to encounter many stressful events. From a cultural perspective of mental health, external and internal stressors should be considered. External stressors are derived from cultural diversity, language differences, and aspects of the individual's environment such as socioeconomic status (SES), generational differences, reasons for migration, length of residency after migration, and social networks. All these factors have been hypothesized to cause mental illness. Internal stressors are produced by the individual and depend on the individual's level of expectation toward a new culture, self-esteem, locus of control, and personality structure. Because culture continually interacts at both group and individual levels of behavioral organization, cultural issues can only be understood from a dynamic biopsychosocial viewpoint. In this section, we review culturally mediated stressors and their relation to psychopathology by focusing on a few of these stressors.

The first of these stressors is migration, which is fairly prevalent in the United States. In Los Angeles, California, alone, over one hundred nationalities are represented. Immigrants overall experience greater psychological stress than indigent groups. A new culture may come in conflict with mainstream cultural systems for several reasons. First, the mainstream culture, which usually has a more advantageous power position, may insist that an immigrant discard conflicting cultural characteristics. The Japanese culture in American society exemplifies this kind of cultural conflict. Japanese culture may be characterized as a collective culture. Japanese people emphasize harmony with persons of authority, such as parents, older siblings, or a superior at their place of work. They sacrifice themselves by refraining from expression of emotion and by being patient, modest, and formal. Family members have rigid roles, and the extended family emphasizes interdependence, favoritism toward males, hierarchical rank status, and cooperation.

On the other hand, the American culture is characterized by individualism. It emphasizes independence and egalitarianism, which favors the nuclear family, flexible roles for family members, and greater power for females. Americans are competitive and feel free to express their emotions. Japanese American adolescents may experience psychological conflict in their attempts to become more independent and "American" because the cultural role expectations of Japanese parents conflict with those of American mainstream society. Likewise Mexican adolescents may find it cumbersome and even embarrassing to interact intensively with grandparents because the American adolescent peer group demands heavy investments of time and allegiance to friends. Thus, cultural factors may intensify generational conflicts.

Language itself may differentiate between first and later generations. Although first-generation elders speak their native language fluently, they may have little or poor command of the dominant language. Conversely, their grandchildren may have much better command of the English language than of the native language. This communication gap is likely to have adverse psychological effects especially in the Chinese, Japanese, Mexican, and similar cultures, where interdependence with the extended family is intrinsic to the group's integrity. In these situations, the elderly experience loss of self-esteem because imparting knowledge and love to the young ones is difficult, while the young lose the stabilizing context and sense of direction provided by family and culture. This may contribute to anxiety, poor self-esteem, and acting-out behavior among these young people.

The relation between social class and psychopathology is important in transcultural child psychiatry because economic disadvantage makes many cultural minorities vulnerable to severe family stress, single-parent family status, residential overcrowding, and poor housing. Children who are raised in poverty that leads to family discord and fragmentation may be at higher risk for mental disorder. Although cultural status does not necessarily predispose people to antisocial activities, some age group such as adolescent Black or Hispanic boys may be at greater risk of becoming involved in violence and substance abuse as a function of the poor social and economic prospects facing them.

Acculturation is another stressor that professionals must consider for an understanding of immigrant and minority children and adolescents. Stressors associated with acculturation encompass both the loss of cultural identity and potential difficulties in achieving competence within the absorbing culture. Barriers to acceptance include lower socioeconomic status and racism (Canino & Spurlock, 1994). Native American youths not only experience their adolescence as a developmentally normative time to become independent of one's parents but concurrently have the opportunity to leave the cultural and ecological milieu of the reservation in their quest for adulthood. They may seek acceptance in mainstream American society only to find that they are poorly educated, have a value system different from that of the larger society and may encounter racist attitudes that effectively bar their entry into the mainstream (Sue & Sue, 1981; Thompson, Walker, & Silk-Walker, 1993).

Acculturation may also be thought of as a complex process with significantly different experiences for each generation. Among Japanese Americans, first-generation individuals experienced the stress of being new to rejection and outright racism. The second generation, or *Nisei*, furthered acculturation through higher education and occupational challenges, whereas the *Sansei*, or third generation experienced stresses associated with intermarriage, as well as encountering problems like those of other native-born Americans (Yamamoto, 1978).

Understanding acculturation may depend on knowing the effect of major historical events on individuals. Many Cambodian refugees lost their families and their cultural infrastructure as well. Not only migration but also the genocidal annihilation of their society destroyed their cultural roots. Such refugees may find it difficult to convincingly transmit the positive aspects of their culture and may concurrently suffer from the guilt of having survived (Yamamoto, Silva, & Chang, in press). Some children of Holocaust survivors may tacitly accept the guilt of their elders and at the same time find it difficult to fully adopt their parents' culture because it failed to optimally prepare them for life in modern society (Epstein, 1979).

No discussion of culturally associated stressors can be complete without considering prejudice and racism and their deleterious effects on human beings. In an excellent review, Adams discusses the history of the changing patterns of racism in the United States. Adams (1990) differentiates between attitudinal and structural racism. He describes institutionalized racism as affecting one's "economic life chances, honor chances and power chances" (p. 371). In institutionalized racism meaningful dialogue and opportunities for belonging to the power structure of society are severely limited for the affected minority group, including its children. Barriers in educational attainment ensure that minority people feel inadequate early in their emotional and intellectual development. Racist ideologies complement institutionalized racism by promoting insults and hatred.

Racism is linked to racial awareness, the latter phenomenon beginning during early childhood. Therefore, minority children learn early that their ethnic-identity may not be a source of self-respect. Because of this, the self-esteem of the minority child suffers. Moreover, racism and diminished economic opportunity go hand in hand. Spurlock and Norris (1991) make this point when they discuss African American identity:

> Being Black means different things to different African Americans and may mean different things at different periods of the life cycle. It is most likely to mean being poor. . . . Regardless of the nature of one's employment, an African American is likely to be questioned. (p. 594)

Racism, in turn, leaves cultural minorities with an increased risk of experiencing mental disorder. It may occur in conjunction with poverty, which in turn may lead to premature births, poor nutrition and prenatal care, and increased risk of attention deficit disorders. Parents who are victims of institutionalized racism and are poorly educated may have no time and lack the discipline necessary to care effectively for their children. These situations may be a fertile ground for the development of conduct disorder. The lack of culturally competent teachers and mental health professionals also leads to a failure to provide children and adolescents, as well as adults, with needed services (Spurlock & Norris, 1991). At the ecological level, many Black inner-city communities are not safe environments for children to explore their world. Children who learn that their community is undesirable and unsafe develop a high level of mistrust toward their social environment, which leads to a worldview marked with suspicion (Spurlock & Norris, 1991). There have been significant efforts, however, to link racial awareness with pride and a sense of group cohesiveness. Such programs can help children gain a sense of belonging and give them a chance to focus on the positive self/group identity. In the United States, these efforts often are the product of frustration experienced by non-White cultural groups because racism has played such a prominent role in our society.

Because of this, programs to build the self-esteem of racial minorities have sometimes resulted in a retaliatory stance divided along racial lines, thus increasing the sense of global isolation in minority children, and continuing their risk of psychopathology.

Psychopathology as a Cultural Construct

The identification and measurement of psychopathology is essential for arriving at the correct diagnosis and optimal treatment, and for implementing research studies. Cultural considerations also affect these activities. This is especially true with symptoms, of mental disorders, which frequently reflect the component psychosocial setting in which the patient lives and are explicable in large part as cultural constructs. The conceptualization of this symptomatology as a complex system of cultural symbols has been long acknowledged by transcultural mental health professionals (Fabrega, 1996). However, the successful "translation" of symptoms of mental disorders from one cultural setting to another remains a subject of controversy and intensive study. This issue is prominently highlighted by the increasing use of the fourth edition of the *Diagnostic and Statistical Manual of Mental Disorders (DSM-IV;* APA, 1994) and related instruments (Canino & Spurlock, 1994) across numerous cultural settings amidst constant debate about the appropriateness and limits of such instruments from a transcultural perspective (Kleinman, 1996; Stein, 1993). Nevertheless, *DSM-IV* represents an improvement over its predecessors in that it includes an outline for a cultural formulation that takes into account the diagnosis of mental disorder in part as a function of the cultural identity of the individual, cultural explanations of the individual's illness, cultural factors related to psychosocial environment and level of functioning, and cultural elements of the relationship between individual and the clinician (APA, 1994).

However, understanding psychopathology in a cultural context in both children and adolescents presents many challenges (Canino & Spurlock, 1994; Cervantes & Arroyo, 1994). In part, this is true because systematic studies of *DSM-IV*, its predecessors, and related instruments as they apply to children and adolescents, remain in their embryonic states (Canino, 1996; Fabrega, Ahn, Boster, & Mezzich, 1990). Even in *DSM-IV*, diagnoses in several categories depend on intellectual and cognitive tests whose normative standards on minority children have yet to be developed. These disorders include mental retardation, reading disorders, mathematics disorder, and disorders of writing expression (Cervantes & Arroyo, 1994). Further, the disorders related to reading, mathematics, and written expression are all based on an expectation related to "age-appropriate education" (APA, 1994). This criterion can be difficult to assess because school systems in minority areas frequently lack funding, supplies, equipment, and appropriate personnel. Thus, the expectation that an equivalent grade level means an equivalent set of opportunities educationally is often false and may lead to overdiagnosis of developmental disorders among minority children.

Difficulties in diagnosis are not limited to developmental disorders. In different cultures, the prevalence of diagnostic categories involving major mental disorders may vary and the reasons for this variance are not clear. Depression as diagnosed by *DSM-III* and *DSM-IV* criteria has been found to be uncommon in the Chinese (Hwu, Yeh, & Chang, 1989; Yamamoto, Takeuchi, Sue, & Kurasaki, 1995). This does not necessarily mean that the Chinese have fewer problems than Americans, although this is one interpretation of the epidemiological data (Helzer et al., 1990). It is possible that these findings are correct and that the results reflect the Chinese having fewer mental disorders than Americans and that this may be a function of traditional cultural characteristics emphasizing the family, kinship, and community as well as harmony with others, filial piety, and the high value of interpersonal relationships. The results, however, may also reflect specific culturally mediated ways of expressing emotions and/or symptoms of mental disorders. Thus, the evaluative process increases in complexity as expected symptomatology is assessed in the face of behavioral norms that differ from the culture that created the diagnostic instrument.

In children and adolescents, developmental issues add to this complexity. To continue with the example of depression, there is an ongoing debate among child mental health professionals regarding the diagnosis of depression in children. Though we have moved beyond the concept of depressive equivalents, and agree that children can be depressed, the expression of this disorder may not always follow the adult criteria exactly (Weller & Weller, 1991). Children may show only diminished play with peers and so not demonstrate complete anhedonia, or they may be too young to understand or fully describe death or suicidal ideation. Insufficient verbal skills also may limit their ability to describe worthlessness and guilt or poor concentration. They may have a poor or absent concept of time, which limits assessment of that criterion.

Finally, especially in younger children, the lack of social skills and alternatives for self-expression may limit the behavioral manifestations available for demonstrating the underlying mood, and thus lead to misdiagnosis. In young children with poor verbal skills, poor concentration may mimic attention-deficit/hyperactivity disorder (ADHD), acting-out behavior secondary to irritability may suggest oppositional defiant disorder or conduct disorder, and lack of achievement of proper weight may cause a presumption of failure to thrive.

Furthermore, stressors and precipitants for depression may vary for different cultural and ethnic groups, and these may also be dependent on developmental stages. Among some Hispanic groups, overvaluing interdependence may cause adolescents to experience greater conflict with their parents leading to greater feelings of depression and detachment, as well as anger and resentment toward the family unit (Steinberger, 1989). The validation of diagnostic assessment tools is not limited to clinical diagnostic purposes; most research diagnostic instruments have not been tested in minority children or in those children with cultural backgrounds different from mainstream American culture (Canino, Canino, & Bravo, 1994). In Puerto Rico, *DSM-III* diagnostic criteria by child mental health professionals resulted in a prevalence rate of mental disorder of 49.5%. It is unlikely that half of Puerto Rican children are mental disordered. Rather, other factors besides symptomatology of mental disorder likely resulted in those implausible prevalence rates, for when severity of criteria was taken into account by using the children's global assessment scale, the prevalence rate diminished to 18.2 (Bird, Canino, et al., 1988; Bird, Yager, et al., 1990). Therefore, research studies must take into account severity of illness as perceived by clinical cultural measures to ensure adequate research and treatment among pediatric minority populations.

Epidemiology and Utilization of Services

Because there is a dearth of epidemiological studies in virtually every area of transcultural child psychiatry, we are currently unable to discuss the prevalence of mental disorder among children and adolescents of ethnic and cultural minorities. However, the perception and treatment of mental illness during childhood and even adolescence is heavily dependent on parental help-seeking behavior. It is known that certain minorities such as Asian and Hispanic groups tend to avoid mental health services, and consequently these minorities appear to underutilize mental health services for both child and adult disorders. Although a lack of presence among Hispanic and Asian patients in treatment centers may be a function of a relatively low prevalence of mental disorders among them, a reluctance to use these services is an alternative explanation.

As the United States becomes an increasingly culturally diversified society, there will also be a greater need for culturally competent professional and appropriately responsive settings to optimize the delivery of mental health services for minority groups. Utilization of mental health facilities by such groups has increased in recent years but for some minorities does not appear to be proportionate to the population at large. In California, for example, Hispanics and Asians appear to underutilize mental health services (Mochizuki, 1975; Yamamoto & Silva, 1987). The extent of this utilization remains unclear, especially for Spanish surnamed groups, because census tracts reflect the underreporting of undocumented individuals.

As previously mentioned, use of mental health care by minorities may be a function of how well mental health professionals can identify mental disorders in these groups. In the past, the absence of minorities seeking help for their medical problems was explained as a function of "protective" aspects of the culture including its own "folk" health care system. (Madsen, 1967). Although some cultures may in several respects be better adapted to the challenges of their own social and physical environment, other cultures may exhibit less adaptive approaches (Edgerton, 1992). Extensive epidemiological work in mental illness in the United States nevertheless reveals that ethnic and racial minorities have rates of mental disorders comparable to non-Hispanic Whites (Escobar, 1993). The relative lack of availability of culturally competent mental health professionals in the United States also leads to underutilization by minority groups not only because of difficulties in diagnostic assessment but also because faulty communication and limited cultural knowledge hinder the development of an empathic therapeutic relationship. These problems are also encountered in child psychiatric settings. For example, McMiller and Weisz (1996) studied 192 families about their help-seeking behaviors for children or adolescents in need of mental health care. They found that both Black and Hispanic families, compared with White families, were much less likely to seek help from mental health professionals and agencies as a first step (McMiller & Weisz, 1996).

Child Mental Health and the Law

The interplay between childhood and adolescent psychopathology and the legal system represents an important area of mental health inquiry. This is also true in the area of cultural mental health; however, issues that arise between minority children and adolescents and their families may present unique and special challenges for the mental health professional. Perhaps the most important factor to consider is that the families of minority children and adolescents are not only adjusting to the general influences that affect mainstream society but also are facing the transitional stress generated by the necessary adjustment of a minority culture into American society. This process is complicated by poverty at home, lack of familiarity with English, poor schools, racism, and a community ecology that generates existential frustration, fear, and violence. Domestic violence is a special problem for the emerging area of transcultural child mental health because factors such as poverty, poor parental education, and hopelessness tend to increase child abuse. As is well known, parental child abuse not only causes physical and psychological harm for the victims but also constitutes a strong modeling influence on the developing person. This situation has special repercussions on the intergenerational transmission of learned abusive behaviors and helps perpetuate a cycle of human beings who are unable to achieve optimal psychological development. Furthermore, children exposed to abusive behavior are at higher risk for developing attention deficit disorders, depression, posttraumatic stress disorder, and conduct disorders. The legal system may become involved in attempting to resolve these severe problems. The mental health-legal profession may be called to delineate the causative factors and outcomes involved in domestic child abuse. Cultural, psychological, and socioeconomic factors may need to be clearly delineated to provide optimal assessment and treatment.

Violence outside the household has reached unprecedented proportions in American society especially among ethnic communities in many large cities (Blumstein, 1995). High rates of adolescent-caused violence are endemic among Black and Hispanic American youth. For those who survive, the psychological sequelae are likely to include significant forms of stress disorders, depression, or at least maladaptive attitudes associated with hopelessness, frustration, and chronic low self-esteem.

Future Trends in Treatment, Research, and Social Policy

Although the field of transcultural child and adolescent mental health is still in its embryonic stage, it will continue to grow because of an increasing demand for services for ethnic minority children and youth. At present, about 40% of public school students belong to an ethnic minority, a proportion that is likely to remain high as the United States makes its way into the 21st century. Some minorities—especially the Hispanic and Asian American groups—are likely to increase their proportion of the population. Along with population increases in ethnic minorities, professionals are likely to see associated problems that have traditionally plagued minority children and adolescents as well as any other groups that are or become socially disenfranchised by the mainstream community. Problems such as child abuse, adolescent violence, substance abuse, posttraumatic stress disorder, and other psychopathology are likely to continue to affect ethnic minorities. Although members of mainstream society face these problems, cultural and ethnic minority groups are at greater risk because they represent socioeconomically disadvantaged groups that are likely to be experiencing stress, mental disorders, and incidents of violence. Resolving such problems will necessitate not only novel ways for obtaining optimal diagnoses and treatment but also the continued development of social policies at local, state, and federal levels. Nor can we as mental health professionals expect to overcome these problems by only looking at the confines of the United States. The impact of immigration from other countries, armed conflict, and economic pressures will continue to force our country to resolve its problems as a function of international factors. An international perspective on childhood and adolescent mental disorders is therefore necessary if professionals are to achieve a truly biopsychosociocultural model for understanding early childhood development in terms of the emerging field of transcultural child and adolescent mental health.

References

ADAMS, P. L. (1990). Prejudice and exclusion as social trauma. In J. D. Noshpitz & R. D. Coddington (Eds.), *Stressors and the adjustment disorders* (pp. 362–391). New York: Wiley.

AMERICAN PSYCHIATRIC ASSOCIATION. (1994). *Diagnostic and statistical manual of mental disorders* (4th ed.). Washington, DC: Author.

BARKER, G. C. (1975a). Pachuco: An American-Spanish argot and its social function in Tucson, Arizona. In E. Hernandez-Chavez, A. D. Cohen, & A. F. Beltramo (Eds.), *El Lenguaje de los Chicanos* (pp. 183–201). Arlington, VA: Center for Applied Linguistics.

BARKER, G. C. (1975b). Social functions of language in a Mexican-American community. In E. Hernandez-Chavez, A. D. Cohen, & A. F. Beltramo (Eds.), *El Lenguaje de los Chicanos* (pp. 170–182). Arlington, VA: Center for Applied Linguistics.

BIRD, N. R., CANINO, G., RUBIO-STIPEC, M., GOULD, M. S., RIBERA, J., SESMAN, M., WOODBURY, M., HUERTAS-GOLDMAN, S., PAGAN, A., SANCHEZ-LACEY, A., & MASCOSO, M. (1988). Estimates of the prevalence of childhood maladjustment in a community survey in Puerto Rico. *Archives of General Psychiatry, 45,* 1120–1126.

BIRD, N. R., YAGER, T. J., STAGHEZZA, B., GOULD, M. S., CANINO, G., & RUBIO-STIPEC, M. (1990). Impairment in the epidemiological measurement of childhood psychopathology in the community. *Journal of the American Academy of Child and Adolescent Psychiatry, 29,* 796–803.

BLUMSTEIN, A. (1995). Violence by young people: Why the deadly mexus. *National Institute of Justice Journal, 229,* 2–9.

BOWLBY, J. (1973). *Separation.* New York: Basic Books.

BOWLBY, J. (1982). *Attachment.* New York: Basic Books.

BURNAM, M. A., HOUGH, R. L., KARNO, M., ESCOBAR, J. I., & TELLES, C. A. (1987). Acculturation and lifetime prevalence of psychiatric disorders among Mexican-Americans in Los Angeles. *Journal of Health and Social Behavior, 28,* 89–102.

CANINO, G. (1996). Cultural comments of childhood—onset disorders: II. In J. E. Mezzich, A. Kleinman, H. Fabrega, & D. L. Parron (Eds.), *Culture and psychiatric diagnosis: A DSM-IV perspective* (pp. 279–281). Washington, DC: American Psychiatric Association.

CANINO, G., CANINO, I. A., & BRAVO, M. (1994). Diagnostic assessment with Hispanic children. In S. K. Hoppe & W. H. Holtzman (Eds.), *Search for a common language in psychiatric assessment* (pp. 36–47). Austin: Texas-World Health Organization Collaborating Center.

CANINO, I. A., & SPURLOCK, J. (1994). *Culturally diverse children and adolescents, assessment, diagnosis, and treatment.* New York: Guilford Press.

CERVANTES, R. I., & ARROYO, W. (1994). *DSM-IV:* Implications for Hispanic children and adolescents. *Hispanic Journal of Behavioral Sciences, 16,* 8–27.

DASEN, P. R. (1975). Concrete operational development in three cultures. *Journal of Cross-Cultural Psychology, 6,* 156–173.

DOMINO, G. (1992). Cooperation and competition in Chinese and American children. *Journal of Cross-Cultural Psychology, 23,* 456–467.

EDGERTON, R. B. (1992). *Sick societies. Challenging the myth of primitive harmony.* New York: Free Press.

EPSTEIN, H. (1979). *Children of the Holocaust: Conversations with daughters of survivors.* New York: Bantam Books.

ERCHAK, G. M. (1992). *The anthropology of self and behavior.* New Brunswick, NJ: Rutgers University Press.

ERIKSON, E. (1950). *Childhood and society.* New York: Norton.

ESCOBAR, J. I. (1993). Psychiatric epidemiology. In A. C. Gaw (Ed.), *Culture, ethnicity and mental illness* (pp. 43–73). Washington, DC: American Psychiatric Press.

ESCOBAR, J. I., BURNAM, A., KARNO, M., FORSYTH, A., & GOLDING, J. M. (1987). Somatization in the community. *Archives of General Psychiatry, 44,* 713–718.

FABREGA, H. (1996). Cultural and historical foundations of psychiatric diagnosis. In J. E. Mezzick, A. Kleinman, H. Fabrega, & D. L. Parron (Eds.), *Culture and psychiatric diagnosis: A DSM-IV perspective* (pp. 3–14). Washington, DC: American Psychiatric Association.

FABREGA, H., AHN, C. W., BOSTER, J., & MEZZICH, J. (1990). *DSM-III* as a systemic culture pattern: Studying intracultural variation among psychiatrists. *Psychiatric Research, 24,* 139–154.

FREUD, S. (1966). *Introductory lectures on psycho-analysis.* New York: Norton.

FROMM, E., & MACCOBY, M. (1970). *Social character in a Mexican village.* Englewood Cliffs, NJ: Prentice-Hall.

GRIFFITH, E. E. H., & GONZALES, C. A. (1994). Essentials of cultural psychiatry. In R. E. Hales, S. C. Yudofsky, & J. A. Talbot (Eds.), *American psychiatric press textbook of psychiatry* (2nd ed., pp. 1379–1404). Washington, DC: American Psychiatric Press.

HAYNES, N. M., & COMER, J. P. (1990). The effects of a school development program on self-concept. *Yale Journal of Biological Medicine, 63,* 275–283.

HELZER, J. E., CANINO, G. J., YEH, E. K., BLAND, R. C., LEE, C. K., HWU, H. G., & NEWMAN, S. (1990). Alcoholism-North America and Asia. *Archives of General Psychiatry, 47,* 313–319.

HOFFMAN, C. (1991). *An introduction to bilingualism.* New York: Longman.

HWU, H. G., YEH, E. K., & CHANG, L. Y. (1989). Prevalence of psychiatric disorders in Taiwan defined by the Chinese diagnostic interview schedule. *Acta Psychiatrica Scandinavica, 79,* 136–147.

KARNO, M., HOUGH, R. L., BURMAN, A., ESCOBAR, J. I., TIMBERS, D. M., SANTANA, F., & BOYD, J. H. (1987). Lifetime prevalence of specific psychiatric disorders among Mexican-Americans and non-Hispanic whites in Los Angeles. *Archives of General Psychiatry, 44,* 695–701.

KIRMAYER, L. J., YOUNG, A., & ROBBINS, J. M. (1994). Symptom attribution in cultural perspective. *Canadian Journal of Psychiatry, 39,* 584–595.

KLEINMAN, A. (1996). How is culture important for *DSM-IV.* In J. E. Mezzick, A. Kleinman, H. Fabrega, & D. L. Parron (Eds.), *Culture and psychiatric diagnosis: A* DSM-IV *perspective* (pp. 15–25). Washington, DC: American Psychiatric Association.

LEVINE, R. A. (1984). Properties of culture: An ethnographic view. In R. A. Schweder & R. A. LeVine (Eds.), *Culture theory: Essays on mind, self and emotion* (pp. 67–87). New York: Cambridge University Press.

LEWIS-FERNANDEZ, R., & KLEINMAN, A. (1994). Culture, personality and psychopathology. *Journal of Abnormal Psychology, 103,* 67–71.

MADSEN, W. (1967). *The Mexican-Americans of South Texas.* New York: Holt, Rinehart and Winston.

MATTHEWS, J., & MATTHEWS, L. (1983). *One billion: A China chronicle.* New York: Random House.

MCMILLER, W. P., & WEISZ, J. R. (1996). Help-seeking preceding mental health clinic intake among African-American, Latino and Caucasian youths. *Journal of the American Academy of Child and Adolescent Psychiatry, 35,* 1086–1094.

MCRAE, H. (1994). *The world in 2020: Power, culture and prosperity.* Boston: Harvard Business School Press.

MOCHIZUKI, M. (1975). *Discharge and units of service by ethnic origin: Fiscal year 1973–1974* (Vol. 3, Rep. No, 11). Los Angeles: County of LA Department of Health Services.

OKAMOTO, Y., CASE, R., BLEIKER, C., & HENDERSON, B. (1996). Cross-cultural investigations. *Monographs of the Society for Research in Child Development, 61,* 131–155.

POWELL, G. J., YAMAMOTO, J., MORALES, A., & ROMERO, A. (1983). *The psychosocial development of minority children.* New York: Brunner/Mazel.

SILVA, J. A., & LIEDERMAN, P. H. (1986). The life-span approach to individual therapy: An overview with case presentation. In P. B. Baltes, D. Featherman, & R. M. Lerner (Eds.), *Life-span development and behavior* (Vol. 7, pp. 113–134). Hillsdale, NJ: Erlbaum.

SPURLOCK, J., & NORRIS, D. M. (1991). The impact of culture and race on the development of African Americans in the United States. In A. Tasman & S. M. Goldfinger (Eds.), *American psychiatric press review of psychiatry* (Vol. 10, pp. 594–607). Washington, DC: American Psychiatric Press.

STEIN, D. J. (1993). Cross-cultural psychiatry and the *DSM-IV. Comprehensive Psychiatry, 34,* 322–329.

STEINBERGER, C. B. (1989). Teenage depression: A cultural-interpersonal-intrapsychic perspective. *Psychoanalytic Review, 76,* 1–18.

SUE, D. W., & SUE, D. (1981). *Counseling the culturally different: Theory and practice.* New York: Wiley.

TAN, S. Y. (1989). Psychopathology and culture: The Asian-American context. *Journal of Psychology and Christianity, 8,* 61–75.

THOMPSON, J. W., WALKER, R. D., & SILK-WALKER, P. (1993). Psychiatric care of American Indians and Alaska natives. In A. C. Gaw (Ed.), *Culture, ethnicity and mental illness* (pp. 189–243). Washington, DC: American Psychiatric Press.

WELLER, E. B., & WELLER, R. A. (1991). Mood disorders. In M. Lewis (Ed.), *Child and adolescent psychiatry. A comprehensive textbook* (pp. 646–664). Baltimore: Williams & Wilkins.

YAMAMOTO, J. (1978). Research priorities in Asian American mental health delivery. *American Journal of Psychiatry, 135,* 457–458.

YAMAMOTO, J. (1995). Beyond psychotherapy—community psychotherapy to prevent depression and anxiety in Asian. In L. Cheng, H. Baxter, & F. Cheung (Eds.), *Psychotherapy for the Chinese–II* (pp. 145–150). Hong Kong: Hong Kong Contemporary Development.

YAMAMOTO, J., & SILVA, J. A. (1987). Do Hispanics under utilize mental health services? In *Health and behavior: Research agenda for Hispanics. The Simon Bolivar Research Monograph Series* (Vol. 1, pp. 267–277). Chicago: University of Illinois.

YAMAMOTO, J., SILVA, J. A., & CHANG, C. V. (in press). Transitions in Asian American elderly. In S. I. Greenspan & G. H. Pollock (Eds.), *The course of life.* Madison, CT: International Universities Press.

YAMAMOTO, J., TAKEUCHI, D. T., SUE, S., & KURASAKI, K. (1995, October). *Cross-cultural epidemiology.* Proceedings of the 7th Scientific meeting of the Pacific Rim College of Psychiatrists, Fukuoka, Japan.

PART II

PORTRAITS OF
AMERICA'S CHILDREN

CHAPTER 3

Puerto Rican Children

IAN CANINO and LUIS H. ZAYAS

SINCE THE MAINLAND PUERTO RICAN population comprises the second largest Latino group in the United States, understanding the developmental and psychosocial adjustment issues of their children is of vital importance to mental health professionals, educators, and researchers. Despite their population size, little empirical research on normative developmental processes has been conducted on these children and adolescents. Published research on mental health issues is more common. Due to the paucity of adequate developmental research that would allow contrasting psychopathological conditions with normative, culturally influenced developmental processes, any comprehensive discussion of this population requires drawing on the research done on the general U.S. child and adolescent population and other Latino groups.

Furthermore, any discussion of mainland Puerto Rican children requires that we highlight the contextual influences of their development. Under average expectable conditions, only minor variations in the physical maturation of children across races, cultures, and ethnicities are seen because the organism essentially follows biologically predetermined patterns. When provided with adequate environmental circumstances for the unfolding of maturational capacities, mainland Puerto Rican children do not differ significantly from children of other ethnic and racial groups. Some Puerto Rican children in the United States grow in conditions of relative advantage and stability, in which parents are physically and emotionally healthy and have achieved educational, occupational, and financial success. Among these children, professionals may see few developmental problems. Some mainland Puerto Rican children grow up in contexts of stress and poverty that place their cognitive, psychosocial, and physical development at risk. Others in the same environment possess factors that help guard against or minimize negative developmental outcomes.

In considering the psychosocial development of mainland Puerto Rican children, we are, in fact, considering how culture and other contextual factors influence development. Borrowing from Brooks-Gunn (1995), "whenever the term *children's development* is used, it must stand for children's development in context" (p. 468, italics in original), our focus in this chapter is to place Puerto Rican children's development within a framework that incorporates elements of the Puerto Rican family within the risk and protective factors in their environment.

Context and Development

Puerto Ricans in the mainland United States represent the second largest Latino group. Although concentrated primarily in the Northeast, they have established large communities in the Midwest and increasingly in the Southeast, principally in Florida. Population data indicate that mainland Puerto Ricans number about 2.4 million, constituting 10.6% of the total Latino population of 22.8 million (U.S. Bureau of the Census, 1995a). Compared with the general U.S. population, Puerto Ricans on the mainland tend to be younger (median age 26.9), have lower educational attainment, earn less, and are more likely to be unemployed and live below the poverty level. Compared with other Latino groups, Puerto Rican families have the lowest median income (U.S. Bureau of the Census, 1995a, 1995b), have younger mothers than other Latino families, and consequently have more young children in the household (Wasserman, Brunelli, Rauh, & Alvarado, 1994).

Because of their large migration after World War II, Puerto Ricans in the mainland now represent several generations, from those with decades of residency to those more newly arrived. The phenomenon known as "circular migration" between the mainland and the island, facilitated by U.S. citizenship and affordable air travel, has exposed many Puerto Ricans to both island and mainland cultures. In New York City, which has the largest concentration of Puerto Ricans outside the island, Puerto Ricans now comprise about 50% of all Latinos. New York Puerto Ricans tend to be young (median age 27), have high rates of fertility and female-headed households, and are among the poorest New Yorkers (Hispanic Research Center, 1995).

Thus, after many years of migration and residence in the United States, the socioeconomic conditions of Puerto Ricans remain poor.

RISK FACTORS

Environmental factors associated with negative behavioral outcomes in children are inadequate health care (Paterson, De Baryshe, & Ramsey, 1989), situational stress (Wahler & Dumas, 1986), inadequate treatment of parental psychopathology (Downey & Coyne, 1990; Hall, Williams, & Greenberg, 1985) and marital discord (Jouriles, Pfiffner, & O'Leary, 1988). Rutter (1979) adds low social status, overcrowding or large family size, paternal criminality, and admission of a child to foster care. It is the cumulative effect of these factors, more than the existence of any single factor, that increases the possibility of negative outcomes.

In those children reared in inner cities who are exposed to contexts characterized by the real or possible chronic exposure to injury, multiple traumas, abandonment, or exploitation, a series of behaviors has been reported. These children may indicate action-oriented impulsive behavior, low frustration tolerance, present-time orientation, ambivalent interaction with others, and poor verbal mediation skills for conflict resolution. In addition, they may be hypervigilant and unable to trust, and may indicate core feelings of being bad or worthless (Schaer, 1988). Children facing neighborhoods and schools fraught with danger will develop behaviors that are often attempts at adaptation, as the following case indicates.

Case Example

Juan, a 12-year-old Puerto Rican child born in New York, came to the attention of a mental health clinic because he was impulsive, overreactive, inattentive, and had difficulties monitoring his aggressive feelings. Previous evaluations had concluded that he required medication. This had been partially effective. On closer inspection, he had no history of any of these symptoms before the age of 7, and the symptoms only caused impairment in school. He had no previous history of learning disabilities. The symptoms had started as he entered the middle school of a well-known problematic and poorly funded school two years prior to the present evaluation. The school offered no consistent discipline, the classrooms were large and noisy, and he was exposed to unsupervised and sometimes aggressive youth from the higher grades. Due to the exhausted teachers, there was no true academic stimulation. Juan had been initially abused by the older children and had acquired an offensive and hypervigilant style to defend himself. His previous sense of humor and malleability had been supplanted by a rigid and "tough" style; his initial interest in academic subjects, by a bored and pessimistic approach to "book work." He was already behind one year in his achievement scores. His psychological, social, and cognitive development were clearly at risk. An immediate change to a new school environment was recommended. After this was implemented and on a 2-year follow-up, Juan was doing well and he was no longer on medication.

Risk factors present in the physical environment, in addition, can correlate with the occurrence of central nervous system damage and influence its subsequent development. Murphy and Moriarty (1976) call attention to those sensory motor deficits, deviant body morphology, unusual sensitivities, integrative and adaptive difficulties, poor impulse control, inhibitions, and incapacities to read a caretaker's cues, which place children at risk to adequately cope with stress.

In a study by Werner and Smith (1982), perinatal complications were correlated to future impairment in both physical and psychological development for children in general when combined with persistent poor environmental circumstances. Many children with biological risk factors and difficult temperaments had a worse prognosis for developing learning disabilities when their caretakers were stressed and the home situation was chaotic. Research shows higher than average developmental risks for mainland Puerto Rican children than Mexican American or other children in areas such as birth weight, congenital problems, chronic medical conditions, functional limitations, and physician diagnosis of medical problems (Arcia, Keyes, & Gallagher, 1994).

Other environmental risk factors are created by the conditions in which many Puerto Rican children live. The prevalence of asthma among Puerto Rican children living in poverty in inner-city neighborhoods is greater than Mexican American, Cuban American, and other Puerto Rican children (Carter-Pokras & Gergen, 1993). Many different factors seem to explain this finding. Puerto Rican families in the United States often live in inner-city areas with poor air quality, which are also hosts to industrial sites. Other findings indicate that Puerto Rican children may have greater residential exposure to tobacco smoke due to parental and other household smoking (Pletsch, 1994). Puerto Rican mothers of reproductive age smoke more than other Hispanic women, increasing the risk for asthma and bronchial reactions in themselves and their children (Pletsch, 1991). Compounding the risk of asthma prevalence is the finding reported by Pachter and Weller (1993) that less acculturated Puerto Rican parents of asthmatic children are less compliant with their children's asthma treatment than Puerto Rican parents who are more acculturated or bicultural. One effect of this high asthma prevalence and lack of adherence to asthma treatment regimen is increased school absence which in turn affects academic performance.

PROTECTIVE FACTORS

The same protective factors that mediate ecological stressors, in children and families of other ethnic and cultural groups, also reduce the risk for negative developmental outcomes among Puerto Rican youth.

Protective family factors include homes in which rules are consistently and fairly enforced (Werner & Smith, 1982), good supervision and well-balanced discipline is available as well as a high level of warmth and an absence of severe criticism (Rutter, 1979), a good relationship exists between the parents (Werner & Smith, 1982), and an adequate identification figure is present in the household (Garmezy, 1981). Educational research with Puerto Rican families supports the influence of these universal factors in protecting children's futures. Diaz Soto (1988) reports that parents of high-achieving Puerto Rican children in the fifth and sixth grades hold high aspirations for their children and themselves and are knowledgeable and involved in their children's educational activities.

The family context in which children of any ethnocultural group grow is important for examining the children and adolescents' developmental outcomes. Recent research in child socialization in Puerto Rican families holds some important evidence for understanding Puerto Rican child socioemotional and behavioral development. Across studies, Puerto Rican and other Latino parents often emphasize the child and adolescent's social behavior both in the home and in public. In reviewing the literature on early childhood socialization among Latino groups, Zayas and Solari (1994) point to the emphasis on having children be obedient, follow rules, and conform in classroom settings. Similarly, Latino parents give equal or greater emphasis to their children's noncognitive social skills as they give to the children's cognitive problem-solving skills.

In a study of infant attachment and maternal perceptions of infants' behaviors, Harwood, Miller, and Irizarry (1995) report that in contrast to Anglo-American mothers' concern with instilling in their toddlers an optimal balance of autonomy and relatedness, Puerto Rican mothers focus on contextually appropriate levels of relatedness. One dimension of relatedness that Harwood et al. (1995) term "proper demeanor" refers to Puerto Rican parents' preference for children to exhibit the quality of being *educado*. The well-brought-up child will be one who is *tranquilo, obediente*, and *respetuoso*. That is, "the child is calm, obedient, and respectfully attentive to the teachings of his or her elders, in order to become skilled in the interpersonal and rhetorical competencies that will someday be expected of the well-socialized adult" (p. 98). With this emphasis, Puerto Rican parents appear to express the importance given to the public domain in personal behavior. In addition to rearing children to be *bien educado*, parents' socialization of their children emphasizes that children be *amable* (polite, gentle, kind, and good), which describes a person whose interactions are based on seeking positive relatedness with all people, not just friends and family (Harwood et al., 1995).

Case Example

Natalia, a Puerto Rican second grader, is the oldest of two daughters of an intact Puerto Rican family who had recently moved to a middle-income suburban community. Her mother was expecting a third child and her father was employed as a handyman in a small apartment complex where they resided. Her teacher became concerned with how shy, reticent, apparently anxious, and unassertive Natalia was in the classroom. Natalia seldom spoke up in class and would not initiate conversation with the teacher, never raised her hand, and answered only questions posed to her by the teacher. Natalia did not present any behavioral problems, but in fact was exceedingly cooperative when asked by the teacher to assist her (e.g., running an errand to the principal's office). At recess, Natalia chatted animatedly with other girls, according to the teacher, but would become quiet when an adult approached. In a routine teacher-parent conference, the teacher raised her concerns with Natalia's mother, whose English was quite limited. Hearing that the teacher was "worried" about Natalia alarmed the mother. Natalia's mother discussed her concerns with her husband, who had been unable to attend the meeting. More fluent in English than his spouse, Natalia's father spoke with the teacher and could not understand why the teacher was so concerned when Natalia was doing quite well. Tension developed between the parents and the teacher, with the parents feeling that Natalia was being targeted and the teacher feeling that the parents were overlooking Natalia's inhibitions in the classroom. In consultation with a Puerto Rican psychologist, it was apparent that both parents held to relatively traditional Puerto Rican child-rearing beliefs about the importance that children demonstrate respect and deference to adult authority, and that children comply with teachers' requests, conform to rules of the classroom, and not question the teacher or speak out of turn. When the teacher was helped to understand the cultural influences on Natalia's classroom demeanor, she became less concerned with what she had at first thought to be excessive inhibition. The parents were also assisted in understanding the value held by American teachers that pupils be assertive, creative, and independent in their learning.

Although focusing on the child's public demeanor, this child-rearing belief that encourages appropriate social behavior does not diminish the intensity of a family-centered socialization or its maintenance as children mature. Latino adolescents have been reported to indicate greater satisfaction with family life than non-Latino adolescents (Schumm et al., 1988) and respect their parents' views (Coombs, Paulson, & Richardson, 1991) more than Anglo-American adolescents. Ramirez and Price-Williams (1976) reported that Latino children tend to express achievement motivation in the form of family achievement, indicating the cultural emphasis on the importance of the family as a collective unit. In short, one member's achievement is the family's achievement. Similarly, Martinez and Dukes (1987) noted that when traits associated with self-concept were grouped according to whether they existed in the "private" domain (e.g., satisfaction with self based on family-based standards) or "public" domain (e.g., satisfaction with self based on standards of social success bestowed by extrafamilial sources),

Latino adolescents showed higher levels of self-esteem in the private domain than in the public domain.

It is well known that across social class, ethnicity, and race, effective parenting, in which parents supervise their children closely and establish clear-cut rules and values, attenuates children and adolescents' involvement in negative social behaviors. In the Puerto Rican culture two elements are traditionally associated with decreased risk for antisocial behavior: social control (Hirschi, 1969) based on strong family attachments (Hagan, 1989) and direct parental control based on strict discipline and coercion (Paterson, 1982). When compared with Anglo-American adolescents, father-absent homes in Latino adolescents had a greater effect on delinquent behavior (Wilkinson, 1980). Sommers, Fagan, and Baskin (1993) conclude that high levels of adherence to a familistic orientation contribute to the avoidance of delinquent behavior in mainland Puerto Rican adolescents.

These adolescents, like other Latino adolescents in the United States, are pulled at times by competing culturally patterned value systems: one that emphasizes family closeness and obligation to parental demands and another that emphasizes greater physical and psychological independence from the family. The capacity of some Puerto Rican families to adapt to their adolescent's social and developmental needs while remaining a cohesive unit provides the adolescent with the skills to balance these competing demands. In other families in which demands for adherence to cultural beliefs about family ties are rigid, the potential for problematic behaviors is increased.

So-called invulnerable children display appropriate levels of sociability, dominance, endurance, high activity level, demonstrativeness, reflectiveness, and impulse control (Garmezy, 1981; Werner, Hough, Golding, Burnam, & Karno, 1961). Resilient adolescents possess an internalized set of values and are more socially perceptive and mature, more responsible, more appreciative and nurturant and possess better verbal communication skills than those who succumb to stress (Werner & Smith, 1982). For resilient, well-functioning Puerto Rican children and adolescents a core appreciation of their ethnic identity, familistic values, and the appropriate adaptation to a bicultural and often bilingual environment are additional factors.

An important aspect of healthy psychosocial development for children of migrants is a solid sense of ethnic identity. Research has shown that ethnic and racial concepts emerge through childhood and adolescence (Goodman, 1964; Porter, 1971; Rotheram & Phinney, 1986) and that developmental changes in a child's ethnic awareness and identity often occur in response to change in generational or sociocultural group, developmental growth, or the interaction among these influences (Aboud & Mitchell, 1977; Canino & Spurlock, 1994; Katz, 1976).

In addition, the development of a sense of ethnicity and culture in children often implies two processes: enculturation and acculturation (Berry, Trimble, & Olmedo, 1986). Enculturation is defined as the awareness and acquisition of the social norms of one's own cultural group. Acculturation includes one of two processes; assimilation or biculturalism. Assimilation is the desire or the attempt by a group to give up its own identity and culture and adopt fully that of the majority culture, whereas biculturalism implies retaining important aspects of the original culture while adopting characteristics of the host culture as well (Oetting & Beauvais, 1990; Rogler, Cortes, & Malgady, 1991). Although acculturation occurs in many children of different ethnic groups, Puerto Rican children who are exposed to many different cultural groups may define their ethnic identity through mechanisms that differ from those of Puerto Rican youth who are less exposed to a multicultural grouping. For example, Rodriguez-Cortes (1990) studied the social practices of ethnic identity among 60 students in two groups of Puerto Ricans. Mainland Puerto Rican adolescents based their ethnic identity on motivational factors such as how they felt or thought about themselves, whereas island-based adolescents based ethnic identity on behavior. In short, those on the island defined Puerto Rican ethnic identity on the basis of a repertoire of social behaviors, but the mainland group, exposed to the behavioral repertoires of many different groups (and acculturation to them), considered their socioemotional identification of being Puerto Rican as evidencing their ethnic identity.

Case Example

Maria, a 16-year-old, third-generation Puerto Rican adolescent from a large urban center, was quick, assertive, and outspoken. She spoke little Spanish but was expressive and passionate in her ideas and her strong opinions of the woman's role in society. Her taste in music and clothes as well as her idiomatic expressions reflected the strong influences of Central American, African American, and Asian American youth to whom she had been exposed growing up. Even though she felt Puerto Rican, was proud of her heritage, and had often visited "the island," she confessed she had recently gone through a crisis in her self-perception and identity. On a recent trip to Puerto Rico, she had difficulties with her assertive style, was ostracized for her lack of Spanish skills, and the boys there had misconstrued her social behavior and independence and thought her "easy." Initially, she was deeply disappointed and wished to deny her heritage. After much thought, many conversations with her family who were at multiple levels of acculturation, and extensive reading of books recently authored by Puerto Rican women raised in the United States, she decided she belonged to a special and new generation of Puerto Rican adolescents. She could share certain aspects of herself with island friends but was most comfortable with those friends she grew up with and fully identified with those Puerto Rican women who had similar experiences.

Furthermore, how well children and adolescents go through this process is often related to their level of self-esteem. In a study by Phinney (1989), high school students with a clear sense of their ethnicity had higher levels of self-esteem than those that did not. Adolescents who are unable to integrate their bicultural exposure well and indicate high levels of

assimilation have been correlated with greater risk for psycho-
pathology and delinquent behavior among Latino adolescents
(Fridrich & Flannery, 1995; Rogler et al., 1991; Vega, Gil, Warheit,
Zimmerman, & Apospori, 1993).

In a study comparing Latino and African American third
and sixth graders from lower and lower middle-class groups,
Rotheram and Phinney (1990) found that Latino children were
more group oriented, more reliant on authority figures for solving problems, more likely to respond to a correction by a peer by
doing nothing or feeling bad, and were less assertive in expressing themselves to peers and adults. Children with response patterns similar to their own ethnic group indicated higher
self-esteem. Sixth graders, consistent with norms of social behavior (Eisenberg, 1986) reported less emotional responses and
were more likely to take direct action, intervene to stop a fight,
and lend money to a peer.

Research evidence suggests that a second language does
not compete with the first language during language acquisition but that both languages build on a common cognitive base
that is the same for many languages. All other things being
equal, young Puerto Rican children demonstrate typical second
language behaviors (Shannon, 1990) such as rhyming, singing,
and repeating jingles that are associated with successful English
acquisition (Wong-Fillmore, 1983). The acquisition of a second
language often enriches the native language and bilingualism
is associated with higher levels of cognitive attainment (Hakuta
& Garcia, 1989).

In a study of Puerto Rican children in a bilingual program
in New Haven, Connecticut, Hakuta (1987) concluded that there
are some correlations between bilingualism and nonverbal measures of cognitive ability in the younger groups of kindergarten
and first graders but not on metalinguistic performance. In a
study of Latino bilingual children, Gonzalez (1994) concluded
that the children construct a representational system that is similar and nonverbal across languages. In addition, they create a
second representational system that is verbal and culturally
linguistically bound. They concluded that based on gender-based
point assignments areas, bilingual children construct two

culturally linguistically bound representational systems for verbal concepts that are different between languages.

In recently migrated Spanish-speaking children, both the rate of English language acquisition and the context and frequency of language utilization may vary. The child may use language in an active or interactive setting or in a passive and receptive one (Shannon, 1990). Some Puerto Rican children may use English at school but not at home or in their communities; others may use English at school and in their neighborhoods but not at home; and still others may use both languages interchangeably in all or some settings. Some Puerto Rican children may act as "language brokers" and expose themselves to both languages. In the process, they acquire the additional language skills of translation and interpretation. This, nevertheless, may have the unpleasant effect of leading to parentified roles in their families. The more acculturated children and families eventually become English-dominant, and in second and third generations the children often are monolingual in English. Veltman (1983) reports that the eventual widespread use of English occurs among Latinos as in other migrant groups, but in Latinos it occurs at a slower pace.

Those children with language-processing problems, cognitive disabilities, or those exposed to the current chaos of many of our public school systems certainly do not do as well. Many Puerto Rican children in the inner cities are in the process of becoming bilingual in a context in which the second language is developing at the expense of the native language and are not learning either language well.

Case Example

Ramon, a 4-year-old Puerto Rican child born in San Juan, had been in the United States for the past two years in a bilingual preschool program. He indicated difficulties understanding words and sentences, had a limited vocabulary, and his sentence production was limited both in length and complexity for a boy his age. There had not been any early signs of language developmental delays prior to his arrival in the United States. A teacher had alarmed the parents by stating that the child had a receptive and expressive language disorder and that they should apply to a special education school for the next year. The parents sought further advice and a battery of standardized measures were administered by a bilingual and bicultural psychologist. No disorder was identified, and the parents were informed that the delay seemed to be related to the acquisition of two languages in a child who was within the normal range of ability but was not particularly adept in language and verbal tasks. After an additional six months, the child was developing well.

Conclusion

This chapter has reviewed those developmental and clinical factors associated with the psychosocial adjustment of mainland Puerto Rican children and adolescents.

Normal development is a complex phenomenon that attempts to explain the maturational stages of the growing child. Multifactorial influences support and enhance as well as hinder the outcomes on any individual's adjustment and achievement. Constitutional and environmental factors are in constant interplay producing a large variety of developmental paths and temporal sequences. This chapter thus addresses those ecological family and social factors that seem to be particularly relevant but not exclusive to the development of Puerto Rican children. Social stressors are underlined because they reflect the socioeconomic reality of this population on the mainland. Through case illustrations and a review of the existing literature, the ethnic, linguistic, and social developmental aspects of these children are discussed.

Many of these factors are shared by children of other ethnic and racial groups. The present body of research on Puerto Rican children's development does not allow for adequate comparisons with children of other ethnic groups and limits the conclusiveness of some of the present findings. Studies are needed that identify the interactions of sociocultural and neurobiological variables on development as well as more research that examines inter- and intraethnic differences and similarities between children of different groups.

References

ABOUD, F. E., & MITCHELL, F. G. (1977). The effects of preference and self identification. *International Journal of Psychology, 12,* 1–17.

ARCIA, E., KEYES, L., & GALLAGHER, J. J. (1994). Indicators of developmental and functional status of Mexican-American and Puerto Rican children. *Journal of Developmental and Behavioral Pediatrics, 15,* 27–33.

BERNAL, G. A., MARTINEZ, C., SANSEBASTIEN, D., BERNAL, M. E., & OLMEDO, E. E. (1983). Hispanic mental health curriculum for psychology. In J. C. Chunn, P. J. Dunston, & R. Ross-Sheriff (Eds.), *Mental health and people of color.* Washington, DC: Howard University Press.

BERRY, J. W., TRIMBLE, J. B., & OLMEDO, E. L. (1986). Assessment of acculturation. In W. J. Lonner & J. W. Berry (Eds.), *Field methods in cross-cultural research: Cross-cultural research and methodology series* (Vol. 8, pp. 291–324). Beverly Hills, CA: Sage.

BROOKS-GUNN, J. (1995). Children in families in communities: Risk and intervention in the Bronfenbrenner tradition. In P. Moen, G. H. Elder, Jr., & K. Luscher (Eds.), *Examining lives in context* (pp. 467–519). Washington, DC: American Psychological Association.

CANINO, I. A., & SPURLOCK, J. (1994). *Culturally diverse children and adolescents: Assessment, diagnosis, and treatment.* New York: Guilford Press.

CARTER-POKRAS, O. D., & GERGEN, P. J. (1993). Reported asthma among Puerto Rican, Mexican-American, and Cuban children, 1982–1984. *American Journal of Public Health, 83,* 580–582.

CITIZEN'S COMMITTEE FOR CHILDREN. (1993). *Keeping track of New York's children* (Status Report). New York: Author.

COOMBS, R. H., PAULSON, M. J., & RICHARDSON, M. A. (1991). Peer vs. parental influence in substance use among Hispanic and Anglo children and adolescents. *Journal of Youth and Adolescence, 20,* 73–88.

DIAZ SOTO, L. (1988). The home environment of higher and lower achieving Puerto Rican children. *Hispanic Journal of Behavioral Sciences, 10,* 161–167.

DOWNEY, G., & COYNE, J. C. (1990). Children of depressed parents: An integrative review. *Psychological Bulletin, 108,* 50–70.

DUSENBERRY, L., EPSTEIN, J. A., BOTVIN, G. J., & DIAZ, T. (1994). Social influence predictors of alcohol use among New York Latino youth. *Addictive Behaviors, 19,* 363–372.

EISENBERG, N. (1986). *Altruistic emotion, cognition, and behavior.* Hillsdale, NJ: Erlbaum.

FRIDRICH, A. H., & FLANNERY, D. J. (1995). The effects of ethnicity and acculturation on early adolescent delinquency. *Journal of Child and Family Studies, 4*(1), 69–87.

GARMEZY, N. (1981). Children under stress: Perspectives on antecedents and correlates of vulnerability and resistance to psychopathology. In A. I. Rabin, J. Aronoff, A. M. Barclay, & R. A. Zucker (Eds.), *Further explorations in personality* (pp. 196–270). New York: Wiley.

GONZALEZ, V. (1994). A model of cognitive, cultural, and linguistic variables affecting bilingual Hispanic children's development of concepts and language. *Hispanic Journal of Behavioral Sciences, 16*(4), 396–421.

GOODMAN, M. E. (1964). *Race awareness in young children* (Rev. ed.). New York: Collier.

HAGAN, J. (1989). *Structural criminology.* New Brunswick, NJ: Rutgers University Press.

HAKUTA, K. (1987). Degree of bilingualism and cognitive ability in mainland Puerto Rican children. *Child Development,* 1372–1388.

HAKUTA, K., & GARCIA, E. (1989). Bilingualism and education. *American Psychologist, 44*(2), 374–379.

HALL, A., WILLIAMS, C. A., & GREENBERG, R. S. (1985). Supports, stressors, and depressive symptoms in low income mothers of young children. *American Journal of Public Health, 75,* 518–522.

HARWOOD, R. L., MILLER, J. L., & IRIZARRY, N. L. (1995). *Culture and attachment: Perceptions of the child in context.* New York: Guilford Press.

HIRSCHI, T. (1969). *Causes of delinquency.* Berkeley: University of California Press.

HISPANIC RESEARCH CENTER. (1995). *Nuestra America en Nueva York: The new immigrant Hispanic population in New York City, 1980–1990.* New York: Fordham University.

JOURILES, E. N., PFIFFNER, L. J., & O'LEARY, K. D. (1988). Marital conflict, parenting, and toddler conduct problems. *Journal of Abnormal Child Psychology, 17,* 513–525.

KATZ, P. (1976). The acquisition of racial attitudes in children. In P. A. Katz (Ed.), *Towards the elimination of racism* (pp. 125–154). New York: Pergamon Press.

MARTINEZ, R., & DUKES, R. (1987). Race, gender, and self-esteem among youth. *Hispanic Journal of Behavioral Sciences, 9*, 427–443.

MCGOLDRICK, M., PEARCE, J. K., & GIORDANO, J. (Eds.). (1982). *Ethnicity and family therapy.* New York: Guilford Press.

MURPHY, L. B., & MORIARTY, A. E. (1976). *Vulnerability, coping, and growth from infancy to adolescence.* New Haven, CT: Yale University Press.

OETTING, E. R., & BEAUVAIS, F. (1990–1991). Orthogonal cultural identification theory: The cultural identification of minority adolescents. *International Journal of Addiction, 25*(5A/6A), 655–685.

PACHTER, L. M., & WELLER, S. C. (1993). Acculturation and compliance with medical therapy. *Journal of Developmental and Behavioral Pediatrics, 14*, 163–168.

PATERSON, G. R. (1982). *Coercive family process.* Eugene, OR: Castalia Press.

PATERSON, G. R., DE BARYSHE, B. D., & RAMSEY, E. (1989). A developmental perspective on antisocial behavior. *American Psychologist, 44*(2), 329–335.

PHINNEY, J. (1989). Stages of ethnic identity development in minority group adolescents. *Journal of Early Adolescence, 9*, 34–49.

PLETSCH, P. K. (1991). Prevalence of cigarette smoking in Hispanic women of childbearing age. *Nursing Research, 40*, 103–106.

PLETSCH, P. K. (1994). Environmental tobacco smoke exposure among Hispanic women of reproductive age. *Public Health Nursing, 11*, 229–235.

PORTER, J. D. W. (1971). *Black child, white child: The development of racial attitudes.* Cambridge, MA: Harvard University Press.

RAMIREZ, M., & PRICE-WILLIAMS, D. (1976). Achievement motivation in children of three ethnic groups in the United States. *Journal of Cross-Cultural Psychology, 7*, 49–60.

RODRIGUEZ-CORTES, C. (1990). Social practices of ethnic identity: A Puerto Rican psycho-cultural event. *Hispanic Journal of Behavioral Sciences, 12*, 380–396.

ROGLER, L. H., CORTES, D. E., & MALGADY, R. G. (1991). Acculturation and mental health status among Hispanics. *American Psychologist, 46*, 585–597.

ROTHERAM, M. J., & PHINNEY, J. S. (1986). Introduction: Definitions and perspectives in the study of childrens' ethnic socialization. In

J. S. Phinney & M. J. Rotheram (Eds.), *Children's ethnic socialization: Pluralism and development* (pp. 10–28). Newbury Park, CA: Sage.

ROTHERAM, M. J., & PHINNEY, J. S. (1990). Patterns of social expectation among black and Mexican American children. *Children Development, 61,* 542–556.

RUTTER, M. (1979). Protective factors in children's response to stress and disadvantage. In M. W. Kent & J. E. Rolf (Eds.), *Primary prevention of psychopathology: Vol. 3. Social competence in children* (pp. 49–74). Hanover, NH: University Press of New England.

SANCHEZ-AYENDEZ, M. (1988). The Puerto Rican American family. In C. H. Mindel, R. W. Habenstein, & R. Wright, Jr. (Eds.), *Ethnic families in America.* New York: Elsevier.

SCHAER, I. J. (1988, August). *A theoretical conceptualization of the multiply traumatized inner-city child of poverty.* Paper presented at the annual convention of the American Psychological Association.

SCHUMM, W. R., McCOLLUM, E. E., BUGAIGHIS, M. A., JURICH, A. P., BOLLMAN, S. R., & REITZ, J. (1988). Differences between Anglo and Mexican American family members on satisfaction with family life. *Hispanic Journal of Behavioral Sciences, 10,* 39–53.

SHANNON, S. M. (1990). English in the Barrio: The quality of contact among immigrant children. *Hispanic Journal of Behavioral Sciences, 12*(3), 256–276.

SOMMERS, I., FAGAN, J., & BASKIN, D. (1993). Sociocultural influences on the explanation of delinquency for Puerto Rican youth. *Hispanic Journal of Behavioral Sciences, 15*(1). 36–62.

TARNOWSKI, K. J., & ROHRBECK, C. A. (1993). Disadvantaged children and families. In T. H. Ollendick & J. Prinz (Eds.), *Advances in clinical child psychology* (Vol. 15, pp. 41–80). New York: Plenum Press.

U.S. BUREAU OF THE CENSUS. (1995a). *Current population reports* (pp. 23–189). Washington, DC: U.S. Government Printing Office.

U.S. BUREAU OF THE CENSUS. (1995b). *Statistical brief: The nation's Hispanic population—1994* (SB 95-25). Washington, DC: U.S. Government Printing Office.

VAZQUEZ-CALZADA, J. L. (1988). *La poblacion de Puerto Rico y su trayectoria historica* (pp. 283–312). Unpublished manuscript, University of Puerto Rico, School of Public Health, Medical Science Campus, San Juan, Puerto Rico.

VEGA, W. A., GIL, A. G., WARHEIT, G. J., ZIMMERMAN, R. S., & APOSPORI, E. (1993). Acculturation and delinquent behavior among Cuban American adolescents: Toward an empirical model. *American Journal of Community Psychology, 21*(1), 113–125.

VELTMAN, C. (1983). *The assimilation of American language minorities: Structure, pace and extent.* Washington, DC: National Center for Education Statistics.

WAHLER, R. G., & DUMAS, J. E. (1986). Maintenance factors in coercive mother child interactions: The compliance and predictability hypothesis. *Journal of Applied Behavioral Analysis, 19*(1), 13–22.

WASSERMAN, G. A., BRUNELLI, S. A., RAUH, V. A., & ALVARADO, L. E. (1994). The cultural context of adolescent childrearing in three groups of urban minority mothers. In G. Lamberty & C. Garcia Coll (Eds.), *Puerto Rican women and children: Issues in health, growth, and development* (pp. 137–160). New York: Plenum Press.

WERNER, E. E., & SMITH, R. S. (1982). *Vulnerable but invincible: A study of resilient children.* New York: McGraw-Hill.

WERNER, K. B., HOUGH, R. L., GOLDING, J. M., BURNAM, M. A., & KARNO, M. (1961). *Personality characteristics of men and women who successfully assimilated stress during their formative years.* Paper presented at the biannual meeting of the Society for Research in Child Development, State College, PA.

WILKINSON, K. (1980). The broken home and delinquent behavior. In T. Hirschi & M. Godttfredson (Eds.), *Understanding crime.* Beverly Hills, CA: Sage.

WOLFGANG, M. E., FIGLIO, R., & SELLIN, T. (1972). *Delinquency in a birth cohort.* Chicago: University of Chicago Press.

WONG-FILLMORE, L. (1983). The language learner as an individual: Implications of research in individual differences for ESL teacher. In M. A. Clarke & J. Hamescombe (Eds.), *TESOL 82: Pacific perspectives on language training and teaching.* Washington, DC: TESOL.

ZAYAS, L. H., & BRYANT, L. H. (1984). Culturally sensitive treatment of adolescent Puerto Rican girls and their families. *Child Adolescence Social Work Journal, 1,* 235–253.

ZAYAS, L. H., & SOLARI, F. (1994). Early childhood socialization in Hispanic families: Context, culture, and practice implications. *Professional Psychology: Research and Practice, 25,* 200–206.

CHAPTER 4

Central American Children

WILLIAM ARROYO

THE PSYCHOSOCIAL DEVELOPMENT OF Central American children and their families who reside in the United States will be the focus of this chapter, which is intended to assist service agencies, individual providers of service, researchers, and policymakers in their efforts to improve the quality of life for these populations. As is the case for the other unique populations discussed in this book, a discussion of important health problems found in this population is beyond the scope of this chapter. Normal psychosocial development is closely intertwined with normal physical development. Other sources (Magar, 1990; Salas, Heifetz, & Barrett, 1990; Zambrana, Ell, Dorrington, Wachsman, & Hodge, 1994) address this area in depth.

The term *Central American* in this chapter refers to either immigrants or descendants of immigrants from Central America who now reside in the United States. Central America proper consists of the seven sovereign states of Guatemala, Belize, El Salvador, Honduras, Nicaragua, Costa Rica, and Panama. This term, Central American, therefore is more of a geographic descriptor than one that addresses national origin such as Salvadoran or Nicaraguan. There are many differences among these countries including government structures, economics, political histories, political relationships with the United States, customs, race, and even language (e.g., many different native languages are spoken by Guatemalan Indians). In the United

States, it is not uncommon for these populations to be included under the rubric of Hispanic or Latin American in both the lay and research literature despite the many differences among the groups. The inclusion of these populations with the other Latin American groups in the U.S. research literature jeopardizes the validity of the findings for these unique populations.

The racial makeup of the Central American populations is diverse. The predominant ancestries are native and European. African slavery was introduced on the Caribbean coastline in the 1500s and 1600s, however, and substantial migrations of people of African descent from the Caribbean area occurred at the turn of this century.

Between 1987 and 1990, 1,031,752 foreign-born children came to the United States with a large proportion from Central America (U.S. Bureau of the Census, 1993). Prior to 1975, the migration of Central Americans to the United States was relatively minimal. Emigration from Central America began to increase in the late 1980s and remains relatively high. This upswing was triggered by simultaneous intense civil strife and war in the countries of Guatemala, Nicaragua, El Salvador, and Honduras, which at times became a controversial focus of U.S. foreign policy (Ropp & Morris, 1984).

U.S. Census data combines population data of Central and South America and further classifies these two categories within the umbrella term *Hispanic*. Therefore, it is virtually impossible to identify population estimates from each of the Central American countries. Data from the Immigration and Naturalization Service indicates the Central American contingent accounted for approximately 5% of legal immigration to the United States between 1993 and 1995 (U.S. Immigration and Naturalization Service, 1997). During the 1995 fiscal year, El Salvador and Guatemala accounted for more than 50% of legal immigration from the Central American region. During the 1980s, under the status of political asylum, a large portion of legal Nicaraguan immigrants entered relative to the other Central American countries, which arguably was a reflection of U.S. foreign policy. There is no reliable data regarding the estimates of undocumented entrants from this region.

U.S. census data indicated that the Central American population in 1994 appeared to be a younger population than that of the general U.S. population with 30.5% under the age of 18 (includes South American immigrants) compared with 26.9% for the general population.

The U.S. Census Bureau data suggests that Central Americans (and South Americans) are an undereducated population relative to the U.S. population, as indicated by the estimated percentage of the population aged 25 years old or older who have not attended college. For the total U.S. population, the 1994 estimate is 53.5%, and for the Central and South American group, it is 65.9%.

The Central American population of children below the age of 18 also appears to be greater than that of the general population. The 1994 U.S. Census Bureau estimates in percentages are 42.4% (for Central and South American) and 40.1% (for the general population) (U.S. Bureau of the Census, 1996).

Psychosocial Development

Virtually no research is available in the United States on the psychosocial development of Central American children. Some of the research cited in the chapter on Mexican children and families has varying application to these populations. I will discuss some of the salient developmental themes that have been evident in clinical experience.

The socialization of Central American children in the United States has been largely influenced by the customs practiced in their country of origin or the country of origin of their ancestors. Some of these practices may also be regionally influenced given the degree of variation among some of the isolated native Central Americans within the same country. However, the influence of mainstream U.S. socialization has penetrated the beliefs, customs, and practices of many Central Americans; this is commonly referred to as acculturation. As in other Latin American countries, Roman Catholicism remains a powerful influence; however, active recruitment by fundamentalist religious sects is ongoing in major urban areas in the United States.

It is likely that a greater proportion of Central American children are fluent in Spanish than are other Latin American groups because of the recent immigration surge from this geographic area. As in the case of the Mexican children in the United States, Spanish-speaking children (Bernal, Knight, Garza, Ocampo, & Cota, 1990) will likely identify with their ancestral heritage. It has also been my observation that a child of Central American descent who is among a large group of non-Central American Latinos will readily identify him- or herself as being different from the group.

The awareness of racial and ethnic identity has not been studied among the Central American groups. However, it is probable that ethnic identification parallels that of the Mexican population (Bernal et al., 1990); its constancy similarly emerges at age 8 or later. Racial awareness would likely occur earlier (between ages 3–5) as in the African American and European American populations.

Cognitive development among Central Americans has not been a focus of research. There are many potential pitfalls (Cervantes & Arroyo, 1995; Figueroa, 1989) encountered in the use of psychometric instruments, especially those used to measure intelligence, on Latino children. The most obvious implications relate to the use of English language instruments with, for example, monolingual Spanish-speaking children. Furthermore, the point at which a bilingual child, whose primary language is not English, is "ready" to be tested in English is unknown; there simply is no standard. Cummins (1984) suggests that it takes five years for immigrant students who arrive after the age of six to acquire peer-appropriate cognitive/academic proficiency in English. Psychological tests that are available in Spanish (Figueroa, Delgado, & Ruiz, 1984) are designed for monolingual students with minimal or no sustained exposure to English. Thus, their validity for non-English speakers who are enmeshed in a predominantly English-immersion educational system, including bilingual programs, is highly questionable. Use of assessment instruments inappropriate for the particular child leads to a "false" interpretation of potential problems.

FAMILY STRUCTURE

Central Americans appear to place high value on family cohesion and loyalty. The roles of individual family members may become compromised in the face of a piecemeal pattern of migration of families to the United States, limited economic resources, limited social resources, and other hurdles faced by newly immigrated impoverished groups. Parenting studies of Central Americans are nonexistent.

CULTURAL IDENTITY AND CUSTOMS

Acculturation, or "cultural identity" as some authors (Felix-Ortiz de la Garza, Newcomb, & Myers, 1995) prefer, is a dynamic process on both a group and an individual level. Various investigators (Franco, 1983; Martinez, Norman, & Delaney, 1984; Olmedo, Martinez, & Martinez, 1978; Olmedo & Padilla, 1978) have developed instruments to measure acculturation primarily in Latino children; none to date have been used exclusively with the different Central American groups. This process and theme is often a salient one for Central Americans. The various members of one family, for example, will proceed at different rates of acculturation; this difference can become a focus of family conflict.

IMMIGRATION

Emigrating from a Central American country to the United States has been a common experience for many Central Americans. For some immigrants, especially those who have made thoughtful preparations, it has been a rewarding endeavor. For others, however, the experience has been fraught with intense suffering.

Relocation to the United States probably has a differential developmental impact; this has not been studied systematically. In general, the success with which the young child adjusts to the move will depend on the parents' successful adaptation. In the case of the unaccompanied minor, many more variables influence the success of the transition. The older adolescent may have a greater challenge establishing a new extrafamilial social network and learning English.

COMMON PSYCHOSOCIAL PROBLEMS AND
CLINICAL IMPLICATIONS

Myriad potential problems exist for a young emigré. Such problems are often a function of development.

Piecemeal migration patterns among families from Central America (i.e., parents emigrate before child), have often influenced children's perception of the family. Young children who remain in their country of origin while the parents emigrate to the United States, may have a difficult adjustment when the family is reunited and the "psychological" parents are left behind (Arroyo, 1996; Arroyo & Eth, 1985).

The rate at which an immigrant child will learn English varies considerably; in part it depends on the child's exposure to English. A young child who has the necessary fundamental resources at home and receives gradual exposure will learn English with relative ease and will acquire it rapidly when immersed in the educational system. In all likelihood, this child will be completely bilingual and bicultural. Older children have a greater challenge when learning a new language. This may not be as detrimental from a social perspective if the older child successfully establishes a satisfying social network with limited English-speaking skills, which may be the case in a neighborhood with many immigrants. Bilingual education programs vary among states and school districts.

The determination of a communication disorder or mental retardation in a bilingual child is challenging for clinicians and school personnel alike. Cervantes and Arroyo (1995) propose several cultural considerations in making these and other diagnoses of mental disorders. For example, many Latin American groups generally value interdependence among family members much more than appears to be the norm in American society. In some children this may be mistaken for a symptom of Separation Anxiety Disorder. Most of the diagnostic categories in *DSM-IV* that are applicable to children have criteria that are language dependent; a clinician who is neither bicultural nor bilingual may falsely assume that a communication problem due to limited English proficiency is a symptom of a mental disorder.

In a clinical sample of Central American children who had immigrated to the United States, Arroyo (1996) found that some of their symptoms could be directly related to their exposure to war-related violence, (e.g., injury, witness to trauma, direct impact on family). Less stressful events were also apparent including separation from other family members, disruption of social networks, disruption of education, political persecution, and general impoverishment. Urrutia-Rojas and Rodriguez (1996), who studied a large group of children apprehended by the Immigration and Naturalization Service, similarly found an extensive list of potential sources of stress prior to emigration from Central America. For example, the travel route by land from their country of origin to the United States proved to be potentially traumatic for both groups (Arroyo, 1996; Urrutia-Rojas & Rodriguez, 1996); these events included physical and sexual assaults by strangers and apprehension by the INS in some cases. In addition, some reported being fearful of deportation to life-threatening environments and prolonged separation from family. Postemigration stressors included exposure to community-related violence that triggered haunting memories of war zones, discrimination in school, and adaptation to their general community. Adolescents were often stressed by having their families solely depend on the adolescent to procure services and other resources that the family needed; this was in large part due to the adolescent's facility with English. Arroyo (1996) found that the incidence of stress-related disorders (adjustment disorders and posttraumatic stress disorder) was much higher in a clinical group of Central American children exposed to high doses of war-related events than a clinical sample of Latino children.

There are no published epidemiological studies regarding mental disorders among Central Americans. Bird et al. (1988)

completed the sole epidemiological study on Latino youngsters from Puerto Rico.

Substance abuse has also been a problem in the Central American community. Tommasello, Tyler, Tyler, and Zhang (1993) found greater exposure to alcohol and illicit drugs in Central American youth in the Washington, DC, area than among Latinos sampled in the National Household Survey (SAMHSA, 1995). A study on alcohol use by Central American adults (Marin & Posner, 1995) has implications for family-related stress. In this comparison study with Mexican Americans, the Mexican American population was found to drink more often and have more heavy drinkers than the Central American population. In this study, the women from both groups were infrequent users of alcohol.

There are no arrest data and delinquency rates for Central Americans. Morales (1992) reports that there is a differential treatment of culturally diverse populations by the juvenile justice system; Latin Americans and African Americans are disproportionately overrepresented in the juvenile justice system.

Gang activity has impacted the Central American community. In Los Angeles, youth gangs have been formed based on the Central American country of origin. Belitz and Valdez (1995) discuss some of the psychological preconditions and complications of gang activity; some of the youth have treatable conditions such as posttraumatic stress disorder, depression, and substance abuse.

Adult studies of psychological stress among Central American adults have implications for parenting, economics, and the welfare of their children. In several adult studies (Cervantes, Salgado de Snyder, & Padilla, 1989; Padilla, Cervantes, Maldonado, & Garcia, 1988) with Central Americans who immigrated to the United States during the past decade, posttraumatic stress disorder, depression, and anxiety were commonly found. Leslie and Leitch (1989) report that these immigrants were unlikely to use community resources to seek help for their problems. Plante, Gerdenio, Menendez, and Marcotte (1995) found that even after 5 years the war-related stress for Salvadoran immigrants remained high; effective coping strategies included learning English, maintaining a positive and hard-working attitude, perceiving support, and having religious faith.

Conclusion

Central American children account for a significant portion of the recent increase in Latino children who have emigrated to the United States. This recent surge can in large part be attributed to the instability of the governments in some of the Central American countries. The psychosocial development of these children may be jeopardized by remnants of war-related stress in addition to the adaptation to American society.

The ongoing provocative controversies regarding immigration, particularly of the Latino populations, generally center around short-term costs and societal impact but rarely address issues related to the well-being and the contributions that will be made by these immigrant populations (Center for the Future of Children, 1995). Service providers and policymakers need to consider the unique problems and attributes of this youthful population. Research about these populations is long overdue.

References

ARROYO, W. (1996, December 2). *War trauma in Central American children and youth.* Paper presented at the workshop of the Ethnographic Research on the Health and Well-Being of Immigrant Children and Families, Irvine, CA.

ARROYO, W., & ETH, S. (1985). Central American children traumatized by warfare. In S. Eth & R. S. Pynoos (Eds.), *Post-traumatic stress disorder in children* (pp. 101–120). Washington, DC: American Psychiatric Press.

BELITZ, J., & VALDEZ, D. M. (1995). Clinical issues in the treatment of Chicano male gang youths. In A. M. Padilla (Ed.), *Hispanic psychology* (pp. 148–165). Thousand Oaks, CA: Sage.

BERNAL, B. E., KNIGHT, G. P., GARZA, C. A., OCAMPO, K. A., & COTA, M. K. (1990). The development of ethnic identity in Mexican American children. *Hispanic Journal of Behavioral Science, 12*(1), 3–24.

BIRD, H. R., CANINO, G., RUBIO-STIPEC, M., GOULD, M. S., RIBERA, J., SESMAN, M., WOODBURY, M., HUERTAS-GOLDMAN, S., PAGAN, A.,

SANCHEZ-LACAY, A., & MOSCOSO, M. (1988). Estimates of the prevalence of childhood maladjustment in a community survey in Puerto Rico. *Archives of General Psychiatry, 45,* 1120–1126.

CENTER FOR THE FUTURE OF CHILDREN. (1995, Summer/Fall). *The future of children: The David and Lucile Packard Foundation* (Vol. 5).

CERVANTES, R. C., & ARROYO, W. (1995). Cultural considerations in the use of *DSM IV* with Hispanic children and adolescents. In A. M. Padilla (Ed.), *Hispanic psychology* (pp. 131–147). Thousand Oaks, CA: Sage.

CERVANTES, R. C., SALGADO DE SNYDER, V. N., & PADILLA, A. M. (1989). Posttraumatic stress in immigrants from Central America and Mexico. *Hospital Community Psychiatric, 40,* 615–619.

CUMMINS, J. (Ed.). (1984). *Bilingual special education: Issues in assessment and pedagogy.* San Diego, CA: College-Hill.

FELIX-ORTIZ DE LA GARZA, M., NEWCOMB, M. D., & MYERS, H. F. (1995). A multidimensional measure of cultural identity for Latino and Latina adolescents. In A. M. Padilla (Ed.), *Hispanic psychology* (pp. 26–42). Thousand Oaks, CA: Sage.

FIGUEROA, R. A. (1989). Psychological testing of linguistic-minority students: Knowledge gaps and regulations. *Exceptional Children, 56,* 145–152.

FIGUEROA, R. A., DELGADO, G. L., & RUIZ, N. T. (1984). Assessment of Hispanic children: Implications for Hispanic hearing impaired children. In G. L. Delgado (Ed.), *The Hispanic deaf: Issues and challenges for bilingual special education* (pp. 124–153). Washington, DC: Gallaudet College Press.

FRANCO, J. N. (1983). An acculturation scale for Mexican American children. *Journal of General Psychology, 108,* 175–183.

LESLIE, L. A., & LEITCH, M. L. (1989). A demographic profile of recent Central American immigrants: Clinical and service implications. *Hispanic Journal of Behavioral Science, 11,* 315–329.

MAGAR, V. (1990). Health care needs of Central American refugees. *Nursing Outlook, 38,* 239–242.

MARIN, G., & POSNER, S. F. (1995). The role of gender and acculturation on determining the consumption of alcoholic beverages among Mexican-Americans and Central Americans in the U.S. *International Journal of Addiction, 30,* 779–794.

MARTINEZ, R., NORMAN, R. D., & DELANEY, H. E. (1984). A children's Hispanic background scale. *Hispanic Journal of Behavioral Science, 6,* 103–112.

MORALES, A. T. (1992). Latino youth gangs: Causes and clinical intervention. In L. A. Vargas & J. Koss-Chionino (Eds.), *Working with culture: Psychotherapeutic intervention with ethnic minority children and adolescents* (pp. 129–154). San Francisco: Jossey-Bass.

OLMEDO, E. L., MARTINEZ, J. L., & MARTINEZ, S. R. (1978). Measure of acculturation for Chicano adolescents. *Psychological Reports, 42,* 159–170.

OLMEDO, E. L., & PADILLA, A. M. (1978). Empirical and construct validation of a measure of acculturation for Mexican Americans. *Journal of Social Psychology, 105,* 179–188.

PADILLA, A. M. (1988). Life experiences, stress, and adaptation of immigrant adolescents. In J. W. Berry & R. C. Annis (Eds.), *Ethnic psychology: Research and practice with immigrants, refugees, native peoples, ethnic groups and sojourners* (pp. 47–84). Boulder, CO: Westview Press.

PADILLA, A. M., CERVANTES, R. C., MALDONADO, M., & GARCIA, R. E. (1988). Coping responses to psychosocial stressors among Mexican and Central American immigrants. *Journal of Community Psychology, 18,* 418–427.

PLANTE, T. G., GERDENIO, M. M., MENENDEZ, A. V., & MARCOTTE, D. (1995). Coping with stress among Salvadoran immigrants. *Hispanic Journal of Behavioral Science, 17,* 471–479.

ROPP, S. C., & MORRIS, J. A. (1984). *Central America: Crisis and adaptation.* Albuquerque: University of New Mexico Press.

SALAS, S. D., HEIFETZ, R., & BARRETT, C. E. (1990). Intestinal parasites in Central American immigrants in the United States. *Archives of Internal Medicine, 150,* 1514–1516.

SUBSTANCE ABUSE AND MENTAL HEALTH SERVICES ADMINISTRATION (SAMHSA). (1995). *National Household Survey on Drug Abuse: Main Findings* (DHHS Publication No. SMA 95-3020). Washington, DC: U.S. Department of Health and Human Services, Office of Applied Studies.

TOMMASELLO, A., TYLER, F. B., TYLER, S. L., & ZHANG, Y. (1993). Psychosocial correlates of drug use among Latino youth leading autonomous lives. *International Journal of Addictions, 28,* 435–450.

U.S. BUREAU OF THE CENSUS. (1993, July). *The foreign-born population in the United States. 1990 census of population.* Washington, DC: U.S. Department of Commerce.

U.S. BUREAU OF THE CENSUS. (1996). *Current population reports* (Series 25-1130). Washington, DC: U.S. Department of Commerce.

U.S. IMMIGRATION AND NATURALIZATION SERVICE. (1997). *1995 statistical yearbook.* Washington, DC: Author.

Urrutia-Rojas, X., & Rodriguez, N. (1996, December 2). *Unaccompanied migrant children from Central America: Socio-demographic characteristics and experiences with potentially traumatic events.* Paper presented at the workshop of the Ethnographic Research on the Health and Well-Being of Immigrant Children and Families, sponsored by the National Research Council of the Institute of Medicine, Irvine, CA.

Zambrana, R. E., Ell, K., Dorrington, C., Wachsman, L., & Hodge, D. (1994). The relationship between psychosocial status of immigrant Latino mothers and use of emergency pediatric services. *Health and Social Work, 19,* 93–102.

CHAPTER 5

Children from the Middle East

WALID O. SHEKIM

Historical Background

GEOGRAPHIC DEFINITION

EUROPEAN GEOGRAPHERS ecogentrically divided the vast territories of the Orient into three parts according to their distance from Europe: The Near East—the land east of the Mediterranean Sea; the Middle East—the territory from western Iran to Burma and Ceylon including India and Pakistan; and the Far East—the territory of Southeast Asia including China and Japan (Deighton, 1972). The Near East erroneously came to be known as the Middle East when the British military command was set up in Egypt just prior to World War II. The term Middle East now applies to territories originally identified as the Near East and to some of the old Middle East, including the lands east of the Mediterranean Sea and north of Africa, the Arabian Peninsula, the Persian Gulf, Iran, Turkey, and Greece. Afghanistan and Pakistan are sometimes included in the Middle East. The perimeters of the Middle East have changed from time to time according to the strategic needs of the colonial European West and, more recently, American interests. The people of the Middle East, which is an artificial term, lack homogeneity; however, if the inner core of the Middle East is considered to be the Arab world, then some homogeneity starts to appear.

The people of the Middle East do not have a single identity. They comprise different cultures, religious sects, and nations that have fought each other throughout history. There are Asians and Africans; there are Arabs, Iranians, Berbers, and Turks; there are White Middle Easterners and Black Middle Easterners; there are Jews, Christians, and Muslims; there are members of sects—Sunnis, Shi'ites, Catholics, Greek Orthodox, and Protestants. Overall, the Middle East offers a rich variety of geographic, racial, religious, social, political, and cultural similarities and differences.

The Arab world, which makes up the largest bloc of land in the Middle East, comprises 21 countries; most of the people are Muslims. Christianity exists as a minority religion in Syria, Jordan, Egypt, and Iraq, and to a somewhat greater extent in Lebanon.

Afghanistan and Pakistan are sometimes considered Middle Eastern countries united by the Muslim religion, but they are geographically removed from the Middle East and are culturally and historically different people.

EARLY HISTORY

Recorded history started in the Middle East around 3000 B.C., in two lands: Egypt and Sumer (the lower part of Mesopotamia, now in Iraq). The Sumerians developed some of the earliest arts of civilization and established small city-states, while the Egyptians organized the first national state with a central government (Bottero, 1972; Cottrell, 1972). The major religions of humankind—Christianity, Judaism, and Islam—originated in the Middle East. Since ancient times, the Middle East has attracted conquerors because it constitutes a land bridge with rich natural resources between the three continents of Europe, Asia, and Africa.

Over many centuries, Europeans have consistently portrayed the Middle Easterners, the Arabs, or the "Orientals" as their antithesis (Musallam, 1983a). In the Middle Ages, this sense of otherness focused on religion. In the West, Islam appeared to be a terrifying combination of heathenism and heresy.

The prophet Muhammad was labeled an "imposter," and his followers (Saracens, Assassins, and Moors) loomed as a threat to everything that was virtuous and Christian.

The first Crusade was launched in 1096 to free Jerusalem from the "wicked infidels," initiating a series of wars between Europeans and people of the Middle East that continued for 200 years. French and British scholars known as Orientalists searched for knowledge about the people of the Middle East, but their information was often inaccurate. The Middle East was described as a land of mystery, luxury, cruelty, anarchy, ignorance, and depravity in contrast to Europe's self-image as a bastion of morality, order, enlightenment, and renaissance (Musallam, 1983a).

An additional factor in Middle Eastern history is the influence of Persia (Iran), a large Muslim non-Arab country that fought the Arabs throughout the ages. Turkey ruled most of the Arab world during the rise and fall of the Ottoman Empire (1300–1920). Toward the end of this period, many Christians felt outnumbered and disadvantaged and started migrating to North and South America. In addition, many Arab Muslim independent thinkers and activists migrated to the New World, escaping Ottoman oppression and seeking new freedom and life in America.

RECENT HISTORY

The state of Israel was established in 1948 from the partitioning of Palestine. The Israelis and their sympathizers hailed the birth of the Jewish nation, but to the Arabs, the "birth of Israel" meant that 130,000 Jewish inhabitants of British-occupied Palestine seized Arab land with the help of Britain, France, and the United States. The Arab-Israeli wars that grew out of this conflict are still not resolved and have displaced many people on both sides. Palestinian refugees into Arab countries, many of them seeking a better life in the Western world, ended up in the United States. Jews of Arab countries and other Muslim countries such as Iran immigrated to the United States and Israel.

Some immigrants from the Middle East may have come to the Americas as early as the late 19th century. At that time, most emigrés were Syrian Arabs and Christian Lebanese who escaped the Ottoman Turkish oppression and went to South America, where many of them are now the elite of countries such as Brazil, Argentina, and Ecuador. Egyptian Christians (Copts) came to the United States escaping poverty and unrest. The Palestinian exodus out of Palestine after the Arab/Israel War of 1967 resulted in another wave of immigrants to the United States. The Lebanese Civil War (1975–1992), with its religious, political, and economical roots, devastated Lebanon and its people for over 15 years, and resulted in another wave of migration by Lebanese people into the United States. Tension between the Arab countries and Israel resulted in the influx of both Arabs and Israelis into the United States, in an effort to avoid another war. Thus, during the late 19th century people from Middle Eastern countries, both Arabs and non-Arabs, attempted to escape poverty in their native land and hoped to gain financial security for themselves and their families. Family stories abound with anecdotes of young men who immigrated to the United States, found jobs, and then saved enough money to bring their families to the New World.

Middle Eastern Identity in the United States

The history of immigration to the United States from the Middle East does not lend itself to a Middle Eastern identity. Instead, Middle Easterners in the United States comprise several communities with tensions among them that may make them suspicious of each other and their intentions. It is not unheard of that an Israeli immigrant to the United States who served in the Israeli Army and fought the Arabs more than once finds himself fixing the air conditioning unit of a Palestinian family. An Arab-Jewish family from Algiers may find its neighbors include a southern Lebanese family. Many people in Middle Eastern communities have relatives back home who are still in conflicts. The resonance of this violence has created many local heterogeneous communities that harbor fear and distrust. However, these people had and continue to share similarities in many ways. Arabs and Jews are Semites, and many Arabs see anti-Semitism as affecting them. Lebanese Christians and Muslims share the same history; they eat the same foods, dance to the same music, and sing with the same language. Arabs and Jews both claim foods like hummus, tabbouleh, and falafel as theirs ethnically. Syrians and Muslim and Christian Egyptians share the same history and traditions although they may pray in different houses of God.

FAMILY VALUES

Muslim, Christian, and Jewish Middle Eastern people share similar family values including a deep sense of closeness and emotional ties (Musallam, 1983b). Individuals do not end their dependence on their family at the age of 18 or 21, but rather are considered to be adults when they get married. The extended family continues to be involved in the lives of the young couple, and they may combine their financial and close familial ties for decades. In some ways, the extended family in the Middle East, and the social support system associated with it, is more effective than the Western government-funded welfare system (Musallam, 1983b). The Western welfare system ensures the minimal material needs of the individual, such as food, medical care, and shelter, but often at the expense of psychological needs such as self-respect, acceptance, and affection (Musallam, 1983b). The extended family functions as a welfare system: It makes sure family members are cared for if widowed or orphaned and takes care of the ill and unemployed. In the Middle East, nursing homes, if they exist, are for the destitute and the indigent, and for those who do not have living family members, because family elders are always cared for at home. "The warmth of a Middle Eastern family envelops you like a heavy cloak on a freezing day. Though I and many others might feel like casting the cloak off for a while when the sun is shining, I would never want to see it packed away for good," said Nadia

Hijab, a Palestinian journalist who is the editor of *The Middle East* magazine in London (Musallam, 1983b). Immigrants from the Middle East lost the support of their extended family when they came to the United States. Many tried to persuade as many family members as possible to come with them. If family members were not available, they sought their compatriot supportive communities. If the American mainstream seemed hostile, Middle Eastern immigrants often withdrew and still do into their little communities and isolated themselves from the society that had rejected them. This created many adjustment problems for the immigrants in school, with friends, and in their portrayal by the media.

THE IMPACT OF PREJUDICE

Middle Eastern immigrants to the United States found an unfriendly environment. Often the Middle Easterners are portrayed as dark people with bushy hair and moustaches whose ancestors where slave traders, and whose compatriots are plane hijackers, bomb-throwing terrorists, murderers, and thugs, called "Camel Jockeys." Men are pictured as evil, and as uncivilized, cunning womanizers. Middle Easterners also are seen as foreigners with alien religions. Islam has been depicted as an enemy religion since the time of the Crusades. Even before the rise of the American Jewish lobby for a U.S. policy in favor of Israel, many people viewed the Arabs as infidels who would slash people's throats and take their money while they were asleep. Dr. Edmond Ghareeb, Professor of Contemporary Arab Studies at Georgetown University, Washington, DC, conducted an opinion study surveying a sample of the California population about the impression of Arab Americans (Sharqawi, 1997). The study found that Arabs were perceived as terrorists, wearing non-Western clothes and without underwear; owners of convenience stores like 7-11 and fast-food restaurants; belly dancers, and grocers. There were some positive images. However, few perceived the Arabs as generous, good-natured, and having a rich cultural heritage. It was found that the people who had negative images about the Arabs learned it from movies, TV, and the press, while those with positive opinions learned about the Arabs from books or from a positive, first-hand experience.

Professor Ghareeb also reported that Arabs were seen in late 19th century as Syrians coming from Central Asia and from the Ottoman Empire. They were perceived as Turks from Oriental ancestry and considered to be the least desirable of the undesirable immigrants.

Many Jewish Middle Eastern people, such as Iranian Jews, face anti-Semitism in the U.S. and even experience discrimination by American Jews in Jewish school settings, where they are seen as second-class Jews because of their origin from the Middle East.

DIFFICULTIES IN ASSIMILATION

Unlike the Koreans, Taiwanese, or Greek immigrants, Middle Easterners do not make up an entity of people who can be studied and discussed as a group. Because there is not an overarching Middle Eastern identity, it is difficult to do research and to understand the psychological adjustment problems of a diverse group of children and adolescents from Middle Eastern origin. The immigrants find it difficult to assimilate in the new society so they form homogeneous groups: Jordanians, Armenians, Lebanese, Maronite Egyptian Copts, Iranian Muslims and Jews, Palestinians, Iraqis. Many times when Middle Eastern families feel discriminated against, they become more cohesive to gain identity, strength, and security. They may attempt to form Arabic or religious groups such as Muslim groups consisting of Arabs and non-Arabs from different Middle Eastern countries. Sometimes they may overreact and reject the New World culture and civilization. Because they become more rigid, mistrusting teachers, neighbors, and coworkers, they may come across as an angry people reinforcing existing stereotypes. On the other hand, many enlightened Arabs, American Jews, and Israelis are rising above decades of conflict and war and fanaticism, stretching arms to each other and joining in ventures such as "Peace Now." Ironically, by doing this, they face the wrath of their fanatic brethren in their homelands.

Adjustment of Middle Eastern Immigrants to Life in the United States

Immigrant children from the Middle East often grow up in a family that feels rejected, degraded, and discriminated against by the mainstream society, and that faces serious economical hardship. These circumstances can create emotional tensions in the family members that lead to more tension, strife, and maladjustment. The children are faced with similar circumstances at school. They may not be accepted at school by peers because of their color, dress, religion, funny names, and different-looking parents who speak to them in a strange language in front of their peers at school. Some immigrant children may find it hard to identify with their parents' traditions, may deny their origin, may want to change their name, eat different foods, listen to American music, and try to learn a completely new American life. Other children may conform to their family norms and traditions and strongly identify with their origin, isolating them more from their peers and leading to more emotional maladjustment, insecurity, rejection, and ridicule. The children may withdraw or excel in school to compensate. Many of these children are among the best students in high school and college; however, some are depressed, withdrawn, and worried. They may rebel against family norms and traditions and reject their values, unable to tolerate what they see as extreme conservatism or reactionary values. Young adolescents may deny their parents' identity and values becoming very much influenced by their peers. They refuse to bring their friends home, dislike being seen with their parents, and may get involved with the wrong crowd. To be accepted, they may use alcohol and drugs, and because Middle Eastern families are traditionally extended, grandparents, uncles, and aunts may get involved and make it harder for the teenagers. They don't trust school counselors and psychologists; they feel they are being picked on, discriminated against, and neglected. Many of them are unfamiliar with the idea of psychological adjustment and do not perceive the psychological difficulties immigrant families face in their new life. Often parents do not speak English well so they find it hard to communicate with the school personnel or mental health professionals.

PROBLEMS WITHIN FAMILIES

The generation gap in the Middle Eastern family is wider than in other immigrant communities and this leads to much strife. Families may decide to go back to the homeland or face breakups or the introduction of "unwanted" elements into the family by the marriage of grown-up children. Sometimes, a family member may become a fundamentalist Muslim to counteract the evil that seems to be afflicting the family. Such a family member may escape into religious fanaticism as a defense against the apparent moral disintegration in other family members; religion serves as a soothing agent for inner turmoil and suffering.

The gap between parents and children in Middle Eastern immigrant families continues to grow. Many immigrants cannot identify with Christmas or Valentine's Day although their children are bombarded by these and other holidays year after year. Many immigrants are torn by the conflict between the United States and their homeland, and find it hard to accept what appears to be aggression against their Middle Eastern country or bias of the U.S. government. They and their children often end up on different sides of the issue leading to more frustration, isolation, and negativism. Middle Eastern families tend to be overprotective, sometimes to the extent of infantalizing, making it harder for youngsters to gain independence, which also leads to more isolation and more frustration for these children.

Siblings of the same family often react to social adjustment in different ways. The conformist identifies with family values and traditions, whereas the rebellious child may reject them, leading to alienation of one sibling from the other. Older brothers may threaten to kill a younger teenage sister who wants to date or attend school parties. Teenage years are the most difficult for families immigrating from the Middle East, especially for girls, who generally do not have as much freedom in their homeland as male siblings and whose parents were brought up with more authoritarian and rigid rules.

The Middle East itself now offers mixed standards. Many women in cities appear to be emancipated and seem to enjoy more freedom and equality than the women in the rural areas (Musallam, 1983b). There are still issues of education and work, and challenges such as combining career and family. Even though more and more Middle Eastern women are joining the workforce, many remain at home awaiting arranged marriages. The traditional view that the woman belongs at home to raise her children and take care of her family is still strong although it is being contested by the new generation in the United States. Young Middle Eastern girls resent the lack of equality with their brothers and feel restricted in their movements. They reject the concept of family honor relating to sexual morality, virginity, and fidelity of the female sex (Musallam, 1983b). Often parents themselves feel confused, lost, and unsure of their beliefs. In addition, they are often divided. Teenagers easily perceive this uncertainty and assert their independence. This can become a learning experience for the whole family, but more often it leads to family pain and strife.

Future Directions

Middle Easterners perceive mental illness as a stigma preferably to be disguised or hidden. Because family members deny mental illness in their families when interviewed, it is harder for the clinician to formulate a diagnosis and treatment plan. At the clinics, these families complain of physical symptoms, and often are not willing to discuss their psychological turmoil, because they are mistrusting, paranoid, and feel coerced. It is usually the school system that insists that the child see a mental health professional. However, most Middle Eastern families firmly believe that these professionals are not aware of cultural differences between Middle Eastern peoples' family environment and the schools and families of mainstream society.

Much of the adjustment or maladjustment of children, adolescents, and families from the Middle East remains unresearched and unstudied. Attempts at studying Middle Eastern families are being made. But research is hampered by the lack of mental health professionals from the Middle East. In many Arab countries, child psychiatrists or clinical child psychologists do not exist. In the United States, there are only a handful of Arab child psychiatrists and child clinical psychologists.

Research into the mental health adjustment of Middle Eastern families may have to await the elimination of the stigma that exists about mental illness in the minds of Middle Easterners. We may have to see an increase in the awareness of the difficulties Middle Eastern families face culturally. Many of these families attribute their maladjustment to political reasons and to discrimination rather than to problems that all immigrant families must cope with in their new environment. Finally, we need many more mental health professionals of Middle Eastern origin.

References

COTTRELL, L. (1972). In S. G. F. Brandon & F. Heer (Eds.), *Gift of the Nile in forty centuries* (pp. 13–21). Brittanica Society.

DEIGHTON, H. (1972). Middle East. In *Encyclopedia Britannica* (Vol. 15, pp. 407–408). Chicago: Encyclopedia Britannica.

MUSALLAM, B. (1983a). The shadow of the West. In *The Arabs: A living history* (pp. 153–176). Harvil Press.

MUSALLAM, B. (1983b). Women and the family. In *The Arabs: A living history* (pp. 135–152). Harvil Press.

SHARQAWI, M. (1997). *Arab immigration to the west: After 100 years* (America without borders) [Video]. Arlington, VA: ALEF Teleproductions.

CHAPTER 6

Asian Indian Children

VIJAYALAKSHMI MANDAYAM RANGANATH and
VEENA KITTANE RANGANATH

LIKE MANY OTHER ASIAN countries, India has a rich past and now is experiencing the same rapid change and technological advances that are sweeping through the world. These social and economic changes are having a major impact on culture and tradition. The exposure to American television has exerted a particularly strong influence.

India, with 930 million people, is one of the most densely populated countries in the world. Only China exceeds this figure. Since 1900, it is estimated that at least 10 to 15 million Asian Indians have immigrated to other countries. In 1980, the population of Asian Indians in the United States was 382,000; by 1990 it had reached 815,000 (U.S. Census Bureau, 1990). The Indian Consulate Office estimates that the number was close to 1.3 million in 1996. When the U.S. Census Bureau designation of "Other Asians" is included, the number increases further. Approximately 19 countries are listed in this category including Pakistan, Burma, Sri Lanka, Bangladesh, Bhutan, Sikkim, and Nepal. Immigrants from these countries totaled 779,991, according to the 1990 census (Lavin 1996).

To understand the Asian Indian children who immigrated with their parents as well as children born in the United States to Asian Indian immigrants, one needs to understand the immigration process, culture, family structure, and interaction of these children with the new environment and its culture. The Chinese and Indians entered the immigration pool post-World War I as indentured laborers and subsequently as free immigrants. Most Asian Indians came to the United States in the late 19th or early 20th century. In 1943, the Chinese were allowed to immigrate under a quota system; this opened the door for other Asians. In 1946, the U.S. Congress applied the Chinese formula to Filipinos and "Natives of India," who were still under British rule (Daniel, 1990). The 1965 amendment to the Immigration and Nationality Act, signed by President Lyndon B. Johnson, lifted the racial barrier in the immigration process. Since then, there has been a steady immigration of Asian or East Indians to the United States, which peaked in 1980.

Three groups of immigrants from India stand out. The first group (in 1900) consisted of poor laborers who worked in the lumber mills and on the railroads of the Pacific Northwest, and on the farms of California. Most of these Asian Indians were Punjabi, who wore their traditional turbans. They were referred to as "Ragheads" or "Hindoos" and were subject to mob attack and ridicule. The farm laborers eventually settled in central and northern California, where they interacted with the Mexican field-workers and other ethnic groups. Interracial marriages resulted as well as second and third generations of Asian Indians, many of whom live in Yuba City, California.

From 1940 to 1950, the student group came to the United States seeking higher education and often returned to India at the end of their educational goal. These students often were isolated and seldom interacted with the mainstream culture. Many early Asian Indian students who came to this country were involved in the Indian Freedom Movement and shipped arms to India to help overthrow British rule. These activists were numerous at the University of California–Berkeley; student uprisings led to arrests and some deaths.

The third group of immigrants were representatives of India's major religious groups—primarily the Hindu, Buddhist, or Muslim—and established centers for worship wherever they settled.

Most Asian Indian immigrants have legal status and are often sponsored by relatives who have settled in the United

States. Approximately 80% of Asian Indian immigrants are professionals. The average Asian Indian immigrant has had 16 years of education compared with U.S.-born, who have 12 years or more of schooling. Immigrants without a professional degree usually work and go to school to obtain one. Professional Asian Indians who tend to be affluent and do well in their professions in the host country are predominantly males. The educational level of females is less than that for males, even though there are many more Asian Indian female professionals than in most immigrant groups.

The size of the Asian Indian immigrant family is 3.6 persons compared with the American-born family size of about 5 persons. A 1979 survey showed that 79% of the 14- to 24-year-old Asian Indians living in the United States were born here; this number is steadily increasing. In 1988, the number of U.S.-born increased to 87% (Ananth & Ananath, 1996; Dutt, 1989). This provides a nucleus of Asian Indians who have either successfully or unsuccessfully dealt with the process of acculturation. The Asian Indian children who are born in the United States and those who immigrate with their parents straddle two cultures, one at home and another in the school. Data are inadequate and unreliable regarding the assimilation of immigrant and refugee children, especially the factors that protect or deter their adaptation to the host culture as well as the rates of mental disorders. Beiser, Dion, Gotowiec, Hyman, and Vu (1995) propose a model that takes into consideration the pre- and postimmigration stressors, personal resources, personal characteristics, and social resources. The economic and political situation in the host country influences the patterns of adjustment to immigrant status and the immigration rates.

Family and Child Development

RELIGION

An understanding of the Asian Indian family and the developmental aspects of children requires a knowledge of India's religions and cultures.

India is a secular country with several major religious denominations. About 80% of the population are Hindus; Muslims, the next major group, represent about 12%, closely followed by Christians. There are other groups such as the Jains, Sikhs, Buddhists, Parsees, and Jews.

Hinduism is not just a religion, but a philosophy or a way of life. The Hindu culture is rich in mythology, which is intricately woven into daily life. Hindus have innumerable deities to represent different aspects of life. Brahma is the creator, Vishnu preserves life, and Shiva is the destroyer, who deals with death. Likewise, several goddesses both protect and destroy life. One of the major belief systems that is essential to a Hindu is fate, or karma, which determines a person's destiny. This deeply held belief encourages the graceful acceptance of misfortune and hardship, an attitude that mental health professionals have sometimes interpreted as passivity and failure to exercise autonomy in one's life. The other major Hindu belief is reincarnation that is illustrated by the varying forms that deities take at different times to carry out their goal of destroying evil. The belief in reincarnation involves a person going through phases of evolution at each birth to a higher or lower status as determined by his or her actions (i.e., good or bad). Karma represents the sum of past actions that a person must work through during cycles of births and deaths. The life cycle of a Hindu has several stages or phases similar to the conceptualization of psychosocial development outlined by Erik Erikson. These stages are all defined by religious beliefs. Kakar (1978) noted: "At birth or infancy the prehistory of the individual prepares the person with the capacity to understand his or her Dharma [which means their moral obligation or duty]."

Boys between the ages of 7 and 12 were previously sent to live with a guru or teacher and mastered whatever subjects the teacher provided.

In India today, children attend schools much like those in Europe and the United States. Because the acquisition of knowledge is highly valued, parents stress education and achievement in school and reward their child's efforts. To ensure success in a focused quest for knowledge without the distraction of social comingling, adolescents are coached to control sexual impulses by the family, teachers, and the community. This phase of childhood and early adolescence is referred to as *brahmacharya*. Marriage in young adulthood ushers in the stage of *grahasthya* (householder), in which the main goal is to provide and care for the family and carry out the prescribed dharma (the duty or job). Following this phase, the person enters late adulthood and old age, the stages of *vanaprastha* and *samanysa* (withdrawal and renunciation), which refer to preparation for death. This belief system and these phases of life do not easily mesh with the Western emphasis on individualism and other psychological concepts that underlie most therapeutic approaches.

SOCIAL CHANGE AND CHILD REARING

In India's urban areas, social changes have been rapid with dissolution of the caste system and rigid gender roles, as well as economic growth reflected by two parents in the workforce. In the rural areas of India, however, these changes have been slower. There are now more nuclear families, and a decreasing number of traditional family systems with the father being the head of the household (a patriarchal society). There are a few states in the southern part of India where matriarchal society remains predominant and where property is transferred from the female head of household to the female offspring, the maternal uncle being the executor of the estate. In addition, the child carries the mother's maiden name. Despite the rapid changes, the Indian family is an extended one with immediate family members such as sisters, mothers-in-law, sisters-in-law, maternal grandmothers, and aunts taking a major role in the development of the child.

The concept of a babysitter is foreign to Asian Indians, who rely heavily on the extended family for the care of the young. Because family members often help the mother, she avoids the stress of being the sole care-provider and is less likely to abuse her children. For example, if a mother is frustrated with a crying infant, an aunt or grandmother may take the infant from the mother and assist her in soothing or caring for the child. Unlike

American families where the primary caregivers often work to support the family and do not have easy access to extended family, the unwritten code of conduct in Asian Indian families dictates that a woman's primary role is to care for her children, which puts an unusual burden on the professional woman. Consequently, the conflict for professional Asian Indian women who raise children in North America revolves around the perception of abdication of their maternal role to a stranger versus their own career growth. The Indian woman is socialized from very early in life to care of the family at the cost of giving up her needs and ambitions. When an Indian professional woman breaks this strong taboo, she is often depressed and may not be able to provide optimum care for the infant. To overcome some of these conflicts, affluent Indian families in North America have their extended family members visit them and assist with the child rearing. However, it is emotionally traumatic to the visitors, the parents, and the child when a family member has to return to India. In some Indian families, the child is sent with the extended family member to India in the hope that he or she will be raised in the proper Indian tradition and not corrupted by Western culture. When they are adolescents, the children return to the United States to complete their education. Conflict with the biological parents may ensue because the child is emotionally attached to the extended family members and has difficulty negotiating the cultural change.

Although these attempts to resolve child-rearing issues through involvement of the extended family may impose financial and emotional burdens, the grandparents, aunts, and other family members provide some relief from stresses of infant care and household chores. At the same time, they continue the tradition of storytelling and introduce the young children to Indian cultural norms and values by drawing from personal experiences and traditional child-rearing practices.

In India, the extended family system encourages the development of the infant's ability to deal with different care providers. Kurtz (1992) points out that this type of child rearing helps the child move away from the exclusive one-to-one relationship with the biological mother toward a mature and cooperative interaction with the family group, resulting in a more harmonious collective living situation. As the Hindu mother gently encourages the child to separate from her and interact with other family members, this child-rearing pattern subtly helps the child develop a sense of self-motivated renunciation.

Most Asian Indian children live in two-parent families. The men from India in North America play a major role in the care of the infants and children, which is often missing among their counterparts in India. This sometimes is a difficult transition for men who were raised in India and socialized to expect that their main duty or role in life would be the provision of financial stability for the family. It would be degrading for the head of an Indian household to engage in day-to-day care of an infant, a role clearly assigned to the mother. With the assimilation of the Asian Indians into the majority culture, the Indian fathers in North America are much more involved in the care of their children and appear to enjoy the contact.

Members of Asian Indian families have assigned gender roles and, in this well-developed hierarchy, the father is the head of the system. Conformity to authority is stressed at the cost of creativity, and when a family member deviates, he or she is shamed or made to feel guilty.

A comparative study of Asian Indian and American college students regarding the perception of parental behavior and its relationship to depression, self-esteem, and ego development was measured by Suniya and Quinlan (1993), who found that Asian Indian women perceived their mothers as caring and less overprotective. The Asian Indian women were similar to the American women in reporting that fathers had a strong effect on their self-esteem. Both groups reported that intrusive or restrictive behavior of fathers negatively affected the women's self-image and, subsequently, achievement.

Like many other ethnic groups, the Asian Indians try to solve family problems in privacy and are not eager to seek the assistance of mental health professionals until the problem can no longer be contained within the confines of the family. And again like other immigrant groups, the most stressful times for Asian

Indians in North America occur when adolescents begin to test or doubt all their cultural values, eventually breaking away from the traditional value system.

RITES OF PASSAGE

The Indian culture includes many rituals that serve psychological purposes, and to help children and adolescents who are straddling two different cultures—one at home and another in school—it is important to understand these rites of passage and their significance. As soon as a young Asian man establishes himself financially, the family actively searches for a "suitable" bride. This process is carried out in different ways, but there is often an element of coercion to marry the girl the family chooses.

This practice is followed more often by first-generation Asian Indian immigrants, who often choose to marry a girl born and reared in India rather than Asian Indian women born and raised in North America. Interracial marriages are no longer a novelty and are not unfavorably perceived by families or the Indian community. Interestingly, first-generation females of Indian origin tend to marry Caucasians, but the males usually marry Indians, whether raised in this country or in India. Although it is commonly believed that pressure is placed on first- and second-generation Asian Indian females to carry on the tradition and values of the culture, Sharma's (1984) study of assimilation of first- and second-generation Indian girls in England showed that autonomy, gender role, and parental expectations were different for the second-generation Indian girls, compared with those for Indian boys, and approximated those of British boys and girls.

Both in India and in the United States, marriages occur after the male and female complete their basic education, which often prevents early marriages. In India, however, class and rural or urban setting have a bearing on child marriages. Failure to fulfill these expectations may foster depression in Asian women who are childless.

All married couples are expected by their respective families to have children. These expectations may not be openly stated, but it is often hinted that those who lack children lack purpose in life. Asian Indians value children as an essential part of the life cycle. A couple without offspring is looked on as a failure, and the blame is placed on the woman. Families welcome pregnancy with great eagerness. In some parts of India, it is still customary for the pregnant woman to return to her family of origin for childbirth and postpartum care. She goes back to her husband's home when the baby is 4 to 6 months old.

In the United States, couples awaiting the birth of a child often invite their parents, especially the girl's mother, to come and help the expectant mother until she delivers her baby and regains her strength. The seventh month of pregnancy is marked with a festive occasion, *Seemantham*, during which the maternal grandparents invite relatives and friends, give gifts to the mother-to-be, and perform rituals for the welfare of the mother and fetus. This symbolic tradition validates the rite of passage to motherhood. It resembles the American baby shower but is not the same because the emphasis is on the mother-to-be rather than the baby. Traditionally, the Hindu belief is that the developing fetus is responsive to environmental cues and emotions of the mother; hence the mother-to-be should not be agitated or upset and often is exposed to music and philosophical and religious discourses. The Hindu epic *Mahabharata* includes an episode that illustrates this belief: A young prince (Krishna's nephew), while in his mother's womb, listens to the plans of a military formation and as a young warrior enters this formation but does not know how to extricate himself and is killed. This story illustrates the belief that the fetus is capable of hearing and retaining some memory of significant events. Pregnant women are exposed to pleasant situations, rather than traumatic events, to minimize the effect on fetus.

LANDMARKS OF NORMAL DEVELOPMENT

Infancy

The birth of a child is a very joyous event, especially if the first-born is a male. Males are much more valued than females because males carry the family name. In addition, the eldest son performs the final religious rites at the death of his father, a matter of vital importance to Hindus. If the last rites are not conducted, Hindus believe that they will not attain *moksha* (go to heaven).

Graves' (1978) study of infant behavior and maternal attitudes in West Bengal noted that the exploratory and attachment behaviors of boys were similar to those of American children, whereas girls showed less exploratory behavior and increased physical proximity to the mother. Mothers interacted more with boys than with girls after the children had reached the age of 2 years. In part, this may be because female children are not seen as a part of the family but are viewed as transients who will move away. This is well illustrated by Verma (1995) who noted, "An unmarried girl is a guest in her parents' home" and "an unmarried girl is like a bird sitting in the branches of the tree in her father's courtyard, ready to fly to her husband's home." Throughout India in the past, and in certain rural and urban areas even now, female infants are perceived as an unwelcome burden because of the unwritten laws of dowry and marriage expenses. As a result, infanticide is still practiced. For families who can afford to pay for ultrasound or amniocentesis, the confirmation of the female sex of the fetus may result in termination of pregnancy by abortion. Otherwise, after the birth, the unwanted infant is starved or fed raw rice with the husk, which causes suffocation. The Indian government has passed laws and has made efforts to crack down on clinics that provide such services; in spite of this, the practice continues.

The future of the newborn child is often mapped by an astrologer, who follows planetary movements and creates a horoscope based on the position of the stars at the time of the child's birth. The horoscope serves as a document of birth much like the birth certificate in North America. Unlike the American custom, the baby is not given a name immediately after birth. In the traditional Hindu family, the child is given a name, *Namakaran,* on the 12th day following birth, which is celebrated with families and friends.

Traditionally, the firstborn males and females are given the paternal grandparents' name so that the lineage can be easily established. With the name comes the expectation that the child will be like his or her grandparents and will embellish the family myths. In recent years, however, the media and Western influence have disrupted this process. Names now are based on famous movie stars, politicians, and other prominent persons.

On the 15th or 16th day, the infant is placed in a cradle separate from the mother; this event is also marked by ceremony and celebration. Infants and toddlers, for the most part, sleep in the same bed with their parents and are frequently in close physical proximity to the mother or the grandparent. Most Asian Indian women breast-feed their infants, a practice that is encouraged by tradition. Demand feeding is the norm, although this pattern must be modified by working mothers. All the milestones in the child's development are celebrated as an achievement. For example, introduction of solid food is a special event; the family and friends gather along with the priest to celebrate the first few spoonsful of rice porridge, which is first offered to God for blessing. This ceremony is called *Annaprasana* and done before the first birthday. Breast-feeding may continue to overlap the feeding of solid food.

Toilet training starts early with the mother or other female members of the family taking the child at fixed intervals and coaxing him or her to urinate or defecate. Accidents are not punished, and a lot of praise is lavished when the child is successful. The child is trained by 2½ to 3 years. Older children are shamed by peers or made to feel guilty if they lose their bowel or bladder control. If the infant or toddler is playing with or exposed him- or herself, the elders in the family do not react with anxiety, but gently persuade the child to stop such behavior. As the toddler develops fine and gross motor control and develops into a preschooler (2 to 5 years), writing is introduced in a traditional ceremony *Aksharabhyasa;* the first word, usually *OM*, is written in a plateful of rice. Around the same time, the first haircut, *Choulam,* is a special occasion for a male child. Through the storytelling methods, children are exposed to the great Hindu myths with hidden psychological symbolism similar to that found in Western epics.

The relevance of all these traditional practices was to recognize the child as an important person in the family structure and to provide support to the new mother and her physical and emotional well being. However, with nonavailability of an extended family in the United States and the pressure of financial security forcing the mother into the workforce, more stress is on the mother, who is unable to handle the child, demands of workplace, demands of the housework, and the expectation to care for her husband. This can produce depression and increase difficulty in handling the child.

School-Age Children

The Asian Indians like other Asian ethnic groups, emphasize learning and mastery of knowledge; a child who performs poorly in school is often shamed. The parents are deeply involved in their children's education, to the extent of coaching them in completing homework assignments. Achievement and excellence in school are a source of pride for parents who see their children as an extension of themselves and also a measure of their successful parenting. To please their parents and earn approval, the children often struggle hard to study and prove their worth. This can cause difficulty for both the parents and their children. The parents often withhold praise and recognition if the child does not follow their expectations. This active ignoring of the child may result in the child's poor performance and affect their self-esteem and worth. The parents may show differential treatment among sisters and brothers, with the child who excells in school being more acceptable to the family, praised more, and on display to the community as a high achiever. In addition to academic subjects and extracurricular activities, such as sports, Asian Indian children are immersed in cultural activities, such as traditional music, dance, and instruction in native languages and traditional scriptures. In the parents' anxiety to maintain their Indian heritage, they urge their children to excel in all spheres, often compare their children to others, and subtly pressure the children to achieve.

School-age children are exposed to the mainstream culture, which offers alternate ways of problem solving that may
not conform with the family's value system. This is the begin
ning of a journey through two cultures for these children, one
at home and the other at school. For the parents, the questioning
of their authority and values poses difficulty in disciplining and
expectations for their child. Asian Indian parents, however, have
certain advantages over many other ethnic immigrant groups
because they usually know the English language, are aware of
the major cultural values that conflict with Indian traditions,
and are better prepared to counter such influences.

Adolescence

For a male child, the traditional Hindu rite of passage into adolescence is *Upanayanam,* a ceremony that is performed sometime
between the ages of 7 and 16 years. This ceremony signifies a
promise of celibacy and complete devotion to acquiring knowledge, with the expectation that sexual urges will be contained
until the young person is married. In the south Indian state of
Kerala where matrilineal family systems still exist, female adolescents go through a similar ceremony called *Kettu Kaliyanam,*
or pseudomarriage ceremony (Gokalnathan, 1976).

In other parts of India, the menarche is marked by the
preparation of special food, and the girl's entrance to adolescence is celebrated by close family members. At the same time,
orthodox Hindu families consider menstruating females to be
unclean; they are isolated from other family members and are
not allowed free access to the kitchen and other parts of the
house. This practice often results in conflicts with the teenager
who feels lonely and devalued.

Asian-Indian immigrants—both parents and children—
find that adolescence is a difficult time because conflicts in the
value systems come to the forefront. Asian Indian families do
not believe in dating or premarital sex; they do not believe in
fostering independence at the cost of harmony; and they stress
interdependence of the family group even in areas of career

choice and marriage. Teenagers perceive their parents as intrusive, whereas their parents feel that they have the right to exercise authority because they supply emotional and financial support and are fulfilling their parental duty by providing guidance. This perceived intrusion and the demands placed on the youth could lead to suicidal attempts or acting-out behaviors (e.g., alcohol abuse), which are particularly common if the parents discover the adolescent has been sexually active or is performing poorly in school.

Asian Indian youth are under great pressure by their parents who want them to become professionals (e.g., physician or engineer) and do not value other choices. This often presents a dilemma for the young person who needs the family's support when making other choices. However, most Asian Indian youth assimilate the values of both cultures, similar to other immigrant populations. There is a great need for research in epidemiology, culturally competent psychotherapy, and ethnopsychopharmacology, especially for children and adolescents. Research on the outcomes of different modalities of therapy in the immigrant population is also needed.

ASIAN INDIAN CHILD-REARING PRACTICES AND CHILD MENTAL HEALTH

The psychoanalytic literature includes long-standing debate as to child-rearing practices and subsequent personality development of Hindus that give rise to pathology (Carstairs, 1978; Kakar, 1978; Roland, 1978). Any attempt to fit non-Western child-rearing practices into a Western way of thinking is certain to fail and result in a perception of pathology. Kurtz's (1992) analysis of the child-rearing practices in India indicated that such psychoanalytic studies do not take into consideration the multiple mothering that is present in the Indian family structure. In addition, the close physical proximity of the mother does not necessarily mean a close emotional tie between the mother and the infant. Instead, the mother subtly helps the infant to establish other attachments and to renounce the intense mother-infant relationship that is characteristic of Western child-rearing practices. Consequently, the system of defense mechanisms in Hindus is one of renunciation rather than the repression that is the cornerstone for the Western psychoanalysis.

Asian Indians emphasize the need to soothe infants; the mother or other caretakers immediately respond to the needs of a crying infant. Sinha (1995), in her writing has illustrated that the predominant pattern of child rearing in India is one of nurturance, responsiveness to the needs of children, and the promotion of synchrony with the infant. Kopp, Khoka, and Sigman (1977) compared the sensorimotor development of infants in the United States and India. Although Indian mothers were physically close to their infants, tended to soothe them with nursing, and allowed them less physical freedom than American mothers gave their infants, who were placed in a playpen or on the floor, Indian infants did not show large differences in their sensorimotor development. It was also noted that visual exploration and social interactions of infants in the family group is valued by the Indian mothers.

Until the age of 4 or 5 years, children are subject to few demands, and their needs are immediately attended to by family members. When a child turns 5, the expectations of the parents and the family group change with the introduction of discipline and chores appropriate for their age and gender. This change is not as abrupt as claimed nor traumatic enough to cause problems in personality development. Kurtz (1992) found that a gradual and subtle process of emotional weaning starts early on, and separation is not as traumatic as portrayed. Carstairs and others believe that the intense relationship with mother during the child's infancy and toddler stage, and followed by the abrupt separation with the arrival of a sibling or other reason is traumatic and results in difficulties in adjustment and affecting the personality development of the children. Carstairs and others believe that the intense relationship to the mother influences the development of the personality of the male child. Whereas Kurtz disagrees with them and believes that the process of separation/individuation begins slowly and is subtle (Carstairs, 1978; Kakar, 1978). Rogoff,

Jayanthi, Artin, and Christine (1993) examined toddlers and the caregivers from four cultures (Mayan Indian town in Guatemala, middle-class urban neighborhood in Turkey, a tribal village in India, and middle-class urban group in the United States) and focused on child-rearing practices, observation of caregivers helping toddlers operate novel objects, and self-dressing by the toddlers. The purpose was to understand the cultural differences in teaching styles among parents. Unlike their American counterparts, the Indian caregivers facilitated the activity of the toddler but did not engage in interactive play; instead they allowed the child to attend to the task. The authors concluded that in cultures that allow children to learn through participation in ongoing activity, children tend to develop a keen power of observation and can attend to different events at the same time.

The Asian Indian child is made a part of the family group and, through modeling, is taught to delay gratification, work toward the welfare of other members, and sacrifice his or her needs to the good of the entire group. At the same time, the individual is provided with stability, nurturance, and emotional support by the family. Deviations from the prescribed norms are curbed by shaming and inducing guilt. Conformity and obedience are often rewarded by the family group and a sense of loyalty and identification is fostered. Values are inculcated subtly by nonverbal communication such as a disapproving glance or nod of the head and are not explicitly stated as in the majority culture.

The development of the identity of the children and youth depends on the child-rearing practices of the Asian Indian families. Table 6–1 illustrates some of the differences in patterns of child rearing and family structure for Asian Indian and mainstream American cultures. These differences in the Indian and American family structures are tentative because of the changing social structure in India and the United States. Another consideration is that both India and the United States have very diverse populations, and the major themes referred to here may not be applicable to the individual family or person.

TABLE 6–1
Patterns of Culture

	Asian Indian	American
Family Structure	Highly hierarchical, mostly joint or extended; provides stability; harmony and interdependence encouraged	Less hierarchical; mostly nuclear; independence stressed; individualistic, aggressive competition
Child Rearing	Intense relationship between mother-infant within frame-work of multiple parent surrogate; infant in close proximity to caretaker; infant crying quickly attended to; feeding in response to crying	Exclusive domain of the parent; hired help or day care; proximity to parents not encouraged; crying not regularly assuaged with feeding
Child and Adolescent Behavior	Children expected to be respectful, obedient, and rarely rebellious	Children not expected to be totally obedient; allowed to question authority, express opinions and display feelings freely

Mental Disorders among Asian Indian Children and Adolescents

Literature is scarce regarding the epidemiology of mental disorders in the Asian Indian children and youth who live in North America. First, there are no studies from the United States on Asian Indian children and youth although there are many child mental health professionals from the Indian subcontinent. The cross-cultural studies looking at normal development and child-rearing practices among different cultures do not address the behaviors or disorders that are frequently encountered among recent Indian immigrants, and subsequent generations of Asian Indian children and youth. Most of the studies that have focused on issues of behavior disorders involve children from the United Kingdom. These studies do not tease out the disorders that are unique to immigrant children and subsequent generations. Second, there are few studies looking at adults with mental disorders and/or at their treatment. The problems in conducting research in this area are many because of the narrow categories in the *Diagnostic and Statistical Manual of Mental Disorders (DSM-IV)* and the use of culturally and linguistically unsuitable scales and other measures. Third, the basic tool of mental status examination does not take into consideration the sociocultural background of the person being assessed. In the basic mental status examination, the abstractability of similarities are heavily dependent on the sociocultural and educational background of the person being assessed.

There is not an integrated approach within the mental health field toward assessment of patients from different cultures, except for the culture-bound syndromes, which are unique and are assigned a separate status. Linguistically, India is diverse. A person from one state may be unable to communicate with a person from a neighboring state; the unifying language, whether acceptable or not, is English. Given these variables, even an Indian psychiatrist may have difficulty in communicating with patients from different parts of India unless those patients are fluent in English.

The concept of normality or deviant behavior as perceived by children and parents will differ based on their culture and belief systems. This is well illustrated in the paper by Hackett and Hackett (1993), who studied parental ideas of normal and deviant behavior among English and Gujarati populations in East Manchester, England. They found that the Gujarati parents were more stringent, less tolerant of physical aggression in their children, and not tolerant of bed-wetting, which was often punished. The Gujarati children showed less tantrum behaviors compared with the English and exhibited more fear, anxiety, and avoidance, which their parents did not perceive as a problem. This raises an interesting question: Should therapists who encounter such culturally different children attempt to change the child's behavior to meet the expectations of the parents or should they try to change the expectations of the parents? Often, what can be termed as self-assertive behavior in school may indeed be perceived by Indian parents as increased aggressive behavior. Thus, a child exposed to two sets of expectations—one in school and another at home—may experience confusion and conflict.

Although England has a large Asian Indian population, they are underrepresented in the local mental health clinics. Kallarackal and Herbert (1976) found that the rates of disturbance were low because Asian Indian parents do not recognize certain behaviors as problems and also tend to contain issues within the family because of cultural norms and language barriers (Stern, Cottrell, & Holmes, 1990). Thus, the rates of disorder may be the same or higher.

In a study of Asian families' attendance in a child mental health outpatient service, the dropout rate for preschool Asian referrals was 50%. The range of problems reported in the Asian group was narrow (primarily depression and somatic complaints) compared to the non-Asian group, which reported a broad range of disorders. Also, referrals for Asian children originated from pediatricians, or general practitioners, and very rarely from social or school services, perhaps because Indian parents find psychological distress couched in somatic complaints more acceptable. Similarly Roberts and Cawthorpe (1995) noted in their 5-year retrospective study of children and adolescents of Asian and White families referred to the Bradford Child Psychiatry Clinic that a large percentage of White families were referred from social service agencies; the children and adolescents of Asian families were referred by general practitioners and health visitors. Asian families may be reluctant to seek external help from social agencies because of a sense of alienation and lack of trust in the system. In addition, the parents tend to focus more on the child's physical health. The diagnosis of adjustment disorder was frequent among Asian females and the diagnosis of conduct disturbance more frequent among the White children. In contrast to White parents, Asian parents' failure to recognize conduct disorder in males may be explained by their perception of such behavior as naughtiness, stereotypical toughness, and bravery.

It is well documented that Indian females between the ages of 15 and 24 are at higher risk for suicide than are the males (Patel & Gaw, 1996). According to Patel and Gaw, meta-analysis of the literature on suicide among Asian Indians showed no published studies in the United States despite the increase in number of Asian Indian immigrants. Violent methods such as hanging and burning were frequently used by Indian females with notably higher rates for Hindu females than for Muslims, who have a stronger prohibition against suicide. Cultural conflicts between parents and child are a common instigator of suicide attempts.

However, other factors have to be considered, such as the stress of immigration and separation from family of origin. Deliberate self-poisoning is frequent among Asian adolescents as well as among Whites and usually results in hospitalization. McGibben, Ballard, Handy, Mohan, and Silveira (1992) showed that self-poisoning was more common in females of both White and Asian groups. Among the probable cause of self-destructive behavior is that the Asian group showed more intergenerational conflict around the type of dress, religion, and outside family relationships. Mental disorders among Asian Indian children and youth are infrequently diagnosed for numerous reasons, such as the failure to understand mental illness or rejection of emotional problems as weakness. Sometimes, the health care provider may collude with families in ignoring an underlying illness.

Conclusion

Asian Indian families in North America will have to adapt to new ways to handle the emancipation of the youth, a social change that is supported by peers and reinforced by the media. Kurian (1976) in his survey and interview of Asian Indian families in Canada notes that there are several areas in which the families must adjust to the cultural changes that they encounter with immigration.

It is important to look closely at the factors that afford some protection and facilitate better mental health among immigrants. Positive indices for mental health include strong self-esteem, a firm sense of identity, acceptance of sex role, capacity for healthy interpersonal relationships, optimal tolerance for stress or tension, and a sense of trust (Khatri, 1970). These positive indices can be integrated into therapy and education of parents to decrease the risk of mental illness in both immigrant and native populations.

It is not clear whether the incidence of childhood disorders for the Asian Indian population residing in the United States is comparable to that of other ethnic groups. Most studies did not differentiate between the subgroups of Asians. On a personal note, I have been consulted by persons in the Asian Indian community for treatment of first-onset schizophrenia, bipolar disorder, substance abuse, and other mental health problems.

References

AMERICAN PSYCHIATRIC ASSOCIATION. (1994). *Diagnostic and statistical manual of mental disorders* (4th ed.). Washington, DC: Author.

ANANTH, J., & ANANATH, K. (1996). *East Indian immigrant to the U.S. life cycle issues and adjustment.* East Meadow, NY: Indo-American Psychiatric Association.

BEISER, M., DION, R., GOTOWIEC, A., HYMAN, I., & VU, N. (1995). *Canadian Journal of Psychiatry, 40*, 67–72.

CARSTAIRS, G. M. (1978). Changes in Indian village societies and their impact on child development: A personal perspective. In E. J. Anthony & C. Chiland (Eds.), *The child in his family* (Vol. 5, pp. 345–356). New York: Wiley.

DANIELS, R. (1990). *A history of immigration and ethnicity in American life.* New York: Harper Perennial.

DUTT, E. (1989, October). Becoming a second generation. *India Abroad, 20*(2), 13–16.

GOKALNATHAN, K. S. (1976). Adolescence in a matriarchal society: Changing cultural and social patterns after industrialization. In E. Fuchs (Ed.), *Youth in a changing world: Cross cultural perspectives on adolescence* (pp. 253–257). The Hague, Paris: Morton.

GRAVES, P. L. (1978). Infant behavior and maternal attitudes: Early sex difference in West Bengal, India. *Journal of Cross-Cultural Psychology, 9*(1), 45–60.

HACKETT, L., & HACKETT, R. (1993). Parental ideas of normal and deviant child behavior: A comparison of two ethnic groups. *British Journal of Psychiatry, 162,* 353–357.

KAKAR, S. (1978). In E. J. Anthony & C. Chiland (Eds.), *The child in his family* (Vol. 5, pp. 319–332). New York: Wiley.

KALLARACKAL, A. M., & HERBERT, M. (1976, February). The happiness of Indian immigrant children. *New Society, 26,* 422–424.

KHATRI, A. A. (1970). Personality and mental health of Indians (Hindus). In E. J. Anthony & C. Chiland (Eds.), *The child in his family* (pp. 389–412). New York: Wiley.

KOPP, C. B., KHOKA, E. W., & SIGMAN, M. (1977). A comparison of sensorimotor development among infants in India and the United States. *Journal of Cross-Cultural Psychology, 8*(4), 435–451.

KURIAN, G. (1976). Problems of socialization in Indian families in a changing society. In E. Fuchs (Ed.), *Youth in a changing world: Cross cultural perspectives on adolescent.* The Hague, Paris: Mouton.

KURTZ, S. (1992). *All the mothers are one: Hindu, India, and the cultural reshaping of psychoanalysis.* New York: Columbia University Press.

LAVIN, M. R. (1996). *Understanding the census: A guide for marketers, planners, grant writers and other data users* (pp. 138–139). New York: Epoch Books.

MCGIBBEN, L., BALLARD, C. G., HANDY, S., MOHAN, R. N. C., & SILVEIRA, W. R. (1992). Deliberate self-poisoning in Asian and caucasian 12–15 year olds. *British Journal of Psychiatry, 161,* 110–112.

PATEL, S. P., & GAW, A. C. (1996). Suicide among immigrants from the Indian subcontinent: A review. *Psychiatric Services, 47*(5), 517–521.

ROBERTS, N., & CAWTHORPE, D. (1995). Immigrant child and adolescent psychiatric referrals: A five year retrospective study of Asian and caucasian families. *Canadian Journal of Psychiatry, 40*(5), 252–256.

ROGOFF, B., JAYANTHI, M., ARTIN, G., & CHRISTINE, M. (1993). Guided participation in cultural activity by toddlers and caregivers. *Monographs of the Society for Research in Child Development, 58*(8, Serial No. 236).

ROLAND, A. (1978). The modernization process (and its pains) in the Indian adolescent female as observed in the therapeutic situations. In E. J. Anthony & C. Chiland (Eds.), *The child in his family* (Vol. 5, pp. 357–364). New York: Wiley.

SHARMA, S. S. (1984, September). Assimilation of Indian immigrant adolescent in British society. *Journal of Psychiatry, 118,* 79–84.

SINHA, S. R. (1995). Childrearing practices relevant for the growth of dependency and competency of children. In J. Valsiner (Ed.), *Child development within culturally structured environments: Comparative cultural and constructive perspectives* (Vol. 3, pp. 105–137). NJ: Able.

STERN, G., COTTRELL, D., & HOLMES, G. (1990). Patterns of attendance of child psychiatry out-patients with special reference to Asian families. *British Journal of Psychiatry, 156,* 384–387.

SUNIYA, L. S., & QUINLAN, D. M. (1993). Parental images in two cultures: A study of women in India and America. *Journal of Cross Cultural Psychology, 24*(2), 186–202.

U.S. BUREAU OF THE CENSUS. (1990). *Statistical abstract of the U.S. 1990.* Washington, DC: Superintendent of Documents.

VERMA, J. (1995). Transformation of women's social roles in India. In J. Valsiner (Ed.), *Child development within culturally structured environments: Comparative cultural and constructive perspectives* (Vol. 3, pp. 138–163). NJ: Able.

CHAPTER 7

Filipino American Children

ROLANDO A. SANTOS

Demographic Profile

THERE ARE NEARLY 1.5 million Filipino Americans in the United States today. It is the fastest growing Asian American group in the nation. Relative to all other countries, the Philippines is the source of the second largest group of immigrants to the United States (after Mexico). Immigration accounts for about 65% of all Filipino Americans, 31% of whom came between 1980 and 1990. Since 1980, the immigration rate from the Philippines has averaged about 43,000 immigrants a year. In 1987, the number was 58,300, and in 1988 it was 50,697. At this rate, the Filipino American population will surpass all other Asian American groups in the nation by the year 2000. In 1990, 68% of all Filipino Americans lived on the West Coast (mostly in California, Hawaii, Washington, and Oregon). About 43% lived in California—the largest Asian American group in the state.

The median age of the Filipino American population in 1990 was 29. However, whereas the median age of those born in the United States was 14.1, that of the foreign-born was 38.4 and the latter made up about 65% of the Filipino American population. Almost one-fourth of all Filipino Americans are of school age (5–19 years old), and about 70% of these children were born in the United States. American-born citizens (ABCs) comprise most of the school-age population whose parents and caretakers are immigrant, often referred to as *FOBs* (fresh-off-the boat) or

FOJs (fresh-off-the jet). These figures indicate significant gen-erational- and culture-gap issues. Additional demographic char-acteristics of Filipino Americans, in relation to other Asian American groups, are shown in Table 7–1.

Immigration Patterns

Socioeconomic factors are the chief motives for immigrating to the United States. Although political and family reunification may be cited as reasons for coming to the United States, eco-nomic reasons often underlie these claims. Filipinos started ar-riving in the United States as early as 1763. These immigrants were crewmen on Spanish galleons, plying the route between Manila, Philippines, and Acapulco, Mexico. Known as *Manila-men*, these crewmen jumped ship to escape forced labor and maltreatment and sought refuge in Louisiana. A second wave of immigrants, the *sacadas* or contract laborers, came between 1906 and 1934 to work on the sugarcane plantations in Hawaii. Filipinos became the new source of cheap labor after 1924 when no further Japanese immigration was allowed. These laborers were young (14–29 years of age) and single, with little or no for-mal education, and were from the rural areas of the Ilocos and Visayan regions of the Philippines. During the same period, some Filipino scholars or *pensionados* were sent to the United States for advanced education and training to prepare them for leadership positions in government and education. Most of the Filipinos coming to the United States at that time, however, be-came farm hands in Hawaii and California or workers in Alaskan canneries; they were called *Pinoys*. They were also hired as busboys and janitors and as domestics in homes, hos-pitals, and hotels. Because the Philippines was a U.S. territory, Filipinos were considered to be U.S. nationals and could come to the United States in unlimited numbers.

As the Filipino population grew, they came to be viewed as economic and social threats in American communities where they worked, becoming victims of racial discrimination, segre-gation, and violence. They could not enjoy the privileges of full

TABLE 7–1
Demographic and Socioeconomic Characteristics of
Filipinos and Other Asian Americans

	Filipinos	Chinese	Japanese	Korean	Vietnamese
Population (1990)	1,406,770	1,645,472	847,562	798,849	614,547
Population (thousands), 1980	782	812	716	357	245
Immigrants admitted to United States (thousands, 1988)	50.7	28.7	4.5	34.7	25.8
Median income per full-time worker (in 1979 dollars)	13,690	15,753	16,829	14,224	11,641
Percentage of women (16 and over) in labor force as family householders	79.0	70.3	72.5	71.1	56.0
Percentage of families below poverty level	6.2	10.5	4.2	13.1	35.1
Percentage of households with income from public assistance	10.0	6.6	4.2	6.2	28.1
Average family size	4.2	3.7	3.6	4.9	5.2
Median income (in 1979 dollars)	23,687	22,559	27,354	20,459	12,840
Percentage of unemployed in the civilian workforce	4.8	3.6	3.0	5.7	8.2
Percentage with fewer than 5 years of schooling	7.0	10.3	2.3	4.0	10.3
Percentage with 4 years of high school or more education	74.2	71.3	81.6	75.1	62.2
Percentage with 4 or more years of college	37.0	36.6	26.4	33.7	12.9

Source: U.S. Bureau of the Census, 1991.

citizenship; for example, they were not allowed to vote, own property, start businesses, or marry Caucasians. Socially isolated, Pinoys lived in *Manilatowns* and frequented dance halls and gambling places for entertainment. Most of the few survivors of this period (often called *old-timers*, or OTs) are poor and still living alone in cheap downtown hotels or rest homes. When the Philippines became a commonwealth in 1934, Filipinos lost even their partial rights and became aliens, limited to an annual immigration quota of 50 persons. Some of these OTs married much younger girls in the Philippines, girls who were already in the United States as tourists, or students with expired student visas. Some of these marriages were arranged for fees. Marriages of convenience enabled the women to enter or stay in the United States as permanent residents and eventually assume American citizenship. Children who were born from these unions often had their OT fathers mistaken for their grandfathers.

After World War II, Filipinos immigrating to the United States were war veterans, military personnel and their families, professionals and their families, and students. The doctors, nurses, engineers, accountants, dentists, teachers, businessmen, and lawyers who come are mostly from urban, middle-class families in the Philippines. Although many of these professionals eventually find jobs commensurate with their training, education, and experience, many remain unemployed for long periods or have to settle for jobs for which they are overqualified (e.g., dentists working as dental technicians, medical doctors as medical technologists, lawyers as security guards, teachers as teaching assistants and hotel chambermaids, architects as cab drivers or short-order cooks). Credentialing and licensing laws, limited English proficiency, prejudicial stereotypes, age, subtle and overt racism, lack of appropriate marketable skills, and a tight job market are factors that have contributed to unemployment or underemployment. Another segment of the Filipino American population consists of illegal aliens (*tago-ng-tago* or TNTs, literally "hide and hide"), who may have come as tourists, businesspersons, or students, or with temporary work permits, but whose visas have expired.

Cultural Values

The 1.5 million Filipino Americans are not a monolithic group but an aggregation of individuals, each occupying a different point on the continuum from traditional Filipino to modern American. Age, length of residence in the United States, educational background, socioeconomic status, occupational history, urbanicity, ethnic physical characteristics, English proficiency, place of residence, and ethnicity of spouse are major factors determining the pace, direction, and degree of Americanization of these individuals. Regardless of a person's place on this continuum, however, a core of recurrent themes underlie the socialization of Filipino Americans.

In what has become a watershed in subsequent studies of Filipino values, Jaime Bulatao (1964) describes three major values and some common themes that permeate Filipino thought and behavior—family, authority, economic sufficiency, and patience. These values, in varying degrees, underlie the socialization of Filipinos and Filipino Americans:

Value 1. Emotional Closeness and Security in a Family. "The family is seen as a defense against a potentially hostile world, as insurance against hunger and old age, as a place where one can be oneself without having to worry too much about maintaining smooth interpersonal relations with others" (Bulatao, 1964, p. 57). The following themes attend this value: (a) The interest of the individual must be sacrificed for the good of the family; (b) parents should be very strict in watching over, protecting, and curbing their children, who might otherwise meet with disaster; and (c) women are highly valued for their qualities as mothers and housekeepers.

Value 2. Approval by Authority Figures and by Society. There is a great concern for what an important authority figure may be thinking about oneself and a tendency to shape one's behavior accordingly. (Bulatao, 1964, p. 64) For the family to remain close and secure, someone must exert firm authority, which is respected and obeyed, within limits. Authority figures provide other benefits including help in obtaining a job. To secure approval in this culture, one must follow tradition and keep in mind what the neighbors may be thinking regarding oneself.

Value 3. Economic and Social Betterment. This value usually appears as a wish to increase the standard of living of one's family to repay one's debt of gratitude to parents and relatives. Usually, economic sufficiency and security are the primary goals. More rarely, the value is expressed as a desire for individual success, to make good in one's career (Bulatao, 1964, p. 74). Some subthemes are that (a) everyone should strive to obtain economic sufficiency for the family, (b) one must study and work hard to improve one's economic situation, (c) social recognition is a major aim in one's going to school and to work, and (d) a person must suffer before gaining happiness.

Frank Lynch's study (1964) also frequently quoted in studies and discussions on Filipino values, defines *social acceptance*— being taken by others for what one is, or believes oneself to be, and being treated in accordance with that status—as an important Filipino value. A Tagalog proverb says, in translation, "It doesn't matter if you don't love me; just don't shame me." Filipinos place great importance on being able to get along well with others in ways that avoid outward signs of conflict even though it may mean being agreeable under difficult circumstances. It means sensitivity to the feelings of others and a willingness and ability to change tack or direction so as not to cause others any inconvenience or hurt feelings. This characteristic ensures highly valued *smooth interpersonal relations* (SIR).

There are three ways of maintaining SIR. *Pakikisama* means "getting along well with others." It could involve making concessions or giving in or following the lead or suggestion of others to achieve and maintain group consensus. Euphemisms—the use of an agreeable or inoffensive word or expression for one that is harsh, indelicate, or otherwise unpleasant or taboo—are a second means of maintaining SIR. Lynch quotes Juan Delgado, who wrote in 1754, that the Filipino would rather suffer 100 lashes than a single harsh word. He also quotes Rizal, the Philippine national hero, as writing in 1609, "The Filipino today prefers a beating to scolding or insults." The use of a go-between or middleman is a third way to avoid possible embarrassment or bad feeling, or to remedy conflict. This intermediary communicates embarrassing requests, complaints, or decisions to avoid the shame of a face-to-face encounter.

Culture Conflict and Mental Health

Since most Filipino Americans are immigrants, there is a strong carryover of traditional Filipino values, customs, and traditions to the United States. Although this may help in cushioning the culture shocks of immigration, it also heightens culture conflicts, resulting in cognitive and behavioral disequilibrium, dysfunction, and pathology. The 1990 Tompar-Tiu study of clinical depression among Filipino Americans indicates that clinical depression is more prevalent among Filipino Americans than in the general U.S. population. The depressive symptomatology and psychosocial profiles of clinically depressed (CD) versus nondepressed (ND) Filipino Americans delineate in bold relief the cogency of Filipino traditional values. According to Tompar-Tiu and Sustento-Seneriches (1995): "The most common stressors believed to be causes of depression were geographical separation or alienation from family and financial difficulties. Significant psychosocial stressors—were divorce; separation from spouse or partner; parents', children's, and other family members' inability to understand or communicate with one another; decreased closeness among family members; unemployment; significant worsening of financial and social status; having no one to share leisure time with; significant decreases in sleep; and inability to have children" (p. 52). Stress, she continues, "erodes feelings of social competence and self-esteem; when nothing seems to work out, learned helplessness may become an issue and a stressor in itself." According to the same study, "one of the most important social-environmental resources is the availability of supportive individuals, such as close family members, loved ones, friends, and religious counselors." Other findings indicate that cognitive symptoms (e.g., worrying too much, guilt feelings, feelings of not being understood, feelings easily hurt), affective symptoms (e.g., easily annoyed or irritated, loneliness, nervousness, fearfulness, and temper outbursts), and motivational symptoms (e.g., feelings of worthlessness, thoughts of death or dying, feelings of inferiority to others, and feelings of hopelessness about the future) are better predictors of clinical depression among Filipino Americans than somatic symptoms (e.g., headaches, chest pains) and vegetative symptoms (e.g., poor appetite, trouble falling asleep, low energy, loss of sexual interest or pleasure). The latter may be hard to differentiate from symptoms of physical illness. Any problems, perceived or real, among Filipino Americans, are very likely underreported because of the cultural tendency of Filipinos to deny the existence of such problems, at least to outsiders, or to somatize them. Tompar-Tiu and Sustento-Seneriches (1995, p. 35) point out, "It is common among Filipino Americans, depressed or not, to smile even when relating sad events or reporting hurt feelings." This nervous smile should not mislead clinicians into believing that the Filipino patient is not depressed.

There is a compelling need for mental health education in Filipino American communities and for mental health and other professionals who provide services—educational, social, economic, and mental—to ensure culturally relevant diagnosis and remediation of problems facing their clientele. What sometimes might be viewed as pathology could merely be sociocultural dysfunction in the new environment for the immigrant, or what might be brushed aside as simply manifestations of adjustment problems that will eventually go away, could indeed indicate a serious psychiatric problem. An awareness of Filipino customs and values as well as proficiency in the language of clients with little or no proficiency in English is necessary in diagnosing and treating any mental or behavioral problems. Although English is a second language in the Philippines, there can be serious communication problems between new immigrants and their caseworkers. Nonverbal cues and culturally embedded language, although using English words, might distort, instead of clarify, issues to those not familiar with Filipino values and their manifestations. A Filipino American clinician, or a trained Filipino interpreter to assist the clinician who does not understand the client's primary language and culture, would be the ideal arrangement. The mere fact that the clinician is Filipino American, however, may not mean that he or she speaks the language or dialect of the client or understands the nuances of the Filipino culture involved. Tompar-Tiu and Sustento-Seneriches (1995) also caution that the Filipino American therapist might complicate matters with "countertransference phenomena" such as "overidentification with the patient and the patient's family, denial of painful acculturation issues common to both patient and therapist, and boundary problems." Acquaintance with what is normal behavior among Filipinos and Filipino Americans could spell the difference between appropriate, humane, and effective remediation and what is inappropriate, cruel, and ineffectual.

Child Rearing and Mental Health

Traditional Filipino values help shape the children's concept of what constitutes mental health and mental illness. They influence the children's manifestation of symptoms, coping styles, help-seeking strategies, and utilization of and response to treatment. Tseng and Hsu (1991, p. 149) observe, "The manifested individual abnormality or disorder is a part of the display of the total family psychopathology."

Current literature has much to say about traditional Filipino American parental expectations and behaviors in child rearing, but causal relationships between parental behavior and children's behavior are still highly speculative. Also, Jocano and Policarpio (1974) observed that, after two-and-a-half years of intensive field research of family life in an urban community in the Philippines, data gathered with questionnaires did not tend to reflect what the respondents actually did in real situations.

AGE LEVELS AND CHILD REARING

Erik Erikson's (1963) stage-related theory, which proposes five stages of psychosocial development from birth to late adolescence (birth–18 years), will be used as a framework in describing Filipino child-rearing practices.

There are several criticisms of Erikson's theory. In the context of transcultural child mental health, however, the most relevant is the observation of Gibbs and Huang (1989, p. 5) that although the theory is "quite relevant for children reared in a nuclear family in highly industrialized societies, it may be less applicable to children reared in extended families in industrial societies where different psychosocial outcomes might be emphasized." Despite this and other limitations, the scheme provides a useful framework in the study of psychosocial development, even if only as a basis for cross-cultural analysis. The five stages of psychosocial development described by Erikson (1959) are:

1. Trust versus mistrust (birth to 1 year).
2. Autonomy versus shame and doubt (2 to 3 years).
3. Initiative versus guilt (4 to 5 years)
4. Industry versus inferiority (6 to 11 years).
5. Identity versus role confusion (12 to 18 years).

The first year of life fosters the development of trust versus mistrust. Later on, the child-rearing practices encourage autonomy, and later still, freedom to explore is encouraged. Misbehavior, however, brings sharp correction by adults, and children are taught to respect adults. Although Filipino children experience Erikson Stages 1 through 3, the following section describes their occurrence according to beliefs and practices regarding respect for adults and family and immediate intervention if these values are ignored.

Infancy and Early Childhood (Birth–5 years)

"After birth, the newborn is physically cuddled, fondled, sung to, talked to, and rocked to sleep. The baby is picked up immediately and nursed whenever he cries and for as long as he wishes. The first four weeks after [a child's] birth, the mother's time is wholly devoted to the infant" (Aquino, 1981, p. 174). Relatives and friends visit mother and child and often help with household chores so the mother will not overexert herself in her weakened condition. In Jocano's 1974 study, 73% of the respondents used either bottle feeding or feeding from both breast and bottle. This was especially true with working mothers, who often had live-in help. Lack or insufficiency of mother's milk was also a major reason for the mixed-feeding practice. In the rural sample, however, over 66% of the mothers breast-fed. Usually, weaning takes place within one year. Some children, however, are breast-fed up to their third year, until the child just stops suckling, or until the mother gets pregnant again.

Even among those with advanced education, many still retain their rural beliefs in witches and supernatural beings as possible sources of illness, deformities, or death. The child learns early to trust the family but to beware of strangers and outsiders. Typically, during the first few months after birth, the baby sleeps with the mother to facilitate feeding, protection, and diaper changing. As a rule, strangers are not hired as babysitters. Relatives, in-laws, older siblings, or *yayas* (maids) provide child care in the absence of or in cooperation with the mother. Turning over, sitting, and crawling are encouraged and are accomplished by the child during this period without any help from others.

Baptism is an important ritual during the child's first year, especially among Roman Catholics. Sponsors (*ninong* and *ninang*) are chosen and considered as second parents and expected to help in the care and upbringing of the child. This practice also links the *compadres* (coparents) in a quasi-kinship relationship. The occasion is celebrated with feasting and merrymaking. Jocano and Policarpio's Philippine study (1974) points out that when the child is between 4 and 5 years old, the attention, overt manifestations of affection, and privileges slowly make way for more strict disciplinary measures to ensure conformity and obedience to elders, male or female. Scolding, shouting, reprimanding (about 74%), and corporal punishment (about 11%) are most frequently used to correct an errant child. Shaming is also used, as is threatening with dire consequences (e.g., the "*aswang* [witch] will come and get you!"). Children who do well are seldom rewarded because such behavior is expected. Praise or rewards are usually not given in public. Although parents do not flaunt children's success, they are anxious to minimize damage to the family's reputation by punishing children in the presence of any offended party to show the latter that such behavior is not tolerated in the family.

Generally, children in a dangerous situation are simply physically removed from it without explanation (Aquino, 1981). Often a child does not develop an insight into the situation and may not recognize the danger when alone. Additionally, children are taught as early as possible not to talk back to elders or to look into the elder's eyes while being reprimanded. Both are signs of disrespect and might result in more serious consequences.

As children grow older, they increasingly share in household chores, (e.g., cooking, setting the table, dishwashing, cleaning the yard, folding clothes, and doing errands for elders in the household). In the Jocano and Policarpio study (1974), two other important aspects of child rearing at this age level seem to be dealing with bed-wetting and learning to sleep alone, after having slept with the mother for so long. Bed-wetting elicits reactions ranging from spanking, to rationalizing for the child (e.g., he had had too much to drink), or to viewing the occurrence as a normal part of growing up that will soon go away. Up to this age level, the typical Filipino child will not have had any formal school experience (e.g., prekindergarten or nursery school). Until recently, children started compulsory schooling in the Philippines at the age of 7 years. Now, children must enter school when they are 6 years old.

Elementary School Age (6–11 years)

According to Erikson, between 6 and 11 years children must win recognition by producing things. They should be encouraged to make and do things well, to persevere, and to finish tasks; and they should be praised for trying. These tasks may be difficult for newly immigrant children who find it difficult at first to compete with peers who have had preschool education. Although typically a child is to "be seen and not heard," Filipino parents are proud to show off a child's accomplishments (e.g., musical skills, athletic and academic achievements). Often, however, the parents do not have the resources—know-how, finances, and time—to facilitate such accomplishments, and many children start their formal education with very few of the physical, social, and academic skills that facilitate transition from the home to the school culture. In the United States, many are placed at inappropriate grade levels because of their ages. A 7-year-old may be placed in the second grade although in the Philippines, he would just be starting in the first grade. Most of his American classmates will have had at least two or three years of schooling (pre-kindergarten, kindergarten, and first grade). On top of that, the child is saddled with other problems that hinder academic achievement—little or no facility in English, lack of acquaintance with the American culture, minority status, and parents who are not familiar with the American educational system and their role in it. Immigrant children find themselves without the physical skills to participate in school sports such as football or baseball, and may be the butt of ethnic jokes from both non-Filipino and, more cruelly, U.S.-born Filipino Americans, who are anxious to be accepted by the majority population and do not want to be identified with the recent immigrants. Although many survive and excel despite these difficulties, others skip school, develop psychosomatic disorders, become withdrawn, or overcompensate by bullying, vandalizing, fighting, or engaging in other aggressive behaviors. Thus dysfunction, unless appropriately diagnosed and remediated early, may unnecessarily lead to more serious pathological disorders calling for mental health treatment.

Adolescence (12–18 years)

In a 1974 Mendez study of a Philippine rural population, menstruation is a critical period and with it come some prohibitions, most important of which is for the girls not to take baths during their period. Sponge baths are fine, but washing of the hair is not. For boys, circumcision is viewed as a rite of passage to manhood.

Traditionally, parents are not involved in the procedure. The peer group makes all necessary arrangements with, usually, a local person who has been performing the rite and this is usually done without the parents' knowledge. In a few cases, the operation is performed by a medical doctor. Uncircumcised boys become the object of ridicule and shaming. Among Filipino Americans, these two concerns may not be viewed as seriously.

At this stage, the *barkada* or the peer group is mainly social in nature: The members share similar backgrounds and interests. On some junior and senior high school campuses or on street corners or malls, Filipino Americans may be mistakenly viewed as gang members and treated as such. This causes problems for these teenagers, who may be good students, student leaders, and law-abiding adolescents, but look "hoody."

Like most other ethnic groups, Filipino Americans also have their gangs. Kang and Saar (1996, p. 3) cite the 1990 Enriquez study in Honolulu indicating that Filipino Americans are "overrepresented in Honolulu gangs" compared with other ethnic groups. Gang members are predominantly male, although girls are sometimes members. Girlfriends may form their own gangs to support those of their boyfriends. The gang members in this study mostly lived in crowded areas with inadequate recreational facilities. Their parents had come from rural areas in the Philippines and had two to three low-paying and nonprofessional jobs. The main reason given for joining gangs was protection from other gangs. Boredom, lack of things to do, and deprivation of love and attention were other reasons cited. Behaviors of youth at risk for gang membership include "poor performance in school, truancy, lack of hobbies, nothing to do during leisure time, problems at home, frequent negative contacts with police officers, living in a neighborhood where gangs exist, having friends who are gang members or in gang attire, having tattoos, and dressing in gang-style clothes" (Kang & Saar, 1996, p. 1). The same article quotes Rodel Rodis, a Filipino American attorney who has represented many Asian youngsters in trouble with the law in California, as saying, "Back home, there are aunts and uncles, grandparents and neighbors who all take part in raising the young. But in the United States they return to empty houses after school and, for some, the gang becomes the extended family that provides its members comfort and solace."

Sexuality is another issue at this stage of development. Most Filipino American youth grow up with minimal direct sex education from parents and other elders. Much of what they know, they learn in school and from peers. Recent census data show that, compared with the Chinese and Japanese American groups, Filipino Americans have the highest percentage of births to teenage mothers (6.1% vs. 1.1% and 2.7%, respectively), the highest percentage of births to unmarried mothers (16.8% vs. 5.5% and 9.8%, respectively), the lowest percentage of mothers beginning prenatal care during first trimester, and the highest percentage of mothers who do not start prenatal care until the third trimester or do not get prenatal care at all.

A serious area of role confusion is ethnic identification, especially during adolescence, when physical appearance, image, and social acceptance are so important. A strong rejection of ethnic physical characteristics and ethnic background is common among Filipino American youth. Their minority status, the negative and derogatory stereotypes of Filipinos among their classmates and others, coupled with the colonial mentality of immigrant parents engender resentment, embarrassment, jealousy and, often, a denial and rejection of their ethnic background. Many try to pass as members of more prestigious groups to enhance their self-esteem and their chances for social acceptance.

Another major source of role confusion is what Tseng and Hsu (1991) refer to as the "premature 'parentified' role often assumed by the first generation immigrant child, who may serve as an interpreter and mediator between parents and the dominant society."

Case Example

The extreme cases of Lisa and Roberto, both of whom are 18-year-old Filipino Americans, illustrate the range of possible intracultural variations within the overarching general values earlier discussed. Lisa is a student in an expensive and exclusive private secondary school in Pasadena, California, and a world traveler.

She lives in a mansion with her parents and two siblings in a predominantly White neighborhood. Both parents are immigrant medical doctors from wealthy families in the Philippines. Both were graduates of exclusive private universities in Manila. Lisa speaks English only but understands Tagalog, the first language of the parents. Lisa looks forward to attending Stanford University or an Ivy League university. She plans to go to medical school. So far, she has dated only White boys.

Robert, another Filipino American, lives in Hawaii. He is a high school dropout and works as a busboy in a luxury hotel. Both parents started working as domestics in the same hotel after the sugarcane plantations, where they had worked for years, closed down their operations. They immigrated from the Ilocos region in the Philippines, where they managed to eke out a living as tenant farmers. Both had completed the sixth grade in a barrio school; they speak mostly Ilocano and very limited English with a heavy Ilocano accent. From rural Philippines, they went directly to Hawaii to join relatives in the sugarcane plantations. The family—parents, five children, an aunt, and two in-laws—live in a small plantation house. Roberto's 16-year-old girlfriend is pregnant but his family does not approve of his marrying an Afro-Samoan American girl. Roberto looks forward to owning his own car soon. He says he has no definite plans for the future: "Time will tell."

Both Lisa and Roberto are Filipino Americans. Mental health and social welfare workers, however, will more likely have the Filipino American Robertos, and not the Filipino American Lisas, as their clients. Thus the importance of the concept of the "culture of poverty" in understanding Filipino American clientele. Thus, too, the importance of understanding the traditional values that most Filipino immigrants bring with them and with which they rear their children in the United States.

References

Aquino, C. J. (1981). The Filipino in America. In A. L. Clark (Ed.), *Culture and child rearing* (pp. 167–190). Philadelphia: Davis.

BULATAO, J. (1964). Manileno's mainsprings. In F. Lynch (Ed.), *Four readings on Philippine values* (pp. 50–86). Quezon City: Institute of Philippine Culture, Ateneo de Manila University Press.

ERIKSON, E. H. (1963). *Childhood and society.* New York: Norton.

GIBBS, J. T., & HUANG L. N., et al. (1989). *Children of color.* San Francisco: Jossey-Bass.

JOCANO, F. L., & POLICARPIO, P. (1974). *The Filipino family in its rural and urban orientation: 2 case studies.* Manila: Centro Escolar University Research and Development Center.

KANG, C. K., & SAAR, M. (1996, January 25). Asian gangs rise strikes a paradox. *Los Angeles Times,* 1–3.

LYNCH, F. (1964). Social acceptance. In F. Lynch (Ed.), *Four readings on Philippine values* (pp. 1–21). Quezon City: Institute of Philippine Culture, Ateneo de Manila University Press.

SANTOS, R. A. (1983). The social and emotional development of Filipino-American children. In G. J. Powell (Ed.), *The psychosocial development of minority group children* (pp. 131–146). New York: Brunner/Mazel.

TOMPAR-TIU, A., & SUSTENTO-SENERICHES, J. (1995) *Depression and other mental health issues: The Filipino experience.* San Francisco: Jossey-Bass.

TSENG, W., & HSU, J. (1991). *Culture and family.* New York: Hawthorne Press.

U.S. BUREAU OF THE CENSUS. (1990). *Asian and Pacific Islanders in the United States: 1990 census of population.* Washington, DC: U.S. Government Printing Office.

U.S. BUREAU OF THE CENSUS. (1994). *Statistical abstract of the United States* (114th ed.). Washington, DC: U.S. Government Printing Office.

CHAPTER 8

Native Hawaiian Children

FAYE F. UNTALAN, ANDREA W. GUILLORY, and
CAROL TITCOMB HARTLEY

THE HEALTH AND SOCIAL STATUS of Native Hawaiian children compares unfavorably to that of all other ethnic groups in the state of Hawaii. To some degree, this is the product of their cultural endowment. To a greater degree, this has been brought about by social change within the Hawaiian community in response to pressures from the West. Both are influential in contemporary patterns of child rearing and parental expectations of child development. Selected developmental and educational outcomes among Hawaiian children are presented. Findings are interpreted using the Structural/Behavioral model (Horowitz, 1987), which allows for characterization of outcomes vis-à-vis organism and environmental characteristics.

Historical and Cultural Overview

The Hawaiian Islands were populated circa 300 A.D. by Marquesan Islanders as part of the Polynesian migrations. The basic unit of the society they established was the *'ohana*, or extended kin group. The *'ohana* was composed not only of its living members, but of ancestors who assumed the forms of plants and animals to give inspiration, guidance, warnings of danger, and punishment for offenses (Puku'i, Haertig, & Lee, 1972). Thus, the people had a sense of connectedness to their family of flesh and of the spirit, and to the flora and fauna of their land. They practiced conservation of resources from the land. They also practiced *aloha,* as shown in value for affiliation, devaluation of achievement and acquisition, and avoidance of conflict and confrontation. Social relations were characterized by reciprocity, mutual interdependence, and mutual help (Puku'i et al., 1972). Sharing and free exchange was the basis for the distribution of goods and services.

Between 800 and 1200 A.D., invaders from Tahiti brought the *kapu* (taboo) system to Hawaii. *Kapu* provided rules of conduct that regulated political, spiritual, and social behavior. There was no ownership of private property. The *ali'i* (chiefs, or highest ranking class) directed the use of the land, which was held in public trust. They were responsible for the welfare of the people and the preservation of natural resources. In return, the *maka'ainana,* or commoners, repaid their chiefs with labor and loyalty. The highly structured, stable society flourished. In 1778, the English ships *Resolution* and *Discovery,* under the direction of Captain Cook, sailed into this ancient, insular culture (Stannard, 1989) and introduced the instruments of social and political change: commerce, muskets, and microbes.

POLITICAL AND SOCIAL CHANGE

Political rivalry among chiefs often spawned battles, and eventually escalated into a civil war. In 1795, with the help of muskets and armies furnished by foreigners, Kamehameha forcibly united the islands. Under King Kamehameha I, rivalry between chiefs moved from the political to the economic arena, as each vied for trade with the sailing ships. The flourishing civilization of the Hawaiians had been based on shared goods and services, conservation of natural resources, and the interdependence of chiefs and commoners (Kelly, 1956). With the advent of the lucrative fur and sandalwood trade between the Pacific Northwest and the Orient, Hawaii was visited more and more often by vessels offering barter and seeking refreshment (Stannard, 1989). The introduction of a competitive, consumption-based, market economy led to the corruption of the chiefs, exploitation of the people, and despoilment of the land. The chiefs ordered the people into the forests to cut the fragrant sandalwood trees for trading. As a result, fields lay fallow and fishing nets gathered dust. Provisions became so scarce that many were driven to eat moss and other famine foods (Stannard, 1989).

Disease

By virtue of their geographic isolation, Hawaiians were susceptible to tuberculosis, syphilis, and gonorrhea, all of which are known to have been carried by the crews of the *Resolution* and the *Discovery*. At the time of first contact, observers aboard the vessels admired a robust, well-nourished race. A mere seven years later, debilitating health problems were prevalent. In the 19th century, the islands were visited by epidemics of cholera, typhoid fever, bubonic plague, influenza, and smallpox (Stannard, 1989).

Depopulation

The population of the Hawaiian Islands at the time of first contact was estimated to have been 500,000. The first credible census of Hawaiians, taken by the missionaries in 1832, was 130,000. One hundred years after contact, the census counted 48,000 Hawaiians, representing a population collapse of greater than 90% (Stannard, 1989).

Overthrow of the Government

In 1819, King Kamehameha II abolished the *kapu* system, further weakening the structure of Hawaiian society. This set in motion a chain of events that led to the overthrow of the Hawaiian monarchy in 1893 by a coalition of American planters, roughly 100 years after initial contact with outsiders. The Republic of Hawaii was annexed to the United States in 1898.

Land Alienation

The Great Mahele of 1845 (refers to the legislation in Hawaii which established the Board of Land Commissioners and the decisions that resulted) dismantled the traditional concept of land tenure in public trust in favor of the American system of private ownership. Newcomers could now have a stable land base for their investments. Hawaiians were dispossessed as lots were quickly sold.

Acculturation

In 1820, the missionaries arrived and a campaign of cultural abnegation began. Hawaiians were required to adopt Christian names and the English language. They were asked to destroy their temples, renounce their gods, and disavow their ancestors. They embraced colonial culture to the point of internalizing Western perceptions of themselves as lazy, idolatrous, licentious heathens (Puku'i, Haertig, & Lee, 1979). With the introduction of tourism in the 20th century, Hawaiians adopted stereotypes of themselves as happy-go-lucky beachboys.

CURRENT POPULATION

Hawaiians are now a minority in their ancestral land, making up only 13% of the state population. In Hawaii today, there are more Caucasians than any other group, followed by Japanese and then Filipino. The 1990 U.S. Census showed that the fourth largest group in the state was Hawaiian/Part Hawaiian. Intermarriage with other groups has contributed to changes in the population of Native Hawaiians. Of the 138,742 Hawaiians self-identified in the 1990 census, it is estimated that only 8,134 are Pure Hawaiian. Less than 6% of Hawaiians and less than 1% of residents in the state are Pure Hawaiians. Lacking land, driven by the high cost of living and the search for better employment and educational opportunities, many Hawaiians have emigrated to other states (Untalan Munoz, 1976). The 1990 census found 72,272 persons of Hawaiian ancestry scattered throughout the United States, with the majority in California (34,447), Washington (5,423), Texas (2,979), Oregon (2,415), and Florida (2,049).

Health Status

In the title of its 1990 annual report, *The Health State*, the Hawaii State Department of Health alluded to the favorable health status of its population through lower age-adjusted mortality attributable to motor vehicle accidents, cardiovascular disease, suicide, and homicide; smaller proportion of families with incomes below federal poverty level; lower rates of violent crime when compared with national norms; and greater life expectancy. However, the overall data mask significant ethnic variation, in particular that Hawaiians have the poorest status in the state.

Since data were first reported in 1910, the life expectancy from birth of Hawaiians has trailed the state population by 5 to 10 years. Pure Hawaiians experience the highest mortality rates in every major disease category (Johnson, 1989). Chronic conditions and behavioral risk factors are more prevalent among Hawaiians than the state average, including obesity (42% vs. 22%), cigarette smoking (33% vs. 21%), and alcoholism (9% vs. 6%)(Hawaii State Department of Health, 1990).

Maternal health status has particular relevance to child health outcomes, and here again Hawaiians trail other ethnic groups. Hawaiians occupy the highest obstetric risk category with the highest crude birth, teen pregnancy, and illegitimacy rates, and the lowest levels of educational attainment (Hartley, 1992). Although Hawaiians constitute 13% of the state population, they are responsible for 24% of live births, and half of these births are to teen mothers. Hawaiian women are more likely to smoke or drink during pregnancy and least likely to seek elective abortion. As might be expected, Hawaiians have the poorest pregnancy outcomes, with the highest rates of infant mortality and of birth defects. Infant mortality rates have been up to 50% greater than average, with rates among Hawaiian children of Hawaiian mothers higher than those among Hawaiian children with non-Hawaiian mothers (NHEA, 1993).

Hawaiians make up a disproportionate 42% of the caseload of the Children with Special Health Needs Branch of the Department of Health (Hawaii State Department of Health, 1990). Hawaiians have the second highest rate of preterm birth after

Blacks. This pattern is all the more pronounced among Pure Hawaiians who have the highest relative risk of teen pregnancy (3.8), absent prenatal care (3.5), fetal death (1.7), preterm delivery (1.6), and infant mortality (2.1) (Hartley, 1992).

Socioeconomic Status

Poverty being a powerful correlate of adverse health outcomes, it is not surprising to find Hawaiians disproportionately distributed across the lower socioeconomic strata. The Native Hawaiians Study Commission (1983) reported that in 1977 Hawaiians had lower ($13,615), and Pure Hawaiians the lowest ($9,278) median family income compared with Japanese ($19,431) and Caucasians ($19,005). The U.S. Bureau of the Census (1992) revealed that Hawaiian families were twice as likely to live below the federal poverty level. Hawaiians comprise a disproportionate 31% of the households receiving Aid to Families with Dependent Children (Hartley, 1992).

Family income is directly related to educational attainment and occupational status of its wage earners. In 1977, 4% of Hawaiians over the age of 25 had completed four or more years of college, compared with 14% of the state population 25 years of age and over (Native Hawaiians Study Commission, 1983). Hawaiians are overrepresented in service and labor fields, and underrepresented in executive and professional positions (U.S. Bureau of the Census, 1992). Less than 1% of doctors and lawyers are of Hawaiian extraction (Kanahele, 1986).

Mental Health

Hawaiians are a people divided and diverse, a shifting and amorphous group. Barred from political, economic, and social leadership in their own land, Hawaiians are plagued by an excess of psychosocial problems. Suicide, substance abuse, criminal and domestic violence may be conceptualized as acts of aggression arising out of self-loathing, frustration, and powerlessness.

On statewide surveys, students of Hawaiian ancestry reported heavier use of alcohol and drugs than did other students.

In 1992, Hawaiians accounted for 46% of drug-related arrests among juveniles (NHEA, 1993). They were disproportionately represented among arrests for violent crimes such as murder, manslaughter, rape, assault, and robbery; and responsible for 24% of adult and 33% of juvenile (10–17 years of age) arrests (*Crime in Hawai'i*, 1990). Hawaiians make up a disproportionate 31% of confirmed reports of child abuse and neglect in Honolulu. Current prevalent mental health diagnoses in a Hawaiian community include oppositional defiant disorder (primarily male adolescents), attention-deficit/hyperactivity disorder (primarily males), and posttraumatic stress disorder (equal frequency for males and females).

Hawaiian men surpass all other groups in rates of suicide (Takeuchi, 1987). Hawaiian adolescents showed 6-month prevalence rates for suicide of 4.13% for males and 4.49% for females (Yuen et al., 1996). Although depressive symptoms were the most important risk factor, the degree of perceived family support was an independent predictor of suicide attempt. This may reflect the importance of the sharing and unity found in the *'ohana* for Native Hawaiian adolescents (Yuen et al., 1996). Both male and female Native Hawaiian adolescents continue to experience family support as a mature form of attachment during adolescence. This connectedness seems to be a protective factor for psychosocial risks (Nahulu et al., 1996).

Thus was the ancient prophesy of Ka'opulupulu fulfilled "that the nation would be taken by white men, and that the people would dwell landless in the houses of the fish, that there would be an end to the line of kings, leaving but bare shelves, and that a stubborn disobedient generation was coming which would cause the native race to dwindle" (Bushnell, 1933, p. 274).

CHILD-REARING PATTERNS AND
DEVELOPMENTAL EXPECTATIONS

In contemporary Hawaiian society, *'ohana* has been redefined to refer to the extended family, typically for about three generations and lacking its associations with the spirit world and homeland. Nonetheless, connectedness to the *'ohana* remains important, and the *'ohana* continues to play a primary role in child rearing.

High Value on Children

Despite the escalating costs of fertility (diminished academic achievement and occupational advancement, as well as eroding supports of shared child care traditionally provided by the *'ohana*), children remain a ubiquitous feature in the Hawaiian community. The strong value place on children may help explain behaviors that characterize the Hawaiian maternal population, including higher than average rates of birth and adoption, of illegitimacy and teen pregnancy, multiparity and short birth spacing, together with lower than average rates of contraception and abortion.

Indulgent Infancy: Birth to 2 Years

As in the past, infancy remains a time in which attention and affection are lavished through lots of warm, close, physical contact. Much of an infant's waking time is passed being cuddled in someone's arms. At family gatherings, it is common for an infant to be passed from one to another. Holding a baby is a privilege shared by all, even teenage boys and belligerent men (Howard, 1974).

Caregiving strategies reflect the Hawaiian value of nurturance. Infants are fed on demand. Food has symbolic value and is offered even when it is clear that the child is not hungry, and even when the child may be distressed due to overfeeding. Diapers are changed frequently (24 a day by informal count), even before soiling has occurred. Cosleeping with parents, grandparents, "aunties," or siblings is practiced because of the value placed on physical and emotional intimacy (Howard, 1974).

In the past, such standards of care were made possible by the diffusion of responsibility among multiple caregivers. Many people were on hand to help indulge the infant (Ritchie, 1981). Taking part in shared caregiving reaffirmed the cultural values of affiliation and the related tradition of reciprocity. In contrast, Western society does not yield parental authority within an extended family.

Early Childhood: 2 to 7 Years

Traditionally, newly mobile and verbal toddlers encountered a distinctly different set of parental expectations. They were obliged to become self-sufficient and to function independently of adults. The degree of autonomy granted to young children in Hawaiian households differs markedly for Western practice and is regarded as parental neglect (Ritchie, 1981).

Among contemporary Hawaiians as well, the indulgence of infants ends abruptly. Although it is acceptable for infants to cry and fuss until their needs are met, whining, clinging, demanding toddlers are not acceptable (Howard, 1974). Toddler dependency overtures are at first ignored. When adults are sufficiently provoked, punishment is swift, unpredictable, and usually physical (Howard, 1974). In the traditional setting, Hawaiians preferred thrashing to tongue-lashing, seeking above all to minimize conflict and avoid confrontation (Puku'i et al., 1979). Good behavior, on the other hand, was seldom showered with praise. Rather, children were censured from being boastful and, in this manner, learned the ideals of humility and modesty. Even today, Hawaiian parents aim to produce a friendly, helpful person who accepts situations as they are and gets along well with others without calling unseemly attention to personal needs, problems, or ambitions (Boggs, 1968).

Today, as in the past, toddlers develop new strategies to avoid punitive responses. They turn from adults to older children in search of substitute social rewards. Among their peers, young children become sensitive to the feelings of others, attentive to nonverbal nuance, and adept at interpersonal negotiation. They learn modulation of personal goals within a group context (Ritchie, 1981).

As dwellings have changed from rural villages to suburban apartments, the *'ohana* has contracted into isolated nuclear family units. A lonely mother is shut up with too many preschool children in an overcrowded house (Ritchie, 1981). With cousins dwelling in separate households and other siblings away in school, fewer opportunities are available for sibling child care and peer socialization. When the dependency needs of toddlers and young children clash with parental expectations of early independence, the absence of a protective peer group places young children at risk for child abuse and neglect.

Latency: 7 to 13 Years

Traditionally, children were socialized in gender-specific roles from the age of 7 years. Boys were ceremoniously thrust into the world of men where it was their duty to gather and prepare foodstuffs and to make offerings to the gods and ancestors. Girls remained with the women, to receive instruction in the weaving of mats, the beating of barkcloth, and other domestic endeavors.

In contemporary Hawaii, parental expectations of boys and girls are clearly differentiated by gender. The responsibilities of girls continue to be domestic and typically include cooking, cleaning, laundry, and child care. Because family life revolves around these tasks, girls have opportunities to earn social rewards, including approval, affection, and status. First, in the performance of these duties, girls win parental approval, softening somewhat the harsh rejection of early childhood. Second, girls bask in the affections of their younger siblings, who provide a nonthreatening opportunity for intimacy in a society in which it is risky to initiate interaction with adults (Howard, Heighton, Gallimore, & Jordan, 1967). Third, as valued and vital members of the family, adolescent girls may achieve near-adult status. For girls, traditional cultural expectations have remained valid.

In contrast, there is neither status nor security in the traditional male occupations of fishing and cultivation, the ancient skills of navigation and canoe making, the arts of dance and chant. Typically, boys are assigned to work in the yard or to take out trash, chores that contribute less to family life. In these, they are poorly, if at all, supervised. Parents are likely to be tolerant of boys who go surfing, work on cars, *talking story,** pal around, and eat with their friends (Boggs, 1968). As a result of this exemption from and avoidance of responsibility, boys are ill equipped for assuming mature adult roles as partners and providers.

Adolescence: 13 to 18 Years

In both traditional and contemporary Hawaiian cultures, the birth of a child confers adult status to adolescent parents. Grandparents assumed much of the burden of child care in the past, ensuring the transmission of traditions from one generation to the next, while parents devoted their youthful energies to cultivation, fishing, and other labor-intensive tasks.

Today, however, a young woman assumes the authoritative role in the household, whereas the peer group continues to be the dominant social influence for a man. The lack of male roles and models is perpetuated into the next generation of Hawaiians so that boys have no opportunity akin to that of girls to prepare for adulthood. With the birth of each child, pressure is brought to bear by a man's wife and parents to settle down. As he enters his 30s, a man is drawn into greater participation in and attachment to the family (Howard et al., 1967).

In Western society, the period of adolescence reaches well into the 20s as a time for self-discovery through academic pursuit and vocational experimentation. Teen pregnancy and parenting are regarded as adverse health and social outcomes that jeopardize personal development.

Developmental and Educational Outcomes

The multidimensional Structural/Behavioral model (Horowitz, 1987) permits conceptualization of developmental outcomes in

---

* "Talking story" is a conversational style and social pastime among Islanders who chat about people and events, sharing gossip and telling stories. The spoken word has the power of truth; language is descriptive, rich in imagery; meaning is conveyed through innuendo, and direct references. Stories of a personal nature are eschewed.

relation to both the support afforded by the environment for a particular outcome and the contribution of organism character-istics for that same outcome. Developmental outcomes are char-acterized along with a continuum of Minimal to Optimal. The environment extends along a continuum of Nonfacilitative to Fa-cilitative. The organism dimension (reflective of genetic endow-ment and cumulative biological/environmental experience) is characterized along two independent continua: (a) Impaired to Unimpaired and (b) Vulnerable to Invulnerable.

Early Development

The Infant Child Monitoring Questionnaire (ICMQ) is a screen-ing tool that has been specially tailored for the state of Hawaii's unique cultural groups. The ICMQ provides a parent report of gross motor, fine motor, communication, personal–social, and adaptive development for children 4 to 48 months of age. Items reflect developmental milestones. The 30-item ICMQ is similar to the recently published Ages and Stages Questionnaire (ASQ): A Parent-Completed, Child-Monitoring System. The ICMQ and the ASQ were developed by the same group, in-cluding Diane Bricker, Jane Squires, LaWanda Potter, and Linda Mounts at the University of Oregon Center on Human Devel-opment. The ICMQ was developed for use in Hawaii through grant funding. The Zero-to-Three Hawaii Project advocates use of the ICMQ for screening with all children in the state of Hawaii.

Current ICMQ data on Hawaiian children ages 4 to 48 months who were enrolled in an early education program re-veal that referrals were made primarily for suspected delays in the areas of communication, fine motor, and adaptive develop-ment. Development in the areas of gross motor and personal social development was much less likely to show suspect de-lays. Native Hawaiian children seem to make efficient and ef-fective use of experiences that shape their social development; the majority of Hawaiian children appear to be Unimpaired and Invulnerable. Strong social skills and self-sufficiency are pro-moted within the culture and by parents, and reinforced within the system of sibling child care. The environment is Facilitative in the social domain.

However, strong cultural emphasis on keeping the child and the home clean tends to limit a child's opportunity to experience and practice in a variety of tactile and fine motor skills. Playing with mud or modeling clay, drawing with crayons or paint, and using scissors may be prohibited to avoid making a mess. The environment may be viewed as Nonfacilitative of early fine motor and adaptive skills. Many Hawaiian children seem to be Vulnerable (not resilient) to a Nonfacilitative environment in these areas.

Language Development

More than 70% of Hawaiian children entering kindergarten scored in the lowest levels of achievement (stanines 1–3) on the Peabody Picture Vocabulary Test-Revised. Even those in schools where socioeconomic status was higher showed an unexpectedly high (41%) distribution in the lowest stanines of 1–3 (NHEA, 1993).

Speaking pidgin in the home has been reported to result in poor language development and affects vocabulary, comprehension, and reading skills. The pidgin dialect in Hawaii (Hawaii-English-Creole) is viewed as an underlying problem related to limited language proficiency in that it may be used to the exclusion of standard English and may create confusion over standard English grammar and vocabulary. The use of pidgin in the home has been found to have more detrimental effects on English language proficiency than speaking a foreign language in the home (Werner, Bierman, & French, 1971). Hawaii-English-Creole is a language and/or style of speaking developed by the many non-English-speaking immigrants as they arrived in Hawaii and began to use English. This pattern of speaking is maintained as a new generation continues its use. Hawaii-English-Creole is not to be confused with Hawaiian pidgin used by the earlier Hawaiians and is likely no longer in use.

The tradition of sibling child care and peer socialization together with the diminished parental role for caregiving beginning in toddlerhood has the effect of limiting exposure to adult language models and opportunities for increasing vocabulary (Werner et al., 1971). Additionally, children in families with low incomes (where there is an overrepresentation of Hawaiian families) have fewer opportunities for many kinds of experiences, including language (Hart & Risley, 1995). Frequency of language experience in the first 2 to 3 years of life is critical for optimal language development (Hart & Risley, 1995). Many Hawaiian children seem to be Vulnerable to the Nonfacilitative lack of a supportive, stimulating environment for language development.

Kau'ai Longitudinal Study

Werner et al. (1971) found that Hawaiian children at 2 and 10 years of age had significantly lower mean scores on the Cattell and Primary Mental Abilities Tests, and more achievement and behavioral problems than White and Japanese children, even when social class was controlled. Differences were apparent on infant tests even before age 2. Hawaiian children also had the largest percentage of language problems, defined as verbal scores far below nonverbal subtest scores on intelligence tests administered at age 10.

Werner et al. (1971) found that Hawaiian (along with Filipino) children had the largest percentage of poor grades in basic skills subjects, and attributed this to lack of achievement motivation rather than to ability. Traditional Hawaiian culture values humility, modesty, and the acceptance of situations without calling attention to one's own needs or ambitions; it devalues achievement (Puku'i et al., 1972). The environment appears to be Nonfacilitative of individual achievement, and Hawaiian children seem Vulnerable to the lack of support from the environment in developing achievement motivation.

School Success

The 1983 Native Hawaiian Educational Assessment (NHEA) Project found that Native Hawaiian students were behind their non-Hawaiian peers on most educational outcomes. They were overrepresented in special education, underrepresented in programs for the gifted and talented, and well behind in standardized scores of reading and math.

Hawaiians are at risk for school success not only due to the clash in values and expectations between their culture and school, but to their overrepresentation in lower socioeconomic strata and the psychosocial burden of cultural displacement.

The 1993 Native Hawaiian Educational Assessment showed that in public schools in the state of Hawaii, Hawaiian students continued to score below national norms, and consistently scored below the other non-Hawaiian groups in Hawaii public schools, on achievement tests. Hawaiian students educated in private schools performed at or above national norms. When compared with other students in private schools, however, Hawaiian students were underrepresented in the highest achievement stanines (NHEA, 1993).

School Completion

In the 1991–1992 school year, the dropout rate for public schools in Hawaii, grades 9 through 12, was 9.5% for Hawaiian students compared with 7.9% for all students. Regardless of socioeconomic setting, Hawaiians showed higher rates of absence, grade retention, and dropouts. Absenteeism among Hawaiian students has been alarmingly high. One in four Hawaiian public high school seniors showed an excessive rate of 20 or more absences from one class during a single semester (NHEA, 1983). At the high school level, one in eight Hawaiian students had to repeat a grade. This accounts for the large number of students who have reached 18 and dropped out of school without completing requirements for graduation. Most who remain in high school until the senior year do graduate, but many graduate with severe disadvantages such as low reading scores and math (NHEA, 1993).

Hawaiians have a higher rate of high school completion than other American ethnic minority groups. Since the time of the missionaries, there has been a tradition of strong support for education and literacy. However, Hawaiian students are less likely to graduate from college. The rate of college graduation among Hawaiians at the University of Hawaii is 38% lower than the overall rate, regardless of public or private school background (NHEA, 1993).

SPECIAL PROBLEMS

Hawaiians continue to be overrepresented in special education enrollment in Hawaiian public schools. Specific Learning Disabilities was the most common diagnosis. Mild Mental Retardation, Severely Emotionally Handicapped, and Speech Impaired were other frequent diagnoses. Hawaiians were also strongly represented in the Partially Sighted and Hard of Hearing categories. Hawaiians continue to be underrepresented in gifted and talented programs (NHEA, 1993).

HOME ENVIRONMENT AND SCHOOL PERFORMANCE

In Martini's (1995) studies of the relation between home environment and school performance among ethnic groups in Hawaii, she found that a child's chances for success in school are greatly influenced by the home environment. American schools mirror middle-class culture. Children reared with these goals and values are better prepared for success when they enter school because they are familiar with the operating principles of middle-class schools, which emphasize verbal reasoning, literate discourse, high mental activity, and specific metacognitive strategies. The extent to which parents understand and support schooling, and are involved in the life of the school, also predicts a child's success.

Werner et al. (1971) examined educational stimulation in Hawaiian homes, based on research addressing the relation among home environment, intelligence, and school achievement. They adapted the methods for Kau'ai and found high reliability in their ratings. They found that the majority of Hawaiian households were below average in providing educational stimulation such as language models, chances for children to improve vocabulary, intellectual interests and activities, work habits emphasized in the home, value placed on education by family, and opportunities to explore the larger environment (e.g., library use, special lessons). Emotional support in the home for the child was also rated (e.g., kind and amount of reinforcement used, presence or absence of traumatic experiences, and methods of discipline). Hawaiian families received a high percentage of below-average ratings, although the majority of homes were rated as providing at least adequate support.

CULTURE: ORGANIZER OF DEVELOPMENT

Traditional Hawaiian cultural emphasis on the group rather than the individual, on social cooperation rather than individual industry, and on sibling child care, which reduces exposure to extensive adult language learning opportunities, puts the Hawaiian child at risk in regard to school success and also puts the family at risk for decreased understanding and support of school. Thus, the Hawaiian child enters school without adequate preparation and skills to succeed, and is likely also to be hampered by conflicts between values encountered at home versus school. When Hawaiian youth grow up as independent members of multihousehold extended family systems having limited contact with their birth parents, they are at particular risk for social and academic difficulties during adolescence (NHEA, 1993).

Cultural continuity in educational experiences for Hawaiian children may provide the facilitative environment needed to afford greater opportunities for Hawaiian children to achieve optimal development. Hawaiian children and youth seem especially vulnerable to succeeding in environments where demands for performance are not consistent with cultural expectations. Culturally sensitive early intervention with families and their young children in the first 3 years of life is especially important for a strong foundation for all facets of development, and for language development in particular (Hart & Risley, 1995). Examples of cultural continuity in educational experiences for older children include the use of cooperative learning strategies rather than an individual achievement orientation in the classroom (NHEA, 1993), Hawaiian language immersion programs, and the Native Hawaiian Gifted and Talented Program that provides educational experiences consistent with Hawaiian children's cultural experiences. In these settings, where cultural values are honored and promoted, Hawaiian children seem to thrive.

References

BOGGS, J. (1968). Hawaiian adolescents and their families. In R. Gallimore & A. Howard (Eds.), *Studies in a Hawaiian community: Na Makamaka o Nanakuli* (Pacific Anthropological Records No. 1). Honolulu, HI: Bernice Pauahi Bishop Museum Press.

BUSHNELL, O. A. (1993). *The gifts of civilization: Germs and genocide in Hawaii.* Honolulu: University of Hawaii Press.

HART, B., & RISLEY, T. (1995). *Meaningful differences in the everyday experience of young American children.* Baltimore: Brookes.

HARTLEY, C. T. (1992). *Needs assessment in maternal and child health: Wai'anae District, State of Hawaii (census tracts 96-98).* Unpublished master's thesis, University of Hawaii, Honolulu.

HAWAII CRIMINAL JUSTICE DATA CENTER. (1990). *Crime in Hawaii.* Honolulu: Author.

HAWAII STATE DEPARTMENT OF HEALTH. (1990). *The health state* (Annual Report Statistical Supplement). Honolulu: Author.

HOROWITZ, F. (1987). *Exploring developmental theories: Toward a structural/behavioral model of development.* Hillsdale, NJ: Erlbaum.

HOWARD, A. (1974). *Ain't no big thing: Coping strategies in a Hawaiian American community.* Honolulu: University of Hawaii Press.

HOWARD, A., HEIGHTON, R., GALLIMORE, R., & JORDAN, C. (1967). *Traditional and modern adoption patterns in Hawaii.* Honolulu: Bernice Pauahi Bishop Museum Press.

JOHNSON, D. B. (1989). An overview of ethnicity and health in Hawaii. In E. Wegner (Ed.), *The health of Native Hawaiians: Social process in Hawaii* (Vol. 32). Honolulu: University of Hawaii Press.

KANAHELE, G. (1986). *Ku kanaka.* Honolulu: University of Hawaii Press.

KELLY, M. (1956). *Changes in land tenure in Hawaii 1778–1850.* Unpublished thesis, University of Hawaii, Honolulu.

MAKINI, M. (1995). Features of home environments associated with children's school success. *Early Child Development and Care, 111,* 49–68.

NAHULU, L., ANDRADE, N., MAKINI, G., YUEN, N., McDERMOTT, J., DANKO, G., JOHNSON, R., & WALDRON, J. (1996). Psychosocial risk and protective influences in Hawaiian adolescent psychopathology. *Cultural Diversity and Mental Health, 2*(2), 107–114.

NATIVE HAWAIIAN EDUCATIONAL ASSESSMENT (NHEA). (1983). Honolulu, HI: Kamehameha School Bernice Pauahi Bishop Estate Office of Program Evaluation and Planning.

NATIVE HAWAIIAN EDUCATIONAL ASSESSMENT (NHEA). (1993). Honolulu, HI: Kamehameha School Bernice Pauahi Bishop Estate Office of Program Evaluation and Planning.

NATIVE HAWAIIANS STUDY COMMISSION. (1983). Honolulu.

PUKU'I, M. K., HAERTIG, E. W., & LEE, C. A. (1972). *Nana I Ke Kumu* (Vol. 1). Honolulu: Hui Hanai.

PUKU'I, M. K., HAERTIG, E. W., & LEE, C. A. (1979). *Nana I Ke Kumu* (Vol. 2). Honolulu: Hui Hanai.

RITCHIE, J. (1981). Child rearing and child abuse: The Polynesian context. In J. E. Korbin (Ed.), *Child abuse and neglect: Cross cultural perspectives.* Berkeley: University of California Press.

STANNARD, D. E. (1989). *Before the horror: The population of Hawaii on the eve of Western contact.* Honolulu: University of Hawaii, Social Science Research Institute.

TAKEUCHI, D. (1987). Native Hawaiian mental health. In A. Robillard & A. Marsella (Eds.), *Contemporary issues in mental health research in the Pacific Islands.* Honolulu: University of Hawaii, Social Science Research Institute.

U.S. BUREAU OF THE CENSUS. (1992). *1990 Census of population, general characteristics, United States.* Washington, DC: Author.

UNTALAN MUNOZ, F. (1976). Pacific Islanders—a perplexed, neglected minority. *Social Case Work, 57*(3), 179–184.

WERNER, E., BIERMAN, J., & FRENCH, F. (1971). *The children of Kau'ai.* Honolulu: University of Hawaii Press.

YUEN, N., ANDRADE, N., NAHULU, L., MAKINI, G., McDERMOTT, J., DANKO, G., JOHNSON, R., & WALDRON, J. (1996). The rate and characteristics of suicide attempters in the Native Hawaiian adolescent population. *Suicide and life-threatening behavior, 26*(1), 27–36.

CHAPTER 9

Hmong Children

JOSEPH WESTERMEYER, MAYKA
BOUAFUELY-KERSEY, and CHENG HER

Historical Background

THE HMONG ARE A DISTINCTIVE Sinitic people who have inhabited remote and mountainous areas of east and southeast Asia for thousands of years (Lemoine, 1972; Mottin, 1979). Numbering in the tens of millions, their homelands have ranged from Hainan Island and Vietnam on the east, China on the north, Burma on the west, Thailand on the south, and Laos in the center. The Hmong gradually migrated southward, as population pressures and incursions of lowland peoples forced them into the harsh, sparsely populated Annamite Mountains in Southeast Asia.

Even in modern times, the Hmong have migrated back and forth across national boundaries. Although they have not organized as a nation among themselves, they have established social, economic, and political liaisons with lowland peoples and governments, resulting in much diversity. The Hmong in Hainan Island and in areas of China have adapted Chinese ideographic writing, two-story houses, mercantile industry, trading, and paddy-rice agriculture. In contrast, those in Laos adapted certain aspects of Lao, French, and American culture and technology due to their alliances with those groups (Bernatzik, 1970).

Indochina, including the areas of Laos, Cambodia, and Vietnam, was a colony of France from 1893 until the military defeat at Dien Bien Phu in the mid-1950s. The three countries of Indochina rejected French domination of the area. During World War II, they were dominated by Japan for several years. In the 1950s, the Hmong people allied themselves with the French and later the Lao and Thai peoples in opposing the Vietnamese domination of Indochina. In addition, many Hmong people migrated out of China into Indochina when the Communist Chinese regime prohibited their growing opium poppy as a cash crop. For these historical reasons, the Hmong largely united under the leadership of Vang Pao, who had fought with the French forces. He rose to the rank of general in the Royal Laotian Army, commanding all military efforts in northern Laos (including home guard, regular army, and special guerrilla units). Following the establishment of a communist regime in Vietnam, regular Vietnamese army units invaded northern Laos in force, soon subduing Vang Pao's forces. Consequently, many Hmong people fled Laos into Thailand. Subsequently, most of this group emigrated to the United States as refugees (Geddes, 1976; Westermeyer, 1971).

Prior to 1955, the Hmong had much interaction with the French. Many Hmong had fought side by side with the French against the Vietnamese. Hmong soldiers fought at Dien Bien Phu, a major battle involving the invasion of eastern Laos by the Vietnamese. The French loss at Dien Bien Phu marked the initiation of American involvement in Southeast Asia. The President of the United States, John F. Kennedy, sent Special Forces army units into Laos, where they organized local tribal militia among several groups, including the Hmong.

For another two decades, from 1955 to 1975, the Hmong struggled with other tribal groups, the lowland Lao, Thai volunteers, and the Royal Laotian Government (RLG) against the North Vietnamese. During this period, the United States was a major supplier of military and refugee assistance to those peoples of Laos involved in the war. The French also provided military officer training, some medical assistance, and limited supplies. The English coalition (including the United Kingdom,

Canada, Australia, India, Malaysia, Singapore) also provided varying degrees of military and civilian assistance. In early 1975, with the withdrawal of the United States and other allies from South Vietnam, a relatively bloodless coup led to the establishment of a communist regime in Laos. Within hours, tens of thousands of Hmong began fleeing Laos for Thailand. As stories of Vietnamese and communist Laos atrocities against the Hmong spread, and as life became more harsh in Laos, other Hmong subsequently fled over the following decade and a half (until around 1990).

This history led to certain unique attributes regarding the Hmong who fled to the United States. They came as a defeated army and as allies of a defeated United States. They had a two-decade history of relying on the United States for material support, although they decided major aspects of their own destiny. Having lost two wars in alliances with Western countries, they had reasons to distrust Westerners, or at least Western society.

Hmong Culture in Laos

The Hmong and their cultural cousins, the lu Mien, were known as the "high Lao" *(Lao sung)* because they lived in the mountain ranges of northern Laos. They raised upland rice, corn, vegetables, opium poppy (as a cash crop), cattle, and pigs. A few Hmong became merchants (bringing manufactured goods from the valley towns to mountain villages with mule trains) (Bernatzik, 1970).

Until recent times, most Hmong remained illiterate. Some younger Hmong had begun to attend government schools, becoming literate in the Lao language. A few Hmong elite studied in Francophone schools in Laos and even France, achieving professional status in several fields. Most older Hmong had been raised as animists, but Christian, Buddhist, and Catholic influences produced a rash of conversions from 1960 on. These educational and religious changes resulted in occupational changes. Traditionally farmers-hunters-warriors, men could elect to join the army, become skilled workmen, or enter a profession. Women could become nurses, teachers, office workers, truck gardeners, or shopkeepers (Westermeyer, 1983; Yang, 1974).

The Hmong lived in autonomous villages, affiliating themselves in larger groups only when necessary. They might cooperate with another nearby village to build a bridge or exchange bridal partners, but would compete for hunting territory or acquisition of wealth. Even within a village, members of different clans (approximately 12 to 15, depending on local convention) might be wary of each other. Major dialectical subgroups (e.g., the White, Green, Multicolored Hmong which reflect different colored clothing worn by subgroups) kept to themselves, usually living in villages apart from each other and refusing to exchange their sons and daughters in marriage. Faced with an outside threat, however, they formed strong alliances. Their experiences negotiating alliances with one another served them well in their efforts at allying with other tribal groups, the Lao, the Americans, and even the Thai. This culturally valued skill was manifest in the tight military organization developed by Vang Pao to oppose the North Vietnamese (Geddes, 1976).

Those Hmong reaching the United States from 1975 to 1995 shared many characteristics (Westermeyer, Vang, & Lyfong, 1983). They realized from both their ancient and recent history that their survival lay in organizing themselves, staying together, negotiating and mediating their differences, and presenting a common front to the outside world. Their language, their core cultural values, their race, and their common history tied them together, although they were worshipping different gods. Their educational backgrounds ranged from no formal education to formal occupational training to university degrees. Although many continued their economic dependency in the United States, most entered the local workforce in a great diversity of occupations—reflecting within their small population virtually the entire occupational range of their communities. Some individuals and families had been devastated by the war, with many deaths and lost connections. Other individuals and families remained largely intact, with minimal loss of life and regular contact with one another (Downing & Olney, 1985; Hendricks, Downing, & Deinard, 1986; Westermeyer, Neider, & Callies, 1989).

Hmong Culture and Cultural Conflict in the United States: Family, Community, and School

FAMILY

Whether in Asia or the United States, Hmong families organize more along extended family lines than nuclear lines (Dunnigan, 1982). Family decisions regarding place of residence, large purchases, and crisis management tend to be discussed among several family elders, perhaps with a patriarch (sometimes a matriarch) eventually deciding the matter after all the participants have had their say. Although most family groups consist of nuclear family members, it is not unusual for a single, widowed, divorced, or separated grandmother, aunt, uncle, or cousin to live with a nuclear family. Living alone has been traditionally considered unworkable, lonely, and even socially deviant.

In a residence type called *patrilocal*, married sons tend to live close by one another and near an elder male family member—grandfather, father, uncle, or brother. This means that newly married brides must leave their relatives and come to live as strangers among their new husband's family—at times a difficult transition. Predictably, the relationship between a daughter-in-law and her mother-in-law poses opportunities for cooperation and collaboration, or considerable antipathy. A man and his children inherit their clan name from the man's father—a practice called *patrinymy*. In Laos, women retained their own clan names throughout their lives despite marriage, although some women have been taking their husband's clan name in the United States, in keeping with common American practice.

In Laos, the groom's family paid a sum of money or other wealth (e.g., pigs, cattle) to the bride's family. This was less the purchase of a wife than the purchase of a quitclaim by the groom's family, so that the children of the union would belong to the groom's rather than the bride's clan. Bride price also represented a commitment of the husband's clan to the relationship and symbolizes the prestige or status of the couple and their extended families. The practice of bride price continued widely among the Hmong in the United States. A man or woman could not marry anyone from his or her own clan, regardless of the closeness or distance of the relationship—a practice termed *clan exogamy*. Conversely, marriage to someone of another clan, even a first cousin (e.g., mother's niece or nephew or aunt's offspring) was permissible. Although marrying a distant cousin from the same clan would be permitted by American law, it would be considered incest and a great crime against nature in Hmong society.

Ideally, the family should choose, or at least approve, the marital union. Marriage against one's parents' wishes may result in "marriage by elopement," but this is a risky procedure. In theory, the "kidnapping" man may be attacked, or even killed by the "stolen" woman's male relatives—although this rarely happens. In practice, it is up to the man's clan to "make right" the union by paying a bride price (and perhaps a bit more, for the emotional distress imposed). Failure of the man's family to make such an offer, or failure of the woman's family to accept it, results in a common-law, or unapproved, marriage. In Asia, Hmong couples unable to obtain their respective parents' approval to marry have been known to commit suicide rather than risk an elopement (Westermeyer, 1972).

Common clan names are Her (Hauh), Kue (Ku), Lee (Ly), Moua, Vang, Vue (Vuh), Xiong, Yang. At times, clan names have been lengthened to honor a great clan leader (e.g., Lyfong to honor the greater leader, Ly Fong). Those with the same last name have a claim on one another's goodwill and hospitality, even if they have never known one another. By the same token, loyal friendships sometimes evolve among members of different clans.

From the Hmong perspective, an ideal marriage is to a close relative in one's mother's clan. Such a union reinforces family ties. One should marry within one's dialectical/clothing group (i.e., Green Hmong to Green, White Hmong to White). Families tend to be aggrieved if one marries a non-Hmong, although such unions occurred even in Laos to ethnic Khamu, Chinese, Lao, and French. The number of "out marriages" has greatly increased in the United States, as education and work provide opportunities to meet partners of other ethnic origins.

Relocation to the United States has disrupted many traditional aspects of Hmong life, resulting in greater or lesser degrees of acculturation (Westermeyer, Bouafeuly, & Vang, 1984; Westermeyer, Neider, & Vang, 1984). For example, inheritance laws in the United States and Hmong tradition differ widely. In most states of the United States, a man's estate goes to his spouse, as well as his children. By Hmong tradition, however, a man's father, paternal uncles, and brothers would inherit his wealth. This point of conflict has produced family dissension, with offspring forced to choose between their mother (who is not of their clan) and their paternal relatives (who are their clanspeople).

Case Example

In a marriage between a Green Hmong and a White Hmong, the man's relatives had harbored antipathy for his wife, who was not of their choosing. On the man's premature death, his relatives took over the household, threatened to evict the wife, and discussed how they would divide his wealth. It came as a considerable shock to them that the wife had inherited his estate, further alienating their relationship.

Before arriving in the United States, many polygynous households were forced to disband. This created hardship for many families, some of which split into separate families and some of which reunited.

Case Example

A Hmong man became depressed in the Thailand refugee camp to which he had fled. Mutual friends asked him to take an orphaned 14-year-old as a minor wife. The girl was looking for a mother and mentor, as well as a family, and agreed to the union. The husband found her attractive and agreed to the union without consulting his wife. Some months later, when the family decided to come to the United States, the extended clan decided the first or major wife (a competent woman and mother) would accompany her four children as one family, and the husband would accompany the new wife (by now pregnant) in another family. Soon after arrival in the United States, the husband and minor wife were referred to a mental health clinic after expressing suicidal intent to their relatives. As both were recovering from their major depressive disorders, it became apparent that they wished to reunite as a polygynous family. Informed that a man legally could have only one wife, but such a complex union could proceed if all agreed, they moved into two adjacent apartments. The man negotiated the second marriage with his major wife, who was happy to reunite with her husband, have a minor wife around for help, and have a new baby in the household. The new wife, who had attended school in Asia, matriculated in high school. The husband found a stable job, which augmented the family's sparse income, and experienced a return of his attraction to his major wife. Several years later, this family arrangement continued to serve its members.

Changing residences, sources of income, and finances disrupted many families in the United States. Some elderly parents were forced to live alone in high-rise apartments to maximize pensions and governmental income programs. Some elderly parents became lonely or ashamed at this prospect.

Case Example

A 60-year-old mother had been urged by her children to move into a high-rise building to live alone. The purpose of this move was to bring more money into the extended family coffers from welfare services. The family provided the mother with food on a daily basis, and saw that she had necessary transportation to family events and health services. However, the woman spent most of the day by herself, isolated from her neighbors because of her inability to speak English. After several months, she was treated for a major depression.

On the other hand, some seniors have chosen to live alone.

Case Example

A 58-year-old widowed Hmong woman had been estranged from her husband for about two decades in Laos. During this period, she moved among her children's homes, spending a few months with each of her married children. She provided child care and homemaking services in each home, never complaining about her social situation. On coming to the United States, she chose to live alone in her own apartment. Although the family was shamed by her choice, and her grandchildren missed her regular visits to their homes, she would not move out of her own apartment.

As these cases indicate, the clinician, counselor, or behavioral scientist working in the context of the Hmong family must be able to suspend his or her own assumptions about family organization and function. Some non-Asians have found it instructive to read novels by Pearl Buck (based on her experiences in China, where she grew up) and by Amy Tan (e.g., *The Joy Luck Club*) in addition to several books and articles describing family interviews and therapy (Kim, 1985; Leong, 1986; Shon & Ja, 1982).

COMMUNITY

In the two decades since their arrival in the United States, the Hmong have regrouped in communities ranging in size from a few hundred people (the population of a good-sized mountain village in Laos) to over 20,000 people (the size of the major Hmong town of Long Cheng). Large communities are centered in the Sacramento Valley of California, Montana, St. Paul-Minneapolis, and several communities in Wisconsin, Colorado, and Rhode Island. These large Hmong groups have resulted from "secondary migration"—the gathering of Hmong with their clans and relatives after they were scattered across the United States. Some Hmong have formed communities where they were first placed, from the states of Hawaii to Oklahoma to Pennsylvania.

In virtually all the large and medium-size Hmong communities, Hmong organizations have been established. Some of these groups have received public funding; others have developed around a Christian church. These diverse associations serve numerous purposes: They provide a meeting and courting place for youth, a site to play music and sports, and a venue for sharing job information, news from Asia, personal problems, and future plans. Guided by parents and elders, older children and teenagers have undertaken projects serving the Hmong community as well as the mainstream society, including preparations for the Hmong New Year celebration and neighborhood cleanup projects.

Hmong gangs have also sprung up in many communities. These youth gangs manifest some of the same warrior behaviors and social dynamics of mountaineer Hmong villagers faced with an outside threat. Among the factors associated with youth gangs have been intergenerational conflict, separation of the generations during daily activities, and the apparent inability of some parents to serve as role models for a successful lifestyle in the United States.

Case Example

A Hmong mother and father were shocked when their eldest son, at the age of 14, was arrested for a crime and found to be a gang member. The father worked a full-time job and a weekend job, spending 56 hours per week at work, plus an additional 12 hours in travel. In addition, the mother left home at noon and returned home from work at 10:00 P.M. Their eldest son was left in charge of the home and his five younger siblings, and was expected to purchase groceries, cook, and manage the household, in addition to attending school. Exposed to a gang in high school, he began to model himself after youths a few years older than himself. Faced with this family crisis, the family had to decide whether to spend more time with their family by making sacrifices in their lifestyle (their incomes largely paid for a mortgage on their home and payments on two cars), or risk having their son continue in his self-destructive behavior.

Some of these troubled adolescents represent families that are working hard to survive in the majority society. Other cases represent families that are not adapting to life in the United States. In either case, the parents often rely on their children in a way that would have been commonplace in Asia—where most children did not attend school beyond the age of 10 or 12 and where such home-centered activities prepared them for adult roles. In Asia, the assignment of such responsibilities often involved close interaction with Hmong adults and other Hmong youth performing similar tasks. However, such responsibility in the United States often involved social isolation, little or no supervision by adults, lack of preparation for adult work roles, and lack of contact with peers.

Case Example

A 16-year-old boy was evaluated by the court after he had threatened a schoolmate with a knife. He lived with several younger siblings and his mother; the father had been absent from the family for several years. Family assessment revealed that his mother had been living in terror of this young man, who threatened her physically when she tried to set limits. When she threatened to inform the family social worker or police, he warned her that he would accuse her of "child abuse," which would result in her losing her children and going to prison. For several years, the mother had relied increasingly on this son to serve as a translator (because she did not speak English), set limits with the younger children, shop for the family, and manage the family finances.

SCHOOL

Prior to 1950, Hmong children in Laos learned from their parents of the same sex, from extended family members, and from adult villagers. Young children remained at home, assisting with light household chores and (once reaching the age of 4 or 5 years) caring for younger siblings. Sibling rivalry was remarkably absent, or at least minimal by American standards.

Preteens and early teenagers worked alongside their parents. Girls would assist their mothers and grandmothers in carrying water and firewood, tending the gardens, caring for small animals (chickens, pigs, goats), sewing and mending clothes, preparing meals and stitching artful *pangdau* embroidery. Boys would accompany their fathers in slash-and-burn agricultural chores, hunting and fishing, home building, tending of large animals (cattle, horses), and various home defense activities. Adolescents might also learn special skills from parents, relatives, or other adults (e.g., herbal healing shamanism, iron and silver working, working with wood, playing any one of several musical instruments).

Although adjacent ethnic groups had traditions for formal education in schools, enrollment usually meant leaving Hmong culture for another religion and language (e.g., attending school in a Buddhist monastery, using the Lao language). French, Vietminh, and American influences introduced the idea that the Hmong could attend schools that retained the Hmong culture. Typically, Hmong girls did not attend school. Many young Hmong women in the United States today remain illiterate. From the beginning of access to education, however, some Hmong girls did attend school or became literate through the efforts of their siblings or friends. Some Hmong parents foresaw that their daughters would need as much education as their sons. However, many Hmong people perceived education primarily for its vocational value—largely involving vocations that had been male occupations in Asia (e.g., teaching, administration).

As a consequence, the Hmong today have family patterns of education not unlike those of other Americans a few generations ago. Grandparents are apt to be illiterate, with parents either being illiterate or having only a grade school education. Those who came to the United States as young children are apt to have educational goals, from some high school exposure to advanced university degrees. Children with learning or behavior problems may have learning disabilities much like those of indigenous American children, but they may have acquired these problems through exposure to war, refugee flight, or infectious diseases common to southeast Asia (Carlin, 1979;

Harding & Looney, 1977; Williams & Westermeyer, 1984). Listening to the parents' view of the world can help in understanding their child's experience (Cheng, Leong, & Geist, 1993; Takeuchi, Kuo, Kim, & Leaf, 1989).

Case Example

A 10-year-old Hmong boy was referred because of his threatening behavior during episodic temper tantrums. Additional history revealed that the boy had failed to learn more than several words in English, although he had been in English-as-a-Second-Language (ESL) training daily for two years. In special education classes, where a Hmong translator was available, he had acquired knowledge and skills. His level of knowledge-skill acquisition was behind his agemates, but was well ahead of his poor English acquisition. The mother related that the family had been intercepted by soldiers of the Laotian government as they tried to flee Laos into Thailand. All of the family members had been beaten about the head with rifle butts and left for dead. Nearby Lao villagers found the family; the father and two sons had died from the beatings. The patient and his mother were brought to a Laotian hospital, where they were found to have skull fractures. The mother was unconscious for about one day, and the son was unconscious for several days. Although before the beating he had been quick to learn new things, afterward he learned things only slowly. He also became more easily frustrated and upset. Electroencephalography and computer tomography of the head revealed scattered lesions. We recommended to the school that they continue the special education classes in Hmong, but supplement these with individual instruction in English related to the content in the special classes (eliminating the ESL classes, where he was not progressing). We also recommended that he have more opportunity to interact with English-speaking children, perhaps in a summer program that would include both Hmong and local children in a day camp that included play and handicrafts. Our clinic staff assisted the mother in understanding her son's special needs, including limit setting and behavioral modification, resulting in reduction of the tantrums.

Case Example

An 11-year-old Hmong boy was referred following a fight at school, in which he had harmed another Hmong boy. Additional history revealed that he was obtaining D and F grades in school, where he was thought to be possibly retarded. His family had been in the United States since he was 1 year old, and the family spoke English in the home. The boy was fluent in English and knew minimal Hmong. He also had occasional temper tantrums and threatened children smaller than himself. History revealed that, during the flight from Laos, the boy had extremely high fevers over a 2-week period when he was about 1 month old. During the period of high fevers, he had two prolonged episodes of generalized tonic-clonic seizures. On evaluation, he had an IQ of 119. However, he was observed to have a remarkably short attention span and to become easily frustrated. Following the evaluation, the school placed the boy in a special program for children with learning problems, including attention deficit disorder. He rapidly achieved B and C grades in the new learning environment. Once his learning had stabilized over a period of 2 months, a course of methylphenidate (Ritalin) was tried. Within a few weeks, his grades rose to A's and B's. His self-esteem improved notably, and his temper tantrums were ameliorated.

In both of these cases, the treatment of these children required changes in the school program. Without such changes in the educational program, it is unlikely that the psychological and medical interventions would have been nearly as successful. These cases also demonstrate the need to consider psychological evaluation for Hmong children. In both cases, the school and family had tolerated serious learning and behavioral problems for years before intervention was prescribed. Three general factors appear to account for such delay in adequate care:

1. Hmong parents lack familiarity with the American school system. Some Hmong parents have never attended school and consequently have no personal experience to draw on. Even those Hmong parents who did attend school in Laos cannot always apply their experience there to the American school system. For example, if a child in Laos could not sit still and pass examinations, the child was told to stay home (since universal education did not exist, schools were overcrowded, and no special services existed).

2. The school staff often has difficulty identifying children in need of services when many non-English speaking children are in competition for help. The compliant, quiet child receives little or no attention under these circumstances unless a crisis occurs. In the two preceding case examples, a behavioral crisis led to consultation with a mental health professional rather than a learning specialist (i.e., the mother of the first child was becoming afraid of her growing son, and the second child had injured another child in a fight at school).

3. Parents are unable to obtain professional mental health services, either through lack of such resources nearby or lack of finances to pay for such consultation.

Several other school problems have been commonplace in areas with large numbers of Hmong children. One of these relates to the children becoming disinterested in school during their early teenage years, with a shift in affiliation to teenage gangs. This problem resembles that of other ethnic groups, whose teenagers cannot identify with the school staff or the school's overarching educational goals. By the same token, some Hmong students clearly identify with the staff and the school goals—usually because their families know the staff and support those goals. This can set up conflicts among Hmong adolescents, whose attitudes and values vis-à-vis education differ vastly.

Some Hmong students learn to use school contacts as a weapon against parental authority. They threaten their parents that they will accuse them of physical abuse if they restrict their activities, refuse allowances, or punish them. Parents unfamiliar with American laws or school resources have been cowed by such threats.

Case Example

A 15-year-old child of mixed Hmong-Lao parents objected to her parents' requirement that she be at home by dark and that she stop seeing a 20-year-old man. When her parents physically restrained her from leaving the home, she complained to a school counselor that her father was abusing her sexually. She was immediately placed in a distant home, and her father was arrested and charged with incest. This was not the outcome that she had planned on, since she could not see her boyfriend while in the foster home and she did not want her father to be in prison. During the evaluation (in our clinic), she admitted that her accusations were false. Moreover, there were no additional data to indicate that incest had occurred—and much information to support that it had not occurred.

The preceding case demonstrates how the school can contribute to problems and alienate parents. The following case exemplifies how the school might aid in bringing a problem to light.

Case Example

A 14-year-old Hmong girl stayed after school one day and told her favorite teacher that she wanted to die. The girl went on to explain that her father had just betrothed her to a 20-year-old man, whom she did not know. Moreover, she wanted to go on to college and eventually become an airline stewardess; and she perceived that marriage would not permit her to follow her plans. Further evaluation in our clinic revealed that the father thought he had taken a responsible course, since his daughter had recently been expressing interest in boys and asking to go to boy-girl activities (e.g., sports events at school, movies). The father interpreted her interest as an indication of her wanting to marry (the usual process at the age when he grew up in Laos) and had done what he thought a responsible father should do. He was quite willing to negotiate a release from the betrothal, much to his daughter's relief.

PREVENTION AND PARENTAL INVOLVEMENT

Clinical facilities are accustomed to dealing with problems like these, but little effort has been devoted to prevention (Williams, 1989; Williams & Berry, 1991). However, such prevention can be undertaken in the school setting. Recently, one school with a large number of Hmong children (20% of students) recognized the gap between the school and their Hmong parents—blue-collar workers who were either illiterate or had a grade-school education. They have started a program in which mothers of Hmong students come to the school two mornings a week. Mothers of preschool children are invited to bring them (a pre-school program was arranged). The program focuses on two general activities during each half-day session:

1. Learning to speak English through practicing it (all have had ESL but do not practice their English because they have no American friends).
2. Learning about the school—its processes, rules, educational mission, and values—so that they perceive it as an adjunct to their parental responsibilities (rather than as an outside agent that could become antagonistic or threatening).

Activities to enhance familiarity included touring the class-rooms and other locations (e.g., library, gym), spending time observing in the classrooms while their child and the other children are learning, getting to know their child's teachers, learning how the school is organized, becoming acquainted with special staff (e.g., counselors, librarian, social workers, psychologist), and becoming familiar with disciplinary measures. Although this program is in its initial stages, the ultimate goals are for this core of Hmong parents to become active in school endeavors (e.g., volunteer parents, PTA) and to educate other Hmong parents about the school.

Conclusion

The Hmong migration to the United States greatly resembles the migration of other ethnic groups, while also possessing certain unique features. Until relatively recently, these independent mountaineers living in a subsistence economy practiced animism and had no need for literacy. Changes beginning a century ago and accelerating over the past five decades have resulted in major changes affecting Hmong culture. These changes have continued in the United States. Against this background of change has been continuity with family values, strong ethnic affiliation, mutual support, and adaptation.

Although the family comprises a great support to Hmong people, family traditions can also pose dilemmas for Hmong children and adolescents. Changes in inheritance, choice of a marriage partner, and means of financial support can precipitate crises, and even mental or emotional disorders. Hmong social organizations can facilitate individual and family adjustment to these changes. At the same time, evolution of Hmong gangs has caused problems for Hmong communities as well as the larger society.

Hmong children and adolescents may have learning and behavioral problems related to their experiences as refugee children. They may have been wounded or injured during warfare or other violence, malnourished, or ill for prolonged periods with inadequate medical care. Identifying such problems is a critical first step in ameliorating them. Recommendations affecting parenting skills and educational programs can often contribute to improved psychological function and social stabilization of these children. Clinicians serving Hmong families can provide the highest standard of care through understanding the perspectives and experiences of Hmong children and their parents.

Prevention should receive greater attention than in the past. Involvement of Hmong parents in the business of the school is a crucial step. Until parents perceive the school as an ally in educating and developing their children, schools and parents are apt to work at cross-purposes. And a few children are apt to pit parents and school against one another, if given the chance to do so. A strong, mutually supportive relationship between Hmong parents and their community schools will contribute to optimal maturation and, if needed, timely mental health evaluation.

References

BERNATZIK, H. A. (1970). *Akha and Miao*. New Haven, CT: Human Relations Area Files.

CARLIN, J. E. (1979). Southeast Asian refugee children. In J. D. Call, J. D. Noshpitz, R. L. Cohen, & I. N. Berlin (Eds.), *Basic handbook of child psychiatry* (pp. 290–300). New York: Basic Books.

CHENG, D., LEONG, F. T., & GEIST, R. (1993). Cultural differences in psychological distress between Asian and Caucasian American college students. *Journal of Multicultural Counseling Development*, 21(3), 182–190.

DOWNING, B. T., & OLNEY, D. P. (1985). *The Hmong in the West: Observations and reports*. Minneapolis: University of Minnesota Center for Urban and Regional Affairs.

DUNNIGAN, T. (1982). Segmentary kinship in an urban society: The Hmong of St. Paul-Minneapolis. *Anthropological Quarterly, 55*, 126–134.

GEDDES, W. R. (1976). *Migrants of the mountains: The cultural ecology of the Blue Miao of Thailand*. Oxford, England: Clarendon Press.

HARDING, R. K., & LOONEY, J. G. (1977). Problems of Southeast Asian children in a refugee camp. *American Journal of Psychiatry, 134*, 407–411.

HENDRICKS, G. L., DOWNING, B. T., & DEINARD, A. S. (1986). *The Hmong in transition.* New York: Center for Migration Studies.

KIM, S. C. (1985). Family therapy for Asian Americans: A strategic-structural framework. *Psychotherapy, 22,* 342–348.

LEMOINE, J. (1972). *Un Village Hmong Vert du Haut Laos.* Paris: Centre National de la Recherche Scientifique.

LEONG, F. T. L. (1986). Counseling and psychotherapy with Asian-Americans: Review of the literature. *Journal of Counseling Psychology, 33,* 196–206.

MOTTIN, J. (1979). *Fetes du Nouvel An: chez les Hmong Blanc de Thailande.* Bangkok: Don Bosco Press.

SHON, S. P., & JA, D. Y. (1982). Asian families. In M. McGoldrich, J. K. Pearce, & J. Giordano (Eds.), *Ethnicity and family therapy* (pp. 108–228). New York: Guilford Press.

TAKEUCHI, D. T., KUO, H. S., KIM, K., & LEAF, P. J. (1989). Psychiatric symptoms dimensions among Asian American and Native Hawaiians: An analysis of the Symptom Checklist. *Journal of Community Psychology, 17*(4), 319–329.

WESTERMEYER, J. (1971). Use of alcohol and opium by the Meo of Laos. *American Journal of Psychiatry, 127,* 1019–1023.

WESTERMEYER, J. (1972). A comparison of amok and homicide in Laos. *American Journal of Psychiatry, 129,* 703–709.

WESTERMEYER, J. (1983). *Poppies, pipes and people: Opium and its use in Laos.* Berkeley: University of California Press.

WESTERMEYER, J., BOUAFEULY, M., & VANG, T. F. (1984). Hmong refugees in Minnesota: Sex roles and mental health. *Medical Anthropology, 8,* 229–245.

WESTERMEYER, J., NEIDER, J., & CALLIES, A. (1989). Psychosocial adjustment of Hmong refugees during their first decade in the United States: A longitudinal study. *Journal of Nervous Mental Disease, 177*(3), 132–139.

WESTERMEYER, J., NEIDER, J., & VANG, T. F. (1984). Acculturation and mental health: A study of Hmong refugees at 1.5 and 3.5 years postmigration. *Social Science Medicine, 18*(1), 87–93.

WESTERMEYER, J., VANG, T. F., & LYFONG, G. (1983). Hmong refugees in Minnesota: Characteristics and self perceptions. *Minnesota Medicine, 66,* 431–439.

WILLIAMS, C., & WESTERMEYER, J. (1984). Psychiatric problems among adolescent Southeast Asian refugees: A descriptive study. *Journal of Nervous Mental Disorders, 171,* 79–85.

WILLIAMS, C. L. (1989). Prevention programs for refugees: An interface for mental health and public health. *Journal of Primary Prevention, 10,* 167–186.

WILLIAMS, C. L., & BERRY, J. W. (1991). Primary prevention of acculturative stress among refugees. *American Psychologist, 46,* 632–641.

YANG, D. (1974). *Les Hmong du Laos Face au Developpement.* Vientiane: Edition Siaosavath.

CHAPTER 10

Korean American Children

WUN JUNG KIM, LUKE I. KIM, and DAVID S. RUE

KOREA IS AN OLD BUT rapidly changing country. Since 2333 B.C., Koreans have preserved their own history, language, and culture. Contact with Western culture began slowly in the 18th century and a diplomatic relationship with the United States was established in the late 19th century. The first small wave of Korean immigration brought a total of 7,226 Koreans to Hawaii by 1905 (L. Kim, 1993). The Japanese occupation of Korea from 1905 to 1945 halted the flow of Korean immigration. The Korean War, which started in 1950, initiated the second wave of Korean immigration. It included young orphans of the war and the wives of American servicemen. The continued presence of the military forces in Korea after the war resulted in the immigration of more than 100,000 Korean wives of U.S. servicemen. The initial humanitarian adoption of Korean war orphans evolved into more systematic adoption arrangements through which about 100,000 Korean children have been brought to the United States over the past four decades.

The passage of the Immigration and Naturalization Act of 1965 marked the beginning of the third, larger wave of Korean immigrants. The act opened the door to many Korean graduate students and physicians-in-training in the United States who were reluctant to return to their homeland for the lack of opportunities for their professional advancement. It also offered an opportunity for highly trained professionals and skilled workers and their families in Korea to immigrate to the United States. Most of them were young, with a mean age of 27.3, coming from urban, middle-class backgrounds (Hurh & Kim, 1988). Many of these young, highly educated immigrants had to experience a downgrading of their occupational status and to assume labor-intensive work such as dry cleaning shops and other small retail businesses. Many endured the hardships of immigration to ensure that their children would have better educational and occupational opportunities.

An average of 30,000 Korean immigrants annually entered the United States in the 1970s and 1980s. The 1990 U.S. census registered 798,849 Korean Americans in the United States. The figure represents more than a 100% increase from the 1980 census count of 357,393 and a 1000% increase from the 1970 census count of about 70,000 (U.S. Bureau of the Census, 1995). Of this number, about one-third are children and adolescents. A 1990 unpublished report by the Korean Foreign Ministry estimates that an additional 200,000 or more Koreans reside in the United States for educational, business, or diplomatic affairs. Korean immigrants have preferred to settle on the West Coast—44.4% are in the West, 22.8% in the Northeast, 19.2% in the South and 13.7% in the Midwest. In contrast to the steady increase of Korean immigrants in the 1970s and 1980s, the flow of Korean immigration slowed down in the 1990s, to below 20,000 per year on average (16,011 in 1994). This downward trend reflects the political and economic climates in both countries: economic development and political stabilization in Korea and unfavorable social and political atmosphere toward immigrants and economic strains in the United States. It is also of significance that reverse immigration has increased, with about 50,000 Koreans returning to Korea in the past 15 years.

The educational backgrounds and family characteristics of the three different waves of Korean immigrants vary widely. The degree of their acculturation into the United States also varies greatly depending on the length of residence and circumstances of their immigration (e.g., adoption or marriage). The time of their departure from Korea for immigration is also a significant factor in understanding the degree of traditional Korean culture's influence on family life, child rearing, and child development; for Korea has been actively transforming from an old agrarian society to a modern industrial nation in the past three decades. The poverty-stricken and war-torn Korea of the 1950s transformed itself to an affluent, dynamic, industrialized society, evidenced during the International Olympics in Seoul in 1988. The customs and cultural habits have changed so much that one has to struggle to grasp what the modern Korean identity is about. This chapter attempts to describe traditional cultural influences that are still operating in conscious or unconscious lives of Korean Americans, especially with respect to child rearing and child development. The discussion will focus on the immigrants of the third wave, who have arrived in the United States since the passage of the 1965 immigration law and who constitute the majority of Korean Americans. References from both studies of child development in Korea and studies of Korean American families and children in the United States are cited.

Family and Child Development

RELIGION AND ETHICS

Christianity has gained rapid acceptance in postwar Korea. Close to one-third of Koreans are said to be practicing Christians. About 60% to 70% of Korean immigrants attend Korean ethnic churches in the United States for social and psychological support in addition to religious functions (Hurh & Kim, 1988). Churches have played a central role for initial settling and networking among Korean immigrants. For example, there are more than 300 Korean churches in the Los Angeles area. This may hinder the acculturation of immigrants as they comfort themselves by settling into a close-knit Korean community. Despite the rising popularity of Christianity, Taoism, Buddhism, and Confucianism have provided the religious and ethical teachings most influential in Korean culture. About one third of Koreans reported affiliation with Buddhism (Park & Cho, 1995). Confucianism was the prevailing ethics that guided 500 years of the Yi Dynasty before the Japanese occupation and is still dominant in the social and emotional lives of Koreans, especially in family and kinship relations. Table 10–1 lists somewhat arbitrary contrasts between Korean traditional values and American mainstream values that illustrate the traditional culture's influences on Korean American children (modified from L. Kim & G. Kim, 1994).

FAMILY STRUCTURE

Confucian teachings carefully defined the hierarchy of the traditional Korean family. The father was in charge of the household, and the grandfather was revered in the extended family. The gender role dynamics assigned the son as a bearer of the family name and procreator of the family. Ancestral worship and the channeling of inheritance to the firstborn son were emphasized. The Korean model of kinship is that of father-son dominance with the attributes of continuity, inclusiveness, authority, and asexuality, whereas in American kinship the husband-wife dyad is dominant with the attributes of discontinuity, exclusiveness, volition, and sexuality (C. Kim, 1989). The emphasis of continuity underscored the importance of a strong family identity and loyalty to clan. Individual identity was overlooked in the atmosphere of collective family identity. Individual failure was perceived as a family shame while individual success was a source of family pride. Children's disabilities, whether physical or mental, often were not addressed openly (Y. Kim, 1986).

Cultural changes in modern Korea, however, have transformed old values and customs. The preference for sons and institutionalization of male chauvinism are changing to a degree (Park & Cho, 1995). Family planning results in no male child in some families. The desire for sons had a lot to do with the old-age security value of children (Kagitcibasi, 1982), but now in the United States, some Korean elders plan their own retirement communities rather than relying on their children (Koh & Bell, 1987). Despite these changes, kinship remains an important resource within the United States and across the Pacific for both premigration and postmigration support and adjustment, economically and emotionally (Min, 1984).

TABLE 10–1
Korean versus American Values

Korean Traditional Values	American Mainstream Values
Family Values	
Family-oriented	Individual-oriented
Interdependency	Autonomy and independence
Vertical, authoritarian structure	Horizontal, democratic structure
Family loyalty and filial piety	Separation and individuation
Family discipline via shame/punishment	Discipline by external authorities
Life Philosophy	
Collectivism	Individualism
Sense of stoicism and fatalism	Sense of optimism and opportunism
Reciprocity and obligation	Avoidance of obligation (go Dutch)
Status conscious and face-saving	Self-realization and pragmatism
Holistic living in harmony with nature	Control and conquering of nature
Communication Style	
Subtle, nonverbal, body language	Emphasis on verbal language
Control of feelings	Free expression of feelings
Flowery, indirect expression	Direct, explicit expression
Little eye-to-eye contact	Eye contact important
Honorific language	Equality in language
Responsive	Assertive
Self-effacing	Self-promoting
Little physical contact	Uninhibited physical contact

CHILD REARING

Traditionally, gender role differences were emphasized by different tasks ascribed to a male and a female child. A male child was given academic lessons by the grandfather after three years of nursing by the mother, whereas a female child was taught domestic routines by the mother and grandmother. The Koreans have placed great demands on their children in the mastery of developmental tasks. Parents often sacrifice their financial resources and time to educate their children. Child care and education still are largely the responsibilities of the mother while the father stays busy as a breadwinner and a spokesperson of the family. Nurturing and discipline by parents are important hallmarks in the child-rearing practices of Koreans. Children are expected to be passive, obedient, and self-disciplined. Achievement-oriented child rearing has had its drawbacks in terms of discontinuous developmental progression and neglect of psychosocial development.

Ironically, children in the modern Korean culture are sometimes overstimulated and uninhibited because parents want to promote confidence and assertiveness that will protect the child's spirit. The social collectivism of families has been transforming into or has been modified by Western individualism in a unique Korean way. This transformation is more evident among Korean immigrants than in Korea. Korean fathers in the United States contribute significantly to child care and help their wives with household chores, and mothers often work as wage earners (Yu & Kim, 1983). The changing family structure adds a strain to the family life in terms of adequate child-care arrangements, traditional gender roles of parents, and parent-child relationships.

Developmental Perspective

CONCEPTION AND BIRTH

Child rearing is an important and serious task for Korean couples. Legitimacy of childbearing is emphasized, and therefore, illegitimate pregnancies are disdained in the Korean community, often resulting in abortion. Failure to procreate may result in the dissolution of a marriage. Meticulous mating practices reflect this cultural regard for genetic importance in conception. *Tae Mong* is a dream about conception. Once a Korean woman has had Tae Mong, she follows the *Tae Kyo* ritual for pregnancy—a set of rules for safe and easy childbirth that, when closely followed, protects the infant from disease and retardation, and the family from misfortune. Stimulative activities and foods are avoided during pregnancy (Pritham & Sammons, 1993). Positive attitudes toward pregnancy are maintained by the whole family and pregnant mothers receive special consideration from the extended families. Immigrant young families may not receive such support. Prolonged morning sickness is often experienced by young Korean American pregnant women in a less supportive environment. Prenatal support for pregnant mothers continues into the postnatal period. A study comparing Scottish mothers and Korean mothers reported that Korean mothers received more postnatal social, emotional, and physical support than Scottish mothers (Park & Dimigen, 1994). The birth of a child itself is celebrated in a quiet, private manner. The Korean tradition used to prohibit strangers from visiting the newborn for the first 21 days, to allow both the baby and the mother to recuperate and adjust to a new life and to form a bond.

INFANCY

Mothers are expected to provide full-time care for their infants for continuous bonding and nurturing. Only close family members may substitute for the mother in providing infant care. Grandparents often travel from Korea to the United States to care for their grandchildren, or infants may be sent to Korea to be cared for by grandparents and other relatives. In a series of surveys of infants in Korea, Lee (1992, 1994) found that 90% of infants slept with their mothers. On the average, 83% awoke and 28% cried more than once per night. Sixteen percent (16%) of the mothers indicated that their baby's crying constituted a problem for them. However, no infant was identified as having colic, and no infants received medication. Compared with Western studies, the duration of crying of Korean infants was shorter and the time of holding and/or close contact with the mothers was longer. The most common responses of mothers toward their baby's crying were feeding, patting/holding, and changing diapers. Ignoring or delayed responses often observed in Western culture were not used by Korean mothers.

In general, Korean children are indulged and overprotected by their parents and extended family. Immediate gratification is fostered. Feeding and weaning schedules, and even toilet training, tend to be liberal. On the other hand, children experience greater contact with and supervision by caretakers. In a study comparing the play of Korean and American infants, the two groups exhibited similar levels of mastery behaviors in exploration of toys; however, the American children used general exploration significantly more than did the Korean American children (Hupp, Lam, & Jaeger, 1992). The difference was influenced by the parental perceptions of their children's play and their child-rearing attitudes. The Korean American mothers guided infants for goal-oriented play rather than allowing them free play. This may promote the development of basic trust and object relations, but delay the development of autonomy and separation or individuation.

EARLY CHILDHOOD

In the traditional Korean society, sex role differentiation and social learning took place within the family through identification and imitation. Preschool group learning away from the family is beginning to take on importance in Korean culture but social and emotional independence or Eriksonian initiative is not promoted. Specific performance-oriented developmental tasks are targeted by parents. Two separate contrary dimensions of warmth and control are observed in parental attitudes and children also perceive these dual aspects (Yi, 1993). Collectivism and familism derived from Confucianism coexist with individualism of Western culture in contemporary Korean families. Mutual interdependence is fostered through a great deal of physical contact and emotional nurturing. In an immigrant Korean family, however, the traditional child-rearing practice may not be maintained because of the parents' own accultura- tion process and a lack of physical and emotional availability. Language acquisition may be delayed when both Korean and English are spoken. True bilingualism may be hard to ac- complish, perhaps due to dissimilar language structures and phonetics. Korean American children reared by primarily Ko- rean-speaking parents may have difficulties with socialization and early learning experience. In addition, emotional expres- sion and cooperative play may not have been encouraged enough to help them with social adaptation of schooling.

LATENCY

Yu and Kim (1983) reported that Korean pupils in U.S. class- rooms were described by teachers as being quiet, obedient, re- spectful, studious, and likable. Some teachers also observed that they were less verbally expressive, less assertive, more sensitive to approval, and less self-confident than European American students. In general, the Koreans are viewed as emo- tionally stable children, who thrive on academic work and re- spond well to concrete and specific instructions. The Korean American children's low verbal expression may have to do with language as well as cultural factors. In Korean families, there tends to be a relatively low level of verbal communica- tion and more reliance on nonverbal implicit modes of com- munication between children and parents. Although warmth by parents is transmitted implicitly to children, verbal de- mands and discipline for achievement-oriented development in this age period call for obedience and conformity on the part of the children. If children succeed in school, they are consid- ered to be progressing satisfactorily.

In a comparison of Korean and British 9-year-old children, researchers found that Korean children scored higher in general intelligence, especially in visual-spatial abilities, but lower in ver- bal tests (Lynn & Song, 1994). A series of studies (Fuson & Kwon, 1992; Miura, Kim, Chang, & Okamoto, 1988; Miura, Okamoto,

Kim, Chang, Steere, & Fayol, 1994) found that Korean children, like other Asian children, had greater flexibility of mental number manipulation and more efficient computing abilities than American children. Whether it is a genetic effect or a child-rearing effect, Korean American children do well in mathematics and science subjects, helping them to achieve a sense of confidence or Eriksonian sense of industry. In a study comparing Korean American children with African American children of an urban school district, Chang (1975) found that Korean American children in third to sixth grades scored higher in behavior, intellectual and school status, and happiness and satisfaction on Pierce-Harris Self-Concept Scales, but scored lower in physical appearance and attributes, and popularity, than African American children. When children struggle academically, they have difficulties in both school and family, experiencing feelings of inferiority and parental disappointment. Social discomfort related to ethnic minority status, low verbal expression, and lack of social skills may induce ostracism from peers. Early development of ethnic/racial identities in these children may be seriously compromised, and they may begin to manifest signs of emotional and behavioral maladjustment.

EARLY AND MIDDLE ADOLESCENCE

Korean American adolescents may be pulled to an adhesive (closely-knit) mode of adaptation (Hurh, 1990) when parents maintain Korean customs, culture, and intraethnic networking, and adolescents face dilemmas in peer relationships and self-identity in the dominant culture. The second phase of separation/individuation in this period may be as unencouraging as the earlier one. Adolescents who have not learned to assert themselves, to express different options, and to deal with anger or aggression appropriately will experience difficulties in coping with the sexual, impulsive, and aggressive drives of adolescence. Adolescents frequently challenge parental authority. Emerging sexuality and physical changes of puberty are not openly discussed in the traditional Korean culture. Whereas sexuality and aggressive conflicts may be universal phenomena during early adolescence, they present a unique dilemma to Korean American adolescents, especially boys. Gender identity disorders and homosexuality seem to be less prevalent in Korean culture, which defines and enforces clear gender roles, but Korean American boys may struggle with their body image and related self/gender concept because of their physical characteristics, (e.g., small size, less masculine appearance) and societal stereotypes. Korean American girls tend to do better in this area.

LATE ADOLESCENCE AND YOUNG ADULTHOOD

Dating is a sensitive issue in the Korean American family. Parent-child relations may undergo strained periods during this stage of development for various reasons. Many Korean parents wish their children to date and eventually marry a member of their own ethnic community. Some may be threatened by the overt expression of affection and sexuality in teenagers. Cultural, generational, and language barriers sometimes hinder effective communication and supportive relationships between parents and adolescents when dealing with extracurricular activities, college planning, peer relationships, and family problems. Parents may have attained financial and occupational stability but not be good role models because of their poor command of English and failure to assimilate into mainstream society. Role models and group support from the Korean American community are not readily available to Korean adolescents because of the short history of Korean immigration. Korean American adolescents are sometimes left alone in their search for identity, struggling with their own inadequate and ineffective biculturalism. When parents demand only academic excellence while neglecting other important developmental tasks of their somewhat lost adolescent children, both parents and adolescents may experience alienation and take defensive postures ranging from acting out to suppression or inhibition.

College entrance sometimes brings relief to the parent-adolescent tension. Despite the physical separation, however, close family ties are still expected. Adolescent moratorium and interdependence are prolonged by mutual needs and cultural tradition. Korean American college students often receive full financial support from their parents. Korean parents in both Korea and the United States feel obligated to support their grown-up children through their wedding, which is viewed as a last rite or duty of parenting. As young adults enter college or the workforce, they may feel isolated and become more acutely aware of their minority status. They may blend themselves well into the mainstream society academically and occupationally, but finding their own voice and place in a competitive and sometimes hostile environment may be daunting. Some may turn their attention to finding their roots by learning or rediscovering the Korean language and adopting customs that they had resisted in earlier years; they may even visit Korea. They sometimes find themselves being caught in two opposing value systems—between the Korean penchant for homogeneity and hierarchical structure and the diverse idealistic pursuit of an open U.S. society. Interracial marriages provide a good example of this conflict; even casual interracial dating often causes a family crisis, although it is now more often tolerated by Korean American parents as inevitable.

Clinical Perspectives

SPECIFIC POPULATIONS

Recent Immigrants

Immigrant families undergo the strains of uprooting, which undoubtedly affect the family dynamics, parent-child relationships, and child development. Kuo (1984) reported that Koreans as a group in the Seattle area exhibited the highest depression scores compared with those of Chinese, Japanese, and Filipino Americans. Kuo attributed this finding to a shorter length of residence in the United States, higher rates of underemployment (i.e., lower-level jobs despite higher educational status), limited proficiency in English, and a higher concentration in small businesses located in high-risk minority districts. Hurh and Kim (1990a) described gender differences in the dynamics of depression: Although Korean males who were married and employed in a high-status occupation showed better subjective mental health than others, no distinctive set of variables accounted for the female respondents' mental health. Two-thirds of Korean women sampled in the Chicago area were employed, and most of the employed wives carried a double burden of performing the household tasks and working outside the home. Changing gender roles add stresses to marriage. In a survey of 150 Korean women residing in Chicago, 60% were reportedly battered by their husbands or partners, 75% of them within 3 to 5 years of immigration (Song-Kim, 1992). Children may also suffer from adjustment stresses in school and inadequate communication between school and parents, in addition to all the losses they experienced by leaving their friends, extended family, and all the familiar surroundings of their homeland. Parents' erroneous expectations of the community and educational system of the United States may leave the school-age children's needs unattended and leave the parents disappointed and bewildered. For example, children going through the Korean educational system learn not only academic skills but principles of moral behavior. As seen in Korean adults (Hurh & Kim, 1990b), the first few years seem to be an especially vulnerable period for children as well. Timing of immigration in relation to the developmental stage of children will affect their adjustment and development. The younger the age at immigration, the higher the level of the immigrant's assimilation into English language and American culture. On the other hand, the younger the age at immigration, the less likelihood that true bilingualism and biculturalism will develop. Language deprivation following immigration to the United States during later childhood years can initially cause withdrawal and despondency before adaptive integration (Marcos, 1982).

Children Separated from Their Parents in Korea

As mentioned earlier, some Korean immigrants have returned to their homeland, leaving their children in America to continue their education. Many Korean parents are eager to send their children for schooling in the United States. Some families have immigrated ostensibly because of the educational opportunities; 80% of parents in Korea want to send their children to college and beyond, but only 39% of children in Korea are allowed to enter the limited college quota system through a very competitive entrance examination. Financially strapped private secondary schools and colleges of the United States have even hired recruiters in Korea to bring in eager Korean children and adolescents. Some American boarding schools and college language courses are said to be filled by many Korean students who failed college entrance examinations in Korea or opted not to face such a competitive examination and instead pursue their education abroad. These children and adolescents separated from their parents, unsupervised or inadequately supervised by school personnel, relatives, and family friends are at high risk for school failure, isolation, or acting out. Freed from highly demanding and regimented college preparation beginning from even early elementary school years, they are often unable to cope with independent pursuit of academic, social, and emotional tasks of development.

1.5 Generation

The term *1.5 generation* has been used in the Korean American community since 1980 to describe a group that is sandwiched between generations; it includes older adolescents and young adults who were born in Korea and immigrated to the United States before their adulthood. On the positive side, they attained a higher degree of comfort with bilingualism and biculturalism than the first, second, or third generation. But on the whole, they have to work harder to succeed as Koreans, Korean Americans, and Americans, all at the same time. These abstract, confusing ethnic identities are hard to reconcile internally and to operationalize in real life. As a result, they may achieve limited assimilation into either culture. This structural marginality produces two possible modes of adaptation—the cosmopolitan or the marginal personality (Hurh, 1990). The cosmopolitan personality emerges from the positive resolution of biculturalism and displays creativity, motivation, leadership potential, and active participation in both the ethnic and mainstream community and a strong sense of Korean American identity. The marginal personality is a product of the negative resolution of the external pressure and internal conflict, and exhibits ambivalent personal identity, inferiority conflicts, hypersensitivity, social isolation, and feelings of powerlessness.

Biracial Children

Between 1945 and 1985, 68,296 Koreans were admitted to the United States as spouses of U.S. citizens, primarily U.S. servicemen stationed in Korea (Thornton, 1992). The continued presence of the U.S. military forces in Korea has been a steady source of biracial Korean American children, estimated to be well over 100,000. Many Korean women married to U.S. servicemen are described as a high-risk group, and experience a high rate of marital conflict and marital failure (B. Kim, 1977). The risks include the likelihood of backgrounds from the disadvantaged segments of Korea, traumatic life experiences, and communication and cultural barriers such as language, different modes of emotional expression, and different expectations of marriage (Ratliff, Moon, & Bonacci, 1978).

Stephan (1992) proposed the benefits of mixed heritage status such as increased contact with the members of both races, enjoyment of two cultures, bilingual development, and intergroup tolerance. Biracial status, however, may act as a risk factor for Korean American children, although no research has been conducted on this group. In Korea, as in other Asian cultures, biracial children are often scorned by peers and society in general, and suffer from social ostracism. Even after immigration to the United States, biracial children are not well accepted by and seem to shy away from the Korean community. Since the parents' marriage is often conflicted or ends in divorce, the disadvantages rather than advantages of mixed heritage will be magnified, including emotional instability and conflicts with ethnic/racial identity.

Korean Adoptees

Since the Korean War, the number of Korean children adopted by American families steadily increased until the 1990s, peaking in 1986 with 6,150 children, which represented 59% of all foreign children adopted in the United States that year. The number has been decreasing since then, with only 1,666 documented in 1995. This marked decrease is attributed to the Korean government's efforts to promote domestic adoptions and the international sociopolitical changes. Korea is now the third leading sender nation of the U.S. international adoptees following Russia and China. The question has been raised as to how 100,000 Korean adoptees have fared in the United States (W. Kim, 1995), in view of the general notion that adopted children are at risk to develop psychological problems for various reasons, both preadoption genetic and environmental factors, and postadoption relationship problems. Transcultural/transracial adoption of African American children has been openly discouraged in the United States for political and social reasons, although there is no good research evidence against it (W. Kim, 1996). A recent review of all the published data on Korean adoptees in both the United States and Europe indicated that Korean adoptees have adjusted well (W. Kim, 1995). Although it is encouraging to find out that they have done better than other adoptees from within the United States and from other foreign countries, they are still at higher risk than average children and adolescents, especially during the early postadoption period and adolescence.

A case study reported an observation of transient regressive features, such as temper tantrums and excessive crying among Korean children during the initial postadoption period (Kim, Hong, & Kim, 1979). Learning disabilities in the group of children adopted after the age of 3 appeared to be related to the problem in language acquisition and acculturation. In contrast to earlier adoption problems, later adoption problems may have to do with the lack of understanding of the children's unique ethnic cultural background and identity. Compared with the emphasis on the African American heritage of Black children adopted by White families and White adoptive parents' familiarity with Black culture, there has been little discussion of ethnic heritage of foreign-born children adopted by American families. It appears that a genuine interest in their ethnic roots should be stimulated, fostering historic continuity and cultural linkage with the adoptees' background, although the mainstreaming of these children into American culture is equally important.

CLINICAL SYNDROMES

A few available epidemiological and clinical studies have shown similar rates of mental disorders between Korean and American subjects, both adults and children. Lee et al. (1990) reported comparable prevalences of adult disorders observed by the same methodology of the Epidemiological Catchment Area (ECA) studies in Korea and St. Louis, Missouri, although the rates in Korea tended to be lower except for alcoholism and somatization disorder. *Hwa-Byung* (Lin, 1983) is the only culture-bound syndrome known for Koreans. The term literally means "anger syndrome" and is attributed to the suppression of anger; phenomenologically, it is a spectrum of affective and somatization disorders. According to the *Diagnostic and Statistical Manual of Mental Disorders (DSM-IV;* APA, 1994), the symptoms include insomnia, fatigue, panic, fear of impending death, dysphoric moods, indigestion, anorexia, dyspnea, palpitations, generalized aches and pains, and a feeling of a mass in the epigastrium. It is prevalent among married women and often occurs in the context of family conflict. It does not manifest in young children and only rarely in older adolescents.

A World Health Organization (WHO) collaborative study of primary schoolchildren in Korea, Japan, and China (Matsuura et al., 1993) reported higher rates of emotional and behavioral problems among Korean children. However, the overall rates of deviance found in Rutter's questionnaires were comparable to the rates found in England, New Zealand, and other Western countries, except for a higher rate of somatic complaints. The characteristics of childhood disorders, even such as selective mutism (Hong & Chung, 1996) and learning disorders (Kim, Lim, & Kim, 1996), were found to be quite similar to the findings in the United States, showing few cultural influences. On the other hand, a cross-cultural study of self-report depressive symptoms among college students in Korea, the Philippines, Taiwan, and the United States found that Korean students reported high levels of depressive symptoms (Crittenden, Fugita, Bae, Lamug, & Lin, 1992). They also exhibited more somatic symptoms, whereas the students of the United States and Taiwan exhibited more psychological symptoms. One may surmise that there is a prevalent manifestation of somaticizing symptoms among Korean youths.

SPECIFIC ISSUES

Adolescent Alienation Syndrome

As described earlier, immigrant adolescents face a daunting task of coping with different disruptive forces. When autonomous and independent development does not progress in a supportive manner in a distressed family, the adolescent becomes at risk. Immigration may be particularly stressful when teenagers have to leave social and peer network and support behind and face a somewhat hostile environment in school and the community. They often experience a sense of rejection, not only in school but at home where their parents struggle, themselves, with the stresses of immigration. Some turn to a peer group within the Korean community or a group of other rejected youths, joining in gang activities in reaction to the sense of alienation from the parents and community. In the New York and Los Angeles metropolitan areas, Korean youth gang activities have attracted much attention. In addition to delinquent acts and substance abuse, withdrawal, depression, and suicide attempts may result in referrals of adolescents to physicians, clergy, and counselors in the Korean American community. Regardless of whether they exhibit externalizing or internalizing behavioral problems, the underlying dynamics of intergenerational tension, alienation between parents and adolescents, and identity conflicts are evident. Such dynamics are not unique to recently immigrated adolescents but may also be observed in the second- or third-generation Korean American adolescents.

Child Abuse and Neglect

The Korean culture used to and, to a degree, still promotes stern discipline of children including the use of corporal punishment. Therefore, child maltreatment and legitimate physical discipline by caring and concerned parents are not easy to distinguish. However, a survey of primary school children in Seoul, Korea, revealed that 8.2% of them had been seriously battered at least once in a one-year period, constituting child abuse according to the investigators (Kim & Ko, 1990). These children came from broken homes and families of low socioeconomic status. Boys were far more likely to be battered than girls (42% vs. 24%). A cross-cultural study of U.S. and Korean children found no differences in the use of physical punishment and related symptoms of anxiety, such as nail biting and nightmares (Englehart & Hale, 1990). In general, child abuse is viewed as a family affair rather than a social issue, rarely reported to the authorities in Korea (Chun, 1989). There are no reported data on child maltreatment in Korean American families. It is presumed that children in the first few years of immigration are at risk for child neglect and abuse due to parental immigration-related stressors. The marital conflicts of parents partly due to the changing gender role dynamics in the process of acculturation and disruptions in the continuity of family life also play a role. However, one should not overlook the cultural differences and the child's perceptions of parental discipline. In sharp contrast to the findings in North American youths, Korean youths' perceptions of parental control are correlated positively with perceived parental warmth and low neglect (Rohner & Pettengill, 1985). Similarly, physical touching, even touching of young boys' genitalia by older people (as a sign of affection and adoration of a male gender), and expectations of girls assuming more household responsibilities than boys at a relatively young age should be viewed in light of cultural customs. The practice of delegating responsibilities to children and issues of dominance and submission should be viewed with awareness and sensitivity on the part of child protective services dealing with Korean American families, as with other ethnic minority groups (Gray & Cosgrove, 1985).

KOREANS' VIEW OF MENTAL ILLNESS
AND TREATMENT

Herbal medicine and acupuncture are still popular in Korea for various physical as well as mental conditions. In fact, these traditional healing methods are becoming popular not only in Asian American communities but in the mainstream culture of the United States. Faith healing, religious counseling, special prayers and fasting, have also been widely practiced as Christianity gained rapid acceptance in Korea. Religious counseling is especially relevant in Korean American families as two-thirds of them are reportedly churchgoers (Hurh & Kim, 1988). Stigma of mental illness is a prevalent problem among Koreans, too. Fear of chronic mental illness and shame delay timely evaluation and treatment. Secrecy surrounds the mental illness of a family member. Although educated and more acculturated Korean Americans become cognizant of the need for psychological help and more tolerant of the stigma associated with such help, Koreans tend to be less receptive than other Asians (Atkinson & Gim, 1989). Underutilization calls for greater understanding of the cultural dynamics of Korean American family issues and their needs.

Conclusion

There is a paucity of cross-cultural studies in general, and data on children and adolescents are even more scarce. Whether

Korean children living in the United States show a greater resemblance to Korean children living in Korea or American children with respect to their normal development and psychosocial deviation is a question that has not been addressed. A clue may be sought through an informative study on transitional objects, such as pacifiers and blankets, to which children become attached. Hong and Townes (1976) reported that 53.9% of American children, 34% of Korean American children, and 18.3% of Korean children have transitional objects. It was also observed that a greater number of Korean infants slept in the same room with mother, experienced more physical contact with mother, particularly at bedtime, and were breast-fed longer than the American infants. Thus, the phenomenon of attachment to an inanimate object appears to be closely associated with child-rearing practices, especially those related to the time of going to sleep. In these respects, Korean American children fell between the Korean and American children.

Despite the dearth of research on Korean American children, it appears that they are not any more vulnerable than other ethnic American children: Even the most vulnerable group (i.e., transcontinentally and transracially transplanted Korean adopted children) have adjusted well. A review of available research indicates that Korean American boys may be at higher risk than girls for various problems. However, normative developmental data in relation to different ethnic groups need to be accumulated and studied for better understanding of intricate gender, migration, and cultural dynamics.

Cross-cultural studies have reported higher rates of depressive and somatization disorders among Korean youths and adults in both the United States and Korea. The finding of high somatic complaints in clinical conditions and in a general population may imply high utilization of medical services for their emotional distresses. Therefore, culturally sensitive mental health services need to be developed to prevent, to identify early, and to provide effective interventions for the immigration-related and other psychosocial problems of Korean American families and their children.

References

AMERICAN PSYCHIATRIC ASSOCIATION. (1994). *Diagnostic and statistical manual of mental disorders* (4th ed., p. 846). Washington, DC: Author.

ATKINSON, D. R., & GIM, R. H. (1989). Asian-American cultural identity and attitudes toward mental health services. *Journal of Counseling Psychology, 36,* 209–212.

CHANG, T. S. (1975). The self-concept of children in ethnic groups: Black American and Korean-American. *Elementary School Journal, 76,* 52–58.

CHUN, B. H. (1989). Child abuse in Korea. *Child Welfare, 68,* 154–158.

CRITTENDEN, K. S., FUGITA, S. S., BAE, H. J., LAMUG, C. B., & LIN, K. M. (1992). A cross-cultural study of self-report depressive symptoms among college students. *Journal of Cross-Cultural Psychology, 23*(2), 163–178.

ENGLEHART, R. J., & HALE, D. B. (1990). Punishment, nail-biting, and nightmares: A cross-cultural study. *Journal of Multicultural Counseling and Development, 18,* 126–132.

FUSON, K. C., & KWON, Y. (1992). Korean children's single-digit addition and subtraction: Numbers structures by ten. *Journal for Research in Mathematics Education, 23*(2), 148–165.

GRAY, E., & COSGROVE, J. (1985). Ethnocentric perception of child rearing practices in protective services. *Child Abuse and Neglect, 9,* 389–396.

HONG, K. M., & CHUNG, S. (1996). Characteristics and treatment courses of the children with selective mutism. *Proceedings of the APA Annual Meeting: New Research Abstracts, 127.*

HONG, K. M., & TOWNES, B. D. (1976). Infant's attachment to inanimate objects. *Journal of the American Academy of Child Psychiatry, 15,* 49–61.

HUPP, S. C., LAM, S. F., & JAEGER, J. (1992). Differences in exploration of toys by one-year-old children: A Korean and American comparison. *Behavior Science Research, 26*(1/4), 123–135.

HURH, W. M. (1990). The "1.5 Generation": A paragon of Korean-American pluralism. *Korean Culture,* 21–31.

HURH, W. M., & KIM, K. C. (1988). *Uprooting and adjustment: A sociological study of Korean immigrants' mental health* (Final report submitted to NIMH). Macomb: Western Illinois University.

HURH, W. M., & KIM, K. C. (1990a). Correlates of Korean immigrant's mental health. *Journal of Nervous Mental Disease, 178,* 703–711.

HURH, W. M., & KIM, K. C. (1990b). Adaptation stages and mental health of Korean male immigrants in the U.S. *International Migration Review, 24,* 456–479.

KAGITCIBASI, C. (1982). Old age security value of children and development: Cross-national evidence. *Journal of Comparative Family Studies, 13,* 133–142.

KIM, B. L. (1977). Asian wives of U.S. servicemen: Women in shadows. *Amerasia Journal, 4,* 91–115.

KIM, C. (1989). Attribute of "Asexuality" in Korean kinship and sundered Koreans during the Korean War. *Journal of Comparative Family Studies, 20,* 309–325.

KIM, J., LIM, Y., & KIM, S. P. (1996). Characteristics of learning disordered children. *Proceedings of the APA Annual Meeting: New Research Abstracts,* 132.

KIM, K., & KO, B. (1990). An incidence survey of battered children in two elementary schools of Seoul. *Child Abuse and Neglect, 14,* 273–276.

KIM, L. I., (1993). Psychiatric care of Korean-American patients. In A. Gaw (Ed.), *Culture, ethnicity and mental illness* (pp. 347–376). Washington, DC: American Psychiatric Press.

KIM, L. I., & KIM, G. S. (1994). *Korean-American immigrants and their children* (p. 20). San Francisco: Many Cultures.

KIM, S. P., HONG, S., & KIM, B. S. (1979). Adoption of Korean children by New York area couples: A preliminary study. *Child Welfare, 58*(7), 419–427.

KIM, W. J. (1995). International adoption: A case review of Korean children. *Child Psychiatry and Human Development, 25*(3), 141–154.

KIM, W. J. (1996). Transcultural/transracial adoption. *American Academy of Child and Adolescent Psychiatry News, 27*(2), 33.

KIM, Y. S. (1986). A comparative survey of anxiety in mothers of mentally retarded children in Tokyo and Seoul. *Japanese Journal of Special Education, 24,* 1–16.

KOH, J. Y., & BELL, W. G. (1987). Korean elders in the U.S.: Intergenerational relations and living arrangements. *Gerontologist, 27,* 66–71.

KUO, W. H. (1984). Prevalence of depression among Asian-Americans. *Journal of Nervous and Mental Disease, 172,* 449–457.

LEE, C. K., KWAK, Y. S., YAMAMOTO, J., RHEE, H., KIM, Y. S., HAN, J. H., CHOI, J. O., & LEE, Y. H. (1990). Psychiatric epidemiology in Korea: Part 1. Gender and age differences in Seoul. *Journal of Nervous and Mental Disease, 178,* 242–246.

LEE, K. (1992). Pattern of night waking and crying of Korean infants from 3 months to 2 years old and its relation with various factors. *Journal of Developmental and Behavioral Pediatrics, 13*(5), 326–330.

LEE, K. (1994). The crying pattern of Korean infants and related factors. *Developmental Medicine and Child Neurology, 36*(7), 601–607.

LIN, K. M. (1983). Hwa-Byung: A Korean culture-bound syndrome? *American Journal of Psychiatry, 140,* 105–107.

LYNN, R., & SONG, M. J. (1994). General intelligence, visuospatial and verbal abilities in Korean children. *Personality and Individual Differences, 16*(2), 363–364.

MARCOS, L. R. (1982). Adults' recollection of their language deprivation as immigrant children. *American Journal of Psychiatry, 139,* 607–610.

MATSUURA, M., OKUBO, Y., KOJIMA, T., TAKAHASHI, R., WANG, Y. F., SHEN, Y. C., & LEE, C. K. (1993). A cross-national prevalence study of children with emotional and behavioral problems—A WHO collaborative study in the Western Pacific Region. *Journal of Child Psychology and Psychiatry, 34*(3), 307–315.

MIN, P. G. (1984). An exploratory study of kin ties among Korean immigrant families in Atlanta. *Journal of Comparative Family Studies, 15,* 58–75.

MIURA, I. T., KIM, C. C., CHANG, C. M., & OKAMOTO, Y. (1988). Effects of language characteristics on children's cognitive representation of number: Cross-national comparisons. *Child Development, 59*(6), 1445–1450.

MIURA, I. T., OKAMOTO, Y., KIM, C. C., CHANG, C. M., STEERE, M., & FAYOL, M. (1994). Comparisons of children's cognitive representation of number: China, France, Japan, Korea, Sweden, and the United States. *International Journal of Behavioral Development, 17*(3), 401–411.

PARK, E. M., & DIMIGEN, G. (1994). Cross-cultural comparison of the social support system after childbirth. *Journal of Comparative Family Studies, 25*(3), 345–352.

PARK, I. H., & CHO, L. J. (1995). Confucianism and the Korean family. Families in Asia: Beliefs and realities [Special issue]. *Journal of Comparative Family Studies, 26*(1), 117–134.

PRITHAM, U. A., & SAMMONS, L. N. (1993). Korean women's attitudes toward pregnancy and prenatal care. *Health Care for Women International, 14*(2), 145–153.

RATLIFF, B. W., MOON, H. F., & BONACCI, G. A. (1978). Intercultural marriage: The Korean-American experience. *Social Casework, 59,* 221–226.

ROHNER, R. P., & PETTENGILL, S. M. (1985). Perceived parental acceptance-rejection and parental control among Korean adolescents. *Child Development, 56,* 524–528.

SONG-KIM, Y. I. (1992). Battered Korean women in urban United States. In S. M. Furuto, R. Biswas, D. K. Chung, K. Murase, & F. Ross-Sherriff (Eds.), *Social work practice with Asian Americans* (pp. 213–226). Newbury Park, CA: Sage.

STEPHAN, C. W. (1992). Mixed-heritage individuals: Ethnic identity and trait characteristics. In M. P. P. Root (Ed.), *Racially mixed people in America* (pp. 50–63). Newbury Park, CA: Sage.

THORNTON, M. C. (1992). The quiet immigration: Foreign spouses of U.S. citizens, 1945–1985. In M. P. P. Root (Ed.), *Racially mixed people in America* (pp. 64–76). Newbury Park, CA: Sage.

U.S. BUREAU OF THE CENSUS. (1995). *Statistical abstract of the United States: 1995* (115th ed.). Washington, DC: Author.

YI, S. H. (1993). Transformation of child socialization in Korean culture. Perspectives on Korean child care, development and education [Special issue]. *Early Child Development and Care, 85,* 17–24.

YU, K. H., & KIM, L. I. (1983). The growth and development of Korean-American children. In G. J. Powell (Ed.), *The psychosocial development of minority group children* (pp. 147–158). New York: Brunner/Mazel.

CHAPTER 11

Chinese American Children

ANN YU LUNG and STANLEY SUE

THE STATUS OF CHINESE AMERICANS raises many important issues concerning ethnic minority group functioning in American society, cultural influences, acculturation, and mental health assumptions and practices. This is particularly true for Chinese American children and adolescents, who constitute a diverse group with special mental health needs. Empirical research in this area is scarce, and much of the available information is derived from clinical observations and personal experiences with this population. However, a growing number of researchers have been focusing their investigation on the prevalence of psychological and psychiatric problems in Chinese American youth, as well as on ways to meet the unique treatment needs of this group.

This chapter begins by giving an overview of the demographics of Chinese American families currently living in the United States. Behavioral and cognitive socialization of Chinese American children based on traditional values is discussed, followed by an analysis of the particular developmental and mental health issues relevant to this group, including culturally based intergenerational conflicts, identity formation, and minority status. To address the problems and treatment needs of Chinese American children and adolescents, an examination of the relationship between members of this group and the current mental health system is provided, with an emphasis on patterns of underutilization, symptom severity, rates of psychopathology, and diagnostic concerns. This chapter concludes with recommendations for improving assessment methodology and suggestions for designing culturally responsive psychotherapy.

Demographic Characteristics

Based on population projections from statistics provided by Ong and Hee (1993), over 2.5 million Chinese ethnics live in the United States, making up the largest Asian American group in the nation. Nearly 23% of all Asian Americans are of Chinese ancestry. The first wave of Chinese immigration to this country occurred around the middle of the 19th century, the second wave emigrated after World War II, and the third wave came after the 1965 Immigration Act was passed. Every year since the Immigration Act became law, tens of thousands of Chinese and their children have come to the United States from Taiwan, Hong Kong, mainland China, and Vietnam, seeking better standards of living and better educational opportunities.

Chinese American children and adolescents are a diverse and ever-changing population. Although some individuals are representatives of the fifth or sixth generation, others are new arrivals in this country, speaking little, if any, English. There is also group heterogeneity in terms of the family's country of origin, whom they reside with in the United States (e.g., parents, grandparents, adult siblings, aunts, uncles, godparents), the languages/dialects spoken at home, religious beliefs, and the parents' educational and socioeconomic status.

Chinese American families who have emigrated to the United States in recent decades come from diverse cultural and language backgrounds. Children from these families typically become bilingual or, in some cases, trilingual (speaking Chinese, Vietnamese, and English) once they start going to American schools (UBA, 1994). Foreign-born children under the age of 5, who simply do not have a stable command of their native language, have more difficulties retaining their first language compared with children who emigrated later in life. It is not uncommon for Chinese children, who are not fluent in the native language of their parents, to answer family members in English when they are spoken to in the ethnic language. When Chinese parents are unable to communicate effectively with their children, they lose the means for socializing and influencing them, which can lead to family rifts and the loss of intimacy that comes from sharing and passing down beliefs and values (Fillmore, 1991).

Cognitive and Behavioral Socialization

Due to the emphasis on social control and academic achievement in the Confucian tradition, many Chinese American children are taught early on a set of normative behaviors characterized by impulse control, emotional restraint, strict discipline, and obedience to authority figures. In the Chinese culture, these behaviors are thought to be preconditions for mastering self-discipline and achieving academic success later on in life (D. Ho, 1994). Studies comparing the parenting practices of Chinese American and European American mothers have found that Chinese Americans tend to be more controlling (Chao, 1983; Hsu, 1981), less expressive of their affection (Bond & Wang, 1983; Hsu, 1981), less likely to encourage independence (D. Ho, 1981; King & Bond, 1985), and more likely to emphasize the value of academic achievement (D. Ho, 1981; Lum & Char, 1985). Chinese American parents also have higher educational expectations for their children. Yao (1985a) conducted a study with 5th- through 11th-grade students who scored above the 90th percentile on achievement tests, and found that the parents of Chinese American immigrant children had higher expectations for their children's grades, and were less satisfied with the grades their children obtained than were the European American parents.

Contrary to the preceding findings, one study by Lin and Fu (1990) found that immigrant Chinese American parenting values and behaviors may be changing. The researchers demonstrated that Chinese American and European American parents of kindergarten and grade school children were equally open to expressing their affection. Although the study showed that ethnic parents indeed had higher ratings on parental control and emphasis on achievement, these parents actually scored higher on encouragement of independence than the European American parents. The authors believed that these results suggest a gradual change among immigrant parents due to acculturation. By adjusting and accommodating to the values and child-rearing practices of the United States, they are facilitating the bicultural socialization of their children, and in effect preparing them to function as effective adults in both the ethnic and mainstream societies.

Parenting practices can have significant impact on the behaviors and temperament of children, even in the very early stages of life. Although few studies demonstrating behavioral and emotional differences between Chinese American and European American infants have attributed these differences to genetic factors (Freeman & Freeman, 1969), most researchers have focused on cultural variations in child rearing and familial experiences. For example, Kagan, Kearsley, and Zelazo (1978) found that Chinese American infants vocalized less, were less likely to smile at external stimuli, and demonstrated more social restraint and inhibition than European American babies. It was hypothesized that Chinese American parents, unlike European American parents, were less likely to reinforce verbal and affective displays by their children. Given the Asian value of social restraint, children raised in such an environment quickly learn that emotional and verbal assertiveness have to be curbed. This study highlights the importance of environmental variables on behavior and temperament, but it is quite possible that both genetic and cultural factors are implicated.

Because many Chinese parents tend to discourage independence and assertive behaviors under any circumstances, Chinese American children are often seen as shy, quiet, or docile. These behaviors can sometimes be misinterpreted by non-Chinese observers, such as classroom teachers, as problems of social isolation, withdrawal, lack of effort, or inattention. Even when a Chinese American child knows the answer to the teacher's question, he or she may not volunteer to respond, choosing instead to sit quietly as though lost. On the other hand, Chinese American parents may perceive any extroverted and independent behavior as problematic and abnormal. A child merely stating his or her opinion is seen by a Chinese parent as talking back, a gesture of disobedience. Consequently, Chinese American children are often less verbal and expressive toward adults in all social settings. A well-behaved child, as defined by many Chinese parents, will actually miss out on many of the social and academic opportunities available to students in American classrooms (Yao, 1985b).

By overemphasizing academic achievement, Chinese American parents may be neglecting other aspects of their child's development. High academic achievement can be misinterpreted by parents as indicating good psychological health. Good grades may give parents the impression that their child does not suffer from any emotional, behavioral, or social problems. This is unfortunate because many Chinese American parents will not even think to seek professional help for their child unless there is evidence of academic decline. The lack of empirical research on the development of Chinese American children and the bicultural nature of Chinese American families make it difficult to draw strong conclusions about what is normal behavior for this group.

Developmental Issues

Although most Chinese American children are socialized by their parents according to the Confucian tradition, they are also exposed to American culture and its values and norms. As a result of these multiple forces of influence, Chinese American children are faced with unique developmental concerns, including intergeneration cultural conflicts, identity formation, and membership in a minority group.

INTERGENERATION CULTURAL CONFLICTS

Given that most Chinese American parents were born in Asian and have been raised with different societal norms and expectations than their bicultural children, many of the problems experienced by Chinese American children and their families arise in the context of this intergeneration cultural gap. Oftentimes, family conflicts occur over divergent views on culturally relevant issues such as academic achievement, appropriate social behavior, parental respect, and familial obligation (Sung, 1985). Interestingly, Lee (1982) observed that in Chinese American families, the oldest son and youngest daughter tend to have the highest rates of psychopathology compared with their siblings. This may be due to the cultural expectations that the oldest son will provide his parents with emotional and financial support in their old age, as well as assume the responsibility for the educational and character development of his younger siblings. Without the guidance of an older sibling, the oldest brother must pave the way for other children in the family. However, the family member most vulnerable to cultural conflicts and arguments is perhaps the youngest daughter because the intergeneration cultural gap is the most pronounced between her and the parents. In addition, the youngest daughter is often left with the day-to-day caretaking of the parents as her older siblings leave home. She also has to endure the constant unequal treatment she receives compared with her brothers.

Cultural and language demands placed on Chinese American children at home have been shown to be associated with mental health problems. Ou and McAdoo (1993) discovered that the levels of self-concept and anxiety among American-born Chinese children were related to their immigrant parents' cultural attitudes. For fifth- and sixth-grade boys, the more Chinese that was spoken at home, the higher the boys' anxiety level. The parents' positive attitudes toward Chinese culture were negatively associated with the boys' self-concept. It appears that the culture clash many Chinese American children encounter at home can be highly stressful.

There is evidence suggesting that cultural restraints against aggression and acting-out behaviors are eroding among subsequent generations of Chinese Americans. Research is showing increasing rates of more aggressive juvenile offenses, such as assault and robbery, committed by Chinese American youths (D. W. Sue & Sue, 1990). As Chinese American children become more acculturated, their sense of familial obligation diminishes, parental authority deteriorates, and parental disciplinary actions become less effective. For many working-class families, both parents work outside the home and have little time to supervise their children. It is not uncommon for parents to call on older siblings, grandmothers, other relatives, and neighbors to provide child care. All of these experiences and cultural demands reveal the complexities that Chinese American children encounter in their growth and development.

IDENTITY FORMATION

During adolescence, the critical task facing an individual involves achieving a healthy sense of continuity and identity that will provide a solid foundation for one's adulthood. For Chinese American adolescents, the issue of identity formation is complicated by their position between two cultures seemingly polarized on the issue of independence versus affiliation. In the Chinese culture, one's sense of identity and belonging is provided within the rigid boundaries of the family. A person's accomplishments, aspirations, roles, and other measures of identity are viewed within the context of the family (L. Huang, 1994). Some Asian American adolescents explain their drive to excel in life in terms of the shame that will befall their family if they fail and the glory they will bring to the family if they succeed (Liu, Yu, Chang, & Fernandez, 1990). European American culture, on the other hand, would more likely expect self-exploration and self-differentiation away from one's parents and family during adolescence. The search for an identity outside the family is encouraged. Therefore, in forging a strong bicultural identity, Chinese American adolescents must learn to successfully negotiate their desire to affiliate and be independent by maintaining their ties with both the Chinese and European American cultures (L. Huang, 1994).

   Having an integrated bicultural identity, where a person simultaneously enters into both the ethnic and the mainstream culture, seems to generate less stress for Asian American adolescents than if they withdraw form the dominant group (Berry, Kim, Minde, & Mok, 1987; Lang, Munoz, Bernal, & Sorensen, 1982). Research findings show that lacking a sense of belonging to either culture can lead to feelings of hopelessness, low self-esteem, and more severe conditions such as depression and suicide (Phinney, Lochner, & Murphy, 1990).

Our discussion thus far has primarily involved cultural influences on values, beliefs, practices, socialization, and conflicts. In addition to these influences, it is also important to consider Chinese Americans in the context of their status as members of a minority group in the United States. Whereas a cultural perspective makes comparisons between Chinese and American cultures, a minority status perspective is concerned with race (or ethnic) relations and the effects of such relationships on the well-being of individuals. It is minority status that distinguishes cross-cultural research, in which different cultural groups are examined, from ethnic minority research, in which cultural differences *and* ethnic relations are critical to consider.

In American society, minority group status has often been associated with stress because of negative experiences such as prejudice, discrimination, and diminished access to resources in society (Moritsugu & Sue, 1983). It has been suggested that racism may lead to feelings of noncontrol, or external locus of control. Ultimately the minority individual may feel a tremendous sense of helplessness and experience severe distress (S. Sue & Chin, 1983). Little in the way of empirical literature has documented the effects of minority group status on Chinese American children and adolescents, but there appears to be little question about the increased stress faced by minority groups.

Mental Health Issues

In the preceding sections, an attempt was made to provide an overview of Chinese Americans and some of the problems and issues confronting Chinese American youths. Socialization, cultural conflicts, identity formation, and minority group status are associated with the well-being of Chinese Americans. Some youths emerge with a strong sense of identity, positive self-esteem, and high achievement levels. Others are less fortunate and may develop emotional and behavioral problems.

RATES OF PSYCHOPATHOLOGY

Estimates of the prevalence of mental disorders are difficult to make for Chinese Americans in general and Chinese American children in particular. Kim and Chun (1993) used data gathered from the Los Angeles County Department of Mental Health in their investigation of the distribution of psychiatric diagnosis among Asian American and European American adolescents. They found ethnic differences in the rates and types of diagnosis, and this difference was more dramatic among the females than males. Diagnostic differences were most pronounced in nonpsychiatric disorders; Asian Americans demonstrated higher rates in academic and personal problems, malingering, and bereavement. Asian American females suffered more affective-oriented disorders than European American females, who were more likely to have behavioral problems. The investigators speculated that this diagnostic asymmetry may be related to Asian cultural norms and values of having high academic achievement expectations and high behavioral restraint.

For the Chinese and Japanese American samples, adjustment disorder was frequently diagnosed in both males and females. The category of "other adolescent disorders," which include oppositional, eating, and identity disorders, was the second most common diagnosis among Chinese American males. Among Chinese American females, nonpsychiatric disorder was the second most frequent diagnosis. The Chinese Americans appeared more similar to the Japanese Americans, compared with the Koreans and Vietnamese Americans, in the percentage of people represented in each diagnostic category. The investigators attributed this finding to acculturation and migrational stress; the Chinese and Japanese Americans both experienced a longer stay in the United States than the more recent immigrants from Korea and Vietnam.

Numerous studies have investigated symptoms of mental disorders in Chinese American children using Achenbach's Child

Behavior Checklist (CBCL). In a study by Touliatos and Lindholm (1980), teachers of children in kindergarten through the
eighth grade filled out the CBCL and reported that their Chinese American pupils exhibited fewer symptoms, including externalizing and internalizing broad-band symptoms, than
their European American students. However, the authors cautioned that the teachers' stereotyped attitudes toward the Chinese American students may have biased their responses.
Reports using the Chinese version of the CBCL have yielded
similar results regarding fewer symptoms (Chang, Morrissey,
& Koplewicz, 1995; Li, Su, Townes, & Varley, 1989). These findings may be due to Chinese children actually exhibiting fewer
symptoms, and/or parents underreporting symptoms due to
stigma and shame. Chang et al. (1995) also reported lower
scores on the Aggressive Behavior, Total Competence, Activities, and Social scales among Chinese Americans. This may reflect the Chinese American family's emphasis on self-control,
respect, and obedience, and lack of emphasis on extracurricular and non-school-related social activities.

Spring, Blunden, Greenberg, and Yellin (1977) compared
teacher ratings of European American and Asian American
children in kindergarten through fourth grade on the Hyperactivity Rating Scale (HRS). The HRS measures 11 categories of
behaviors: restlessness, distractibility, work fluctuation, impul-
sivity, excitability, low perseverance, negativism, poor coordination, fatigue, rapid tempo, and social withdrawal. Compared
with the norms established by non-hyperactive European American children, the Asian Americans scored higher in the direction of desirable school behaviors. Again, these findings are
difficult to interpret because Asian American norms for hyperactivity do not exist and teachers may have been biased in rating the behaviors of Asian American children.

Another telling measure of distress for the youth population is rate of suicide. Yu, Chang, Liu, and Fernandez (1989) examined suicide rates among Chinese American adolescents and
young adults. They found that suicide accounted for a larger proportion of deaths for 15- to 24-year olds in the Chinese American
community (16.8%) than the European American community

(11.9%). For the latter group, accident, illness, and murder were more prominent. In addition, foreign-born Chinese Americans had higher suicide rates than American-born Chinese Americans, which suggests that the process of acculturation for immigrant children and adolescents can be fatally stressful. Although these studies do not permit us to draw firm conclusions about the state of mental health among Chinese American youths, there is evidence that significant mental health problems exist among Chinese Americans and that ethnic differences in symptom patterns are present. However, given the existing data, it is unclear whether rates of psychopathology are similar to or different from those of other Americans.

UNDERUTILIZATION

Compared with European Americans, Asian American children and adolescents underutilize community mental health centers (Bui & Takeuchi, 1992); that is, they do not use mental health services as frequently as would be expected based on the size of their populations. However, judging the rate of psychopathology by the rate of service-seeking can be misleading because Chinese Americans may not be going to therapy even when they have mental health problems. Beginning with Sue and McKinney (1975), experts in the field have identified numerous cultural factors and structural barriers explaining why Asian Americans are underrepresented in mental health services. These factors and barriers would also pertain to Chinese American children and their families.

Cultural inhibition is a major barrier to using mental health services by Asian American families. Many Asians believe that having a psychological problem is shameful and disgraceful (Kitano, 1970; T. Tung, 1985). The less acculturated Chinese Americans tend to feel more stigmatized than their more acculturated counterparts (Atkinson & Gim, 1989). Many Asians are afraid that seeking outside help for themselves or their children will cause their family to feel ashamed and lose honor (Lin & Lin, 1978). Asian Americans are more likely to approach family members, friends, and the church for support rather than seeking out a mental health professional (Chin, 1982). Tracey, Leong, and Glidden (1986) surveyed Asian American college students and discovered that they used campus vocational and academic counseling centers at a disproportionally higher rate and psychiatric services at a disproportionally lower rate given their percentage of the student body. For the Asian American students, talking about academics may have been a less threatening and less shameful way of opening the discussion to more personal issues.

Asian Americans tend to express their psychological problems in the form of psychosomatic symptoms (Owan, 1985), and tend to identify mental health problems as caused by organic (Sue, Wagner, Ja, Margullis, & Lew, 1976) and intrapsychic factors (Wong, 1985). As a result of these preconceptions, Chinese American parents may be more likely to seek treatment from physicians, acupuncturists, herbalists, or spiritualists for their children's problems.

Language barriers also contribute to the pattern of underutilization by Asian American families and children. Many non-English speakers are afraid to seek services from people who do not understand their native Asian language (Shu & Satele, 1977). The language barrier also frustrates therapists (Larsen, 1979), which may lead to ineffectual therapy and potentially harmful outcomes.

In addition, structural barriers to service utilization exist within the current mental health system (Uba, 1994). Asian Americans, including Chinese Americans, receive little information on available mental health resources. It is rare to see large-scale, culturally appropriate mental health outreach programs targeting the Asian American community. Other structural barriers exist as well. Lower class recent immigrants may lack financial resources and health care insurance to obtain adequate mental health services. Existing mental health facilities may be neither highly visible nor accessible to those living in Chinese American enclaves. Last, there is a significant shortage of bilingual and bicultural personnel who are trained to provide culturally sensitive mental health services to Chinese American children and their families.

SEVERITY

Asian Americans who use mental health services have been found to be more severely disturbed than their European American counterparts. One study of Asian and non-Asian Americans at a campus psychiatric clinic compared the two groups' responses to the Minnesota Multiphasic Personality Inventory (MMPI), which assessed levels of psychopathology along several dimensions. Overall, the Asian American students were judged to be more severely disturbed than the non-Asian Americans (S. Sue & Sue, 1974). Brown, Stein, Huang, and Harris (1973) found that Chinese inpatients were more psychologically disturbed than the European American control group. A study of the Los Angeles County Mental Health System has also revealed that Asian Americans who use mental health services are among the most disturbed clients of any ethnic group (Durvasula & Sue, 1996). These findings suggest that it may take more severe levels of psychological disturbances before Asian American parents will seek mental health treatment for themselves and their children.

DIAGNOSTIC AND ASSESSMENT ISSUES

Determining the well-being or the rates of mental disorders among Chinese Americans has been problematic because many difficulties exist in assessment and diagnosis. Defining abnormal behaviors and cognitions is difficult because different cultures have different criteria for what is considered to be pathological. Therapists must be cautioned against overpathologizing culturally sanctioned behavior as indicative of mental illness, and also against underpathologizing by attributing psychiatric symptoms to cultural differences rather than to an actual mental disorder (K. Lin, 1990).

Another assessment and diagnostic concern involves the expression of psychological problems. Asian Americans differ from European Americans in the clusters of symptoms, complaints, and emotions that tend to form syndromes (Marsella, Kinzie, & Gordon, 1973). Chinese Americans who were administered the MMPI reported more somatic complaints than

European Americans, regardless of the severity of their mental disturbance (S. Sue & Sue, 1974). Little is known about the patterns of symptom expression for Asian American children and adolescents. Caution should be exercised when diagnosing members of this population according to the listed symptoms of the *Diagnostic and Statistical Manual of Mental Disorders* (*DSM-IV*; APA, 1994), which is the main diagnostic guide for mental health professionals. Since *DSM-IV* criteria were derived primarily from research and treatment on non-Asian Americans, they may not be as useful for diagnosing Chinese Americans as for members of the mainstream culture.

Language barriers may also impede accurate assessment of psychopathology in Chinese American youths. Chinese American immigrant children and their parents may be unable to express their concerns and emotions in English, leading to distortions in the expression and description of relevant symptomatology. Research has shown that the manifestation of distress and the symptoms of psychopathology may be either reduced or enhanced in a second language (Del Castillo, 1970; Marcos, Alpert, Urcuyo, & Kesselman, 1973). Using lay interpreters or family members may actually pose additional problems. Distortions may arise from the translator's lack of fluency in both languages and ignorance of clinical symptoms. They may be prone to minimize or exaggerate psychopathology (Marcos, 1975). Translators may sometimes miss subtle nuances in what is said between the client and therapist (Wong, 1985). They might end up offering their own opinions to the client rather than translating the therapist's questions verbatim (C. Ho, 1990).

To compensate for their own feelings of discomfort with what is disclosed in therapy, translators may decide to change the comments of the client or the questions of the therapist (Kinzie, 1989). For example, a Chinese American mother may decide to shield her child from the therapist's intrusive questions (e.g., sexual abuse, drug use) by distorting the question for the sake of the child. If certain aspects of family functioning need to be assessed, the therapist should avoid using the child patient as the translator for other family members. First, by giving the child the responsibility of speaking for the family, the family's social hierarchy of authority is disrupted. Second, the parents may be hesitant to disclose any marital problems and feelings of dissatisfaction because they would lose face in front of their child (Lee, 1982).

Inadequate knowledge of the behavioral norms exhibited within the Chinese culture, and the values and beliefs on which these behaviors are based, will inevitably result in biased assessments. It is not uncommon for Chinese American children to make self-deprecating remarks and downplay school achievements, and for Chinese American parents to exaggerate the faults of their children and withhold praise for their achievements. This kind of behavior reflects the Chinese traditional value of modesty and humility, rather than the communicator's actual assessment of their own or their children's self-worth. A therapist unfamiliar with this mode of communication may form the wrong impression and diagnose the child as having low self-esteem or the parents as being overly critical (T. Tung, 1985). Chinese Americans also tend to understate their emotions and imply that their distress is milder than it actually is, which can lead to misdiagnosis. Li-Repac (1980) conducted a study comparing the diagnostic abilities of European American and Chinese American therapists when the target patient is Chinese. The researcher found that the European American therapists, who were less aware of Asian communication patterns, consistently diagnosed the Chinese Americans as being more depressed, inhibited, less socially poised, and having poorer interpersonal skills than the Chinese American therapists assessed these patients as being.

The issue of biased assessment of Chinese American children and adolescents is compounded by the lack of validated instruments for this population. Most of the existing tests and inventories for children were developed through gathering normative data on European American samples. Therefore, comparing Chinese Americans' responses to European American norms on these psychological instruments would likely skew the diagnoses of psychopathology. There is a severe lack of normative data for Asian American children for even the most frequently used psychological tests, even though evidence suggests that the responses/rating of Asian American and European American children are quite dissimilar (Chang et al., 1995; Spring et al., 1977). In addition, existing assessment tools for examining family functioning may not be appropriate for Asian American families. Morris (1990) discovered that as a result of responding to the Family Assessment Device (FAD) according to their cultural values, Asian Americans were seen as more pathological. Behaviors that are typical for Asian American families (e.g., constricted range of affect, authoritarian parental control) were misinterpreted as unhealthy according to the FAD.

Recommendations

Without question, Chinese American youth experience conflict and psychological distress. However, when it comes to evaluating and treating this population, problems and inadequacies continue to exist in the mental health system. The following section offers some recommendations for improving assessment methodology and for providing culturally responsive treatment to Chinese American children and adolescents.

ASSESSMENT METHODOLOGY

To capture the total picture of a Chinese American youth and to accurately interpret the information, assessment should include gathering multiple sources of data within an ecological framework (L. Huang, 1994; Huang & Ying, 1989). Information should be collected on several systems: the individual, the family, the school, and the peer group. In the individual system, it is necessary to determine age, level of acculturation, immigration history, range of affective expression, anxiety and defenses, quality of interpersonal relationships, attitudes toward self and physical appearance, and degree of bilingualism. Information about the family system should cover roles, communication and affective patterns, culture clashes, attitudes about mental health, help-seeking patterns, support networks within the ethnic community, and socioeconomic status. In assessing the child's school system, it is important to address the racial/ethnic composition of the school, attitudes of the teacher, degree of parental involvement, and any differences between the school and the family's expectations for the child. To understand the peer system, the assessor needs to inquire about its ethnic and gender composition, accepted values and behaviors, and the nature and degree of the child's involvement with the group. In addition to investigating these systems, a better understanding of the child's environment can be gained by examining the impact of broader societal issues such as racism, stereotyping, and violence against minorities.

S. Sue (1991) offered several important clinical guidelines for therapists to follow when assessing ethnic clients, including the use of multiple measures or multimethod procedures to see whether tests provide convergent results, the enlisting of consultants who are familiar with the client's background and culture, and the use of test findings as hypotheses for further testing rather than conclusive evidence when the validity of the tests for ethnic populations is in question.

PSYCHOTHERAPY TREATMENT

Many forms of therapy have been reported to be effective for Asian Americans, including psychopharmacological, behavioral, and insight-oriented treatments (M. Ho, 1984; Matsuoka, 1990; M. Tung, 1991). A survey of Asian American therapists revealed that their ethnic clients' somatic problems were most often treated with pharmacotherapy while adjustment problems such as work, school, and acculturation distress, were most often treated with cognitive-behavioral methods. Psychodynamic and other techniques emphasizing self-exploration were used most often in dealing with intrapsychic problems such as identity, self-concept, relationship concerns, and depression (Matsushima & Tashima, 1982). Regardless of orientation, successful treatment adherence and outcome will depend on whether or not the therapist takes into account family structures, culturally based values and expectations, modes of communication, and language match when treating Chinese American youths and their families.

In traditional Chinese families, the father has formal power but the mother has the most influence over her children and the household. She is in charge of making day-to-day decisions for her children. Therapists need to be aware, however, of potential tensions arising from disrupting the family's power hierarchy by deferring only to the mother as the decision-maker. Decisions to be made regarding treatment for a child may actually involve several family members. It is not unusual for parents to ask the advice of their extended family or members of the ethnic community who are more familiar with the mental health system.

Mental health professionals conducting psychotherapy with Chinese Americans, especially those who are less acculturated, need to take cultural values and expectations about treatment into consideration. Chinese Americans with a tradition background will tend to be more familiar with the medical model of treatment. They tend to expect rapid diagnosis, without the need for intrusive questioning (Huang, 1991) and relatively brief interventions (Lin & Shen, 1991). They also expect the therapist, the expert authority, to do most of the talking (Sue & Morishima, 1982). It is not necessarily desirable for them to have an egalitarian relationship with their therapist (Sue & Zane, 1987). Asian Americans are high self-monitors who look for cues about how to behave from their environment and then act accordingly (K. Huang, 1991). They may feel quite anxious when the therapist is silent and expects them to initiate communication. Being nondirective and nonjudgmental might be interpreted as signs of disinterest or incompetence (Lee, 1982; Yamamoto & Acosta, 1982). Unstructured therapy can be uncomfortable, anxiety-provoking, and confusing for those brought up in the traditional Chinese family where roles are highly structured and patterns of behavior are rigid and predictable. In fact, Asian Americans have reported a preference for therapeutic techniques that are directive, structured, and unambiguous because these approaches are more consonant with their values, expectations, and interaction styles (D. W. Sue, 1990).

Asian Americans value preserving interpersonal harmony in social situations and they tend to avoid interpersonal confrontations (Uba, 1994). Compared with European Americans, Asian Americans are more likely to employ nonverbal and indirect means of communication, understate their emotions, and shy away from expressing negative emotions such as anger and depression. If these emotions are expressed at all, it is usually done in a muted or indirect manner (T. Tung, 1985). In therapy, Asian Americans may never openly disagree with the therapist nor disclose that they are confused or dissatisfied with therapy (Lee, 1982; Root, 1989). Clients may find it frustrating and view the therapist as ineffective or insensitive if he or she fails to pick up the subtle cues and nuances they supply (Morrow, 1987).

Many non-English-speaking Asian Americans are afraid to seek services from those who do not speak the same language (Shu & Satele, 1977). For Asian American adults, research has shown that when the therapist and client speak the same language, the client experiences better outcomes. The client will attend more therapy sessions, is less likely to drop out of treatment, reports feeling more rapport with the therapist, and believes that the therapist is more effective and more empathetic (Flaskerud, 1986; Flaskerud & Liu, 1990, 1991; Leong, 1986). Sue, Fujino, Hu, and Takeuchi (1991) found that for non-English-speaking Asian American adult clients, language and ethnicity match between the client and the therapist was positively associated with length of treatment and better treatment outcomes.

Although these findings were based on adults, the benefits of language and ethnicity match may also apply to children and adolescents. A study conducted by Yeh, Takeuchi, and Sue (1994) examined the efficacy of ethnic-specific community mental health centers for Asian American children. Unlike mainstream clinics, these centers were established for the purpose of servicing ethnic populations, were located in close proximity to ethnic communities, and employed a high percentage of bilingual ethnic staff. The researchers found that Asian American children receiving mental health services at these ethnic-specific centers were less likely to drop out after the initial session, utilized more services, and had higher functioning scores at discharge than did those attending mainstream clinics, even when relevant variables were controlled.

CULTURALLY RESPONSIVE THERAPY

The study by Yeh et al. (1994) provides evidence that to improve treatment outcomes for Asian American children, it is important to establish ethnically oriented facilities with staff diversity. Other experts in cross-cultural mental health have proposed guidelines for therapists on how to conduct culturally responsive therapy with Asian Americans.

Matsushima and Tashima (1982) surveyed Asian American therapists who treated Asian Americans and asked them to identify areas of knowledge they considered to be the most important in helping their clients. The therapists emphasized being aware of Asian American cultural values and understanding the specific problems facing Asian Americans. The most important cultural values the therapists reported are (in descending order of importance):

1. Primacy of family.
2. Shame and guilt.
3. Respect for people based on their status and roles.
4. Styles of interpersonal behavior.
5. Stigma associated with mental illness.
6. Restraint of self-expression.
7. Orientation toward group.
8. Achievement.
9. Sense of duty and obligation.
10. Expectations that follow from different roles.

The most prevalent ethnic-specific problems they mentioned are:

1. Immigration experiences.
2. Cultural conflicts in lifestyle and values.
3. Family issues.
4. Racism.
5. Conceptualizations of mental health and attitudes toward mental health services.
6. Behavioral styles and norms.

7. Language.
8. Ethnic identity.
9. Intergenerational problems.

Gaining knowledge and awareness of these values and problems is critical for therapists working with Asian American clients.

Kim (1985) recommended using a strategic-structural family therapy approach for treating Asian American children and their families. This approach is directive, structured, and focuses on external stressors rather than internal conflicts. It emphasizes problem-solving techniques and active problem management rather than process-oriented discussions. It offers concrete, tangible external resolutions rather than internal ones. This type of therapy is more compatible with Asian worldviews and may prove to be highly effective with Asian American families.

The structural component involves the therapist allying with those having power within the family to bring about change in the system. The therapist should start therapy by engaging those higher in the power hierarchy to deflect any confusion, resistance, and shame from family members. It would be in the therapist's best interest to establish him- or herself as an authority, and to not be afraid of using phrases such as "in my professional judgment . . . ." As much information as possible about the family should be gathered ahead of time so the therapist can offer some plausible explanations, even tentative ones, for the "cause" of the family's problems. At the same time, however, it should be made clear to the family that the right solution for them will only be evident after taking the time to carefully assess the extent of the problem.

The first session in a course of therapy is often taken up by questions, and little time is left for actually doing therapy. This may be discouraging for some Asian American families because they may think that subsequent sessions will be the same. Kim suggested that the first session should not be based on time but on some clinically meaningful phenomena, such as successfully instilling hope, or conveying a sense of understanding and faith in improvements. Sue and Zane (1987) advocated "gift-giving" when working with Asian Americans to prevent early dropout from therapy and to reinforce the therapist's credibility. A gift is an immediate and tangible benefit from treatment. They believe that experiencing the following benefits will improve the chances that Asian American clients stay in treatment:

1. Anxiety reduction.
2. Depression relief.
3. Cognitive clarity.
4. Normalization.
5. Reassurance.
6. Hope and faith.
7. Skills acquisition.
8. Coping perspective.
9. Goal setting.

As therapy progresses, the therapist should help the family identify concrete short-term goals, such as relieving symptoms, and then gradually introduce long-term goals. These should consist of a series of visible, achievable, and interrelated short-term goals that are renegotiable within the family.

The strategic component within this framework involves engaging the family in identifying conflicts, emphasizing that each person can contribute to the process as an agent of change, and taking on a nonblaming attitude to prevent anyone in the family from losing face. The therapist must be sensitive about not rushing the family to disclose. The right timing is important, and premature proving can be seen as extremely threatening. The therapist may even consider directing individuals to withhold information until the family is mentally prepared to deal with it.

Conclusion

The goal of this chapter was to address some of the mental health issues facing Chinese American youths, and the ways in which service providers can better accommodate the needs of this population. It was noted that traditional parenting practices may facilitate particular sets of behaviors and attitudes among Chinese American children, such as emotional restraint, impulse control, and the desire for academic achievement. There is some evidence, however, that parenting values in Chinese American families are gradually changing, and parents are teaching their children both traditional and American values that will enable them to become more effective adults in both cultures. Because most Chinese American parents are immigrants and their children are growing up with bicultural influences, intergeneration cultural conflicts and identity formation pose special problems for Chinese American youths. An individual must strike a comfortable balance between the desire for independence and the desire to maintain ties with one's family and cultural heritage. Society's racial attitudes and behaviors toward minorities is another relevant area of concern affecting the well-being of this population. Asian Americans tend to underutilize mental health services and those who end up seeking treatment tend to be more severely disturbed. Some studies show that differences exist in the distribution of mental health disorders between Chinese American and European American children; however, it is difficult to make firm conclusions based on the available research. The accurate assessment of Asian American children and their families is often a challenge for clinicians because of complicating factors such as differential ideas about what is normal behavior across cultures, language barriers, and the lack of validated assessment tools for Asian American children.

Recommendations for improving assessment procedures and mental health treatment include soliciting multiple sources of information when making a diagnosis, and conducting culturally responsive therapy based on techniques that are consonant with the values and beliefs of the ethnic client. Undoubtedly, more empirical research on the psychological functioning and rates of psychopathology of Chinese American children and their families will enhance the mental health community's knowledge and understanding of this population and, in turn, promote the development of culturally sensitive assessment tools and treatments for this group.

References

AMERICAN PSYCHIATRIC ASSOCIATION. (1994). *Diagnostic and statistical manual of mental disorders (4th ed.).* Washington, DC: Author.

ATKINSON, D., & GIM, R. (1989). Asian American cultural identity and attitudes toward mental health services. *Journal of Counseling Psychology, 36*(2), 209–212.

BERRY, J., KIM, U., MINDE, T., & MOK, D. (1987). Comparative studies of acculturative stress. *International Migration Review, 21,* 491–511.

BOND, M. H., & WANG, S. (1983). China: Aggressive behavior and the problems of maintaining order and harmony. In A. P. Goldstein & M. H. Segall (Eds.), *Aggression in global perspective* (pp. 58–74). New York: Pergamon Press.

BROWN, T. R., STEIN, K. M., HUANG, K., & HARRIS, D. E. (1973). Mental illness and the role of mental health facilities in Chinatown. In S. Sue & N. Wagner (Eds.), *Asian-Americans: Psychological perspectives* (pp. 212–231). Palo Alto, CA: Science and Behavior Books.

BUI, K. V. T., & TAKEUCHI, D. T. (1992). Ethnic minority adolescents and the use of the community mental health care system. *American Journal of Community Psychology, 20,* 403–417.

CHANG, L., MORRISSEY, R. F., & KOPLEWICZ, H. S. (1995). Prevalence of psychiatric symptoms and their relation to adjustment among Chinese-American youth. *Journal of the American Academy of Child and Adolescent Psychiatry, 34*(1), 91–99.

CHAO, P. (1983). *Chinese kinship.* London: Routledge & Kegan Paul.

CHIN, R. (1982). Conceptual paradigm for a racial-ethnic community: The case of the Chinese American community. In S. Sue & T. Moore (Eds.), *The pluralistic society: A community mental health perspective* (pp. 222–236). New York: Human Sciences Press.

DEL CASTILLO, J. C. (1970). The influence of language upon symptomatology in foreign-born patients. *American Journal of Psychiatry, 127,* 242–244.

DURVASULA, R., & SUE, S. (1996). Severity of disturbance among Asian American outpatients. *Cultural Diversity and Mental Health, 2,* 43–52.

FILLMORE, L. W. (1991). When learning a second language means losing the first. *Early Childhood Research Quarterly, 6,* 323–346.

FLASKERUD, J. (1986). The effects of cultural-compatible intervention on the utilization of mental health services by minority clients. *Community Mental Health Journal, 22*(2), 127–141.

FLASKERUD, J., & LIU, P. Y. (1990). Influence of therapist ethnicity and language on therapy outcomes of Southeast Asian clients. *International Journal of Social Psychiatry, 36,* 18–29.

FLASKERUD, J., & LIU, P. Y. (1991). Effects of an Asian client-therapist language, ethnicity and gender match on client outcomes. *Community Mental Health Journal, 27*, 31–42.

FREEMAN, D. G., & FREEMAN, N. C. (1969). Behavioural differences between Chinese-American and European-American newborns. *Nature, 224*, 1227.

HO, C. (1990). An analysis of domestic violence in Asian American communities: A multicultural approach to counseling. *Women and Therapy, 9*, 129–150.

HO, D. Y. F. (1981). Traditional patterns of socialization in Chinese society. *Acta Psychologica Taiwanica, 23*, 81–95.

HO, D. Y. F. (1994). Cognitive socialization in Confucian heritage cultures. In P. M. Greenfield & R. R. Cocking (Eds.), *Cross-cultural roots of minority child development* (pp. 285–313). Hillsdale, NJ: Erlbaum.

HO, M. K. (1984). Social group work with Asian/Pacific-Americans. *Ethnicity in Group Work Practice, 7*, 49–61.

HSU, F. L. K. (1981). *Americans and Chinese: Passages to differences.* Honolulu: University of Hawaii Press.

HUANG, K. (1991). Chinese Americans. In N. Mokuau (Ed.), *Handbook of social services for Asian and Pacific Islanders* (pp. 79–96). New York: Greenwood Press.

HUANG, L. N. (1994). An integrative approach to clinical assessment and intervention with Asian-American adolescents. *Journal of Clinical Child Psychology, 23*(1), 21–31.

HUANG, L. N., & YING, Y. W. (1989). Chinese American children and adolescents. In J. T. Gibbs, L. N. Huang, & Associates (Eds.), *Children of color: Psychological interventions with minority children* (pp. 30–66). San Francisco: Jossey-Bass.

KAGAN, J., KEARSLEY, R. B., & ZELAZO, P. R. (1978). *Infancy: Its place in human development.* Cambridge, MA: Harvard University Press.

KIM, L. S., & CHUN, C. A. (1993). Ethnic differences in psychiatric diagnosis among Asian American adolescents. *Journal of Nervous and Mental Disease, 181*(10), 612–617.

KIM, S. C. (1985). Family therapy for Asian Americans: A strategic-structural framework. *Psychotherapy, 22*(2), 342–348.

KING, A. Y. C., & BOND, M. H. (1985). The Confucian paradigm of man: A sociological view. In W. Tseng & D. Y. H. Wu (Eds.), *Chinese culture and mental health* (pp. 29–46). Orlando, FL: Academic Press.

KINZIE, D. (1989). Therapeutic approaches to traumatized Cambodian refugees. *Journal of Traumatic Stress, 2*, 75–91.

KITANO, H. (1970). Mental illness in four cultures. *Journal of Social Psychology, 80,* 121–134.

LANG, J. G., MUNOZ, R. F., BERNAL, G., & SORENSEN, J. L. (1982). Quality of life and psychological well-being in a bicultural Latino community. *Hispanic Journal of Behavioral Sciences, 4*(4), 433–450.

LARSEN, J. K. (1979). Innovations. *American Institutes for Research, 6*(2).

LEE, E. (1982). A social systems approach to assessment and treatment for Chinese-American families. In M. McGoldrick, J. K. Pearce, & J. Giordano (Eds.), *Ethnicity and family therapy* (pp. 527–551). New York: Guilford Press.

LEONG, F. (1986). Counseling and psychotherapy with Asian-Americans: Review of the literature. *Journal of Counseling Psychology, 33,* 196–206.

LI, X. R., SU, L. Y., TOWNES, B. D., & VARLEY, C. K. (1989). Diagnosis of attention deficit disorder with hyperactivity in Chinese boys. *Journal of the American Academy of Child and Adolescent Psychiatry, 4,* 497–500.

LIN, C. Y. C., & FU, V. R. (1990). A comparison of child-rearing practice among Chinese, immigrant Chinese, and Caucasian-American parents. *Child Development, 61,* 429–433.

LIN, K. M. (1990). Assessment and diagnostic issues in the psychiatric care of refugee patients. In W. Holtzman & T. Bornemann (Eds.), *Mental health of immigrants and refugees* (pp. 198–206). Austin, TX: Hogg Foundation for Mental Health.

LIN, K. M., & SHEN, W. (1991). Pharmacotherapy for Southeast Asian psychiatric patients. *Journal of Nervous and Mental Disease, 179,* 346–350.

LIN, T. J., & LIN, M. C. (1978). Service delivery issues in Asian-North American communities. *American Journal of Psychiatry, 135,* 454–456.

LI-REPAC, D. (1980). Cultural influences on clinical perception: A comparison between Caucasian and Chinese-American therapists. *Journal of Cross-Cultural Psychology, 11,* 327–342.

LIU, W. T., YU, E. S., CHANG, C. F., & FERNANDEZ, M. (1990). The mental health of Asian American teenagers: A research challenge. In A. R. Stiffman & L. E. Davis (Eds.), *Ethnic issues in adolescent mental health* (pp. 92–112). Newbury Park, CA: Sage.

LUM, K., & CHAR, W. F. (1985). Chinese adaptation in Hawaii: Some examples. In W. Tseng & D. Y. H. Wu (Eds.), *Chinese culture and mental health* (pp. 215–226). Orlando, FL: Academic Press.

MARCOS, L. R. (1975). Effects of interpreters on the evaluation of psycho-pathology in non-English-speaking patients. *American Journal of Psychiatry, 136,* 171–174.

MARCOS, L. R., ALPERT, M., URCUYO, L., & KESSELMAN, M. (1973). The effect of interview language on the evaluation of psychopathology in Spanish-American schizophrenic patients. *American Journal of Psychiatry, 130,* 549–553.

MARSELLA, A., KINZIE, D., & GORDON, P. (1973). Ethnic variations in the expression of depression. *Journal of Cross-Cultural Psychology, 4,* 435–458.

MATSUOKA, J. (1990). Differential acculturation among Vietnamese refugees. *Social Work, 35*(4), 341–345.

MATSUSHIMA, N. M., & TASHIMA, N. (1982). *Mental health treatment modalities of Pacific/Asian American practitioners.* San Francisco: Pacific Asian Mental Health Research Project.

MORITSUGU, J., & SUE, S. (1983). Minority status as a stressor. In R. D. Felner, L. A. Jason, J. Moritsugu, & S. S. Farber (Eds.), *Preventive psychology: Theory, research, and practice* (pp. 162–174). New York: Pergamon Press.

MORRIS, T. M. (1990). Culturally sensitive family assessment: An evaluation of the Family Assessment Device used with Hawaiian-American and Japanese-American families. *Family Process, 29,* 105–116.

MORROW, R. (1987). Cultural differences—be aware. *Academic Therapy, 23*(2), 143–149.

ONG, P., & HEE, S. J. (1993). In LEAP Asian Pacific American Public Policy Institute and UCLA Asian American Studies Center (Eds.), *The state of Asian Pacific America* (pp. 11–24). Los Angeles: LEAP Asian Pacific American Public Policy Institute and UCLA Asian American Studies Center.

OU, Y. S., & MCADOO, H. P. (1993). Socialization of Chinese American children. In H. P. McAdoo (Ed.), *Family ethnicity: Strength in diversity* (pp. 245–270). Newbury Park, CA: Sage.

OWAN, T. (1985). Southeast Asian mental health: Transition from treatment to prevention—A new direction. In T. Owan (Ed.), *Southeast Asian mental health: Treatment, prevention, services, training, and research* (pp. 141–167). Washington, DC: U.S. Department of Health and Human Services.

PHINNEY, J. S., LOCHNER, B. T., & MURPHY, R. (1990). Ethnic identity development and psychological adjustment in adolescence. In A. R. Stiffman & L. E. Davis (Eds.), *Ethnic issues in adolescent mental health* (pp. 53–72). Newbury Park, CA: Sage.

ROOT, M. (1989). Guidelines for facilitating therapy with Asian American clients. In D. Atkinson, G. Morten, & D. Sue (Eds.), *Counseling American minorities: A cross-cultural perspective* (pp. 116–128). Dubuque, IA: William C. Brown.

SHU, R., & SATELE, A. (1977). *The Samoan community in Southern California: Conditions and needs.* Chicago: Asian American Mental Health Training Center.

SPRING, C., BLUNDEN, D, GREENBERG, L. M., & YELLIN, A. M. (1977). Validity and norms of a hyperactivity rating scale. *Journal of Special Education, 11*(3), 313–321.

SUE, D. W. (1990). Cultural-specific strategies in counseling: A conceptual framework. *Professional Psychology: Research and Practice, 21*(6), 424–433.

SUE, D. W., & SUE, D. (1990). *Counseling the culturally different: Theory and practice* (2nd ed.). New York: Wiley.

SUE, S. (1991). Ethnicity and culture in psychological research and practice. In J. D. Goodchild (Ed.), *Psychological perspectives on human diversity in America: The master lectures* (pp. 51–85). Washington, DC: American Psychological Association.

SUE, S., & CHIN, R. (1983). The mental health of Chinese-American children: Stressors and resources. In G. J. Powell (Ed.), *The psychosocial development of minority group children* (pp. 385–397). New York: Brunner/Mazel.

SUE, S., FUJINO, D., HU, L., & TAKEUCHI, D. (1991). Community mental health services for ethnic minority groups: A test of the cultural responsiveness hypothesis. *Journal of Consulting and Clinical Psychology, 59*(4), 533–540.

SUE, S., & McKINNEY, H. (1975). Asian Americans in the community mental health care system. *American Journal of Orthopsychiatry, 45,* 111–118.

SUE, S., & MORISHIMA, J. (1982). *The mental health of Asian Americans.* San Francisco: Jossey-Bass.

SUE, S., WAGNER, N., JA, D., MARGULLIS, C., & LEW, L. (1976). Conceptions of mental illness among Asian and Caucasian American students. *Psychological Reports, 38,* 703–708.

SUE, S., & SUE, D. W. (1974). MMPI comparisons between Asian American and non-Asian students utilizing a student health psychiatric clinic. *Journal of Counseling Psychology, 21,* 423–427.

SUE, S., & ZANE, N. (1987). The role of culture and cultural techniques in psychotherapy: A critique and reformulation. *American Psychologist, 42*(1), 37–45.

SUNG, B. (1985). Bicultural conflicts in Chinese immigrant children. *Journal of Comparative Family Studies, 16,* 244–269.

TOULIATOS, J., & LINDHOLM, B. W. (1980). Behavioral disturbance in children of native-born and immigrant parents. *American Journal of Community Psychology, 8,* 28–33.

TRACEY, T., LEONG, F., & GLIDDEN, C. (1986). Help seeking and problem perception among Asian Americans. *Journal of Counseling Psychology, 33*(3), 331–336.

TUNG, M. (1991). Insight-oriented psychotherapy for the Chinese patient. *American Journal of Orthopsychiatry, 61*(2), 186–194.

TUNG, T. M. (1985). Psychiatric care for Southeast Asians: How different is different? In T. Owan (Ed.), *Southeast Asian mental health: Treatment, prevention, services, training, and research* (pp. 5–40). Washington, DC: U.S. Department of Health and Human Services.

UBA, L. (1994). *Asian Americans: Personality patterns, identity, and mental health.* New York: Guilford Press.

WONG, H. Z. (1985). Training for mental health service providers to Southeast Asian refugees: Models, strategies, curricula. In T. Owan (Ed.), *Southeast Asian mental health: Treatment, prevention, services, training, and research* (pp. 5–40). Washington, DC: U.S. Department of Health and Human Services.

YAMAMOTO, J., & ACOSTA, F. (1982). Treatment of Asian Americans and Hispanic Americans: Similarities and differences. *Journal of the American Academy of Psychoanalysis, 10,* 585–607.

YAO, E. (1985a). A comparison of family characteristics of Asian-American and Anglo-American high achievers. *International Journal of Comparative Sociology, 26,* 198–208.

YAO, E. (1985b). Adjustment needs of Asian immigrant children. *Elementary School Guidance and Counseling, 19*(3), 222–227.

YEH, M., TAKEUCHI, D., & SUE, S. (1994). Asian-American children treated in the mental health system: A comparison of parallel and mainstream outpatient service centers. *Journal of Clinical Child Psychology, 23*(1), 5–12.

YU, E., CHANG, C. F., LIU, W., & FERNANDEZ, M. (1989). Suicide among Asian American youth. In M. Feinleib (Ed.), *Report of the secretary's task force on youth suicide* (pp. 157–176). Washington, DC: U.S. Department of Health and Human Services.

CHAPTER 12

African American Children

DAVIDO DUPREE, MARGARET BEALE SPENCER,
and SONIA BELL

IT HAS BEEN SUGGESTED that the behaviors and practices evident in contemporary communities where African American children develop have their genesis in African cultures and manifest themselves differently depending on the contexts—social, physical, historical, economic—that African Americans find themselves in (Boykin, 1986). Although this assertion has multiple political implications, it also offers insight into the dynamic nature of culture. Simply by their contrast to mainstream culture, the behaviors and practices that characterize African-American communities are assumed not to be cultural but deviant (Jarrett, 1994; Oyemade, 1985). To gain insight into these behaviors and practices, it is important to focus not only on them but also on their meaning in cultural context (Gordon, 1995). From their differences in meaning alone, diverse developmental outcomes can and should be expected. Kottak (1987) notes that culture is learned and that cultural learning is dependent on "the uniquely human capacity to use symbols, signs that have no necessary or natural connection to what they stand

The research reported in this chapter was supported by funds awarded to the second author from several sources: The Commonwealth Fund, Spencer, W. T. Grant, Social Science Research Council, and Ford Foundations. In addition, supplemental support from the Annenberg Foundation was provided.

for. . . . A person born anywhere begins immediately, through a process of conscious and unconscious learning and interaction with others, to internalize, or incorporate, a cultural tradition through the process of enculturation" (p. 23). As Kottak implies, a great deal of culture is expressed in the human ability to give meaning and value to a thing, activity, or event. Emphasis will be placed on understanding the meaning that is given to experiences that appear to be unique to African American children and families. The African American child cannot be considered in isolation. In discussing African American children and youth, it is imperative to discuss significant others and context because it is in relation to these influences that the children's behaviors take on meaning.

The Ecology of the African American Child: A Culture of Poverty

Despite efforts not to pass judgment on differences among cultures, such well-intentioned efforts often are detrimental because they misplace the focus of research and therapy. For example, a disproportionate number of African Americans in the United States live below the poverty level. According to census figures, 30.9% of Black families lived below the poverty level in 1992. For the same period, 46.3% of all Black children under 18 years of age lived below the poverty level (U. S. Bureau of the Census, 1992). Such statistics include only those who fall below federal guidelines. Nonetheless, there is the implicit association between African Americans and poverty. To avoid the assumption that their experiences in impoverished communities have ethnic or cultural origins, the existence of a "culture of poverty" has been offered (for critiques, see Jarrett, 1994; Oyemade, 1985; Slaughter-Defoe, Nakagawa, Takanishi, & Johnson, 1990). The culture of poverty theory encompasses one view that is important to this discussion: "flawed character."

The flawed character view assumes that although ample opportunities are available to the poor, they do not take advantage of these opportunities due to disorganized behavior, characterized by strong feelings of fatalism and belief in chance, strong present time orientation, the inability to delay gratification, feelings of inferiority, acceptance of aggression and illegitimacy, and authoritarianism (Oyemade, 1985). The very labeling of the theory and its characteristics gives legitimacy to its assumptions because they address issues of seemingly cultural significance such as worldview, accepted practices and behaviors, and belief systems. However, characterizing these descriptors in terms of culture is not useful. Although poverty and its correlate characteristics may take precedence over other factors in predicting the developmental outcomes of children, they *do not* reflect a culture.

On the other hand, the meanings of those predictors in context may be a reflection of culture. One cannot consider a characteristic such as strong present time orientation, the inability to delay gratification, feelings of inferiority, or acceptance of aggression and illegitimacy out of context and expect it to convey any prescriptive significance. As with any characteristic, its mere recognition has no explanatory value. Rather, as a descriptor of a context in which African American children develop, the primary concerns are whether the characteristic is generally present or situation-specific and whether it precludes effective functioning. Thus, its meaning must be elicited.

Jarrett (1994) conducted focus groups with African American women who are single parents. They discussed, among other things, economic impediments to marriage, expansion of the paternal role, expansion of the maternal role, and domestic kin networks. The mothers' narratives indicate that their values are very much mainstream; however, they are cognizant of the circumstances that will require coping and compromise. For example, many African American mothers recognize that the natural father is not the only male who can be a father to their children. Jarrett's ethnography reveals, "Women do not mechanistically respond to economic forces. Rather, they assess their options and make choices that allow them to forge meaningful lives despite the harsh economic conditions in which they and their children find themselves" (p. 45). One cannot look merely at outcomes (e.g., the inability to delay gratification, feelings of inferiority, and acceptance of aggression and illegitimacy) and assume cultural orientation. The meaning in context must be elicited so that instances of resilience can be recognized (e.g., Jarrett, 1995).

Differences in community context alone ensure that development will not be comparable for all children (Bronfenbrenner, 1989). Almost one-third of the African American population live below the poverty level. This usually means that they live in communities with few resources. Furthermore, with little opportunity for upward mobility, they are more likely to be exposed to ongoing environmental stressors. Spencer, McDermott, Burton, and Cole (in press) studied the characteristics of the neighborhoods of a sample of particularly impoverished African American youth participating in a longitudinal study in a metropolitan southeastern area. Their report includes eight dimensions descriptive of their communities: housing characteristics, housing quality (i.e., condition of housing, condition of streets, absence of abandoned structures), security devices, support services (i.e., laundromats, medical/dental offices, religious structures), food services (i.e., fast food places, grocery stores, lounges/bars), retail services (i.e., pharmacy/drug stores, furniture/appliance, all-purpose stores), industrial presence (i.e., industrial plants/warehouse, nontraditional land use), and teenage meeting places (i.e., residence-related areas, traditional recreation centers, convenience stores/liquor stores, street corners).

Spencer et al. developed a typology of neighborhoods based on hierarchical clustering of census tracts by the neighborhood assessment dimensions. Six neighborhood types were identified:

1. Good housing with little business or support services (26.7%).
2. Average housing with considerable business and support services (16.7%).
3. Average housing with little business or support services and many teenage meeting places (13.3%).

4. Below-average housing with some industrial presence (36.7%).
5. Average housing with many businesses and support services (3.3%).
6. Poor housing with many teenage meeting places (3.3%).

The most typical living arrangement for the sample was below-average housing with some industrial presence (36.7%). What is particularly disturbing is that analyses indicate that crimes such as rape, murder, burglary, robbery, and assault were more likely to occur in neighborhoods with few support services, low housing quality, and many informal hangouts for Black teens. That is, such communities were more conducive to crime than daily family functioning.

Although this study offered a description of communities in the southeastern United States, other qualitative studies (e.g., Anderson, 1990; MacLoed, 1995) suggest that many predominantly African American communities in other areas of the United States arguably fall within those typologies. Thus, any discussion must take into consideration how normative developmental outcomes will be manifested differently—cognitively, behaviorally, or physically—as a result of the unique living experiences and conditions of African American children in the United States.

Spencer's Phenomenological Variant of the Ecological Systems Theory

It is our contention that the development of African American children is, ideally, no different from that of other children. However, we also assert that physical and social realities that are specific to African Americans in the United States, as a function of their race (e.g., developmentally-instigative traits) and historical status (e.g., intergenerational poverty), influence them in ways that can lead to fundamentally different developmental outcomes in contrast to other children. It is our hope not merely to present the reader with a body of information to be generalized. To the contrary, our goal in this chapter is to present information that is pertinent to African American children within a theoretical framework that the student or practitioner can employ in the unique situations in which African American children are found. As Comer and Hill (1985) noted over 10 years ago:

> On the whole, psychiatrists are more sensitive to the effects of adverse social conditions on black families and children than the general population. Usually this is so because of the personality factors that attracted them to the field in the first place rather than their psychiatric training. Many psychiatric programs do not provide trainees with a conceptual framework which enables them to understand how economic, educational, health care, housing, racism, and other major environmental conditions—past and present—affect social network, family and child functioning. In the absence of such a framework some psychiatrists conclude, as do more of the general public, that all Americans have the same or a similar experience and that a difference in outcome is due to a difference in inherited skill or will. Without an understanding of the trauma to black institutions and the experiences of black families in the larger political, economic, and social system—and the adaptive mechanisms or responses in the black community—psychiatrists will not be very useful in improving social policy for and in improving the treatment of black families and children. (p. 180)

In response to Comer and Hill's challenge, we offer as a theoretical framework Spencer's Phenomenological Variant of the Ecological Systems theory (PVEST) (Spencer, 1995; Spencer, Cunningham, & Swanson, 1995; Spencer & Dupree, in press). This theory represents an integration of prior and current findings from our research efforts (see Figure 12–1). The word phenomenological is stressed because emphasis is placed on understanding how an individual's unique perception of an

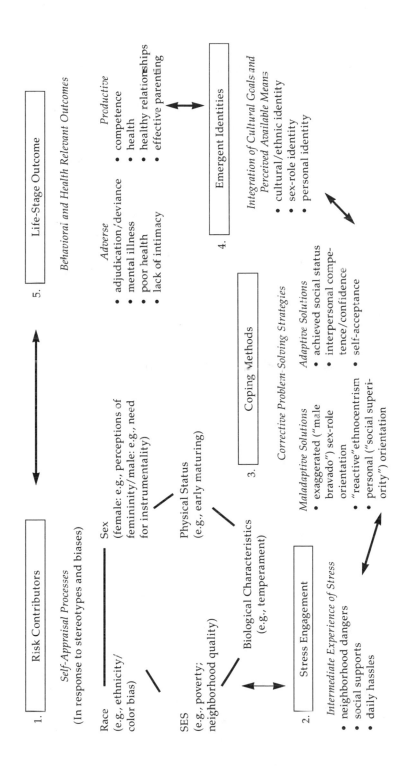

FIGURE 12-1

A Phenomenological Variant of Ecological Systems Theory (PVEST)

243

experience—the meaning given to an experience—can influence coping responses and subsequent development and, in turn, competence (e.g., academic performance) and mental health outcomes. Although the theory is concerned with factors common to other theories that seek to explain child development and resilience such as socioeconomic status, family structure, and self-esteem, the theory is as much concerned with process. That is, it facilitates understanding of the processes by which important factors (including social address variables such as one- versus two-parent families, father or mother's employment status, nationality, or ethnic group) actually influence or interact with coping responses and development. The theory focuses attention on the actual characteristics of and the activities that take place in the environments that the different social address variables describe.

Normative Psychosocial Development for the African American Child

Spencer's Phenomenological Variant of the Ecological Systems theory is distinct from Bronfenbrenner's Ecological Systems theory in its emphasis on identity. The experiences of children and youth have implications for identity development at each stage. Racial identity is not necessarily an explicit concern for African American youth, even in adolescence. However, one does recognize precursors to racial identity. African American children show awareness of color connotations, or concepts, as early as age 3. That is, they often associate negative attributes with black animals or dark-skinned persons when compared with identical white animals or light-skinned persons.

Spencer and Horowitz (1973) found that Black preschool children were as negative concerning the color black and about Black persons as were White preschoolers. Furthermore, 3-year-olds were as negative in their color-racial concept attitudes (i.e., the view of minorities reflected in society at large) as were 4- and 5-year-olds. However, they also found that these attitudes could be changed when alternative attitudes were consistently reinforced. These findings imply that although the attitudes were not yet permanently ingrained, these children have displayed social cognition (i.e., decentration and interpersonal competence) that has influenced their attitudes.

Race awareness is related to the child's social cognitive ability to take the perspective or point of view of another. Spencer (1982b) found that social cognition—as indicated by the child's ability to differentiate affective states—was related to race awareness but not racial attitudes or preference (i.e., the manner in which a minority group views itself). Although race awareness—a social cognitive process—predicted Eurocentric racial attitudes and preferences, racial attitudes and preferences were not correlated with more general social cognitive ability.

However, African American children with Eurocentric attitudes or preferences do not necessarily have negative self-concepts. Spencer (1982a) found that among northern and southern samples of African American preschool children and primary school students, 73% of those showing a White bias also had positive self-concepts. Spencer (1982a) offers that "the minority child's cognitive construction of reality is the intervention which allows and supports identity differentiation and a healthy ego" (p. 81). That is, minority children can be very much aware of color connotations in society (e.g., Black is bad, White is good) as well as societal views of the particular minority group to which they belong (e.g., Blacks are inferior), yet maintain an individual sense of identity that buffers them from such perceptions. They are still cognitively egocentric (Spencer, 1984).

Social cognitive ability does, however, develop with age. There appears to be a developmental pattern in expression of Eurocentric attitudes and preferences and understanding of color connotations as a consequence of increases in social experiences and social cognition (Spencer, 1982a). Three-year-olds are generally Eurocentric in terms of racial attitudes, racial preferences, and color concepts or connotations. However, an Afrocentric pattern of attitudes and preferences begins to appear at age 5 and continues through age 9. These findings become more articulated when examined by age and socioeconomic status (SES). Middle-income children were generally Eurocentric on all dimensions at age 3, while low-income children were neutral on all dimensions at the same age. After age 3, both low- and middle-income children showed a clear Eurocentric orientation for color concepts. After age 3, a different pattern emerges by SES for racial attitudes and preferences; these are more subjectively experienced. Middle-income subjects became progressively more Afrocentric through age 9, while low-income subjects showed a pattern of neutrality. Racial attitudes and preferences at age 9 were significantly different for the two SES groups.

It may be that as socioeconomic status increases, the likelihood of coming into contact with members of the larger society increases. Thus, children are directly confronted with the issue of race and identification. Unlike in earlier stages, it is more difficult to devalue one's own group and feel good about oneself because of changes in the way in which children see themselves between the ages of 3 and 9. Young children distinguish themselves from others on the basis of physical attributes (e.g., I am different from Johnny because I have blond hair) or may describe themselves in terms of typical activities ("I ride a bike"). Older children describe themselves in terms of their active abilities relative to others ("I can ride a bike better than my brother"). During middle childhood, roughly age 8 to 10, they begin to understand mental and volitional aspects of self on their own terms. This ability helps them to appreciate the subjective nature of self. One is distinct from others not only because one looks different or has different material possessions, but because one has different thoughts and feelings. They have more psychological notions of self and will express belief in their own immutable humanity, sexuality, individuality, and continuity but may explain the self in physical terms (Damon & Hart, 1982). For example, they can no longer believe that their skin color—or race—can change.

During adolescence when identity processes are most salient, identity development of African American youth can be further complicated by normative adolescent experiences (i.e., puberty, transition from primary to secondary school); socioeconomic status and its correlates (i.e., chronic stressors such as violence and low resources), as well as their greater visibility as racial minorities (i.e., skin color, facial features) (Spencer & Markstrom-Adams, 1990). Spencer and Markstrom-Adams assert:

> Exploration is a key ingredient for identity formation processes. Furthermore, as supported by a level of cognitive awareness not possible earlier (i.e., social cognition), minority adolescents are faced with an assumed consciousness of prejudicial attitudes and discriminatory practices of the majority group. The relation overall is compounded by color . . . The overall effect may be discouragement from involvement with those outside of one's own reference group and/or a subsequent diminished level of exploration during childhood and use of academic and apprenticeship opportunities during adolescence, which may have life-course implications. (p. 298)

Nevertheless, it must be noted that such negative perceptions are not necessarily indicative of low self-esteem. In fact, research by Hare (1977) on African American and White adolescents suggests that self-esteem may be area-specific. African American males who performed least well on indicators of educational attainment obtained the highest peer self-esteem score but the lowest scores for general, school, and home self-esteem. These findings suggest that youth may respond to negative academic experiences by downplaying the importance of school and becoming more involved with peers who have similar academic experiences or expectations about school. More generally, African American youth may feel more or less valued based on how well they meet the expectations of the people (i.e., friends, parents, teachers, siblings) in the contexts in which they find themselves.

With this overview in mind, the discussion will now turn to issues of importance for African American youth during the different stages of development. The discussion will take place in the context of Spencer's PVEST model to help the reader gain a more holistic understanding of African American child development.

Risk Contributors to the Development of African American Children

INFANCY

As is evident in Figure 12–1, the first concern of the theory is preexisting risk contributors. For African Americans, minority status and its correlates (e.g., low SES) can predetermine risk for poor physical and mental health outcomes. In research on risk, there are variables that, in and of themselves, have no explanatory power yet consistently predict risk. These variables, including race and sex, set individuals at an immediate disadvantage even before birth. For example, there is a persistent difference in preterm delivery among Black and White infants. More Black infants are born prematurely than White infants. Preterm delivery causes low birth weight among infants and is the leading cause of infant mortality. In 1991, the infant mortality rate for Black infants was 16.5 per 1,000 live births compared with 8.9 for all races. More telling, however, is the observation that low socioeconomic status alone does not account for poor pregnancy outcomes among Black women (Blackmore et al., 1993).

Bronfenbrenner (1989) offers that there are developmentally instigative characteristics that are most likely to shape the course of human development because they provoke reactions from the environment. A possible explanation for this precedence in preterm birth is that, for African Americans, race (e.g., operationally defined in terms of skin color, facial features, or hair texture) is a developmentally instigative characteristic, and it directly or indirectly elicits similar experiences (e.g., negative life events, nonoptimal living conditions) that influence birth outcomes (Gaiter, Reynolds, & Mayberry, 1990). Blackmore et al. (1993) suggest that race is actually a surrogate for educational and economic position in the community and a marker for SES and cultural factors. While the implication is that there are correlates of race that actually explain differences in birth outcomes, it must also be inferred that these children are born in a context that existed before their birth (e.g., Davis, 1988;

Oyemade et al., 1994; Reeb, Graham, Zyzanski, & Kitson, 1987) and will continue to exist after their birth and will consequently affect their development. If the new mother received low levels of emotional and material support before the birth of her child, she will probably not receive much more after the birth of her child. As a consequence, the caregiving responsibilities may themselves become stressors. The same factors for which race is a surrogate or marker will continue to influence development over the life course.

Race can also be a proxy for developmental status at birth and during the first year of life. Capute, Shapiro, Palmer, Ross, and Wachtel (1985) found that Black infants are more aggressive in motor development when compared with White infants. Normal motor development does not guarantee normal neurological development; however, failure to attain motor milestones at the appropriate time may indicate central or peripheral neuromuscular disorders. Capute et al. (1985) found that Black children attained gross motor milestones earlier than White children. This difference was, on average, a less than one-month difference before walking. The following order of development was suggested: Black females, Black males, White males, White females. The authors note, however, "If racial differences are not recognized when upper limits are set . . . black children may be classed 'normal' and thereby delay diagnosis and/or treatment" (p. 641). After accounting for race, the differences across SES were markedly diminished and only a slight trend between SES and gross motor achievement remained. There was, however, a relative underrepresentation of Blacks in the upper SES groups; thus motor development for the Black children tended to be motor development for lower SES Black children. Socioeconomic development may affect motor development but additional data will be required to establish SES as a factor independent of race.

Capute et al. (1985) only suggest SES as a possible factor other than race. Spencer's PVEST model suggests that the larger ecology of the African American child must be taken into account. In doing so, Step 2 of the model (stress engagement; see Figure 12–1), becomes important. Stress engagement includes neighborhood dangers and daily hassles. The amount of stress engaged by children is influenced in part by the social support (e.g., nuclear and extended family) available to buffer the children's experiences. When normative parenting activities become a daily hassle, the ability of caregivers to buffer the child from normative (e.g., hunger, noises) and nonnormative (e.g., violence) stressors is diminished.

Nevertheless, one must also recognize that the buffering roles played by caregivers may differ significantly and still be effective (e.g., Jarrett, 1995; Tucker, Brady, Harris, Fraser, & Tribble, 1993). Garcia-Coll's (1990) review of developmental outcomes of minority infants reveals that the caretaking practices of mothers of different ethnic origins may differ qualitatively while having the same ultimate goal: competent children. Mothers have similar developmental and educational goals for their children but the supports for these goals may manifest themselves differently (Garcia-Coll, 1990).

One study reviewed suggested that African American mothers of low SES tended to spend the least time picking up and cuddling their children compared with mothers of other ethnic origins. This was not seen as neglect, however. Another study concerned face-to-face interaction between infant and child; Black mothers of low SES tended to show the least talking and infantized behavior. An anecdotal account helps to give meaning to the practice: The mother's concern was "not to spoil the child by giving him too much attention." The authors suggested that the findings of the study in general were consistent with the mother's expressed objectives. As a practitioner, it is necessary to inquire further into the meaning of behavior for a given group to obtain greater insight for comparison with other groups.

The ecology of the African American child may evolve in response to social trends (e.g., unwed pregnancy, father absence, limited economic resources) that, although not specific to or limited to African Americans, are often associated with this group. One of these trends is nontraditional family structures. It is not unusual for an African American child to be raised in a household that consists of grandmother (e.g., Chase-Lansdale, Brooks-

Gunn, & Zamsky, 1994; Flaherty, 1988; Flaherty, Facteau, & Garver, 1987), aunts, and cousins all of whom may, at different times, take primary responsibility for the care of the child in addition to or, in some cases, instead of the mother (Wilson & Tolson, 1990). This is especially important in light of the Personal Responsibility and Work Opportunity Reconstruction Act of 1996 that requires recipients to work while, at the same time, decreasing supports that were previously offered for child care and transportation (e.g., Family Support Act of 1988).

Problems with the availability, affordability, and quality of child care exist already. Low-income mothers may have fewer child-care choices than higher income mothers. With respect to infant attachment, this is an important trend. There is a body of literature highlighting the potential long-term effects of insecure attachment during infancy including poor social cognition and delinquent behavior (Cicchetti, 1996). However, insecure attachment (e.g., Teberg, Howell, & Wingert, 1983) should not be assumed in the absence of a nuclear family structure or nonmaternal caregiving situation (e.g., Burchinal, Bryant, Lee, & Ramey, 1992).

Multiple caregiving situations do not preclude the existence of a primary attachment relationship between mother and child (Van IJzendoorn, 1993). Jackson (1993) points out that studies of infant-mother attachment were conducted mostly on White and atypical African American infants with mothers who were the infants' unequivocal primary caregivers. Within such studies, less favorable outcomes were reported for African American infants. Some of these studies of infants' attachment were also conducted using criteria derived from the study of White middle-class American infants with nonworking mothers who were their unequivocal primary caregivers. Attachment was not studied within the unique extended family structures of African Americans. Jackson's (1993) own pilot research on multiple caregiver situations in African American families revealed four phenomena that offer insight:

1. There were two to five caregivers with responsibilities designated by the mother for infant care as

well as a larger set of children and adults who also provided care.

2. Caregiving arrangements were constructed to accommodate the demands of parents' unconventional work schedules and conditions as well as the parents' preference for home-based caregivers.

3. The infant's social network was generally large with a range of 4 to 41 familiar individuals being encountered on a recurring weekly basis.

4. The majority of the infants had contacts with many unfamiliar people because most of their caregivers took them out on excursions outside the homes where they received care.

Additionally, caregivers reported that infants were generally sociable and friendly with unfamiliar people except when inhibited or obstructed by the caregiver. Although Jackson's pilot study does not offer stressful enough encounters with strangers to determine attachment status comparable to the "strange situation" (e.g., Ainsworth, 1979), it does effectively assert the need for different methods of determining attachment that are sensitive to cultural context. Jackson's findings describe a social ecology in which the roles of its members have meanings that differ from traditional assumptions.

CHILDHOOD

Although stress engagement may be attenuated by social support, some aspects of social support networks must be seen as having a coping role for the caregivers who are, in turn more effective in support of their children (i.e., minimizing problem behavior) (e.g., Howes et al., 1995; Leadbeater & Bishop, 1994; Myers, Taylor, Alvy, Arrington, & Richardson, 1992). In their study of adolescent mothers, Leadbeater and Bishop (1994) found that adolescent African American mothers reported the highest levels of problem behavior in their male preschool children. The authors suggest that this may reflect a heightened response to the consequences of externalizing behavior for Black inner city males. That is, raising young Black males may be more stressful because of the negative perceptions of Black males in general, which allows even elementary school-age males to be perceived as short, threatening men rather than as children. This is even more intriguing in light of the findings that residing with the child's grandmother as well as the mother resulted in high levels of emotional support and this was associated with fewer child behavior problems being reported with the exception of Black male children.

In Figure 12–1, development is characterized as cyclical, although the pattern of development may differ at different stages of growth. These expectations are in keeping with differences in cognitive, socioemotional, and physical development associated with respective periods of development. Furthermore, what may exist as a life-stage outcome (see Figure 12–1) of the processes taking place at one period of development may essentially be a risk contributor at another point in development. For example, preterm birth in low-SES groups is associated with the later diagnosis of mild mental retardation (Campbell & Ramey, 1994). What was once an outcome, now has implications for peer and teacher interactions as well as academic achievement.

As previously noted, the development of African American children is expected to be comparable to children of other ethnicities given similar circumstances. Nevertheless, race and class differences often preclude the possibility of comparable experiences. Of particular significance to African American children is the overrepresentation in the category of mild mental retardation (Reschly & Ward, 1991; Yeargin-Allsopp, Drews, Decoufle, & Murphy, 1995). This diagnosis is associated with low socioeconomic status and has no known genetic or physiological cause (Campbell & Ramey, 1994; Yeargin-Allsopp et al., 1995). In fact, a case-control study conducted on a sample of children in the metropolitan Atlanta area (Yeargin-Allsopp et al., 1995) revealed:

> The excess prevalence of mild mental retardation among Black children was reduced by nearly 50% when we controlled for sex, maternal age at delivery, birth order,

maternal education, and economic status. However, the residual excess among Black children does not necessarily indicate that Black children are at higher risk for mental retardation. The true odds ratio might be smaller than 1.8 if other unmeasured confounders shown previously to be associated with mild mental retardation, such as maternal intelligence and housing density, were controlled. We did not control for birth weight in most of our analyses because it was unclear whether birth weight should be considered as a confounder or an intervening variable. (p. 326)

Although the emphasis has been taken off race as an explanatory variable, the prescription remains unclear unless the variables for which race is a surrogate or marker are considered in a conceptual framework that gives meaning to them. While they did not consider birth weight because they were unsure whether it was a confounder or an intervening variable, other studies have shown low birth weight to be a preexisting risk contributor. For example, Ramey and Ramey (1992) found that intensive preschool intervention was more effective for those infants weighing between 2,000 and 2,500 g at birth compared with those who weighed less than 2,000 g at birth.

This important finding helps to illustrate the reciprocal relationship between risk contributors and stress engagement. The developmental status of a child at birth can set the child at risk in terms of cognitive development. However, the level of impact can be mediated by social support such as early intervention involving parents, community, and social service resources (e.g., Blair, Ramey, & Hardin, 1995; Breitmayer & Ramey, 1986; Campbell & Ramey, 1994; Ramey & Ramey, 1992). With support in facilitating the transition from home to school (e.g., intensive preschool intervention involving parents), the potential effects of low birth weight on cognitive development (e.g., Liaw & Brooks-Gunn, 1993) can be mediated. This has been revealed in studies comparing low SES, low birth weight African American children who showed significant differences in IQ scores based on their long-term participation in an intensive preschool intervention program (Blair et al., 1995; Breitmayer & Ramey, 1986; Campbell & Ramey, 1994; Ramey & Ramey, 1992).

In many cases, entrance into the school system marks the beginning of problems related to competence and identity that can have long-term implications for the African American child. Developmental tasks are subject to negative influences or are exacerbated as a result of the contact of one culture with another without proper scaffolding or preparation. In such instances, self-esteem and self-perceived competence are placed in jeopardy (Spencer, 1987). Allen and Boykin (1992) offer that for many African American children, there is a cultural discontinuity between the home and school environment of the child. The implication is that the expectations of children by teachers and administration in terms of behavior and competence are often incongruent with their home and community experiences. However, this discontinuity is also linked to the child's level of cognitive development (Spencer, 1984, 1985; Spencer & Dornbusch, 1990; Spencer & Markstrom-Adams, 1990) and socialization by the parents (Spencer, 1983, 1990).

There are some intriguing findings regarding the relationship between rap music and aggression, which addresses the disfranchisement of African Americans from the schooling process. Of the many potential influences on the aggression of African American youth, perhaps the most controversial to date is that of rap music—in particular, gangster rap. The concern with the influence of music on youth is not new. However, the debate over the influence of rap music is particularly sensitive because rap music is, at once, a manifestation of African American culture and experience as well as an assumed progenitor of violence. We suggest that, as with any behavioral phenomenon, the relationship between rap music and aggression or violence must be considered from a phenomenological perspective. That is, one must consider the significance of the music to those who listen to it.

There have been relatively few empirical studies of the relationship between rap music and aggression (i.e., Epstein, Pratto, & Skipper, 1990; Hansen, 1995; Johnson, Jackson, & Gatto, 1995; Took & Weiss, 1994), and even so, methodological concerns limit their generalizability. Nevertheless, it is their methodological shortcomings that provide the best basis for discussion. A few of these studies have considered the musical preferences of youth who have received clinical attention for their delinquent or violent behavior. Whereas White youth showed a greater preference for heavy metal music with some preferring rap music, African American youth preferred rap music. This does not, however, suggest a cause-effect relationship. Musical preference may be an indicator of problem behavior, but only in the context of other indicators.

Took and Weiss (1994) found that when youth receiving clinical attention were compared based on their musical preference (i.e., heavy metal, rap, or pop music), there were no significant differences in delinquency based on preference. However, significant differences were found based on poor performance in school during the elementary school years. This suggests that a certain degree of marginalization, or rather alienation from the school context, took place early on and then manifested itself in more externalizing behaviors. African American youth who become disfranchised as a result of negative schooling experiences may be more receptive to media (i.e., television, movies, music) that offer alternative worldviews or that represent their own feelings of disfranchisement (e.g., Johnson et al., 1995).

ADOLESCENCE

In adolescence, feelings of disfranchisement may lead boys and girls to seek out or be recruited into alternative peer groups (i.e., gangs) (Curry & Spergel, 1992). Gangs provide an alternative culture and security in unsafe communities and can often replace family (Evans & Taylor, 1995; Stallworth, 1994). A qualitative study by Evans and Taylor (1995) suggests that, in contrast to members of earlier gangs, today, members are more likely to engage in violence but also to rent loyalty to their gangs over loyalty to their families—80% said they would choose to protect their gangs over family.

Throughout Spencer's PVEST model, each step is seen as being in reciprocal relationship to both the previous and the following step. This is true for coping methods and emergent identity. In fact, Spencer's PVEST model suggests that the process of developing an identity should be seen as a coping mechanism (Spencer et al., 1995). Identity does not develop in a vacuum. Although coping responses may be maladaptive or adaptive, their identity development will be influenced. Cunningham (1995) found that for the 25% of a sample of African American adolescents who lived in neighborhoods where they personally experienced the highest rate of violence and aggression, males obtained a significantly higher self-rating of machismo—exaggerated stereotypical male gender-role orientation. Furthermore, low emotional support, feelings of alienation, and high contextual hassles (e.g., peer influences, gangs, turf wars) were associated with machismo attitudes. A high machismo orientation may be adopted in response to actual experiences of aggression in one's community; however, actual experiences of violence are also predictive of reactive aggression (e.g., getting into fights often, carrying a weapon, wanting to injure someone).

Dupree (1995) found that in a sample of adolescent African Americans reactive aggression was associated with school-related fear (i.e., I am afraid of going to school, I am afraid I might do something bad, I am fearful or anxious, I have trouble sleeping, I cut classes or skip school). Thus, aggressive attitudes and behaviors may actually be coping strategies in response to fear. These attitudes are influenced by contextual experiences and are expressed as male youth negotiate their personal identity as men (Spencer et al., 1995).

Implications for Intervention

As helping professionals, we may find ourselves asking "What do we know about the development of African American youth?" We must learn first to consider the multiple and varied contexts in which African American youth are found. It is imperative that we acknowledge African American development as, ideally speaking, no different from that of any other group. Nonetheless, the social forces (certain forms of racism and discrimination) that often work against normal development of the African American adolescent must be appreciated. The flawed character view has often served as a model for society's understanding of African American people in general. However, this view is particularly dangerous when speaking of our most vulnerable persons, children and youth. Theory driven, culturally sensitive, empirical evidence of African American youths' experiences in various contexts should be relied on in considering methodology. This approach will enable the helping professional to better relate to African American adolescents as clients and determine which type of intervention would be most appropriate for them.

Sources of stress, such as poverty and low socioeconomic status, neighborhood dangers, and daily hassles, which are often prevalent in African American communities but not limited to these communities, reveal an increasing need for innovative strategies with which to relate to these children and youth. Avoid thinking that the aforementioned factors reflect the experiences of the entire African American community. Similar cultural characteristics may be shared but they are in no way a homogeneous group. In fact, counseling with African American children and youth requires a case-by-case, situation-specific approach. One of the goals of counseling with African American children and youth is to promote resilient coping strategies under unique circumstances. Therefore one should avoid using methods that encourage clients to accept their negative environmental circumstances and adapt to such an environment. Methods providing information that promotes the effective use of underutilized resources or resources that are unattainable within their community should be employed. Help-seeking strategies and greater social mobility will enable them to survive in their environment.

Case Example

A 10-year-old African American male lives in a low-income, high-crime community. He is demonstrating aggressive attitudes and behaviors in school and at home. He has been suspended from school several times and is considered a severe behavior problem. The aggressive behaviors that have been displayed by this adolescent have contributed to family tensions. At the same time, these behaviors have been supported within his peer network. He appears to exhibit a machismo orientation. The initial assessment showed that he has adopted reactive aggressive methods for coping within his environment. Further, his academic background suggests that he is academically talented, but his grades do not reflect his academic ability. His behavior problems appear to have overshadowed his academic ability.

- Consider the factors that constitute risk for this young man. His race, socioeconomic status, and gender make him vulnerable for certain experiences of stress.
- How do these factors contribute to this adolescent's experience of stress? From where do these stressors originate (i.e., home, school, neighborhood)? Consider the disadvantaged neighborhood in which this adolescent resides. What are his social and familial supports, his perceived hassles both in school and at home?
- Assess methods he has previously used to cope given his circumstances. Have they proven productive or counterproductive for this adolescent? *Proceed with caution.* In the eyes of the client, the coping methods may appear adaptive because they have been effective in the short term (e.g., his fighting may be in self-defense, because of a perceived threat, or a way of "posturing" so that others will leave him alone). These may be normative responses based on contexts; however, they have had a negative impact on his development.
- How does the client think he is perceived by his family members, peers, school personnel? What value does he place on their perceptions? Do they appear to have influenced how he sees himself?

- Acknowledge along with the youth that society's initial response is to believe that he is violent or deviant and beyond reform. Help him to anticipate the perceptions and behaviors of others and develop proactive responses as he actively distinguishes between how others perceive him and how he sees himself.

- The counseling emphasis must be on providing the youth with different options with respect to personal, social, and academic life. These options will allow the adolescent to choose between adaptive and maladaptive coping methods; ultimately he must make a choice between productive or adverse life course outcomes. The counseling professional can aid in this process by providing information in the form of referrals, career counseling, and modeling (i.e., mentoring).

- It is important to remember that the young male will still be concerned with how he is being perceived by others. Therefore, you must also work with him to develop strategies that will allow him to employ alternative coping methods or seek help from formal sources without being singled out and ridiculed or perceived as a "punk."

Case Example

An early maturing 14-year-old African American female, who is placed in an alternative academic setting for delinquent youth, has been referred by school staff for out-of-control behavior. Recently, she has been engaged in physical fights with students and teachers. The school's principal has recommended that this adolescent be sent to a more secure academic setting for juvenile delinquents. Before she can be placed within this facility, she must receive a psychological evaluation. The initial intake session revealed that this adolescent's primary caretaker is her maternal grandmother. Prior to that placement, she was temporarily placed in foster care. She had to be taken out of foster care due to aggressive displays of anger within the foster family's household.

- The caregiving situation should not be thought of as deviant because the adolescent is not being reared by her mother. However, it may be useful to understand the status and nature of the relationship between the youth and her biological parents as well as between the biological parents and the grandparent. The focus should not necessarily be on the fact that she is being raised by a grandparent in a single-parent situation.
- Consider risk contributors of gender and physical status. This adolescent is an early maturer who is experiencing rapid body changes. The fact that she has experienced rapid body development (breast development, etc.) may cause adults and peers alike to expect her to act more like an adult. Older males may pressure her to become sexually active. Students may tease her because of her mature physical status. This would making coping with the changes even more problematic because even though she may look mature, she may still think like a child.
- Often, aggressive behaviors are not considered appropriate behaviors for females. This adolescent has been engaged in physical fights with other students that cause her not to be thought of as "feminine." This may influence how she is perceived and limit her interactions with her female peers.
- Consider other sources of stress. What in her home and school atmosphere could be considered as a potential source of stress for this adolescent? The expectations of others (peers and school personnel) may have caused her considerable stress. Her grandmother may not receive financial support for

the care of her granddaughter. The child may be experiencing problems due to the separation from her mother.

- What methods of coping with her situations have existed previously? Have they been productive or counterproductive?
- Counseling emphasis should be on proper expression of her feelings. The adolescent must realize that her feelings are normal because of her experiences. She must be reassured that she is not abnormal.

Conclusion

Within the framework of Spencer's PVEST model, we have reviewed research specific to African American children and the contexts in which they develop. The research reviewed

TABLE 12–1

Possible Indicators of Psychological Disturbance from a Developmental Perspective

Infancy
> Incongruency between physical development and psychological and cognitive functioning
> Limited exploration behavior even when in company of caregiver(s)

Early Childhood
> Poor affect differentiation
> Poor grasp of color concepts

Middle Childhood
> Eurocentric racial attitudes and preferences
> Dramatic declines in academic performance
> Increases in aggressive or disruptive behavior
> Poor relations with peers

Adolescence
> Limited social mobility
> Fearfulness or anxiety
> Fear of going to school, cutting of classes, truancy

represents different periods of development, all of which have long-term implications and are interrelated. Research concerned with African Americans has not yet reached the level of specificity or breadth of coverage that would allow one to write about culture-specific motor, cognitive, and socioemotional development in any articulated fashion; yet there are lessons to be gleaned with respect to psychological disturbance (see Table 12–1).

In the absence of such a body of literature, it is necessary to provide a framework for understanding the factors that need to be taken into account when assessing African American children.

References

AINSWORTH, M. D. S. (1979). Infant-mother attachment. *American Psychologist, 34,* 932–937.

ALLEN, B. A., & BOYKIN, A. W. (1992). African American children and the educational process: Alleviating cultural discontinuity through prescriptive pedagogy. *School Psychology Review, 21*(4), 586–596.

ANDERSON, E. (1990). *Streetwise: Race, class, and change in an urban community.* Chicago: University of Chicago Press.

BLACKMORE, C. A., FERRE, C. D., ROWLEY, D. L., HOGUE, C. J. R., GAITER, J., & ATRASH, H. (1993). Is race a risk factor or a risk marker for preterm delivery? *Ethnicity Discourses, 3,* 372–377.

BLAIR, C., RAMEY, C. T., & HARDIN, M. J. (1995). Early intervention for low birthweight, premature infants: Participation and intellectual development. *American Journal on Mental Retardation, 99*(5), 542–554.

BOYKIN, A. W. (1986). The triple quandary and the schooling of Afro-American children. In U. Neisser (Ed.), *The school achievement of minority children* (pp. 57–92). Hillsdale, NJ: Erlbaum.

BREITMAYER, B. J., & RAMEY, C. T. (1986). Biological nonoptimality and quality of postnatal environment as codeterminants of intellectual development. *Child Development, 57,* 1151–1165.

BRONFENBRENNER, U. (1989). Ecological systems theory. *Annals of Child Development, 6,* 187–249.

BURCHINAL, M. R., BRYANT, D. M., LEE, M. W., & RAMEY, C. T. (1992). Early day care, infant-mother attachment, and maternal responsiveness in the infant's first year. *Early Childhood Research Quarterly, 7,* 383–396.

CAMPBELL, F. A., & RAMEY, C. T. (1994). Effects of early intervention on intellectual and academic achievement: A follow-up study of children from low income families. *Child Development, 65,* 684–698.

CAPUTE, A. J., SHAPIRO, B. K., PALMER, F. B., ROSS, A., & WACHTEL, R. C. (1985). Normal gross motor development: The influences of race, sex and socioeconomic status. *Developmental Medicine and Child Neurology, 27,* 635–643.

CHASE-LANSDALE, P. L., BROOKS-GUNN, J., & ZAMSKY, E. S. (1994). Young African-American multigenerational families in poverty: Quality of mothering and grandmothering. *Child Development, 65,* 373–393.

CICCHETTI, D. (1996, March). *The consequences of child maltreatment: Research and practice.* Paper presented in colloquium at University of Pennsylvania, Philadelphia, PA.

COMER, J. P., & HILL, H. (1985). Social policy and the mental health of black children. *Journal of the American Academy of Child Psychiatry, 24*(2), 175–181.

CUNNINGHAM, M. (1995, June). The influence of contextual peer-based perceptions on African-American adolescent males' gender-role development. In D. Dupree (Chair), *The development of cognitive structures for sex-role, racial identity, and coping in African-American adolescents.* Symposium conducted at the twenty-fifth annual symposium of the Jean Piaget Society, Berkeley, CA.

CURRY, G. D., & SPERGEL, I. A. (1992). Gang involvement and delinquency among Hispanic and African-American adolescent males. *Journal of Research in Crime and Delinquency, 29*(3), 273–291.

DAMON, W., & HART, D. (1982). The development of self understanding from infancy through adolescence. *Child Development, 53*(4), 841–864.

DAVIS, R. A. (1988). Adolescent pregnancy and infant mortality: Isolating the effects of race. *Adolescence, 92,* 899–908.

DUPREE, D. (1995, March). *The role of coping strategies in the relationship between experience with violence and negative affective/cognitive states.* Poster presented at the biennial meeting of the Society for Research in Child Development, Indianapolis, IN.

EPSTEIN, J. S., PRATTO, D. J., & SKIPPER, J. K. (1990). Teenagers, behavioral problems, and preferences for heavy metal and rap music: A case study of a Southern middle school. *Deviant Behavior, 11,* 381–394.

EVANS, J. P., & TAYLOR, J. (1995). Understanding violence in contemporary and earlier gangs: An exploratory application of the theory of reasoned action. *Journal of Black Psychology, 21*(1), 71–81.

FLAHERTY, M. J. (1988). Seven caring functions of black grandmothers in adolescent mothering. *Maternal Child Nursing Journal, 17*(3), 191–207.

FLAHERTY, M. J., FACTEAU, L., & GARVER, P. (1987). Grandmother functions in multigenerational families: An exploratory study of black adolescent mothers and their infants. *Maternal-Child Nursing Journal, 16*(1), 61–73.

GAITER, J. L., REYNOLDS, G. R., & MAYBERRY, R. M. (1990, October). *Determinants of pregnancy outcome for African-American women: National Survey Data.* Paper presented at the 118th annual meeting of the American Public Health Association, New York.

GARCIA-COLL, C. T. (1990). Developmental outcome of minority infants: A process-oriented look into our beginnings. *Child Development, 58,* 505–529.

GORDON, E. W. (1995). Culture and the sciences of pedagogy. *Teachers College Record, 97*(1), 32–46.

HANSEN, C. H. (1995). Predicting cognitive and behavioral effects of gangsta rap. *Basic and Applied Social Psychology, 16*(1/2), 43–52.

HARE, B. R. (1977). Racial and socioeconomic variations in preadolescent area-specific and general self esteem. *International Journal of Intercultural Relations, 1*(3), 31–51.

HOWES, C., SAKAI, L. M., SHINN, M., PHILIPS, D., GALINSKY, E., & WHITEBOOK, M. (1995). Race, social class, and maternal working conditions as influence on children's development. *Journal of Applied Developmental Psychology, 16,* 107–124.

JACKSON, J. F. (1993). Multiple caregiving among African Americans and infant attachment: The need for an emic approach. *Human Development, 36,* 87–102.

JARRETT, R. L. (1994). Living poor: Family life among single parent, African-American women. *Social Problems, 41*(1), 30–49.

JARRETT, R. L. (1995). Growing up poor: The family experiences of socially mobile youth in low income African-American neighborhoods. *Journal of Adolescent Research, 10*(1), 111–135.

JOHNSON, J. D., JACKSON, L. A., & GATTO, L. (1995). Violent attitudes and deferred academic aspirations: Deleterious effects of exposure to rap music. *Basic and Applied Social Psychology, 16*(1/2), 27–41.

KOTTAK, C. P. (1987). *Cultural anthropology.* New York: Random House.

LEADBEATER, B. J., & BISHOP, S. J. (1994). Predictors of behavior problems in preschool children of inner-city Afro-American and Puerto Rican adolescent mothers. *Child Development, 65,* 638–648.

LIAW, F., & BROOKS-GUNN, J. (1993). Patterns of low-birth-weight children's cognitive development. *Developmental Psychology, 6,* 1024–1035.

MACLOED, J. (1995). *Ain't no makin' it.* Boulder, CO: Westview Press.

MYERS, H. F., TAYLOR, S., ALVY, K. T., ARRINGTON, A., & RICHARDSON, M. A. (1992). Parental and family predictors of behavior problems in inner-city black children. *American Journal of Community Psychology, 20*(5), 557–576.

OYEMADE, U. J. (1985). The rationale for Head Start as a vehicle for the upward mobility of minority families: A minority perspective. *American Journal of Orthopsychiatry, 55*(4), 591–602.

OYEMADE, U. J., COLE, O. J., JOHNSON, A. A., KNIGHT, E. M., WESTNEY, O. E., LARYEA, H., HILL, G., CANNON, E., FOMUFOD, A., WESTNEY, L. S., JONES, S., & EDWARDS, C. H. (1994). Prenatal predictors of performance on the Brazelton Neonatal Behavioral Assessment Scale. *Journal of Nutrition, 124,* 1000s–1005s.

RAMEY, C. T., & RAMEY, S. L. (1992). Effective early intervention. *Mental Retardation, 30*(6), 337–345.

REEB, K. G., GRAHAM, A. V., ZYZANSKI, S. J., & KITSON, G. K. (1987). Predicting low birthweight and complicated labor in urban black women: A biopsychosocial perspective. *Social Science Medicine, 25*(12), 1321–1327.

RESCHLY, D. J., & WARD, S. M. (1991). Use of adaptive behavior measures and overrepresentation of black students in programs for students with mild mental retardation. *American Journal on Mental Retardation, 96*(3), 257–268.

SLAUGHTER-DEFOE, D. T., NAKAGAWA, K., TAKANISHI, R., & JOHNSON, D. J. (1990). Toward cultural/ecological perspectives on schooling and achievement in African- and Asian American children. *Child Development, 61,* 363–383.

SPENCER, M. B. (1982a). Personal and group identity of Black children: An alternative synthesis. *Genetic Psychology Monographs, 103,* 59–84.

SPENCER, M. B. (1982b). Preschool children's social cognition and cultural cognition: A cognitive developmental interpretation of race dissonance findings. *Journal of Psychology, 112,* 275–286.

SPENCER, M. B. (1983). Children's cultural values and parental child rearing strategies. *Developmental Review, 3,* 351–370.

SPENCER, M. B. (1984). Black children's race awareness, racial attitudes, and self-concept: A reinterpretation. *Journal of Child Psychology and Psychiatry, 25*(3), 433–441.

SPENCER, M. B. (1985). Cultural cognition and social cognition as identity factors in Black children's personal-social growth. In M. B. Spencer, G. K. Brookins, & W. R. Allen (Eds.), *Beginnings: The social and affective development of Black children* (pp. 85–111). Beverly Hills, CA: Sage.

SPENCER, M. B. (1987). Black children's ethnic identity formation: Risk and resilience of castelike minorities. In K. S. Phinney & M. J. Rotheram (Eds.), *Children's ethnic socialization.* Beverly Hills, CA: Sage.

SPENCER, M. B. (1990). Parental values transmission: Implications for Black child development. In J. B. Stewart & H. Cheathan (Eds.), *Interdisciplinary perspectives on Black families* (pp. 111–130). New Brunswick, NJ: Transaction Books.

SPENCER, M. B. (1995). Old issues and new theorizing about African-American youth: A phenomenological variant of the ecological systems theory. In R. L. Taylor (Ed.), *Black youth: Perspectives on their status in the United States* (pp. 37–70). Westport, CT: Praeger.

SPENCER, M. B., BLUMENTHAL, J. B., & RICHARDS, E. (1995). Child care and children of color. In P. L. Chase-Lansdale & J. Brooks-Gunn (Eds.), *Escape from poverty: What makes a difference for children?* (pp. 138–156). New York: Cambridge University Press.

SPENCER, M. B., CUNNINGHAM, M., & SWANSON, D. P. (1995). Identity as coping: Adolescent African-American males' adaptive responses to high-risk environments. In H. W. Harris, H. C. Blue, & E. H. Griffith (Eds.), *Racial and ethnic identity: Psychological development and creative expression* (pp. 31–52). New York: Routledge & Kegan Paul.

SPENCER, M. B., & DORNBUSCH, S. (1990). American minority adolescents. In S. Feldman & G. Elliot (Eds.), *At the threshold: The developing adolescent.* Cambridge, MA: Harvard University Press.

SPENCER, M. B., & DUPREE, D. (in press). African-American youth's eco-cultural challenges and psychosocial opportunities: An alternative analysis of problem behavior outcomes. In D. Cicchetti & S. Toth (Eds.), *Development and psychopathology.*

SPENCER, M. B., & HOROWITZ, F. D. (1973). Racial attitudes and color concept-attitude modification in Black and Caucasian preschool children. *Developmental Psychology, 9*, 246–254.

Spencer, M. B., & Markstrom-Adams, C. (1990). Identity processes among racial and ethnic minority children in America. *Child Development, 61*(2), 290–310.

Spencer, M. B., McDermott, P. A., Burton, L., & Cole, S. P. (in press). An alternative approach to assessing neighborhood effects on early adolescent achievement and problem behavior. In J. Brooks-Gunn & G. Duncan (Eds.), *Neighborhood, poverty and youth outcomes.*

Stallworth, R. (1994, February). *The influence of gang culture on American society.* Testimony before the United States Senate Subcommittee on Juvenile Justice on the Influence of Lyrics on Children, Washington, DC.

Teberg, A. J., Howell, V. V., & Wingert, W. A. (1983). Attachment interaction behavior between young teenage mothers and their infants. *Journal of Adolescent Health Care, 4,* 61–66.

Took, K. J., & Weiss, D. S. (1994). The relationship between heavy metal and rap music and adolescent turmoil real or artifact? *Adolescence, 29*(115), 613–621.

Tucker, C. M., Brady, B. A., Harris, Y. R., Fraser, K., & Tribble, I. (1993). The association of selected parent behaviors with the adaptive and maladaptive functioning of black children and white children. *Child Study Journal, 23*(1), 39–55.

U.S. Bureau of the Census. (1992). *Current population reports* (P-20). Washington, DC: U.S. Government Printing Office.

Van IJzendoorn, M. H. (1993). Commentary. *Human Development, 36,* 103–105.

Wilson, M. N., & Tolson, T. F. J. (1990). Familial support in the black community. *Journal of Clinical Child Psychology, 19*(4), 347–355.

Yeargin-Allsopp, M., Drews, C. D., Decoufle, P., & Murphy, C. C. (1995). Mild mental retardation in Black and White children in metropolitan Atlanta: A case-control study. *American Journal of Public Health, 85*(3), 324–328.

CHAPTER 13

West African Children

JULIETTE TUAKLI-WILLIAMS

ACCORDING TO THE 1995 census, 11.5 million persons immigrated to the United States between 1960 and 1990. In 1974, 0.7% of all immigrants were from sub-Saharan Africa, excluding South Africa. By 1985, this proportion had tripled (Madhavon, 1985). In 1980, a total of 13,981 immigrants were admitted to the United States from Africa, of which 7,692 were from sub-Saharan Africa. In 1985, the number of African immigrants to the United States had risen to 17,117; of these, 11,203 were of sub-Saharan descent. Since 1985, there has been a doubling of the rate of immigration. With the exclusion of the years 1975, 1984, and 1985, from 1974 to 1995 the largest numbers of immigrants from sub-Saharan Africa have been Nigerians. Ghanaians have been the second largest group, followed by Kenyans. In 1975, Ugandans were the largest number immigrating into the United States, coinciding with Idi Amin's rise to power in that country. Likewise, in 1984 and 1985, Ethiopians made up the largest number of immigrants, coinciding with that country's political and economic upheavals (Logan, 1987).

The immigrants from sub-Saharan Africa have generally been highly trained and skilled workers (Aderinto, 1978). In 1967, a United Nations study showed that of the 417 Nigerian immigrants admitted to the United States between June 30, 1962 and June 30, 1967, 255 were in skilled occupations, which included 131 professionals and technicians; 31 engineers; 9 physicians and

34 professional nurses (Aderinto, 1978). The "brain drain" has not been exclusively to the United States. The total numbers of skilled workers immigrating to the United States, Canada, and the United Kingdom between 1962 and 1973 (excluding 1970) was 3,246, 1,326, and 10,176 persons, respectively (Adepoju, 1977). Europe was the destination of choice for three times as many immigrants. Nigerians represent the single largest immigrant group from Africa—1.62 million in 1995, according to the 1995 census report. West Africans have consistently been the largest proportion of sub-Saharan Africans immigrating to the United States and Nigerians have been particularly well represented in this group. Nigerians will therefore be used in this chapter as examples of West African immigrant children.

Immigrant Characteristics

Notwithstanding independence in the 1960s, Africa remains a continent in crisis. Peace and prosperity remain elusive because of serious and widespread economic and political turmoil. The oil price shock, drought, and economic recession of the early, mid- and late 1970s has given way to military conflicts and the displacement of people in the 1990s. Twenty-two of the world's 36 poorest countries are in Africa where the per capita income for many of these countries has grown less than 1% per year (Klitgaard, 1990). Infant mortality rates ranging from 48 to 161 per 1,000 live births are among the highest in the world with life expectancies among the lowest, averaging around 50 years.

As noted, there has been a dramatic increase in the number of West African immigrants to the United States, of whom the vast majority are Nigerian. The region's share of total sub-Saharan immigration increased from 47% in 1977 to 65% in 1980. Those who have immigrated have generally been the most skilled and enterprising people. Apraku (1991) has profiled West African immigrants and shows that the average age tended to be 40 years with a preponderance of males. Additionally, 78% are married with children. As a group, they are highly educated: 58% hold doctorate degrees; an additional 19% arrive with master's degrees. Some 60% receive further formal training and education after immigration to the United States. By comparison, the median years of school completed for the American population in 1980 was 12.5 years. Apraku (1991) also notes that West African immigrants have an average of 6 years' work experience prior to immigration and remain in the United States for an average of 12.4 years. The immigrants in his study cited political freedom and economic opportunity as their main reasons for immigration and desire to remain in the United States. They noted racism and discrimination against Blacks, crime, drugs, violence, alienation, and a lack of sense of belonging as main dislikes in America.

Nigeria came into being in 1914 following an amalgamation of three main tribal groupings as decreed by British colonialists. The three groups were the Hausa-Fulani in the north; the Igbo in the southeast; and the Yoruba in the southwest. The three groups are extremely diverse. The Hausa-Fulani are one of the oldest Islamic civilizations and flourished well before the British Empire. Ninety-eight percent of this group are Muslim compared with 42% of Yoruba and less than 1% of the Igbo groups. However, rates of polygyny are fairly constant: 42% among the Hausa-Fulani and the Yoruba; 30% among the Igbo. Female literacy rates differ widely: in the north, approximately 5% of females are literate compared with 42% among the Yoruba and 40% among the Igbo. The age of marriage for Hausa-Fulani girls averages 12 to 14 years compared with 18 to 19 years among the Yoruba and Igbo (Ericksen, 1993). The Hausa-Fulani and Yoruba traditionally have strictly hierarchal societies based on large, highly networked kinship groups. The Yoruba have traveled extensively as traders and artisans between highly centralized kingdoms since the 13th century (Bosman, 1967). The Igbo have, by comparison, a republican community model with more egalitarian relationships between gender, age, and class (personal observation).

Apraku (1991) and Kamya (1994) note the very strong ties among Nigerian immigrants that are maintained with families and home countries. Only 10% of immigrants had not returned for a visit following immigration. Among the participants of Apraku's (1991) study, 55% had returned an average of one or more times in 1 to 3 years; 19% had returned once or more per year. Only 12% did not make remittances to immediate family, other relatives, or friends. Remittance amounts varied from $1,000 to $10,000 per year. Personal investment projects were financed in the home countries by more than half. On inquiry, only 10% planned to remain in the United States permanently. Apraku's (1991) group of immigrants from the 1980s are younger and less well-educated, and have less work experience prior to immigration. Premigratory experiences and expectations exert a significant influence on the mental health of the immigrant. Among nonrefugee immigrants of working age (between 15 and 64 years of age), the percentage receiving welfare subsidies is significantly lower than for African Americans of the same age range. The same pattern holds true for unemployment after an initial transition period (see Figure 13–1). After 10 years in the United States, legal Nigerian immigrants have higher than average incomes. Only 29% of native-born Americans earn between $32,000 and $59,999, whereas 53% of a study sample of West

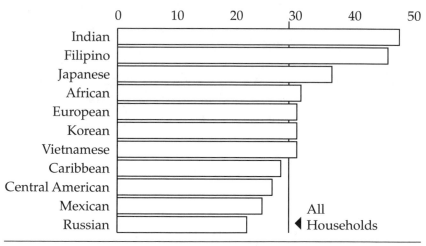

Source: Census Bureau

FIGURE 13–1
The Golden Door. Foreign-Born Median Household
Income, 1989 (in Thousands)

African immigrants had earnings in this range (Apraku, 1991). More than 14% earned over $100,000 compared with only 2.9% of the native-born U.S. population.

Reasons for Emigration

It has been argued that it is not mere poverty or underdevelopment that is responsible for emigration as much as it is the asymmetry between the capacity of a nation to produce numbers of highly trained personnel and its capacity to absorb them (Portes, 1976; Portes & Rumbault, 1990). In addition, Nigeria has increasingly been characterized by a lack of adequate human resources planning, which has resulted in inadequate material and monetary support for the large numbers of high-level professionals produced. The University education system has been modeled along the same lines as that of the West rather than according to the national conditions. This has facilitated the ease with which professionals enter the international labor market (UNESCO, 1983). Okedeji and Okedeji (1973) argue that many African immigrants have been strongly influenced by political instability, authoritarianism, and tribalism. In this context, between 1966 and 1969 no less than 22 African governments were taken over by the military in coup d'états. Aderinto (1978) supports the thesis that a desire to seek further education and a dire economic situation are the main motivations both to immigrate and to remain abroad. In international migration, political factors may be more important than economic factors.

Developmental and Cultural Issues Affecting Children of West African Immigrants

Brooks-Gunn (1995) makes the plea that children's development be assessed in context. In keeping with this concept, this chapter will try to address significant influences on the development of children and adolescents by the Nigerian family and culture. The context within which the norms of family and culture are applied, may vary, as for other immigrant groups, with the degree to which parents have achieved educationally, occupationally, and financially. There is a paucity of developmental research contrasting psychopathological conditions with normative culturally influenced developmental processes for this group. Any comprehensive review of Nigerian children and adolescents must include a review of the research in the general U.S. child and adolescent population, including African Americans and other groups from the African diaspora.

There is a significant correlation between personal and social resources with premigratory psychosocial status. However, one of the most important adaptations that Nigerian families face on arrival in the United States is an abrupt change in social status from a majority group affiliate to a minority group affiliate (McKelvey & Webb, 1996). This change occurs regardless of social status as the stratification is based solely on skin color. The consequences of such stratification may lead to exaggerated attempts to identify with African Americans particularly among the younger adolescent immigrants (Rawlings, 1995). Kamya (1994) supports earlier studies showing that a resentment of racism and discrimination based solely on skin color is a major factor in the decision to return to Nigeria in 90% of returning families. Also, nearly as significant is a feeling of isolation; many families resent their treatment and exclusion by both Black and White Americans. Nigerians are socially heterogeneous with individuals acquiring membership in widely divergent groups, each of which functions only in reference to a certain segment of one's personality (Wirth, 1969). The absence of family and friends becomes increasingly pronounced for parents as the stresses of raising an enlarged nuclear family without the traditional moral, emotional, and financial support of family and friends takes its toll. This interrelationship between stress and self-esteem in immigrant families is explored in some depth by Kamya (1994).

Rutter (1987) has proposed four coping mechanisms in children, including:

1. Reduce the impact of stress.
2. Avoid chain reactions.

3. Establish self-sufficiency and self-esteem.
4. Seek new opportunities.

Protective family factors include homes in which rules are consistently and fairly enforced; where good supervision and well-balanced discipline exists: where a high level of warmth and an absence of severe criticism are maintained; and an adequate identification figure is present in the household (Garmezy, 1981; Rutter, 1979; Werner & Smith, 1982). Children are extremely important to Nigerians. Forty percent of all Nigerian women lose at least one child unintentionally during their childbirth years (Ericksen, 1993). In addition, children are said to represent both the past and present through ancestral and returning spirits. Individuals with children are accorded far more social recognition and respect than those without children. In Nigeria, adult children are expected to care for aged parents. Women particularly seek to enhance their economic security in a polygynous society through the acquisition of children and property. First-born and only children make up nearly 50% of all American children, but only 11% of Nigerian children (LeVine, 1990). These attitudes persist in most Nigerian immigrant families. A baby is considered inhabited by a soul that is accessible to diviners, deities, and ancestors. Ancestral souls are believed to return through children. The returning souls always skip at least one generation; therefore a child may be a grandmother or grandfather reincarnated or from earlier generations. The characterization and development of "the self" are believed to take shape through many child-rearing practices, ceremonies, and rituals. In the United States, immigrant Nigerian families perform attenuated rituals to highlight aspects of family identity and unquestioned cultural absolutes of generations past. It is not uncommon for individual families to apply established rituals to new situations or create new rituals that partake of old ideologies (Drewal, 1992).

Health and disease are considered inextricably linked with socially approved behavior and moral conduct (Appiah-Kubi, 1976). One's psychological development is considered part of one's physical health, as the mind and the body are treated and considered as one unit. Traditionally, great stress is placed on the prevention of ill health with ancestors approached routinely through divination for peace, harmony, and spiritual health (Appiah-Kubi, 1976). In addition, Nigerian parents hold high aspirations for themselves and their children. A peer system exerts strong influences that reinforce high educational aspirations. The children are designated as peers at 3-year intervals of one another or with respect to a temporal relationship with major events occurring within the prior or present year of a child's birth. Where religious influences predominate, as in the predominantly Muslim northern states, smaller peer groups are more common; these are known as "special friendships" or *Kawaye* (Hausa). The following vignette illustrates how Nigerian families in the United States try to establish a peer group close in age to reinforce traditional values and educational aspirations of the family:

> An Atlanta-based cohort of 12- to 15-year-old youngsters recently underwent puberty rites that involved community-based activities such as cleaning local playgrounds and tutoring younger siblings. The timing of these activities was designated by their elders of the home country community and family relations in Onitsha, Eastern Nigeria. Concurrent elaborate masquerades and village sports *(Ibanamor)* were coordinated at the same time in Onitsha to ensure that the Atlanta group retained allegiance with its traditional group. The Atlanta group will become wards of their villages *(Umu ilo)* and be expected to relay their academic and social progress at regular intervals. The threat of being sent back to live with relatives in Nigeria generally serves as motivation for these teenagers where all else fails.

An individual's name reflects the events surrounding that individual's birth. Naming performed with elaborate ritual 3 to 10 days after birth. The elder family members, who are considered to have the closest connections to ancestors, choose names in conjunction with parents. The naming ceremonies may be used to enforce social harmony and order by providing the parents with a program of prescribed actions or behaviors with respect to their child rearing. As will be shown, an individual derives an individual identity, familial and lineage positioning, and inheritance based on this system. The following are examples of the way in which events are used in determining the name of newborns:

> The name *Oladele* was the given name of an infant born to a couple recently reconciled after a long period of separation that was marked by intense acrimony. The name means "Honor comes home" (Yoruba).
>
> The name *Ofili* was the given name of a child born after a couple lost two infants to sudden infant death syndrome. The name means "Born to stay" (Igbo).
>
> The name *Odiakosa* was the given name of a child not expected to survive an adverse pregnancy. The mother was a political refugee who had fled, pregnant, on foot from her village to join her husband in Boston, Massachusetts. The name means "In the hands of God" (Igbo).
>
> The name *Abiku* is traditionally given to a child not expected to live. Such children foster either overprotective or rejecting parental behaviors. It means "Born to die" (Yoruba).

Hausa-Fulani children are named in accordance with the dictates of Islam. Hausa-Fulani are also unique in the strict gender segregation that is maintained domestically. Women and children are cloistered together in an emotionally enmeshed setting. Cultural expectations and knowledge tend to be extraordinarily constant over time in a social environment highly regulated by age and rank. Boys and men have much social power and engage in highly symbolic communications with females while retaining considerable physical distance from their dependent families. As Hausa-Fulani girls are married when very young, their childhoods become truncated and terminate in a profound change in social repertoires at an early age.

The Nigerian kinship system is complex and much like the Aboriginal 8-class kinship system (Mead, 1978). Through this system, families adapt to their physical environment; address problems, stresses, and conflicts; and structure interpersonal relationships (D'Andrade, 1985). The complex kinship system has the effect of strengthening obligations and ties to elders and kin. The highly symbolic communications that refer to consanguineal kinship terms are not only much more numerous than in American culture, but may differ in definition. The patterns of interpersonal relationships affect behavior and cognitive interactions. For example, a junior Hausa would expect to prostrate in greeting a senior while saying *"Ranka dede"* / "May you live long." A Yoruba would expect to genuflect while greeting an elder.

Nigerian parents traditionally provide an early environment for their children that is indulgent and permissive with access to many relations as supportive caretakers. Raising children in the United States frequently is marked by a lack of the security once provided by the community structure and a lack of ready access to the traditionally recognized repositories of wisdom and guidance, for example, elderly relatives. The role(s) of younger relations and siblings with respect to child care may become attenuated by educational or occupational needs. Many parents find their personal capacities inadequate for the restoration of their own psychological well-being. Anxiety and situational stress are not uncommon in families with children. Situational stress, inadequate treatment of parental psychopathology, marital discord, low social status, and overcrowding are significant environmental factors that cumulatively, may exert adverse effects on the normal psychological development of Nigerian children (Downey & Coyne, 1990; Hall, Williams, & Greenberg, 1985; Rutter, 1979; Wahler & Dumas, 1986).

Early maternal-child interactions reflect the traditionally high infant mortality rate (61 per 1,000 live births in 1991, according to the 1991 Nigerian Census), and even higher postneonatal mortality rates: 78–92 per 1,000 live births that families have become accustomed to in Nigeria (Ericksen, 1993). Breastfeeding, permissive, attentive parenting, and an emphasis on the development of self-regulated individual competence for the benefit of a collective system of family and cohorts may mitigate some of the environmental stresses faced.

Biological risk factors such as sickle cell disease, malaria, and maternal malnutrition are prevalent. The effects of such biological risk factors persist among immigrants in the United States. Access to prompt medical care in America ameliorates much of the adverse outcomes however. As shown by Werner and Smith (1982), perinatal complications correlate with future impairments in both physical and psychological development for children when combined with persistent, poor environmental conditions, and practices such as female genital mutilation.

According to concepts elaborated by Hecht, Andersen, and Ribeau (1989), Nigerian culture is a high-context culture. There is less reliance on verbal communications than on understanding through shared experiences, history, and implicit messages relayed through rituals and ceremonies. Nigerians tend to be more attuned to nonverbal cues and messages when communicating. There are more formal relationships with well-defined hierarchies established within the culture, which is more deeply rooted in the past (Hall, 1976). High-context cultures are noted to change slowly, providing a healthy stability. Parents construct learning environments for their children that foster the acquisition of skills and virtues valued in their community. Nigerian parents organize a learning environment for their children that often involves less maternal excitement or stimulation during infancy by American standards, but more praise, structure, and support as the child grows older. Children are generally discouraged from talking to and overly seeking attention from adults. However, older siblings are expected to provide as much attention as needed from the age of 6 to 7 years. This is consistent with a traditional family and community environment organized as an age hierarchy that emphasizes respect and compliance from the young and acceptance of one's proper place in the hierarchy. Social participation in American society has necessitated significantly more self-assertion and exposure to an openly competitive atmosphere. Feelings of excessive vulnerability and great anxiety may result from the relative lack of emotional support for initiative and accomplishment that American children typically get from their parents in the early years and eventually internalize.

Althen (1988) has identified eight values and assumptions that characterize the dominant American culture:

1. Importance of individualism and privacy.
*2. Belief in the equality of all individuals.
*3. Informality in interactions with others.
*4. Emphasis on the future, change, and progress.
5. Belief in the general goodness of humanity.
*6. Emphasis on the importance of time and punctuality.
7. High regard for achievement, action, work, and materialism.
*8. Pride in interactional styles that are direct and assertive.

The five asterisked items are all consistent with the low-context culture of the United States. The seventh item is a shared value in both Nigerian and American cultures.

Goodman (1964) and Porter (1971) state that children become aware of cultural differences by the age of 3 to 4 years. Between ages 4 and 8 years, children develop an ethnic orientation (Goodman, 1964). Changes in a child's ethnic awareness may occur in response to a change in generational or sociocultural group, developmental growth, or the interaction among these influences (Canino & Spurlock, 1994). Both enculturation and acculturation occur; the latter involving assimilation and biculturalism. Enculturation can be defined as an awareness and acquisition of the social norms (Berry, Trimble, & Olmedo, 1986). Nigerian immigrant children undergo both of these processes. Being raised in the United States, immigrant Nigerian children develop a dual consciousness as the ways in which the young are required to behave within their adopted community. However, this awareness is typically at sharp variance with the cultural behaviors of their forebears, parents, and other relatives.

In Nigerian culture, children represent wealth; past and present incarnations of ancestral souls; and social security for their families. There is four times the American rate of twin births: 45.1 per 1,000 births compared with 11 per 1,000 births (Nylander, 1969). The rituals associated with twin births are even more elaborate than for single births. Because many of the attenuated rituals require substitute diviners to take on the roles of the *imams* or priests, elders are appointed within Nigerian community groups in most large cities to which residents further afield may also turn for assistance as required. Rituals associated with birth, puberty, marriage, and death are performed for immigrant families. Counseling and mediation are also provided by these individuals. It is not uncommon for these persons to have become chieftains within their home communities before assuming the role of elder in their American microcommunity. When children are born in America, attenuated forms of the "Stepping into the World" *(Ikose w'aye),* "Outdooring," and "Knowing the Head" *(Imori)* rites are held in conjunction with baptismal, church, and mosque services. As mentioned, names are of extreme importance and serve the following functions: (a) to recognize formally the infant's crucial existential identities of membership within the family lines of one or both parents, (b) to acknowledge events preceding or accompanying the infant's birth, (c) to delineate birth order and gender, and (d) to ascribe a corpus of personal texts to serve as models for self-interpretation and guidance on life's long journey. Thus, inquiry into the meaning of a given traditional name can highlight important psychosocial information about a child, adolescent, and even the family.

Case Example

A child was born to a couple having marital discord because of the husband's gambling habits. The infant's personal text was sent from the husband's community in Nigeria. It was advised that the infant be raised near calm waters from whence much prosperity would emanate. The infant's father was advised to renounce gambling as this would serve to make the waters turbulent and prevent the infant from living up to his given name "Oladele" which means "Honor comes home."

Among the Yoruba, twins of any gender are named Taiwo (1st twin) and Kehinde (2nd twin) from the names *To aiye wo*—"to taste the world first" and *Ko-ehinde*—"to come behind or after."

Children of any gender born after twins are called *Idowu*—"hard, fast" and *Alaba*—"softly, softly," in that order. The Igbo name twins according to gender and birth order for example *Uzo amaka*—"the road is good" (girl); *Uzo echinah*—"the road will never close" (boy).

An infant born after the intercession of a deity (accompanied by prayers, infertility treatments, divination, etc.) will be named in that deity's honor. For example, *Esubiyi*—"Esu gave birth to this one"; *Ogunbiyi*—"Ogun gave birth to this one." (Ogun is the deity of iron and war; devotees are hunters, warriors, or professionals in contact with iron such as taxi drivers, truck drivers.)

For the first three years of a child's life, Nigerian mothers traditionally have sole rights to a child. There is a tremendous amount of physical engagement that is accepted as normal, even desirable. A mother's only duty at this time is to be with her child and to remain soothing, indulgent, and enduring in her affections. In America, economic pressures may necessitate the use of surrogate caretakers. Extreme distress may ensue should an out-of-home, unknown caretaker be the only choice available to parents particularly within the first year of life. By age 4, a child will have a sibling to serve as a primary caretaker, should one be available. The learning of proper social forms of address are stressed, including the correct use of titles, kinship, age, and status terms; appropriate greetings; and the observance of rank, status, and power differences. Children are not considered responsible for their behavior until age 6 years. Older siblings are held directly responsible for any mishaps or infractions committed by their charges. Self-regulatory skills are gently encouraged. However, solitary eating behaviors tend to be strongly discouraged, and toilet training is not considered a priority before the age of 5 years. Although the acquisition of verbal skills is highly encouraged by American families, only verbal skills that reinforce the social obligatory behaviors of the culture are strongly encouraged by Nigerians. Older siblings and adults model social skill development during social gatherings, ceremonies, and rituals. The vocalization of thoughts, wishes, and feelings is considered

inappropriate in many instances because it is believed that to vo-
calize them gives added magical power to the thought or the
thinker. Socialization invariably includes learning how, when,
and where to express oneself. From the age of 6 years, children
are expected to actively reinforce social conventions and moral
rules and are invested with this capacity in the delineation of
chores, responsibilities, and privileges. Social convention takes
precedence over morality. The attainment of education is an important expectation as is the provision of services that enhance
the family unit such as food preparation and child care. In the
traditional realm, the main developmental goal of this period is
to enhance self-sufficiency.

Puberty, the next major developmental milestone, occurs
between 12 and 14 years of age. Somatic maturation typically
occurs later than in America (personal observation). Nutrition, general health, and living conditions exert a significant
influence. Menarche and mature spermatozoa production
occur approximately two years later than in America. For
girls, the onset of menarche is considered the onset of adulthood. Various rites are observed both abroad and in Nigeria
even among those of mixed parentage (American/Nigerian)
(personal observation). These rites are performed by parents
or godparents in lieu of diviners and spiritualists. Parents
typically characterize the transition by social events and by
changing a youngster's wardrobe or jewelry. Parents typically
shelter daughters and focus on educational attainment at a
time when the early adolescent begins to seek out peer approval from mainstream friends and associates. Boys may participate in ritualistic behaviors where a cohort can be
established either in America or Nigeria. For boys, education
is an even more important focus than for girls. Unlike girls,
boys are given much more latitude though not as much as
would be granted in a traditional Nigerian setting. Nigerian
immigrants harbor much concern about crime, violence, drug
use, and unintended pregnancies.

Teens of either gender assume increasing social responsibilities that may place them at odds with peer group activities.
Not infrequently, teens are sent to vacation in Nigeria where

they are imbued with unsolicited advice and familial expectations by well-intentioned relations who seek to reinforce traditional expectations and desires. This practice is known as
"rustication." The extreme importance given to the adherence
to social convention both mitigates and stimulates emotional
conflict in teens. The Nigerian teenager in America has to recognize a different social identity that needs to be incorporated
into familial and host country cultural models. The frame of reference for a comparison of the adolescents' present status and
future possibilities, that is a status mobility framework, depends on the teen's collective identity and the degree of trust retained within the family unit (Ogbu, 1987). A dual-status
mobility framework is generally retained in which education
and behavior conducive to school success are paramount. Where
this does not occur, a teen is commonly returned to Nigeria
should other parental interventions fail.

Case Examples

A 13-year-old teenager had begun to defy her mother at home
and display disruptive behaviors at school. The parents sought
guidance from the chiefs serving the Nigerian community in
that section of the city. A collection was taken up, and the
teenager was enrolled the following year in a private school in
Nebraska. She returned home for school vacations and her parents visited as regularly as able while paying off the debt in-
curred. The teenager performed extremely well at school and
was allowed to re-enroll at the previous school two years later.
She remains an honor student in her senior year. When asked
what changed, she stated that she was afraid she'd be given a
one-way ticket to Nigeria.

An 11-year-old boy engaged in a loud verbal altercation with his
father that resulted in neighbors calling in the police. The father
was charged with disturbing the peace in court. His son returned to Nigeria within the month to complete his school year.
A family emergency was the reason cited to the school for his
abrupt departure.

Clinical Complications

In Nigeria, all education except Islamic religious instruction is conducted in English. Thus, Nigerian immigrants are conversant, to varying degrees, in English. Notwithstanding linguistic fluency, a significant degree of cultural disruption occurs with immigration. It also affects adversely, the social power and status individuals and families have hitherto enjoyed. Cultural discontinuity is of greater significance among Nigerian American children as the collective interpretation of their social reality with the attendant psychosocial adaptations over time that are inevitable, continue to evoke a plurality of cultural models. In addition, the cognizance of being culturally different may evoke feelings of isolation. It would appear that older Nigerians recognize this plurality as a collection of differing right or wrong, superior or inferior systems. However, depression among older Nigerians follows recognition of lessened social status within this society. Teens and children are particularly vulnerable to mixed messages from the media and a relative lack of emotional support for initiative and accomplishment to the degree that they observe in their American counterparts. Teenagers also learn to become more expressive verbally. Where such behaviors are supported by the family or caretaker, less anxiety appears to develop (personal observation). The importance of rituals cannot be overestimated because such behaviors enable a mastery and manipulation of power for a distressed individual in a manner that encourages family and community members to rally and provide needed support and assistance.

Therapists need to inquire about the meanings of given names to obtain perinatal information of importance. Should the client present with a Christian name, the client should be queried about other traditional names, even though they are not ostensibly being used. Gentle questioning about family and community rituals to ameliorate specific concerns is also productive when taking a history. Therapists should remember the Nigerian client's familiarity with high-context communication styles, particularly if little meaningful information is elicited initially. The use of English as a second language may introduce differing understanding of familiar concepts. A family seeking a therapist can be assumed to have engaged in other more traditional therapeutic modalities prior to seeking such tertiary assistance.

Case Examples

O.J., an inner-city resident who immigrated 20 years ago to Boston, and his wife own two busy pharmacies. They have twin teenage boys born with sickle cell anemia. Reluctant to engage an out-of-home caretaker to supplement the caretaking efforts of the older siblings who attended school full-time, Mrs. O.J. deferred the defense of her PhD thesis to be able to attend to her sons' frequent medical crises. Both older children were accepted at Harvard. The twins have had difficulty maintaining adequate high school grades. Mrs. O.J. recently returned from a trip to Nigeria with her twin sons. She admitted to seeking ritual medicines and divination counseling for her twin boys while "on vacation" in Nigeria.

A 16-year-old sophomore began to fall off in her grades at school. She was a gifted youngster who had consistently performed well across the board, seemingly well socialized and popular among her peers. A school counselor with whom she had established rapport invited her to dinner. During their meal, the student broke down and sobbed. She told the counselor of how hard "being a double minority was." She said she felt unable to share important concerns about the political upheaval in Nigeria and the effect of hearing only negative opinions in the media discouraged any casual discussion with any of her friends.

A child's or family's enrollment in *both* American and Nigerian community groups should be encouraged, for example, the Zumunta Association in America for northerners; annual Igbo Congress; the Yoruba Community of Massachusetts, or the Organization of Nigerian Professionals.

Most importantly, therapists would do well to remember that the mind and the body are understood as a single unit in Nigerian culture. A holistic approach to any therapeutic intervention is therefore more effective. To assess the mental and emotional health of immigrant Nigerian children in America, it is important to recognize the children's interpretation of their social reality pre- and postmigration and their own retention of ethnic values and worldview identification (Brice, 1982).

References

ADEPOJU, A. (1977). Migration and development in tropical Africa: Some research priorities. In *African affairs 76* (p. 223). New York: Oxford University Press.

ADERINTO, A. (1978). Toward a better understanding of brain drain. In *Human resources and African development* (p. 324). New York: Praeger.

ALTHEN, G. (1988). *American ways—A guide for foreigners in the United States*. Yarmouth, ME: Intercultural Press.

APPIAH-KUBI, K. (1976). The church's healing ministry. *Ecumenical Review of Mission, 39*(4), 404–412.

APPIAH-KUBI, K. (1993). Traditional African healing versus Western medicine. In J. K. Olupona & S. N. Sulayman (Eds.), *Religious plurality in Africa*. Mouton: De Gruyter.

APRAKU, K. A. (1991). *African Émigrés in the USA: A missing link in Africa's social and economic development*. Boston: Boston University.

BERRY, J., TRIMBLE, J., & OLMEDO, E. (1986). Assessment of acculturation. In W. Lonner & J. Berry (Eds.), *Field method in cross cultural research* (pp. 291–394). Newbury Park, CA: Sage.

BOSMAN, W. (1967). *A new and accurate description of the coast of Guinea*. London: Frank Cass. (Original work published 1705)

BRICE, J. (1982). West Indian families. In R. Barr (Ed.), *Handbook of reading research* (pp. 123–133). White Plains, NY: Longman.

BROOKS-GUNN, L. (1995). Children in families in communities: Risk and intervention in the Bronfenbrenner tradition. In P. Moen, G. H. Elder, Jr., & K. Luscher (Eds.), *Examining lives in context* (pp. 467–519). Washington, DC: American Psychological Association.

Canino, I. A., & Spurlock, J. (1994). *Culturally diverse children and adolescents: Assessment, diagnosis and treatment.* New York: Guilford Press

Chukunta, N. K. O. (1976). *The Nigerian brain drain: Factors associated with the expatriation of American educated Nigerians.* Unpublished PhD dissertation, Rutgers State University of New Jersey.

D'Andrade, R. G. (1985). Character terms and cultural models. In J. Dougherty (Ed.), *Cognitive anthropology* (pp. 88–119). New York: Cambridge University Press.

Downey, G., & Coyne, J. C. (1990). Children of depressed parents: An integrative review. *Psychological Bulletin, 108,* 50–70.

Drewal, M. T. (1992). *Yoruba ritual: Performers, play, agency* (pp. 63–88). Bloomington: Indiana University Press.

Ericksen, K. (1993). *Patterns of infertility in sub-Saharan Africa.* Washington, DC: National Institute of Health.

Garmezy, N. (1981). Children under stress: Perspectives on antecedents and correlates of vulnerability and resistance to psychopathology. In A. I. Rabin, J. Aronoff, A. M. Barclay, & R. A. Zucker (Eds.), *Further explorations in personality* (pp. 196–270). New York: Wiley.

Goodman, M. E. (1964). *Race awareness in young children* (Rev. ed.). New York: Collier Books.

Hall, A., Williams, C. A., & Greenberg, R. S. (1985). Supports, stressors and depressive symptoms in low income mothers of young children. *American Journal of Public Health, 75,* 518–522.

Hall, E. (1976). *Beyond culture.* Garden City, NY: Anchor Books.

Hecht, M. L., Andersen, P. A., & Ribeau, S. A. (1989). The cultural dimensions of non-verbal communication. In M. K. Asante & W. B. Condykunst (Eds.), *Handbook of international and intercultural communication* (pp. 13–185). Newbury Park, CA: Sage.

Kamya, H. A. (1994). *A study of African immigrants in the USA: Interrelationships of stress and self-esteem.* Boston: Boston University.

Klitgaard, R. (1990). *Tropical gangsters* (p. 7). New York: Basic Books.

LeVine, R. (1990). Infant environments in psychoanalysis: A cross-cultural view. In J. W. Stigler, R. A. Shweder, & G. Herdt (Eds.), *Cultural psychology* (pp. 454–473).

Logan, B. (1987). The reverse transfer of technology from sub-Saharan Africa to the United States. *Journal of Modern African Studies, 25*(4), 604.

MADHAVEN, M. C. (1985). Indian immigrants: Number, characteristics and economic impact. *Population and Development Review, 11*(3), 457.

McKELVEY, R., & WEBB, J. (1996). Premigratory expectations and postmigratory mental health symptoms: Vietnamese Amerasians. *Journal of the American Academy of Child Adolescent Psychiatry, 35*(2), 240–245.

MEAD, M. (1978). *Culture and commitment.* New York: Doubleday.

NYLANDER, P. P. S. (1969). *Annals of Human Genetics, 33,* 41–44.

OGBU, J. U. (1987). Optimism, structure, culture boundaries and literacy. In J. A. Langer (Ed.), *Language, literacy and culture: Issues of society and schooling* (pp. 149–177). Norwood, NJ: ABLEX.

OKEDEJI, D. O., & OKEDEJI, F. O. (1973, February). A Consideration of some factors influencing the loss of Nigerian medical and paramedical personnel to developed countries. *West African Journal of Education, 17,* 35–42.

PORTER, J. D. W. (1971). *Black child, white child: The development of racial attitudes.* Cambridge, MA: Harvard University Press.

PORTES, A. (1976). Determinants of the brain drain. *International Migration Review, 10*(4), 496.

PORTES, A., & RUMBAULT, R. G. (1990). *Immigrants in America: A portrait.* Berkeley: University of California Press.

RAWLINGS, J. (1995, Spring). *Home Front Ghanaian News and Views, 14*(1), 41.

RUTTER, M. (1979). Protective factors. In M. W. Kent & J. E. Rolf (Eds.), *Children's responses to stress and disadvantage: Primary prevention of psychopathology: Vol. 3. Social competence* (pp. 49–74). Hanover, NH: University of New England Press.

RUTTER, M. (1987). Psychosocial resilience and protective mechanisms. *American Journal of Orthopsychiatry, 57*(3), 31–331.

U.S. DEPARTMENT OF COMMERCE, BUREAU OF CENSUS. (1995). Washington, DC: U.S. Government Printing Office.

WAHLER, R. G., & DUMAS, J. E. (1986). Maintenance factors in coercive mother-child interactions: The compliance and predictability hypothesis. *Journal of Applied Behavioral Analysis, 19*(1), 13–22.

WERNER, E. E., & SMITH, R. S. (1982). *Vulnerable but invincible: A study of resilient children.* New York: McGraw-Hill.

WIRTH, L. (1969). Urbanism as a way of life. In R. Sennett (Ed.), *Classic essays on the culture of cities* (pp. 143–164). Englewood Cliffs, NJ: Prentice-Hall.

CHAPTER 14

Children and Families of Mexican Descent

WILLIAM ARROYO

THIS CHAPTER WILL ADDRESS psychosocial developmental factors that are pertinent to children of Mexican descent and their families. This discussion of normal psychosocial development as well as common emotional and behavioral problems should enable educators, policymakers, mental health clinicians, and investigators to enhance their skills and knowledge about this mushrooming population. Although a discussion of the health of Mexican American children (Amaro, Messinger, & Cervantes, 1996) is beyond the scope of this chapter, good general health is a prerequisite for normal psychosocial development. I will first provide a portrait of the population of Mexican American children with respect to U.S. census data, education, and economics; this picture has significant implications for development as well as for clinical interventions.

Throughout this chapter, the term *Mexican American* is used to refer to the population of Mexican descent regardless of country of origin (Mexico or United States), generation, and status of citizenship. Many terms, including *Mexican* and *Chicano*, have been used in the field to refer to this population or its subgroups. The term *Latino* (from *Latina*) is the umbrella term used to refer to the various groups of Latin Americans in the United States; other terms including *Hispanic* have been used in the literature to describe this population. The various explanations for the use of the several terms in the scientific and lay literature to describe this population are discussed elsewhere (Arroyo & Cervantes, 1997). The preferred term may vary among regions of the United States. In clinical work, self-identification regarding ethnicity by the child or family is strongly encouraged.

The projected U.S. census for 1996 (U.S. Bureau of Census, 1996) indicates that the Latino (Hispanic) population accounts for 10.5% of the total U.S. population or nearly 28 million people; these figures are based on the 1990 census. Between 1980 and 1990, the Latino population increased by 50%. Approximately 70% of Latinos live in the states of California, Texas, Florida, and New York. People of Mexican origin account for 63% of the U.S. Latino population. Legal immigration from Mexico led all sources of immigration during the 1980s with nearly 1 million individuals. Nearly 90,000 people immigrated legally from Mexico in fiscal year 1995. The estimates of undocumented entrants of Mexican descent vary widely; unauthorized entry into the United States is a recent focus of popular and political controversy.

The Latino populations in the United States tend to be younger (estimated median age of 26.4 in 1996) as compared with the total U.S. population (estimated median age of 34.6 in 1996). The Mexican American group is the youngest of the several Latino groups (Puerto Rican, Cuban, South and Central Americans among others). Furthermore, 38.8% of Mexican Americans are below the age of 18 years in contrast to 26.9% of the U.S. population (1994 estimates). These statistics also have implications for population growth.

The U.S. Census Bureau also reports that Latinos are a relatively undereducated group. The 1994 estimates of high school completion for Latinos and non-Latinos who are age 25 and over in the United States are 53.3% and 83.4%, respectively; the figure for the Mexican American population is 46.7%, the lowest of the Latino populations in the United States. The 1994 estimates for bachelor degree for Latinos, non-Latinos, and Mexican American populations (25 years of age or older) are 6.2%, 15.5%, and 4.4%, respectively; the latter figure represents the lowest among the Latino groups.

A substantial portion of children of Mexican descent live in impoverished conditions despite having made economic gains during the prior decade. The U.S. Census Bureau estimates that in 1994 49.5% of Mexican American children (and 47.7% of all Latino children under 18 years of age) live below the federally established poverty level; in contrast 38.1% of all non-Latino U.S. children are classified as impoverished. The figure for the impoverished Mexican American population is exceeded by that of 52.2% for the Puerto Rican population among the Latino groups.

Psychosocial Development

Although psychosocial elements of development serve as the centerpiece of this chapter, constitutional (or biological) factors of each child are crucial to the process of development. Constitutional and psychosocial factors are intricately woven into the fabric of development; a child's development is highly dependent on the integrity of the factors of both domains. A discussion of the constitutional factors of development is beyond the scope of this chapter.

The empirical research on normative development in general is limited; that body of research relating to Mexican American children is even more so. The research coupled with my clinical experience will serve as the basis for the discussion of child development.

SOCIALIZATION FACTORS

The socialization of children is a protracted process by which children learn acceptable patterns of behavior which include preferred ways of relating to parents, other authority figures, and peers. These lessons or values are inculcated from infancy. The framework for this socialization is built from a plethora of psychological and cultural factors related to morals, religious beliefs, and the parents' own upbringing among others. However, there is a dearth of literature on how these factors influence the development of Mexican American children (Cervantes & Castro,

1985). Another important factor relates to the degree to which the child and/or family adopts the standards of socialization and related beliefs of mainstream United States; this process, which is called *acculturation,* is complex, fluid, and has developmental implications. The developmental implications may affect various domains, including self-esteem, ethnic identity, peer relationships, sex roles, and family relationships. The degree and rate of this process may vary among family members. Garza and Lipton (1982) suggest that the acculturation process also has numerous clinical implications.

Language

Language preference and fluency is another area strongly influenced by multiple factors, including culture, neighborhood, primary language of the home, country of origin, and age of emigration. Spanish-speaking (mono- or bilingual) children will be more likely to identify with their Mexican heritage (Bernal, Knight, Garza, Ocampo, & Cota, 1990) than those who are not fluent. In some neighborhoods, a hybrid language has evolved (so-called *Spanglish*), which includes a mixture of English and Spanish words and grammar. Such phrases are commonly used and understood primarily by the local residents and disparaged by local education authorities.

Racial and Ethnic Identity

The development of racial and ethnic identity awareness in Mexican American children has been the focus of a few investigations. Racial awareness by African American and Euro-American youngsters is evident between the ages of 3 and 5. Bernal et al. (1990) found that Mexican American children are able to identify their ethnic group at 6 to 7 years. The constancy of ethnic identification emerges at 8 years or later.

COGNITIVE DEVELOPMENT

Although the literature on cognitive development is also limited, there are a few studies in the related area of field dependence/

independence. This area of study refers to the presence of significant stimuli, primarily social in nature, that influence an individual's cognitive processes. A person who is field-dependent will tend to rely more on social cues than a field-independent person. Early research often characterized children of Mexican descent as being more field-dependent than their Euro-American counterparts but Buriel (1975) suggests that cognitive development in the areas of field dependence/ independence as well as internal versus external locus of control is largely influenced by the degree of acculturation of the child.

The research on the measurement of intelligence in people of color in the United States has often served as a framework for contentious debate. Numerous studies in a review by Dunn (1987) strongly suggest that Mexican American children are less intelligent than Euro-American children because the former group has scored on the average of 10 to 12 points below that of the latter group. It appears that such differences persist despite the translation of tests and the use of allegedly culturally appropriate instruments. Mercer (1988) found that when adaptive psychosocial functioning is considered, Mexican American children are found to be comparable to their non-Latino counterparts and therefore strongly suggests that the intelligence testing of Mexican American children be expanded to include children's adaptive functioning. Intelligence testing has widespread implications including the areas of educational placement, peer relationships, employment opportunities, and psychological factors such as self-esteem and self-image.

PSYCHOSEXUAL DEVELOPMENT

Psychosexual development and sexual practices have rarely been the subject of empirical investigation in this population. There are many anecdotal and popular notions of behaviors in this area. The high rates of sexually transmitted diseases and the HIV infection rate among Latino adolescents underscore the need to expand this area of research. A study by Padilla and Baird (1991), with implications for health and family planning, suggests that Mexican American teenagers have very limited sexual knowledge. Some of their findings include that both sexes believed that the responsibility of birth control belonged to the female, that it was important to have children, that females be virgins at marriage, and sex was not okay if two people were not in love.

FAMILY STRUCTURE

Each child is a member of a family that significantly influences the child's psychosocial development. Despite what is reported in some of the popular as well as the professional literature, there is no consensus regarding a typical Mexican American family. Some of the published misconceptions include such notions as strict patriarchal structure, rural family structure, and even "culture of poverty traits" (Lewis, 1966). Some of the constructs purportedly under the latter rubric include fatalism, machismo, superstitiousness, religiosity, and female submissiveness. Apart from the negative stereotypes, there is a body of literature that describes Mexican families as having very strong values regarding family unity and family relationships.

The concept of familism or sharing of family functions is a useful one among Mexican American families. Its practice entails the intergenerational and lateral participation of members in sharing responsibilities and duties in child care, companionship, financial responsibility, emotional support, and problem solving. This often supports a decision-making framework that extends beyond the nuclear family. Household management or the organizational structure of the family is often related to age and sex with the older males tending to have more authority.

OTHER SOCIAL FACTORS

Immigration

Prior to the establishment of the U.S.-Mexican border in the late 1840s, migration of people across this area was virtually unrestricted. It was commonplace for people in what is now called the southwestern United States to have strong family and cultural ties to residents of Mexico. Today, similar social and cultural ties remain intact. The numbers of people emigrating from Mexico to the United States, however, have changed due to factors of economics, politics, and wartime, among others, during this century. Undocumented entry (so-called illegal entry) to the United States by Mexican citizens has periodically been a focus of serious political debate at all levels of government throughout this century. At this time, an intense review of immigration policies is being undertaken by Congress as well as by some states. The Welfare Reform Act of 1996 will eliminate many services now available to undocumented immigrants as well as legal immigrants; recent arrivals from Mexico will undoubtedly be affected. In addition, measures such as increased policing by the U.S. Border Patrol have been implemented.

Discrimination and Environmental Stressors

It is not uncommon for people of Mexican descent to report that they have been victims of discrimination for various reasons. Many of the victims, especially those who are undocumented, are fearful of reporting such abuse for fear of repercussions by the abuser and the particular government agency.

The actual experience of emigration may have differential developmental effects. The circumstances of the migration will often provide an important contextual framework for the eventual transition and adjustment from Mexico to the United States for a child or family. These circumstantial factors may be related to the membership of the family with whom the child emigrates, the constitution of the new household, the age of the child, the English language proficiency of the child, the new school environment, the employment prospects of the parents, and the receptivity of the new community. Children who enter without documentation (illegal entry) may be at risk for a more challenging adjustment especially if they fear deportation back to Mexico.

Emigration from Mexico may be more stressful for the older adolescent who has already established an extensive social network outside the family and who has minimal fluency in English. It is not uncommon for adolescent children to emigrate without their parents and/or to become a member of a new household, perhaps that of a relative. Padilla's study (1988) of first-generation Mexican American adolescents revealed that the main sources of stress for the new émigrés were living in a neighborhood with high crime rates, having a family member arrested, and having to negotiate services for a family member in the face of very limited English proficiency. The first two sources of stress in the Padilla study are in marked contrast to studies of adolescents of the dominant society who tend to identify more personalized life events as more stressful (Yeaworth, York, Hussey, Ingu, & Gordman, 1980). In a similar vein, Hovey and King (1996) report that those Latino, primarily Mexican, adolescents who experience acculturative stress are also "at risk" for experiencing high levels of depression and suicidal ideation.

CULTURAL IDENTITY AND CUSTOMS

The process of acculturation generally refers to the influence of one cultural group on another. A common assumption in the literature is that this process is unidirectional. Felix-Ortiz de la Garza, Newcomb, and Myers (1995) have emphasized that not only is it a group process but it also occurs at the level of the individual and is a dynamic process. Developmental implications are also evident. These authors therefore prefer the term *cultural identity* to acknowledge that the construct is multidimensional along various domains and occurs as part of personality formation. Olmedo and Padilla (1978) report that the process may have a crucial role in areas of psychological functioning as well as in the manifestations of psychopathology. Several instruments known as acculturation scales (Franco, 1983; Martinez, Horman, & Delaney, 1984; Olmedo, Martinez, & Martinez, 1978; Olmedo & Padilla, 1978), have been designed to assess cultural identity formation or acculturation in children of Mexican descent. Some investigators (Rueschenberg & Buriel, 1989) have focused on patterns of family acculturation. It may generally be assumed that a youngster who recently emigrated from Mexico will identify more strongly with Mexican cultural elements than a youngster who is third or fourth generation.

Some of the customs and beliefs commonly seen in Mexican culture are rooted in the Roman Catholic religion. *Compadrazgo* (literally coparenting) is a custom by which the *padrinos* (godparents) in certain religious rites, especially baptism, commit to providing assistance to the birth parents of the godchild. There is a special focus on the youngster's religious development, but the child's general welfare also is protected. The coparenting process often engenders a close relationship between the child and godparents. The *Quinceaniera* (15th birthday) is a religious-based milestone for many Mexican American female teenagers. This celebration in some ways is comparable to a debutante ball.

Common Psychosocial Problems and Clinical Implications

There are various challenges in the domain of psychosocial factors that clinicians will encounter in working with Mexican American children and their families. As with any young individual, the child requires a developmental perspective that is framed in a cultural context.

INFANCY AND PRESCHOOL

In light of the high percentage of Latino children living in poverty, every clinician must be concerned with the clinical psychosocial implications of inadequate prenatal care and inadequate nutrition during the early years of development. Insults to the developing central nervous system may result in psychological problems such as cognitive deficits and mental disorders.

Bicultural children who are exposed only to Spanish may initially have some difficulty communicating in English to monolingual English-speaking preschool personnel. Such children tend to learn English quickly. Although some parents may believe that a child with a communication difficulty has the problem because of exposure to two languages, virtually all normal children who are exposed to two languages during this developmental period will learn both languages equally well.

A common scenario is that of emigration from Mexico by a child who is separated from a primary caretaker and siblings; younger children who separate from their families often develop an adjustment problem. Temporary regression to an earlier developmental period may be observed in such cases.

SCHOOL AGE

Elementary school often provides a child with the first exposure to differences in the cultural values of the family and the mainstream United States (the school). The fit between the family's values and those of the school may vary greatly. Children from Mexican American families with a culture similar to that of the mainstream likely will adapt to the school routine better than children whose family's values do not closely correspond to those of the mainstream. A Mexican child whose culture engenders more collaboration among its members than competition may be viewed as passive or defective in some manner unless he or she competes with peers in school activities.

School-age children who immigrate to the United States at this age will be faced with a twofold challenge: adaptation to a new school and to a new neighborhood and community.

A monolingual Spanish-speaking child matriculating into a U.S. school system may be exposed to bilingual education in one of its many forms for an indeterminate period depending on the state and local regulations. A child in a bilingual education program who requires special education resources on the basis of a communication disorder or mental retardation may be overlooked, especially if the communication problem is solely attributed to the child's limited English proficiency. On the other hand, a bilingual child may be erroneously diagnosed as having a communication disorder or mental retardation.

ADOLESCENCE

Psychiatric epidemiological studies of Mexican American children are nonexistent. The sole epidemiological study on Latino youngsters involved Puerto Rican children (Bird et al., 1988). Cervantes and Arroyo (1995) caution clinicians and researchers about cultural considerations in the application of diagnostic criteria to Latino children.

Rates of substance and alcohol abuse as psychiatric syndromes in the Mexican American population are essentially unknown (Gilbert & Alcocer, 1988). The results of the 1993 National Household Survey on Drug Abuse (SAMHSA, 1995) indicate that the reported use (in percentage) of any illicit drug for Latinos, ages 12 to 17, in their lifetime, past year, and past month (21.6%, 21.3%, and 9.3% respectively) was higher than for that of the White (18.0%, 13.5%, and 6.3%) and African American (14.5%, 11.0%, and 6.5%) groups. There was also a significant increase in past year usage between 1992 and 1993 for Latinos. However, data relating to specific Latino groups cannot be gleaned from this body of data. The percentage of alcohol use during the past month for Latinos in this same age group was 17.5%; it was 19.2% for the White group and 13.1% for the African Americans. For heavy alcohol use (5 or more drinks per occasion on at least five occasions during the past month), the rates were 2.2% for Latinos, 1.3% for Whites, and 0.3% for African Americans. The rates for male Latinos were generally higher than the rates for females.

Despite the paucity of information with respect to the adolescent Mexican American population, there is research related to the adult population in this area that has psychosocial implications not only for rates among teenagers but also for the families of this population. Among Euro-Americans, adult males and adult females tend to consume more alcohol than their Mexican American counterparts, with a greater disparity between the female groups than between the male groups according to Mata (1986). There is some evidence (Hispanic Health and Nutrition Examination Survey, 1987) suggesting that the more acculturated Latino adult male has higher levels of substance abuse than the immigrant Latino male. Karno et al. (1987) found a higher lifetime alcohol abuse/dependence prevalence rate among the Mexican American male group than the Euro-American male; the relative rates were reversed with respect to substance abuse/dependence.

Arrest data and delinquency rates falsely suggest that there is a high prevalence rate of disruptive behavior disorders, which are manifested by antisocial behavior. Differential treatment of culturally diverse populations by the juvenile justice system and health service agencies has been well documented (Chambliss & Nagasasawa, 1969; Huizinga & Elliot, 1986; Morales, 1992).

Gangs and related activities have jeopardized the well-being of children in many Mexican American communities. In my clinical experience, an exodus of many families from Mexican American neighborhoods has been triggered by gang-related incidents. Although safety for the families has been achieved by relocation, the social network of the relocating youngsters has been disrupted. Some youngsters report being unable to avoid engaging in the antisocial activities of the local gangs due to their fear of repercussions from their peers who are gang members. The idea that an antisocial lifestyle is so ingrained in gang youth that the youth are not amenable to mental health treatment is a widely held opinion (Morales, 1992). Adler, Orando, and Hocevar (1984) demonstrated that when comparing Mexican American gang members with nongang members, gang members' families differed in terms of the type of family interactions, family patterns of affection, family structure, and attitudes of mother toward males; the mothers had negative attitudes toward father and reported that father was minimally involved in the family activities. Belitz and Valdez (1995) opine that many gang members have been victims of child abuse, and/or have treatable comorbid conditions such as posttraumatic stress disorder, depression, and substance abuse.

Conclusion

Mexican Americans possess a rich culture that will influence their psychosocial development. Such influences may pose challenges for policy makers, clinicians, and investigators alike. Economic, social, and political factors have the potential to jeopardize normal development. This chapter establishes a framework for assisting these children and their families.

References

ADLER, P., OVANDO, C., & HOCEVAR, D. (1984). Familiar correlates of gang membership: An exploratory study of Mexican American youth. *Hispanic Journal of Behavioral Sciences, 6*, 65–76.

AMARO, H., MESSINGER, M., & CERVANTES, R. C. (1996). The health of Latino youth: Challenges for disease prevention. In Kagawa-Singer, Katz, Taylor, & Vanderryn (Eds.), *Health issues for minority adolescents* (pp. 80–115). Lincoln: University of Nebraska Press.

ARROYO, W., & CERVANTES, R. C. (1997). Hispanics of Mexican origin. In J. D. Noshpitz (Ed.), *Handbook of child and adolescent psychiatry: Varieties of development* (Vol. 4). New York: Wiley.

BELITZ, J., & VALDEZ, D. M. (1995). Clinical issues in the treatment of Chicano male youth gangs. In A. M. Padilla (Ed.), *Hispanic psychology* (pp. 148–165). Thousand Oaks, CA: Sage.

BERNAL, B. E., KNIGHT, G. P., GARZA, C. A., OCAMPO, K. A., & COTA, M. K. (1990). The development of ethnic identity in Mexican American children. *Hispanic Journal of Behavioral Sciences, 12*(1), 3–24.

BIRD, H. R., CANINO, G., RUBIO-STIPEC, M., GOULD, M. S., RIBERA, J., SESMAN, M., WOODBURY, M., HUERTAS-GOLDMAN, S., PAGAN, A., SANCHEZ-LACAY, A., & MOSCOSO, M. (1988). Estimates of the prevalence of childhood maladjustment in a community survey in Puerto Rico. *Archives of General Psychiatry, 45*, 1120–1126.

BURIEL, R. (1975). Cognitive styles among three generations of Mexican American children. *Journal of Cross-Cultural Psychology, 6*, 417–429.

CERVANTES, R. C., & ARROYO, W. (1995). Cultural considerations in the use of *DSM-IV* with Hispanic children and adolescents. In A. M. Padilla (Ed.), *Hispanic psychology* (pp. 131–147). Thousand Oaks, CA: Sage.

CERVANTES, R. C., & CASTRO, R. G. (1985). Stress, coping, and Mexican American mental health: A systematic review. *Hispanic Journal of Behavioral Sciences, 7*, 1–73.

CHAMBLISS, W., & NAGASASAWA, R. (1969). On the validity of official statistics: A comparative study of white, black, and Japanese high school boys. *Journal of Research on Crime and Delinquency, 6,* 71–77.

DUNN, L. M. (1987). *Bilingual Hispanic children on the U.S. mainland: A review of research on their cognitive, linguistic, and scholastic development.* Circle Pines, MN: American Guidance Service.

FELIX-ORTIZ DE LA GARZA, M., NEWCOMB, M. D., & MYERS, H. F. (1995). A multidimensional measure of cultural identity for Latino and Latina adolescents. In A. M. Padilla (Ed.), *Hispanic psychology* (pp. 26–42). Thousand Oaks, CA: Sage.

FRANCO, J. N. (1983). An acculturation scale for Mexican American children. *Journal of General Psychology, 108,* 175–183.

GARZA, R. T., & LIPTON, J. P. (1982). Theoretical perspectives on Chicano personality development. *Hispanic Journal of Behavioral Sciences, 4*(4), 407–432.

GILBERT, M., & ALCOCER, A. M. (1988). Alcohol use and Hispanic youth: An overview. *Journal of Drug Abuse, 18*(1), 33–48.

HISPANIC HEALTH AND NUTRITION EXAMINATION SURVEY (HHANES). (1987). *Use of selected drugs among Hispanics: Mexican Americans, Puerto Ricans, Cuban Americans.* Rockville, MD: U.S. Department of Health and Welfare.

HOVEY, J. D., & KING, C. A. (1996). Acculturative stress, depression, and suicidal ideation among immigrant and second-generation Latino adolescents. *Journal of the American Academy of Children and Adolescent Psychiatry, 35,* 1183–1192.

HUIZINGA, D., & ELLIOT, D. S. (1986). *Juvenile offenders, prevalence, offender incidence, and arrest rates by race.* Paper presented at the meeting on Race and the Incarceration of Juveniles, Wingspread Foundation, Racine, WI.

KARNO, M., HOUGH, R. L., BURNAM, A., ESCOBAR, J. I., TIMBERS, D. M., SANTANA, F., & BOYD, J. H. (1987). Lifetime prevalence of specific psychiatric disorders among Mexican-Americans and non-Hispanic Whites in Los Angeles. *Archives of General Psychiatry, 44,* 695–701.

LEWIS, O. (1966, October). The culture of poverty. *Science American, 215,* 19–25.

MARTINEZ, R., NORMAN, R. D., & DELANEY, H. E. (1984). A children's Hispanic background scale. *Hispanic Journal of Behavioral Sciences, 6,* 103–112.

MATA, A. (1986). *Alcohol use among rural south Texas youth.* Austin: Texas Commission on Alcohol and Drug Abuse.

MERCER, J. R. (1988). Ethnic differences in IQ scores: What do they mean? (A response to Lloyd Dunn). *Hispanic Journal of Behavioral Sciences, 10*(3), 199–218.

MORALES, A. T. (1992). Latino youth gangs: Causes and clinical intervention. In L. A. Vargas & J. Koss-Chionino (Eds.), *Working with culture: Psychotherapeutic intervention with ethnic minority children and adolescents* (pp. 129–154). San Francisco: Jossey-Bass.

OLMEDO, E. L., MARTINEZ, J. L., & MARTINEZ, S. R. (1978). Measure of acculturation for Chicano adolescents. *Psychological Reports, 42,* 159–170.

OLMEDO, E. L., & PADILLA, A. M. (1978). Empirical and construct validation of a measure of acculturation for Mexican Americans. *Journal of Social Psychology, 105,* 178–179.

PADILLA, A. M. (1988). Life experiences, stress, and adaptation of immigrant adolescents. In J. W. Berry & R. C. Annis (Eds.), *Ethnic psychology: Research and practice with immigrants, refugees, native peoples, ethnic groups and sojourners* (pp. 47–84). Boulder, CO: Westview Press.

PADILLA, A. M., & BAIRD, T. L. (1991). Mexican American adolescent sexuality and sexual knowledge: An exploratory study. *Hispanic Journal of Behavioral Sciences, 13*(1), 95–103.

RUESCHENBERG, E., & BURIEL, R. (1989). Mexican family functioning and acculturation: A family systems perspective. *Hispanic Journal of Behavioral Sciences, 11*(3), 232–244.

SUBSTANCE ABUSE AND MENTAL HEALTH SERVICES ADMINISTRATION (SAMHSA). (1995). *National household survey on drug abuse: Main findings 1993* (DHHS Publication No. SMA 95-3020). Washington, C: U.S. Department of Health and Human Services, Office of Applied Studies.

U.S. BUREAU OF THE CENSUS. (1996). *Population projections of the United States by age, sex, race, and Hispanic origin: 1995 to 2050* (Current Population Reports, Series P25-1130). Washington, DC: Author.

YEAWORTH, R., YORK, J., HUSSEY, M., INGU, M., & GORDMAN, T. (1980). The development of an adolescent life change event scale. *Adolescence, 15,* 93–97.

CHAPTER 15

Children of Micronesia

FAYE F. UNTALAN and JANET M. CAMACHO

CHILD DEVELOPMENT IS A complex process of adaptation and increased complexity of emerging patterns of behavior that spans the time from early infancy through adolescence. Development occurs in four broad areas during childhood: (a) physical or physiological, (b) neurodevelopmental, (c) cognitive, and (d) psychosocial. Physical development refers to changes in the physical size, shape, and function that occur throughout childhood and that are typically measured. Neurodevelopment comprises changes in behavior that evolve with the passage of time. Cognitive development permits learning, thought, knowing, and problem solving. Psychosocial development comprises the interaction of the infant or child with the environment and interpersonal relationships (Vaughan, 1992). Human development occurs as the interplay between these biological, maturational, and psychosocial processes.

Measuring the development of infants and children does not easily lend itself to a rigid design across age. No one theory accounts adequately for all aspects of the development or behavior of children. There is a limited framework for the analysis of specific cultural rules, boundaries, and expectations for child development or different cultures and societies.

The view of development proposed by Valsiner (1989) is that culture is the major organizer of an individual child's development. This development takes place in a structured environmental context in which physical conditions for life and cultural meanings are intricately related. The process occurs in two directions: (a) It provides culturally appropriate environments for the child; and (b) it fits the birth and development of the child into the cultural system shared by the family, clan, community, and society as a whole. Human psychological development is a multilinear process guided by the structured cultural environments that surround the children (Valsiner, 1989, p. 175).

Micronesian societies are truly developing societies that lack a formal written perspective on their cultural practices. It is an oral culture: Practices and ideas are transmitted verbally from one generation to the next. This practice limits a documented framework for all the islands; also, the islands are distinct cultures in their own way. This becomes a problematic issue in deriving a cultural perspective that accurately depicts each island's concept and practice in the area of child development. Thus, we elected to choose the general framework from the literature and applied those concepts against Micronesian attitudes, values, and perspectives on children.

The Child in Society

Normative indicators of biological, maturational, and psychosocial development have become widely accepted in Western culture. These indicators have become the standard by which to compare children across all ages. There is an increasing awareness though that these indicators may not be cross-culturally relevant. The psychosocial dimension of development is the most complex and difficult to identify because of the influence of cultural variation and behavior of the individual.

The study of normal psychological and behavioral landmarks of Micronesian children is nonexistent in the literature. This chapter describes the context of sociocultural tradition and ongoing transformation among Micronesian societies in an attempt to develop a framework for the examination of normal psychological landmarks of growth and development of children from that region. From the medical perspective, child survival is the primary child health issue of Pacific Islands populations. The rebirth of the sociocultural consciousness of the indigenous populations may provide a vantage point for launching the study of normal child development in Micronesian societies.

The Geography of Micronesia

Micronesia is the name given to the Pacific region that spans a vast ocean area of approximately 3 million square miles, but contains a land mass of only about 970 square miles. Micronesia is situated in the western Pacific Ocean between the Hawaiian and the Philippine Islands. The region encompasses three great island archipelagos known as the Mariana Islands, the Eastern and Western Caroline Islands, and the Marshall Islands (see Figure 15–1). The thousands of islands that compose Micronesia are volcanic islands, coral islands, or atolls.

The name Micronesia is applied to the geography of the region rather than any specific cultural reference. The regional diversity of Micronesian race, language, and culture can be traced to the complex settlement history of the region. Although similar in genetic background, the island nations today are distinct sociocultural and political entities. The languages spoken in this region are Austronesian in origin. Several different languages are spoken throughout the region.

Demographic Distribution

Micronesians are emigrating out of their home islands to seek economic and educational opportunities. The 1990 census of the United States shows 49,345 Chamorros of Guam (identified as Guamanian in the U.S. National Census) now live in the continental United States. The majority are found in California (25,059), Washington (3,779), Texas (2,209), Hawaii (2,120), New York (1,803), and Florida (1,241). The 1990 census of the island of

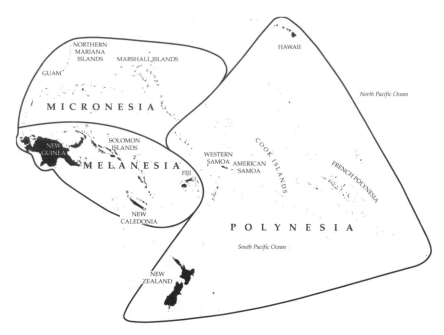

FIGURE 15–1
Map of Micronesia and the Pacific

Guam showed a total population of 133,152. Chamorros, the indigenous population, constitute 43% of the total population. Other groups include Caucasians (14.4%), Filipinos (23%), Koreans (2.95%), African Americans (2.37%), other Micronesians and Pacific Islanders (7%) and unidentified (7.28%). Other Micronesians living in the United States number about 6,808, sparsely distributed in every state (U.S. Bureau of the Census, 1992). Table 15–1 provides a distribution of the total population found in each of the Micronesian island chains, the population growth rate, the percentage of children under 15 years of age, and the infant mortality rate for 1993.

Traditional Micronesian Society

The island societies of Micronesia are embedded in a wave of change that is drastically creating disruptions and disorganization

TABLE 15–1
Population Profile of Micronesian Islands

Country	Total Population	Population Growth Rate	% Under 15 Years	Infant Mortality Rate
Commonwealth of the Northern Marianas	54,000	9.5	24	19
Federated States of Micronesia	114,800	3.6	47	52
Guam	140,100	2.3	30	12
Republic of the Marshall Islands	50,000	4.2	51	63
Palau	21,600	2.2	30	26

Data Sources: United Nations Development Program (UNDP), 1993; UNICEF, 1993.

of the traditional culture. Westernization, the American way, is reshaping many of the customs found among these islands.

Land has been the traditional basis of wealth; a person's land and social identity in Micronesia were rooted in one's hereditary family land (Palfox & Warren, 1980). Micronesians shared similar values and traditions. Primarily matrilineal societies, children were born into membership within the mother's clan. Social position, inheritance rights, kinship structure, residence patterns, and land ownership were determined along matrilineal lines. Traditional life consisted of subsistence economies centered in domestic households that were likely to consist of many extended family members who helped pass on customs and values of the clan. Thus, land ownership and inheritance were determined along kin-based social units (Oliver, 1989b).

Cultural Definitions of Time, Space, and Causality

Beliefs and practices associated with pregnancy, childbirth, and childbearing, vary from one Micronesian island culture to another. Throughout Micronesia, though, high value is placed on children. They are welcomed into the household and community, and treated with love and care throughout infancy. Each culture has divided the individual's life span into sequential stages, defined by criteria that were either physical or behavioral, or both (Oliver, 1989a, p. 662), but the society did not assign specific ages for which developmental milestones are achieved.

Child developmental milestones and expectations in Pacific cultures, such as when the child can walk, talk, and learn basic rules of behavior, are likely not dissimilar to other cultures. The differences are more likely to be in the important and significance of these developmental milestones and the child's response—whether they are encouraged by parental guidance or left to the child's readiness and individual initiative. Infants and children throughout most of the toddler years generally are indulged with care and attention, held, fed, played with, and comforted. Social and physical stimulation are given during these nurturing interactions. No activities or toys are deliberately used to promote development. Toilet training is not formally done but as the child is able to show control, diapers are removed and the child learns by coaxing and from his siblings and peers. It is common to see little boys with only T-shirts on and little girls with only underwear during those early years. Accidents are quickly cleaned and the child is reminded about the proper place to relieve himself or herself. This period usually does not last longer than 2 to 3 months. Because of common beliefs in animism on the islands, children are instructed early to respect nature. Indiscriminate defecation and urination are discouraged. Nature is sacred and certain behaviors are expected in this regard. Otherwise, illness, harm, or misfortune may be attributed to transgressions from this belief system.

In early childhood, many of the values are acquired through socialization. Micronesian children are born into a society of complex values, customs, and practices that have been shaped by Christianity and multiple histories of colonization. Children are loved and cherished, and care is shared by the family, who may include grandparents, aunts, and uncles as well as older siblings. Child rearing in Micronesia is essentially confined to the family who look after all the needs of the child.

Families often live in close proximity allowing siblings and cousins to grow together, play together, and look after each other. This social structure develops strong bonds among related children. Strong values of respect for elders are consciously emphasized throughout the development of children. Elders represent figures of authority and protectors. Modesty, humility, kindness, and generosity also are highly developed social characteristics of Micronesian children.

Family has an important role in Micronesia. Micronesians relational orientation emphasizes strong family and extended family ties; the value of within-group or family cooperation over competition and high sensitivity to interpersonal relations still exist throughout Micronesia (Oliver, 1989b). Increased contact with various cultures, increased mobility of Micronesians through travel, educational opportunities, and industry have blended these traditional values with Western influences.

Micronesians have a deep sense of spiritualism. In many island nations, Catholicism, the predominant religion in Micronesia, has been rooted in society for over 400 years; however, the people still adhere to indigenous beliefs of animism and ancestral worship. The Micronesians believe that they are subject to the environment with little control over their destiny. Death is accepted and is highly ceremonial. The beliefs and customs surrounding death are different from island to island.

Sociocultural Change throughout Micronesia

The modern Micronesian society is an example of the disparity between more traditional family structures and way of life on outer islands and the more modern urban islands of Guam and Saipan. A majority of the traditions have been diluted by the hundreds of years of Western colonialism. Its effect was the alteration of the genetic and cultural composition of Micronesians. Each of the island populations has been racially mixed with people of Spanish, Portuguese, Filipino, Chinese, Japanese, German, and other European descent, now largely referred to as American.

A popular theory explaining the origin of Pacific peoples is that they came out of Africa and southeast Asia following the ocean drift. Micronesians settled the small northerly islands and atolls; Melanesians settled in the central south Pacific, and Polynesians continued easterly and settled in the Polynesian archipelago. Palau and Yap of the Western Caroline Islands and Guam and Saipan of the Mariana Islands were likely the first to be settled in Micronesia. The first contact with Europeans occurred in the 1600s with the settlement of Spanish missionaries in the Mariana Islands. The Chamorros of the Mariana Islands were nearly decimated during the initial Spanish colonization. This was the beginning of the region's long history of colonization, assimilation, and migration. The Chamorro ancestry today reflects the Micronesians' intermarriage with peoples of Spanish, Portuguese, Filipino, Chinese, Japanese, German, other European, and Carolinian descendants.

The Mariana Islands are the most industrialized and commercialized of the Micronesian islands. The modernization of the Mariana Islands began after World War II during political status negotiations, which maintained the division of the Mariana Islands along political and economic boundaries. The most precipitate changes occurred during this period, the result being dramatic transformation of the traditional island way of life. Guam became a U.S. defense center and is now also the urban center of the western Pacific. Its proximity to Asia and the United States has encouraged rapid development of the island. The Commonwealth of the Northern Marianas (CNMI) includes Saipan, Tinian, and Rota. Saipan is the government, tourist, and business center of the CNMI.

The Eastern and Western Caroline archipelago is known today as the Federated States of Micronesia (FSM), excluding independent Palau. FSM comprises four island states; Kosrae and Pohnpei in the east, and Truk and Yap in the west. The islands of FSM number over 600, of which only 65 are inhabited. A majority of the population of FSM are Micronesians. Two of the outer islands are inhabited by Polynesians. Micronesians of each of the FSM island states have a distinct native culture and language; thus, nine different languages are spoken in the FSM.

Previously part of the Trust Territory of the Pacific Islands (TTPI), FSM is the largest and most populous political entity in Micronesia. FSM is associated with the United States through the Compact of Free Association which is providing 1.3 billion dollars over 15 years through the year 2001. The FSM population is expanding at a rapid rate of 3.2% per annum. Their population growth rate continues to outpace that of other islands for the region. This results in less resources for the population. Food and almost all elements of modern life are imported as the region continues to move from a subsistence to a cash-based economy.

Palau consists of six island groups in the Western Caroline archipelago. Of the 200 islands, 10 are inhabited. In 1994, Palau became an independent nation. The entire republic is classified as a rural area, and a medically underserved area.

The Marshall Islands comprise 35 atolls, 24 of which are inhabited. The islands also played a role in World War II. Today, the region is heavily subsidized by the U.S. government. And the islanders rely on imported goods for the majority of their subsistence (Stanley, 1992).

The most pervasive characteristics of Micronesia are the expanse of geography, remoteness of the islands, heterogeneity of the language and culture, and a youthful population that has experienced discontinuity and acculturation throughout the centuries of colonization and migration. The Micronesian islands are also nations in transition both politically and economically. All these factors influence the overall health and social well-being and contribute to the complexity of the demography of the indigenous population today.

Status of Child Health and Health Services in Micronesia

Maternal and child health is often considered the most sensitive indicator of health of the broader population. Women and children in developing countries share a similar health pattern. Health and illness are determined by multiple influences such as the level of progress in areas of education, public health, and available health services; economics; and the sociocultural environment (Williams, Baumslag, & Jelliffe, 1994). Children in developing countries suffer the burden of morbidity and mortality from preventable diseases (Buse & Larson, 1994). Malnutrition, infectious disease, diarrhea, and vaccine-preventable diseases are prevalent and often coexist. Health programs have given priority to decreasing morbidity and mortality of children through the allocation of resources toward efforts to improve child survival.

Micronesia is considered a "developing nation." Micronesia is a very young society. The youth under 20 years of age comprise greater than 50% of the population. With assimilation, the health of the islanders has suffered. Micronesians suffer from an increasing number of acquired diseases such as hypertension, heart disease, diabetes, and communicable disease. The increasing rates of suicide and drug abuse among the youth of Micronesia are modern health issues in the islands.

The health status of children throughout the Pacific Island nations has improved during the past three decades. The infant mortality rate (IMR) has decreased from over 40 per 1,000 live births in the 1960s to less than 30 per 1,000 live births in the 1990s. Survival of a child under 5 years of age is two times greater today than in the 1960s, attributed to the implementation of programs to prevent communicable disease and illness. Today, the leading causes of death among infants and children in the Pacific islands are also the major causes of morbidity (Lewis & Katoanga, 1994). The task of describing child health in Micronesia is hindered by the absence of reliable and comprehensive data of the problems.

To identify specific child health needs of the islands, a review of their 1995 Title V (Maternal and Child Health) block grant applications was conducted. These applications are submitted to the Maternal and Child Health (MCH) Bureau of the U.S. Public Health Service (PHS) for federal funding. This review summarized the needs and conditions as determined by local officials of the islands (U.S. PHS, MCH Bureau, 1995).

Much of the data from these reports illustrate the paucity of conditions among Micronesian societies and the Third World levels of development.

GUAM AND THE NORTHERN MARIANA ISLANDS

Six of 10 prioritized health issues identified on Guam are related to child health:

1. *Low birth weight.* Low birth weight of infants remained around 8% from 1991 to 1993.
2. *Suicide.* A greater number of males commit suicide and a greater number of females attempt it. The goal is to reduce by 18% the incidence of suicide and suicide attempts among youth and adolescents.
3. *Maltreatment.* The goal is to decrease by 25% the incidence of maltreatment and neglect in children ages 0–18 years.
4. *Adolescent drug use and smoking.*
5. *Child communicable diseases.*
6. *Infant mortality.* The IMR in 1994 was 9.5 per 1,000 live births (U.S. PHS, MCH Bureau, 1995).

The Northern Marianas CNMI is designated an underserved area. The IMR is 6.7 per 1,000 live births, low birth weight is 11%, and the suicide rate is 18.3 per 100,000 population. Children with special health needs number approximately 291 cases (U.S. PHS, MCH Bureau, 1995).

THE FEDERATED STATES OF MICRONESIA

The FSM is designated a medically underserved area. The IMR in the FSM is 23 per 1,000 live births. This is an estimate at best because it is believed that many infant deaths are unrecorded. Data collected by the FSM Department of Health Services in 1992 indicated the five leading causes of infant mortality are conditions originating in the perinatal period (25%), respiratory diseases

(14%), complications of labor and delivery (8%), nutritional deficiency (8%), diarrheal and intestinal diseases (6%), and other (39%) (Department of Human Resources (DHR), FSM, 1993). Malnutrition (25% with weight less than the fifth percentile on the growth charts), anemia (32%), and vitamin A deficiency are prevalent in the FSM (U.S. PHS, MCH Bureau, 1995).

THE MARSHALL ISLANDS

The Marshall Islands' IMR in 1994 was 24 per 1,000 population. It continues to be among the highest in Micronesia. A survey of mortality statistics from 1986 to 1989 showed that one third of all deaths in the Marshall islands were children under 5 years. Malnutrition, respiratory diseases, and gastrointestinal diseases are prevalent. Most infant deaths are causes by pneumonia and diarrhea. Malnutrition is identified as the number one killer of children 1 to 5 years of age (U.S. PHS, MCH Bureau, 1995).

Economic and Educational Status

The health problems experienced in Micronesia occur at varying degrees of severity and are primarily dependent on the level of progress, remoteness of some of the populations, and degree of dependence on the Western dollar. Also influencing the health of the populations in the region is the availability and accessibility of health services. The Western models of medicine predominate and may not be culturally appropriate or accessible to all populations.

In Micronesia, children from birth to 5 years are the most vulnerable. Maternal and child health departments focus on developing and implementing primary preventive health services to deal with those issues that affect the growth and development of children from the region. Each nation has in place a child health program and service delivery system that is best characterized as fragmented. Well baby clinics, immunization programs, and growth monitoring programs exist. Each nation has specific tracking, identification, and intervention programs with strategies aimed at identifying children with special health needs.

Level of progress also has cultural implications. The problems encountered such as malnutrition, and other types of preventable diseases have a profound effect on the physical, cognitive, and social development of the young children of Micronesia. The continual influx and experiences of non-Micronesian cultures and modernization in the region have affected social change in the culture. This discontinuity in the socialization process is evidenced in the amount of mental health issues arising in the region. Suicide among the youth, substance abuse, and alcoholism, are major public health issues in Micronesia.

Education, industrialization, and urbanization appear to exert a powerful impact on the degree of modernization of attitudes and social values in a society. The most significant changes have occurred in the area of economic and social progress. The long history of colonization has brought about formal educational systems within each region modeled after Western systems. Most school-age children receive some formal education. However, the data are not adequately reported to determine the numbers in school, dropout rate, or literacy and school achievement in many Micronesian islands. Educational systems and programs patterned under the U.S. system are relatively underdeveloped in many of the islands except Guam. Nevertheless, a major factor in the urbanization and migration of the Micronesian populations has been the expansion of educational opportunities.

To date, there are no studies on the early development of Micronesian children; Micronesia has not approached the study of child development across the age span. The region continues to attempt to find alternative approaches for meeting the basic health needs of the child population. The second issue is that the cultural determinants of health of the Micronesian societies are sketchy beyond the major developmental processes of birth and death. No normative data exist for children from Micronesia. Each island has linguistic references to the physical or behavioral development, and maturational rites of older children.

An Analysis of Changes in Family
Structure and Their Consequences

Many social problems affecting Micronesian societies today can be attributed to changes in the family structure and functions. Family figures of authority no longer have the power and control over the welfare and behavior of the family members. Individual freedom and autonomy led by opportunities to work and earn a living independently, and emerging social norms of personal responsibility and independence are undermining traditional norms of kinship relationships and responsibilities. Thus, erosion of traditional family structure has caused disregard for values and practices which traditionally held families together. Table 15–2 identifies these changing patterns among Micronesian families.

High rates of pregnancies among teens, suicide, and child maltreatment incidence among the islands of Micronesia have been strongly associated with sociocultural changes. Teen pregnancies in the Marshall Islands constitute a major social and health problem. The teenager usually depends on her mother—the infant's grandmother—for child care. In the past, pregnancy in an unmarried teen was dealt with by marriage, or the child was accepted and cared for by parents or other relatives. The pregnancy of an unmarried woman although not socially approved of was usually accepted by the family. The dissolution of the family structure no longer provides the supervision, care, and management of children by older daughters who traditionally had the responsibility and authority to guide the young and were respected by those younger siblings, nieces, and nephews.

Suicide among the youth is increasing throughout Micronesia. Father Francis Hezel, who lived in Micronesia for a number of years, was concerned about the incidence of suicide. His report on suicide from 1975 and 1976 determined that suicide was the leading cause of death for persons between the ages of 15 and 30 years in Micronesia (Hezel, 1976). More recent data from Guam confirm Father Hezel's report. There were 128 cases of suicide reported on Guam between 1988 and 1995 (see Table 15–3).

TABLE 15-2
Changing Family Structure and Conditions in Micronesia

Pre-U.S. Contact* (Prior to World War II)	1960s–1970s	1980s–1990s
Family Structure		
Intergenerational	Intergenerational	Nuclear families
Extended families	families	Parents
Grandparents	Grandparents	Children
Parents	Parents	High divorce rate
Children	Children	
Unmarried	Legalization of	
Aunts/Uncles	divorce	
Mutual marital		
separation		
Rules and Responsibilities for Child Care		
Shared responsibilities	Less authority of	Parents have complete
Clear roles	grandparents	responsibility
Older daughters	Parents taking over	Care and guidance of
responsible for	more of family	children unclear
younger siblings	responsibilities	Nonfamily caretakers
Younger siblings	Children's roles and	
respectful of older	responsibilities not	
siblings and parents	reinforced	
Discipline		
Strict discipline	Lax discipline	Permissive/no
Clear rules for	Confusing rules for	discipline
behavior	behavior	No rules for behavior
Social Problems		
Teen pregnancy	Divorce	High number of teen
unknown or not	Drug and substance	pregnancies
viewed as social	abuse	High alcohol and
problem	Juvenile delinquency	substance abuse
Alcohol and substance	Homicide	High incidence of
abuse unknown or	Suicide	child maltreatment
socially controlled		High suicide
Child maltreatment		
not socially		
significant		
Suicide not socially		
significant		

*Guam was the only U.S. possession in Micronesia prior to World War II. However, very little contact with Americans occurred before the war.

TABLE 15-3
Suicide in Guam, 1988–1995

Age (Yrs.)	Total	Percent
Under 35	128	71
Under 30	98	54
Sex		
Male	159	88
Female	21	12
Race		
Chamorro	92	51
Other Micronesian	22	12
Non-Micronesian	66	37
Employment		
Employed	114	63
Unemployed	24	13
Student	21	12
Methods		
Hanging	98	54
Gunshot	64	36

Data Source: Guam Police Department, 1995.

Seventy-one percent (71%) were under 35 years of age; 54% were under 30 years of age. Eighty-eight percent (88%) of suicides were committed by males and 12% were by females. Fifty-one percent (51%) were Chamorros, the indigenous Micronesian population of Guam, 12% were other Micronesians living on Guam, and 37% were other non-Micronesians. Sixty-three percent were employed, 13% were unemployed, and 12% were students (Guam Police Department, 1995).

In examining the distribution of suicides by village, it is noted by the author, who has been studying patterns of social change among Chamorros, that those villages that have undergone greater change in family land tenure and residency also have the highest rate of suicide, whereas those that are more culturally intact have a lower incidence of suicide. In other words, newcomers and outmigration of original families in the villages have altered the social-cultural support and order of the villages.

Cultural mores and sentiments continue to guide social perceptions and attitudes about social problems associated with some behaviors. For example, alcohol abuse, drift from traditional practices, or unresolved family conflicts are often used to explain personal and family crisis such as suicide. Two cases of teen suicide from Palau illustrate this phenomenon. The first is a 15-year-old female from a broken family who was adopted by an American couple in her childhood. The girl remained in Palau with her adopted family. Suicide was rumored to be a result of sexual molestation by her stepfather. Although interfamilial adoption has been a traditional practice in Micronesia, nonfamilial adoption is more recent. The second case is a 15-year-old male who hanged himself. He was known to be a quiet well-mannered youth, an only child who was then living with his maternal grandmother. His parents were divorced and both had remarried at the time of the suicide. There were allegations of serious problems between his parents.

Child abuse and neglect (CAN) is a problem that is gaining recognition throughout Micronesia. National awareness and federal legislation have prompted U.S.-related territories such as Guam and the Commonwealth of the Northern Marianas to enact child abuse and neglect reporting laws. Islands not affiliated with the United States have not had similar statutory requirements. However, child maltreatment is recognized as a growing serious problem in all the islands of Micronesia. Again, much of the blame is associated with family breakdown and changes in the socioeconomic fabric of society resulting in changes in the structure and functions of the family unit.

In 1989, a conference was held in Hawaii to examine child maltreatment conditions in the Pacific islands. Members of all jurisdictions of Micronesia were gathered to address child maltreatment issues from their island perspectives. Table 15–4 presents a summary of jurisdictional perspectives of child maltreatment in Micronesia including definitions, types of child maltreatment, and some causes.

TABLE 15-4
Perspectives of Child Maltreatment in Micronesia

Jurisdiction	Definition	Types Known	Causes
Commonwealth of the Northern Marianas (CNMI)	Legal: 1982 legislative mandate to report CAN. Physical, emotional, sexual abuse, and neglect. Cultural norms prevalent.	Severe neglect of disabled child. Sexual molestation. Physical abuse resulting in broken bones. Medical neglect. Burns. Educational neglect. Abandonment. Child pornography.	Traditional family breakdown. Women in the workforce. Nonfamilial caretakers.
Federated States of Micronesia (FSM)	Legal: None. Recognize physical abuse, sexual abuse (molestation or intercourse with a child under 14 years old), and neglect. Cultural: acceptable norms used in disciplining the child. (Discipline means care for the welfare of the child.)	Physical abuse. Emotional abuse. Neglect. Sexual abuse.	Disputed family life. Failure of parents to provide needs of the child. Irresponsible parents.

Guam	Legal: 1980 legislative mandate to report CAN. Child whose physical/mental health or welfare is harmed or threatened with harm by acts or omissions of the person responsible for child's welfare. Harm from inflicting injuries, commits or allows sex offense, abandonment, failure to provide.	Physical abuse. Physical neglect. Sexual abuse. Abandonment. Emotional abuse. Educational neglect. Lack of supervision.	Lack of parenting skills. Alcohol or drug abuse. Financial Problems. Mental illness. Changes in traditional child-rearing practices. Single parents. Teen Parents.
Marshall Islands	Legal: None. Cultural norms determine abuse and neglect.	Physical abuse. Neglect. Sexual abuse.	Parental authority. Breakdown of traditional family responsibility for children. Breakdown of extended family. Alcohol and drug abuse. Teen parenting. Population increase.
Palau	Legal: none. Sexual abuse. Cultural norms determine abuse or neglect.	Physical abuse. Sexual abuse. Emotional abuse. Neglect.	Alcohol abuse. Rapid changes. Breakdown of tradition and family.

Source: The First Pacific Islands' Conference on Child Protection. Untalan (1989).

Common types of child maltreatment in the islands include:

- To take advantage of or exploit children.
- To expect or require a child to do something beyond his or her abilities.
- To beat or punish a child without cause or explanation.
- To deny or withhold food, clothing, or other needs of the child.

Parental and adult behavior in the discipline and management of children is still largely viewed from a cultural norm perspective in Micronesia. Infliction of harm to a child without reasonable cause is universally not acceptable. Certain children's misbehavior or misconduct is viewed as warranting punishment. However, there are cultural rules and guides that determine the types of punishment for a child's failure to obey a parental order. Swearing at a sibling may be handled by verbally disciplining or spanking, whereas a child who steals something may be given more severe physical punishment. The age of the child also alters the view of behavioral responsibility and punishment. Corporal punishment is viewed as a corrective measure for bad behavior. Parents who fail to punish their children for wrongdoing, disrespect, stealing, or lying are seen as noncaring or neglectful.

The rapid social changes in the Pacific have caused serious breakdowns in the family and interfamily relationships, as well as in the rules that guided and governed the behavior and care of children. Economic lags in earnings and few opportunities for employment, inadequate or lack of education, stresses, and the inability to adapt to a changing society are factors that contribute to maltreatment of children and neglect in their overall social development.

Although attentive care and indulgence for the young child remain important characteristics of child care in Micronesia, certain emerging developments are altering that traditional practice. These developments include the availability of inexpensive domestic help in some of the islands, and mothers' participation in the workforce. In both cases, child care by nonrelatives is replacing family care and management of young children. Working mothers are very common in many of the islands. As economic pressures continue and as families become entirely dependent on wages for their livelihood, the changes in the familial and cultural fabric will widen and the consequences for children will likely increase.

Studies of Micronesians living outside their islands are rare if available. Information about their coping and adjustment are largely from personal observations, experiences, and reports. In a study on migration and adaptation among Chamorros in California in the 1970s, Untalan (1979) found several issues experienced by Chamorro immigrants such as cultural discontinuity, separation and dissolution of traditional extended family, social isolation, and problems of identity. These are certainly potential roots for stress and psychosocial dysfunction. Lack of organized data limits analysis; however, personal and social dissatisfactions in their lives, social isolation, and alienation from families and friends are common concerns voiced by those living in the United States. On the other hand, there are also observations that indicate Chamorro Micronesians have tremendous resiliency and capacity to adapt in new environments. Crime and unemployment statistics are absent for Chamorros even in communities where they are found in greater concentrations, as in some areas of California. This may be a result of better coping skills or a family or cultural system that provides an effective buffer.

Conclusion

A theoretical framework for the analysis of child development from infancy through adolescence and across societal and cultural perspectives is critical for the determination of normative behavior and development. This is especially problematic when assessing non-Western, non-European groups. Most measurements for child development are derived from Western societies. The major psychological landmarks of child development that are considered normative child behavior are derived also from Western concepts about child development and therefore may be neither appropriate nor applicable to children of different cultures. The task at hand, to define normative psychological behavior of children from a Micronesian society, is a formidable one. It would be difficult to approach the issue from an exclusively historical perspective based on the traditional cultures of Micronesians. The history of the indigenous populations remains sketchy. Throughout the process of acculturation and assimilation, Micronesian societies have experienced a transformation of the genetic heritage, cultural traditions, and social institutions of family, community, and school. The impact of this transformation on the populations has been most dramatic over the past 50 years. Although some traditions have been preserved despite these rapid changes, family traditions of child care and child rearing continue to be challenged.

Changes prompted by colonization, education, new social and economic patterns, and alterations in family relationships and functions are important considerations for the analysis of child caring and child development patterns in changing societies. This situation is a matter of significance in Micronesia, which has gone from relative isolation from the world before 1940 to rapid Americanization in the midst of underdevelopment and lack of economic infrastructure.

References

BUSE, K., & LARSON, H. (1994). Special focus on child health in the Pacific. *Pacific Health Dialog, 1*(2), 4–5.

GUAM POLICE DEPARTMENT. (1995). *Annual report.* Government of Guam.

HEZEL, F. N. D. (1976). *Report on suicide in Micronesia.* Unpublished manuscript.

LEWIS, L. H., & KATOANGA, S. F. (1994). Demographic trends and population issues: Current and potential impact on child health. *Pacific Health Dialog, 1*(2), 4–5.

OLIVER, D. (1989a). *Oceania, the native cultures of Australia and the Pacific Islands* (Vol. 1). Honolulu: University of Hawaii Press.

OLIVER, D. (1989b). *Oceania, the native cultures of Australia and the Pacific Islands* (Vol. 2). Honolulu: University of Hawaii Press.

PALFOX, N., & WARREN, A. (Eds.). (1980). *Cross-cultural caring: A handbook for health care professionals in Hawaii*. University of Hawaii, John A. Burns School of Medicine, Honolulu.

STANLEY, D. (1992). *Micronesia handbook*. Chico, CA: Moon.

U.S. BUREAU OF THE CENSUS. (1992). *1990 census of population, general characteristics, United States*. Washington, DC: U.S. Government Printing Office.

U.S. PUBLIC HEALTH SERVICE, MCH BUREAU. (1995). *MCH block grant applications*. Washington, DC: Author.

UNTALAN, F. (1979). *An exploratory study of island migration: Chamorros of Guam*. Unpublished manuscript, University of California, Los Angeles.

UNTALAN, F. (Ed.). (1989). *The first Pacific Islands' conference on child protection*. Honolulu: University of Hawaii, U.S. Department of Public Health and Human Services.

VALSINER, J. (1989). *Human development and culture: The social nature of personality and its study*. Lexington, NC: Lexington Books.

VAUGHAN, V. C. (1992). Assessment of growth and development during infancy and early childhood. *Pediatrics in Review, 13*(3), 88–97.

WILLIAMS, C. D., BAUMSLAG, N., & JELLIFFE, D. B. (1994). *Mother and child health: Delivering the services* (3rd ed.). New York: Oxford University Press.

CHAPTER 16

Children from the Former Soviet Union

ELEANOR LAVRETSKY, DON MELAND, and
DANIEL A. PLOTKIN

SINCE 1965 WHEN THE U.S. Congress liberalized its immigration policy, the number of foreign-born people residing in the country has more than quadrupled, reaching 22 million (8.5% of the population) in 1994 (Vernez & Abrahamse, 1996). Currently, nearly one million individuals immigrate to the United States every year, accounting for more than 40% of the annual growth in population. Although most current immigrants (approximately 80%) are Asian or Hispanic, this chapter will focus on European immigrants, particularly those from the former Soviet Union.

The different ethnic groups immigrating from Europe to the United States share many common features and face many similar problems related to the stress of immigration, resettlement, and cultural and language barriers. However, they also have important differences involving their cultural and political backgrounds, reasons for leaving the country of origin, adjustment processes, and expectations and motivations for future accomplishments.

Immigrants from different countries of Eastern Europe and diverse ethnic groups of the former Soviet Union (FSU), despite similar political and economic circumstances preceding their emigration, have many dissimilar problems during their resettlement process. Furthermore, even people of the same ethnic group undergoing the immigration process at different times (one or two decades apart) have distinct experiences (Borjas, 1994). Therefore, it is important to consider each ethnic immigrant group separately, in the context of its history, political and cultural background, circumstances of emigration, and the situation in the United States at the time of arrival.

This chapter will focus on immigrants from the FSU, primarily the Russian-speaking Jewish population, which is one of the biggest immigrant groups from Europe. There are few studies of this ethnic group, and there are no publications on Russian immigrant children and their mental health problems. Therefore, we will supplement the limited literature with our own clinical experience in order to make a meaningful contribution.

Russian/Soviet Jewish Immigration from a Historical Perspective

Three waves of Jewish emigration from Russia/FSU can be defined over slightly more than a century: (a) 1881–1912, (b) 1970s, and (c) 1988–1990s (Gitelman, 1995; Larrabee, 1993).

From 1881 to 1912, 1,889,000 Jews emigrated from Russia and Poland, 84% of them to the United States; this was 70% of all Jewish immigrants to America at that time (Gitelman, 1995). The main reasons for emigration were increasingly aggressive anti-Semitism, (e.g., pogroms), and the search for safety, freedom, and better life opportunities. This wave of immigrants came primarily from small towns in what today is Ukraine, Belorussia, and Poland. Their identity was Ashkenazi Jews, their native language was Yiddish, and their religion was Jewish.

These immigrants were poor, with minimal education, and were willing to take any job to survive in America. As a result of their struggle for adjustment, most of them succeeded as small business owners in the food, clothing, and beauty supply industries. They also worked as tailors, hairdressers, or salespersons.

They were able to provide an education for their children, send them to college, and enjoy their achievements as professionals. They, and especially their children and grandchildren, became a natural part of American multicultural society, with a new identity as Americans, their language English, and their religion Jewish. America also gave the necessary freedom and support to the talented and creative people of this wave—composers, musicians, inventors, and scientists—who made a significant contribution to America's culture and economic prosperity.

The song "God Bless America" was written by such an immigrant reflecting his gratitude for the freedom to create. The second wave of Russian immigration (1970s) began when Leonid Brezhnev temporarily opened Soviet borders for certain groups after more than 50 years of closed borders, sealed by Stalin's totalitarian regime and terrorism. The reasons for this wave of emigration were primarily political and religious. It was the first opportunity to leave a country where suppression and lies had become the basis of everyday life. People of this wave (especially those who left in the earlier years, 1971–1974) had been opposed to the regime long before this opportunity became possible and were courageous enough to apply for immigration. They were aware they would have to endure a difficult period of persecution by the Soviet authorities and were psychologically prepared to leave the country. As soon as they applied for immigration, they were fired from their jobs.

Before obtaining their documents of "resignation," applicants were publicly criticized at a meeting of coworkers chaired by a member of the Communist Party. They were blamed for "betraying their Motherland." It was even harder for their children, who were criticized in front of an all-school meeting, labeled as "traitors," and expelled. Thus, this wave of emigration required that parents support and prepare their children for such a process, and find sufficient financial resources to survive while awaiting final emigration. In most cases, it was a period of several months to several years and no one could predict the length of waiting nor the final outcome of the application. The worst scenario was that after applying for emigration, losing their job and social status, they were then denied permission to leave the country, and in many cases the reasons for denial were false allegations (e.g., that they had access to secret strategic information). These *otkasniki,* or *refusniks* actively fought with authorities for permission to leave the country, joined the ranks of dissidents, and frequently went to prison. Others quietly suffered and waited for "better times." Eventually both groups were released when Mikhail Gorbachev started his *perestroyka* and the last wave of emigration began.

A significant number of these emigrants went to Israel. According to Zvi Gitelman (1995), from 1971 to 1974 about 100,000 Jews came to Israel from the FSU, a quarter of them from Georgia and a third from the Baltic Republics—Estonia, Latvia, Lithuania—and other areas annexed by the Soviet Union in 1939 and 1940.

These groups had recent memories of thriving Jewish communities, and some still kept a commitment to Jewish culture and religion; thus Israel was a natural choice for them. By contrast, about 85% of the Soviet immigrants to the United States at the same time came from Slavic Republics—Russia, Belorussia, and Ukraine—where Jews had been cut off from Jewish culture, language, religion, and traditions for several generations.

In the following years, emigration from FSU was divided primarily between Israel and the United States; much smaller numbers of emigrants went to other countries such as Canada, Germany, Australia. Initially, the choice of country was influenced by different factors, including political beliefs, location of their families and friends, standards of life, professions, and issues of safety related to military conflicts in Israel. Later on, the choice was also influenced by information coming from the first groups of emigrants. Many of them had had idealistic expectations of Israel as a free Jewish state, and were disappointed to find a bureaucracy in Israel reminiscent of the Soviet country they had just left. Such information from pioneers of emigration turned many Soviet refugees toward the United States—the traditional country of immigration, "the country of second opportunity." In 1973, 34,733 Jews left the FSU and only 1,449 (less than 5%) arrived in the United States; by 1979, 51,320 emigrated and 28,794 (56%) came to America (Table 16–1).

TABLE 16–1

*Russian Jewish Emigration from the Former Soviet Union and
Arrival in the United States (1965–1995)*

Year	Departures from FSU	Arrivals in U.S.A.
1965	891	12
1966	2,047	36
1967	1,406	72
1968	229	92
1969	2,979	156
1970	1,027	135
1971	13,022	214
1972	13,681	453
1973	34,733	1,449
1974	20,628	3,490
1975	13,221	5,250
1976	14,261	5,512
1977	16,736	6,842
1978	28,865	12,265
1979	51,320	28,794
1980	21,471	15,461
1981	9,447	6,980
1982	2,658	1,327
1983	1,315	887
1984	876	489
1985	1,139	570
1986	914	641
1987	7,776	3,811
1988	19,343	10,576
1989	71,196	36,738
1990	213,437	31,283
1991	178,026	34,715
1992	108,292	45,888
1993	102,134	35,581
1994	99,681	32,622
1995	85,874	21,433
Total	1,138,625	343,774

Source: Data taken from HIAS publications, Israeli Consulate, and Union of Councils.

Although these large numbers of immigrants coming to the United States in the 1970s were prepared to leave the FSU, they were not prepared to start new lives in any new country, and they experienced significant culture shock and a difficult adjustment. For example, they did not know what social services were available to them as refugees in the United States. Many were afraid to apply for government aid ("black welfare" as they called it) because they feared it might negatively influence their professional future. They took any available job to survive and support their families. In contrast to the pre-1917 (prerevolution) Russian wave of immigration, this wave had a high proportion of college-educated professionals—engineers, teachers, physicians, nurses, scientists, artists, and musicians.

Most of the immigrants started working at low-paying non-professional jobs; they worked as housekeepers, windowwashers, taxidrivers, babysitters, and tailors. It was not unusual to find a high-level Russian physician or researcher working as a lab technician at a university vivarium, feeding rats. For many, this situation played not only a negative but also a positive role in their adjustment process. This wave did not rely on welfare support; they quickly learned English as well as the necessary survival skills. They made significant progress in professional retraining, eventually becoming financially successful. The average time of complete adjustment was 5 to 10 years—from initial contact to a confident and comfortable position in the American society (Frumkin, 1995a, 1995b, 1995c).

In 1979 and 1980, Soviet authorities changed their emigration policy and practically stopped emigration. Many who had applied for emigration or who had obtained the necessary invitations from Israel were denied permission to leave and joined the ranks of the *otkasniki*. The number of immigrants to the United States dwindled over the next several years (see Table 16–1).

The emigrants who had reached the United States served as an important source of information and education for the next wave of emigration, which began in 1988 with Gorbachev's policy of perestroika, glasnost, and democratic reforms. The first two years, 1988 and 1989, were similar to the Soviet emigration of the late 1970s, with most people coming to America. In October 1989, however, the United States changed its immigration policy, limiting the annual Soviet immigration to 50,000 (Gitelman, 1995). At the same time, the collapse of the Soviet political system, with its failing economy and rising social and ethnic tensions, pushed great numbers of emigrants from the Soviet Union, most going to Israel rather than the United States.

By 1992 to 1994, however, the total number of emigrants leaving FSU had declined and arrivals in the United States became steady—35,000 to 45,000 per year (Table 16–1). The decline continued in 1995 and 1996. Now, there are new factors influencing immigration. Except for those fleeing war zones (Tajikistan, Georgia, Chechnya, and other areas), individuals are leaving FSU today not out of a fear of immediate threats to their lives and freedom but because of prolonged political and economic crises, instability, and uncertainty about their future.

With Gorbachev's reforms, open borders, and availability of reliable information, FSU citizens are familiar with the conditions, available services, and privileges for immigrants as well as the limitations and difficulties in each country of possible immigration. Compared with earlier waves, there are fewer biases or unrealistic expectations in the decision-making process. Immigrants of the 1970s came to the United States after many years of total isolation and found everything to be surprising, new, and exciting. The immigrants of the 1990s are more knowledgeable about America and are less willing to accept low-paying, nonprofessional, or unskilled jobs.

Psychological Factors Influencing Resettlement of Russian Immigrant Families

It is difficult to understand the problems and treatment needs of Russian immigrants without some knowledge of their cultural, psychological, and political identity and values. The distinctive characteristics of this group are their primarily urban origins, high level of education, and professional identities.

The Jewish population of FSU is 98% urban, with most being from FSU's largest cities—Moscow, Leningrad (now St. Petersburg), Kiev, Odessa, Tashkent—although some come from small towns in Central Asia ("Bukhar Jews"). This is why they feel more comfortable and reside in large American cities: New York, Los Angeles, Chicago, Philadelphia, and San Francisco. They also prefer the most urban parts of each city; in the FSU, downtown was a prestigious area in which to live.

Employment is a critical issue for most FSU Jewish immigrants, who measure their success not by American criteria, but by Soviet standards. In the FSU, housing was always scarce and salaries were low, private businesses were nonexistent, owning a house in big cities was impossible, and people were not very differentiated by material possessions, wealth, or lifestyles. Employment, on the other hand, was universal, and in the majority of families both spouses were employed; there was no problem of unemployment. All efforts were invested in education and professional achievements.

Indeed, profession and work position were the key factors involved in identity and social status, and the main sources of self-esteem, stability, and emotional well-being. Thus, the inability to find an appropriate job in this country means not only financial hardship for these immigrants and their families but, perhaps more importantly, loss of social status, identity, self-confidence, and self-esteem. Unemployment is unacceptable for them.

Many had already achieved significant professional and financial stability in the FSU after decades of hard work and struggle, leaving behind high positions and the respect of coworkers, friends, and family. They may feel trapped, with no way back to the FSU. (In the 1970s, immigrants were not allowed to return; now it is theoretically possible.) The disappointment can give way to bitterness, suffering, clinical depression, and even suicidality.

Anecdotal experience suggests that middle-aged men experience more difficulties with the adjustment than do women. Men seem to have more difficulty accepting the change in status, whereas women are more flexible, learn the language faster, and are more likely to view their situation in the context of their children and grandchildren. This situation may dramatically change the family dynamics, shifting power and decision making from husband to wife and causing family conflicts.

Parenting styles of Russian immigrants are very close to traditional European practices and unlike current American parenting practices. Russian families emphasize early toilet training, impulse control, discipline, and education as a precondition for academic achievements and success later on in life. Russian Jewish parents, especially mothers, tend to be more controlling and protective of their children, less likely to encourage independence, and have more explicit, overt expectations for their children regarding academic achievements and professional training than do American parents.

Russian immigrant parents are fearful that children and grandchildren will become distant, emotionally cold, and less involved with the family and that the diminished sense of familial obligations, and parental authority will make the children prone to socially unacceptable behaviors, such as drug abuse, sexual promiscuity, and juvenile offenses.

Although Russian parents fear American values and child-rearing practices, Russian immigrant children of all ages find them immediately appealing. This can cause conflicts for the Russian child or adolescent whose peers may have more independence and less parental pressure.

Living situations can also be quite different for immigrants compared with those of most other Americans. Russian traditions, economic situations, and lack of housing frequently result in two or three family generations in the same apartment or home until the children grow up, finish their education, and get married. In Russia, it is not unusual for young married couples to live with their parents and grandparents for several years before they get a separate apartment and a more independent life. They are frequently dependent on their parents for financial support, as well, and on grandparents for babysitting for their young children.

On arriving in this country, Russian families frequently continue some of their customs and traditions while giving up others. For example, they will commonly rent one apartment for the entire family (two or three generations) to decrease their expenses and support each other; only later on, after a few years, do they get separate housing. On the other hand, parents generally do not insist on speaking the Russian language to their children and grandchildren. It is quite common that children who came to this country before entering school or elementary school do not speak, read, or write in Russian.

Russian parents (as well as their children) also actively accept American holidays and customs, including birthday celebrations, weddings, and funeral ceremonies. Whereas Russian Jewish immigrants are eager to give up some past customs to integrate into the mainstream American culture, they are very firm in keeping their own understanding of educational values, discipline, and family attachments and obligations.

Intergenerational Conflicts

Older children and adolescents frequently turn to peers for support and confidence and make themselves more distant from family problems. They sometimes lose respect for their parents who cannot learn English fast enough, find a decent job, establish themselves in the community, and provide for the family. They may lose confidence in their family's protective capacities.

As the adjustment and acculturation process progresses, the cultural differences between generations increase. Children, who acculturate more quickly, sometimes have difficulties with following the family's old rules and requirements for academic achievements as well as choice of profession. Conflicts about friends, sexual partners, appropriate social behaviors, and family obligations are common. These bicultural children demand more freedom and independence; at the same time they are comfortable with the "old customary" right to accept financial support from their parents and grandparents whose control they now reject. Their American counterparts are much more consistent in their search for independence, avoiding or feeling uncomfortable with their parents' financial support after separation from them.

The differences that emerge between grandparents and grandchildren are even more dramatic, they sometimes cannot communicate anymore: grandparents who did not learn English may be unable to communicate with grandchildren who do not speak Russian. The connection between generations gets thinner; the elderly feel lonely, abandoned, and isolated; grandchildren lose an important source of information and values. This deterioration in the connection between generations may contribute to the fact that Russian immigrant families are now placing their elderly in nursing homes at an increasing rate. Long-term care facilities for the elderly did not exist in Russia, because the elderly lived with their children until death.

Immigration and Education

Studies of immigrants by the RAND Corporation (Table 16–2) indicate that immigrant students as a whole are more likely to continue their education than U.S.-born youth. They also enjoy enhanced earning power once they enter the job market (Duran & Weffer, 1992; Vernez & Abrahamse, 1996).

These studies (Duran & Weffer, 1992; Kao & Tienda, 1995; Wilson & Justiz, 1988) are consistent with our observations on immigrants from the FSU. Russian children and their parents

TABLE 16–2
Percentage of High School Graduates Participating in Postsecondary Education (Participation Rates)

	Any Postsecondary Education		2- and 4-Year College		At Least 42 Months of College	
	Native	Immigrant	Native	Immigrant	Native	Immigrant
All	65	74	60	68	16	22
Asian	81	86	79	84	33	29
Black	62	73	55	59	11	17
Hispanic	52	70	45	65	8	18
White	67	72	62	67	18	23

Source. Data from Vernez & Abrahamse, 1996.

continue to value education as the main basis for success later in life. Most children plan to attend college after graduating from high school.

Many Russian immigrant parents are disappointed with the American school system through high school, as they feel there is a significant lack of discipline and structure. In contrast, college education and professional training are considered much better and efficient in the United States than in the FSU. The Soviet immigrants of the 1970s were unfamiliar with the American school system, and they sent their children to available public schools. The immigrants of the 1990s are much better informed and educated about available school options: They send their eligible children to magnet schools, and obtain scholarships to private schools; they make all possible efforts to provide the best educational opportunities for their children. In general, Russian immigrant children experience language and academic difficulties in their first 2 to 3 years (depending on age); however, they eventually catch up and demonstrate good performance in high school and college. Children's accomplishments are of great importance to Russian families and may become either a source of pride or of additional stress and intrafamilial conflicts.

Identity Issues

For Russian immigrants, identity formation is complicated by several factors. Besides the usual stresses of immigration to a new country, Russian immigrant children must also struggle with their position in three cultures—Russian, Jewish, and American. They did not know Jewish culture, language, or religion in the FSU; they consider their Jewish identity as a nationality, a genetic and biological makeup rather than a culture or religion. Indeed, in Russia and FSU being Jewish was regarded as a nationality—not a religion.

"Jewish" was written in the Soviet passport under "paragraph 5—nationality" and served as the main reason for different kinds of discrimination. However, after coming to the United States, they are considered "Russian." This causes considerable confusion, as they are expected to join Jewish communities in countries of immigration and feel more comfortable with the very identity that was always a source of suffering. Furthermore, the American Jewish communities find them "not Jewish enough": Most Russian and FSU immigrants do not know and do not observe Jewish customs and traditions; they are not religious and attend synagogue only occasionally; some are indifferent to their Jewish identity. Their political beliefs also differ from those of the traditionally liberal, American Jewish community. After years of disappointment with Soviet socialism, they are conservative and their political and social beliefs are out of step with those of their Jewish American brethren.

After settling in the United States, some young people try to accelerate their learning about Jewish culture. They start to attend temples, The University of Judaism, and other Jewish institutions. However, very soon they find it difficult to maintain religious studies and customs (e.g., keeping kosher) that their families do not follow. Teenagers feel different from American Jewish adolescents who may know a great deal about Judaism and religious Jewish requirements. Russian immigrant children usually learn a minimum of Jewish history and keep only some Jewish holidays and customs.

Russian immigrant children try to give up their Russian identity. Anti-Semitic forces, always very strong in Russia, may have forced their families to emigrate from FSU. They have memories of being constantly reminded that they do not belong to Russian (Ukrainian, Belorussian, etc.) culture, of being blamed for the destruction of Russian culture, and for various failures in Russian history and economy. Although these children may feel that emigration marks the end of their Russian identity, most of them discover that it is impossible simply to give up a culture of several previous generations. Instead, it is a long and complicated process that will take several or many generations to complete.

Many Russian immigrant adolescents seek a fast transition to a new American identity, encouraged by their families. There are no Russian schools and most immigrant children, especially those of younger age who did not learn how to read or write in Russian before coming to the United States, quickly give up this language and English becomes their primary language. They want to speak without accent, and dress and behave like American youth, so they can make friends among American children as soon as possible. Frequently, they succeed in all these tasks but one. Intimate relationships between Russian immigrant and American native adolescents and young adults are often unsuccessful due to significant differences in relationship values.

Russian immigrant adolescents may feel uncomfortable in intimate relationships and quickly terminate them. This can be a great source of frustration, depression, social isolation, and loss of self-esteem for young Russian immigrants who attempted to give up their Russian identity completely. Some may not have easy access to other young Russians because their family resides in an area with primarily American, Asian, or Hispanic population. By the age of 18 or 19 some of them become depressed, pessimistic, and hopeless regarding their ability to find a partner, marry, and have a family life. At this point, they frequently turn back to the Russian community, and to their previous Russian identity, in search of a close friend, sexual partner, or spouse. Others continue denying their Russian identity, remaining lonely and isolated.

Mental Health Issues

The relationship between immigration and mental health problems remains unclear. Indeed, there are reports of both increased and unchanged rates of mental health problems in immigrant children (Boyle et al., 1987; Bradley & Sloman, 1975; Kim & Chun, 1993).

In general, recent studies of immigrant children, using more sophisticated methodology than older studies, do not find significant differences in prevalence of mental health problems among immigrant and nonimmigrant groups. Family dysfunction, poverty, subsidized housing and older child age appear to be risk factors for psychiatric disorder (Munroe-Blum, Boyle, Offord, & Kates, 1989; Murphy, 1977; Rutter, Berger, et al., 1974; Steinhausen, 1985). Hicks, Lalonde, and Pepler (1993) review recent empirical research on issues related to adaptive experiences of immigrant and refugee children. They indicate that although all migrating children experience stresses associated with change and their adjustment to a new country, the hypothesis that these stresses invariably lead to higher rates of emotional problems and maladaptive behaviors cannot be supported.

Instead, research indicates that various adaptive experiences develop in the process of adjustment with outcomes determined by a combination of risk and protective factors (Kopala, Esquivel, & Baptiste, 1994). This is also true for Russian immigrant children. The extreme stresses of the first years of immigration lead to development of adaptive, protective behaviors in most children. According to our observations, family dysfunction in situations of recent immigration becomes the most important stress that may contribute to maladaptive behaviors and psychopathology in 8- to 12-year-old children. In older children, 13 to 16 years old, relationships with classmates, acceptance or rejection by peer groups, and school failures become the more frequent risk factors for psychiatric disorder and behavioral problems.

There are no systematic studies of psychiatric disorders in Russian immigrant children. Clinical experience of the senior author, suggests that each age group may differentially manifest disorders related to immigration. Younger children (2–5 years old) may develop physical symptoms including asthma, tics, or gastrointestinal distress as a reaction to stresses and changes in their environment. In 6- to 10-year-old children, separation anxiety, overanxious disorder, or oppositional behavior may be more common. Adjustment disorders, depression, and behavioral problems may be more frequently diagnosed in adolescents.

Alcohol and drug abuse and dependence are less prevalent in the Russian immigrant community than in American communities. However, recreational use of alcohol and marijuana is now common among Russian adolescents and young adults. Substance dependence is seen more often in 1970s immigrants than in the more recent wave of Russian immigrants (1980s and 1990s). Our interviews of Russian families indicate several possible reasons for this finding:

- The 1970s immigrants were under more stress, and parents who were preoccupied with survival issues were not able to focus on their children; children became "the forgotten victims of immigration."
- Parents were relatively unaware of widespread drug use in schools in this country.
- Parents did not understand the school system and did not attempt to find schools with better environments for their children, as later immigrants did.

Utilization of Mental Health and Social Services

Russian immigrant children do not use mental health and social services as would be expected based on the size of this population. There are several reasons for this apparent underutilization. In the former Soviet Union, mental health care was avoided because of shame and stigma associated with such illnesses. It was also dangerous to be officially under psychiatric care, as this information would follow the patient throughout adult life. A history of treatment for a mental disorder might prevent a person from obtaining education, a chosen job, or even a driver's license. Many colleges and organizations refused to take students and employees who had been seen by psychiatrists and found to have mental disorders.

This was especially true for those diagnosed as schizophrenic, which was widely (and excessively) diagnosed by some schools of Soviet psychiatrists from 1950 until 1980. In view of these factors, only seriously disturbed children and adolescents were referred for psychiatric care in Russia.

From the 1930s through the 1970s, some forms of psychological testing were prohibited by Soviet authorities, including tests assessing intellectual functioning (IQ testing). In Russia, learning disorders were not diagnosed or treated; sometimes children with learning disorders were included in the mental retardation category, which had only a descriptive and qualitative definition. In Russia and FSU, psychotherapies were under developed, and some types were prohibited or discouraged for political reasons, such as psychoanalysis and psychodynamic psychotherapy; indeed, literature on these therapies was not available. The major treatment interventions used by psychiatrists were medication, insulin shock, and long-term hospitalization.

After immigration in this country Russian immigrants continue to underutilize mental health and social services. Children and adolescents who use mental health services have been found to be more severely disturbed than their American counterparts. Russian American parents believe more in medication and other biological treatments and fail to understand the potential benefit of the psychotherapies, especially family and group therapies. When their children are severely disturbed, they expect long-term hospitalization and treatment with injectable medications.

The lack of Russian-speaking mental health professionals (psychiatrists, psychologists, social workers) is another reason for the low utilization of these services by Russian immigrant children. Even children who now speak English better than Russian feel more natural and comfortable with therapists who can understand their family's background and cultural issues. It is even more important for their parents, who may experience difficulties describing behaviors and symptoms of disorders in English.

Conclusion

To define the prevalence of mental disorders and specific mental health needs in immigrants from the former Soviet Union and other European countries, more systematic studies are warranted. Clinical research in transcultural psychiatry and psychology of these populations may help not only to reveal specific problems for each ethnic group but also to develop better methods of diagnosis and treatment.

Education of this population on issues of contemporary psychiatry, available legal rights, services, and treatment modalities will help them to better use these services and achieve beneficial outcomes.

Mental health professionals who work with immigrant children must educate themselves about cultural backgrounds, reactions, and attitudes of these groups. Training programs should expose trainees to transcultural issues so that clinicians will be better able to serve this population.

References

BOARD ON CHILDREN AND FAMILIES. (1995). Immigrant children and their families: Issues for research and policy. *Future of Children, 5*(2), 72–89.

BORJAS, G. J. (1994). The economics of immigration. *Journal of Economic Literature, 32*(4), 1667–1717.

BOYLE, M. H., OFFORD, D. R., HOFMANN, H. G., CATEIN, G. P., BYLES, J. A., CADMAN, D. T., CRAWFORD, J. W., LINKS, P. S., RAE-GRANT, N., & SZATMARI, P. (1987). Ontario child health study: 1. Methodology. *Archives of General Psychiatry, 44,* 826–831.

BRADLEY, S., & SLOMAN, L. (1975). Elective mutism in immigrant families. *Journal of the American Academy of Child Psychiatry, 14,* 510–514.

DURAN, B. J., & WEFFER, R. E. (1992). Immigrant's aspirations, high school process, and academic outcomes. *American Educational Research Journal, 29*(1), 163–181.

FRUMKIN, S. (1995a, July 26). From Moscow to Mercedes. *Almanac Panorama.*

FRUMKIN, S. (1995b, August 18). So what was your American problem? *Almanac Panorama.*

FRUMKIN, S. (1995c, August 31). European reflections: American wannabes. *Almanac Panorama.*

GITELMAN, Z. (1995). *Immigration and identity: The resettlement and impact of Soviet immigrants on Israeli politics and society.* Los Angeles: The Susan and David Wilstein Institute of Jewish Policy Studies.

HICKS, R., LALONDE, R. N., & PEPLER, D. (1993). Psychosocial considerations in the mental health of immigrant and refugee children. Cultural diversity: Voice, access, and involvement [Special issue]. *Canadian Journal of Community Mental Health, 12*(2), 71–87.

KAO, G., & TIENDA, M. (1995). Optimism and achievement: The educational performance of immigrant youth. *Social Science Quarterly,* 76(1).

KIM, L. S., & CHUN, C. A. (1993). Ethnic differences in psychiatric diagnosis among Asian American adolescents. *Journal of Nervous and Mental Disease, 18*(10), 612–617.

KOPALA, M., ESQUIVEL, G., & BAPTISTE, L. (1994). Counseling approaches for immigrant children: Facilitating the acculturative process. *School Counselor, 41*(5), 352–359.

LARRABEE, F. S. (1993). *Eastern Europe and East-West migration* (DRU-566-FF). Santa Monica, CA: Rand.

MUNROE-BLUM, H., BOYLE, M. H., OFFORD, D. R., & KATES, N. (1989). Immigrant children: Psychiatric disorder, school performance, and service utilization. *American Journal of Orthopsychiatry, 59*(4), 510–520.

MURPHY, H. B. M. (1977). Migration, culture and mental health. *Psychological Medicine, 7,* 677–684.

RUTTER, M., YULE, W., BERGER, M., et al. (1974). Children of West Indian immigrants: 1. Rates of behavioral deviance and of psychiatric disorders. *Journal of Child Psychiatry, 15,* 241–262.

STEINHAUSEN, H. C. (1985). Psychiatric disorders in children and family dysfunction. *Social Psychiatry, 20,* 11–16.

VERNEZ, G., & ABRAHAMSE, A. (1996). *How immigrants fare in U.S. education* (MR-718-AMF). Santa Monica, CA: Rand.

WILSON, R., & JUSTIZ, M. J. (1988). Minorities in higher education: Confronting a time bomb. *Educational Record, 68,* 9–14.

PART III

CULTURE AND ASSESSMENT

CHAPTER 17

The Culturologic Interview

Cultural, Social, and Linguistic Issues in the Assessment and Treatment of Children

GLORIA JOHNSON-POWELL

CULTURE PROVIDES THE CONTEXT or environment in which various behaviors are developed and expressed. Thus, behavior is learned in a social context. The earliest and most enduring learning experience occurs in the household in which the infant is reared; such culturally patterned behavior emerges during the first months of life. The early influence of cultural learning on later development is discussed in Chapter 2 and in the Preface, which emphasize contextual variations and their importance in the diagnostic assessment of children from different cultural backgrounds (Canino, 1996; Canino & Canino, 1992; Canino & Spurlock, 1994; Johnson-Powell, 1996).

The absence of well-being is expressed in diverse ways among different cultural groups. Chapter 2 discusses the research that has established the many cultural ways of expressing illness or discomfort and how psychiatric symptoms in part reflect culturally learned behavior. Consequently, cultural attitudes and beliefs often determine the type of help sought by parents for their children as well as the meaning given to the child's symptoms by family members (Canino & Canino, 1992). This chapter provides some guidelines to the diagnostic assessment and treatment of culturally and linguistically diverse children as presented in this book, as well as in the research literature.

The prevalence of childhood dysfunction differs according to age, sex, type of disorder, ethnic background, and geographic region (Kazdin, 1989). Data from research in developmental psychopathology indicate some particular difficulties in identifying childhood psychopathology such as the following: (a) Problem behavior in children may change from one setting to another; (b) problem behavior may be a concern of the parent, but may not be a sign of psychopathology; (c) each child may react to stressors in different ways; (d) problem behavior often differs from one age period to another (Johnson-Powell, 1996). Most importantly, psychopathology in children must be considered along the developmental continuum of childhood.

Because parental information regarding function is crucial, particularly for young children, multiple sources of data are needed and should not be based solely on one observation or informant (Canino, 1996). A comprehensive assessment requires information from the school, the parents, significant family members, and the child; and it must also include the cultural factors related to the psychosocial environment, the cultural identity, and the cultural explanation or meanings given to the child's symptoms or behavior. The cultural assessment then becomes an essential part of the diagnostic process. This book provides an overview of the historical backgrounds and cultural contexts that created the American mosaic in order to indicate the broader sociocultural context in which all children live regardless of ethnic/racial or cultural background.

Three major axioms must be considered in the child mental health assessment process:

1. Boys are different from girls in that boys seem to be at higher risk for developmental and behavioral problems than girls (Offord, Boyle, & Szatmari, 1987).

2. Each child has his or her own way of interacting with the environment, which is most often defined as temperament.
3. A mental health assessment of a child begins with a comprehensive medical examination that includes vision and hearing screening and very often a speech and language evaluation if the child is 10 years old or younger.

Also, it must be remembered that disordered behavior among children has rarely been studied outside Western societies (Johnson-Powell, 1996). Likewise, temperament and behavior in children have not been studied systematically cross-culturally, but significant data implicate culture as a major variable in personality development (Foulks, 1996). Table 17–1 provides an outline of the culturologic interview to use in the formulation of strategies for interviewing culturally different clients.

To enter the world of the client, the clinician *must be familiar with cultural nuances and expressions, cultural beliefs and attitudes, as well as norms and mores.* Clinicians who have not been exposed to such information should make a concerted effort to become more knowledgeable about cultural anthropology and ethnic groups. It will be difficult to know everything about all groups, but sometimes it is helpful to ask the client to describe acceptable and unacceptable behavior and the religious and cultural beliefs that support certain behaviors or practices. This process helps to

TABLE 17–1
Culturologic Interview

---

1. Enter the world of the client.
2. Shape the content and context of the interview.
3. Make the client comfortable.
4. Decrease the social distance.
5. Increase the perception of sameness.
6. Elicit as much information as possible at each contact depending on the level of comfort.

---

shape the content, context, and purpose of the interview and may also help the client feel comfortable. With some basic knowledge about cultural beliefs and interpersonal interactions, the interviewer can then make the effort to decrease the social distance between the client and the interviewer. Learning some greetings in the client's language can help increase the perception of sameness. The client may then begin to perceive and believe that although the interviewer is culturally different and even speaks a different language, there is still some common ground to build a relationship of understanding. Additionally, everywhere in the world, parents are always appreciative of a clinician's interest in their children. Listening carefully in a receptive manner can go a long way to strengthen the perception that the interviewer understands cultural beliefs and practices and is not disdainful of the client's mores and norms.

Table 17–2 gives an outline of the data that need to be obtained during the contact with the client. Chapter 3 through 16 will help the reader to discern the kind of data that should be generated in the interviews over the course of time from many ethnic/racial or cultural groups; space did not permit inclusion of all the cultural groups in the United States that the interviewer or clinician may encounter. In addition to the data outlined in Table 17–2, it is recommended that the clinician elicit the following information:

1. Socioeconomic status.
2. Degree of language proficiency.
3. Educational attainment.
4. Reason for immigration and the time of arrival in the United States (i.e., the wave of immigration with which the family was associated, see Chapter 1).
5. Length of residence in the United States or in the region of the country, including the number of times the family has moved from country of origin to the United States or from one region to another.
6. Information about resources and family support.
7. Proximity to their own cultural group and other cultural groups.

TABLE 17–2
Important Data

---

1. Country of origin
2. Reason for migration
3. Length of time in this country
4. Number of generations in this country
5. Languages spoken
   When and where?
   Predominant
6. Family and kinship network
7. Religious beliefs and beliefs about causality
8. Child-rearing practices
9. Sex roles
10. Kind of community (e.g., diverse ethnic/racial composition or same ethnic/racial community; rural, suburban, urban; residential or commercial; high or low crime rate; degree of community cohesiveness etc.)
11. Life space (what does the individual see or experience in day-to-day life—e.g., numbers of rooms in household; number of occupants in home; number of children and number of adults; single family house or multiple dwelling; utilities)
12. Overt and covert reasons for seeking help
13. Description of help-seeking behavior
14. Educational attainment
    Country of origin
    Country of residence
15. Current and former occupation
16. Experiences with rejection (e.g., racism)
17. Degree of acculturation (e.g., food, dress, social activities)
18. Degree of cultural conflicts

The landmarks of normal psychological development and the typical signs of psychological development are included to provide a guide to the clinician about the kinds of behaviors throughout childhood and adolescence that may be important in the diagnostic assessment (see Table 17–3). Clinicians should use

TABLE 17–3

A Guide to Diagnostic Assessment of Childhood Behaviors

Landmarks of Normal Psychological Development	Typical Signs of Psychological Disturbance
Birth to 1 Month	Birth to 1 Month
	1. Holds head up in prone position
	*2. Anticipatory behavior at feeding
	3. Visual fixation and visual following beyond the midline
	4. Stops crying with novel stimulus, holding, or rocking
	5. Intact vigorous sucking activity in regular bursts
	6. Alert response to light and sound
	7. Begins to play after feeding
8. Holds on with hands to whatever is available during early part of feeding	1. Failure to gain weight
	2. Excessive spitting up
	3. No eye contact
	4. Failure to hold head up
	5. Failure to show anticipatory behavior at feeding
	6. Failure to hold on with hands
7. Ticlike movements of face and head	2 to 3 Months
2 to 3 Months	*1. Social smile with mother, with stranger, and with face mask
	2. Social games ending with smile
	3. Oral imitation (cough game)
	4. Controls breast or bottle with hands
	5. Midline hand use
	6. Prolonged visual tracking

Landmarks of Normal Psychological Development	Typical Signs of Psychological Disturbance
7 to 9 Months	**7 to 9 Months**
1. Mild separation anxiety	1. Persistent sleep problems
2. Subtlety in affect and motor response and in smile	2. Eating problems (e.g., refusing to use hands or hold glass very limited diet)
3. "Dada" or "Mama"	3. Unpatterned sleep and eating (lack of predictability)
4. Hand use	4. Lack of imitation of simple sounds, gestures, or facial expressions
5. Use of "executive finger" (extended index finger in touching and exploring objects)	5. Lack of affect
	6. Bizarre play
	7. Low socialization
	8. Lack of distress with stranger
	9. Excessive self-stimulation and self-destructive behavior
	10. Rumination (i.e., swallowing of regurgitated food)
	11. Withholding BMs
	12. Apathy
	13. Anaclitic depression (grief over a significant caretaker or lack of a consistent caretaker)
10 to 15 Months	**10 to 15 Months**
1. Walks	1. No words
2. Reaches out for, grasps, and manipulates familiar and strange objects	2. Sleep problem
3. Attentive to parent	3. Withdrawn behavior
4. Stops and then goes ahead while saying "no"	4. Excessive rocking, posturing
5. Play and imitation increases	5. Bizarre play
6. Problem solving and investigation increase	6. No separation distress
	7. Night wandering
	8. Excessive distractibility
	9. Bowel disturbance

(continued)

TABLE 17–3 (Continued)

Landmarks of Normal Psychological Development	Typical Signs of Psychological Disturbance
16 Months to 2 Years	**16 Months to 2 Years**
1. Says "no" and responds to "no" 2. Use of about 20 words 3. Primary feminine identification, both girls and boys (e.g., interest in dress, shoes, baby) 4. Separates from parents and reports back 5. Microcosmic play (solitary play with small objects) 6. Imitation of vocal inflection 7. Enjoys and makes use of new experience when conditions are optimal	1. No speech 2. Excessive body rocking 3. Inappropriate play 4. Withholding and other bowel problems 5. Sleep disturbance 6. Retarded development or persistent regression
25 Months to 3 Years	**25 Months to 4 Years**
*1. Parallel play (appropriate play alongside peers) (2½ years) 2. Collateral peer play (3 years) 3. Bedtime ritual (including transitional object) 4. Cooperative play (4 years) 5. Two- and three-word speech (use of speech as a tool to make things happen) (2 years) 6. Creative use of speech (for reflection and organization) (3 to 4 years) 7. Successful toilet training (2 to 2½ years) 8. Accepts reasonable limits (2 to ½ years) 9. Special skills and talents (3 to 4 years) 10. Talks to self (2½ years) 11. "What's this?" (in reference to new objects)	1. Disturbed sleep, animal dreams 2. Persistent soiling and wetting 3. Persistent eating problems 4. Nonspeaking (beyond 18 months) 5. Inappropriate play 6. Fears of dark, ghosts, burglars; shyness 7. Excessive body rocking, finger sucking, and tics

Landmarks of Normal Psychological Development	Typical Signs of Psychological Disturbance
37 Months to 4 Years	
*1. Cooperative play with peers	
2. Sibling truce	
3. Creative use of speech: "3-year prose"	
4. Special skills and talents (e.g., painting, manipulative skills, dance, music)	
5. Some leadership capacity in group	
5 to 7 Years	**5 to 7 Years**
*1. Capacity for group orientation and membership	1. Bowel and urinary problems
2. At ease away from home for part of day (some concern at night)	2. Lying
3. Interest in father's work	3. Persistent fearfulness regarding school, other children, and new situations
4. Early learning skills; knows right from wrong in categorical terms	4. Finickiness with food
5. Can play catch well and solve simple puzzles	5. Persistent phobias
6. More detailed dreams (silly and complicated)	6. Open masturbation or sexual exploration (should normally be private and with consenting peer group members)
7. Interest in procreation	7. Overdependence
8. Ambitious; goal-oriented	8. Fire setting
9. Has clear preferences for friends, TV, clothes, activities, and use of free time	9. Pseudomaturity
10. Appropriate sex identity is clear	10. Running away
	11. Nonadaptive neatness
	12. Persistent thumb-sucking
	13. Strange, bizarre, or withdrawn behavior
	14. Uncommunicativeness
	15. Cruelty to animals
	16. No friends
	17. Lack of interest in appearance or development of skills
	18. Disturbed sleep and frightening dreams
	19. Persistently upset by changes
	20. Excessive clinging to transitional objects

(continued)

357

TABLE 17–3 (Continued)

Landmarks of Normal Psychological Development	Typical Signs of Psychological Disturbance
8 to 10 Years	**8 to 10 Years**
*1. Learns to read and enjoys reading (by third grade)	1. Running away
*2. Has special friends of same sex	2. School failure
3. Belongs to group of friends	3. No friends
4. Knows rules of games and enforces them	4. Persistent fears
5. Can cooperate and help with family plans and activities, including care of siblings	5. Withdrawal
6. Uses scientific observation approach to new situations	6. Persistent finickiness with food
7. Enjoys travel	7. Immaturity
8. Knows right from wrong, with some contingencies and conditions	8. Pseudomaturity
9. Shuns identification with opposite sex	9. Nonadaptive obsessional behavior
10. Tells truth or avoids speaking rather than tell a lie	10. Recurrent nightmares
	11. Language and speech problems
	12. Toileting and bowel problems
	13. Failure to recuperate following physical illness
	14. Hallucinations
	15. Tics
11 to 13 Years	
*1. Peer group identification	
2. One or two close friends	
3. Capacity to joke, be silly, and play with double meanings in language	
4. Experiences events more intensely and more personally and, therefore, shows moodiness	
5. Academic performance may regress for a year or so	

Landmarks of Normal Psychological Development	Typical Signs of Psychological Disturbance
	11 to 16 Years
	1. Depression
	2. Antisocial behavior
	3. Suicidal attempts or rumination
	4. Use of dangerous drugs
	5. Truancy from school
	6. School failure
	7. Reversal of value systems (rather than testing value)
	8. No friends or personal interests
	9. Promiscuous sexual behavior
	10. Anorexia or obesity
	11. Avoidance
	12. Persistence of conforming or passive behavior
	13. Lack of interest in future
	14. Sudden total personality change or deterioration in mental functioning
	15. Acute phobia or obsessional behavior
	16. Excessive bodily preoccupation
	17. Persistent somatic complaints without organic disease
	18. Regressive behavior
14 to 16 Years	
1. Increased intellectual and physical ability	
2. Renewed interest in language	
3. Increasing interest in the wider world and social issues: liberal attitudes with conservative action	
*4. Beginning interest and ease with opposite sex	

(continued)

TABLE 17-3 (Continued)

Landmarks of Normal Psychological Development	Typical Signs of Psychological Disturbance
17 to 19 Years	17 to 19 Years
1. Sexual interests consolidate *2. Short-term educational or occupational choices are made	1. Obsessional neurosis 2. Phobia 3. Suicidal behavior 4. Mental deterioration 5. Depression 6. Use of dangerous drugs 7. Sexual promiscuity 8. Delinquency 9. School failure 10. Persistent regressive episodes

*Most significant psychological achievement for this age period.

caution in that these behaviors conform to Western nosological considerations and may apply to fully acculturated clients, but not to those who are still in various stages of acculturation. The assessment process should yield the kind of data described in Table 17–4 in order to begin consideration of the diagnostic categories in the *Diagnostic and Statistical Manual of Mental Disorders* (*DSM-IV*; APA, 1994).

Canino (1996) found that Axis IV of the *DSM-IV*, the Severity of Psychosocial Stressors, and Axis V, the Global Assessment of Functioning (GAF), are essential components of the classification of culturally diverse children and asserted that the diversity in symptom expression and the multiple cultural pathways in developmental psychopathology often result in over diagnosis on Axis I and Axis II. Canino and Canino (1992) have observed that psychiatric epidemiological surveys in different parts of the world have shown higher rates of psychiatric disorders for children and adolescents than reported previously and suggest such higher rates may be due to overinclusiveness of the *DSM* classification system for children and adolescents. In the Puerto Rico epidemiology study, 49.5% of children and adolescents met the criteria for a *DSM* disorder, which was highly unlikely (Canino, 1996; Canino & Zayas, this volume). With further scrutiny of the data, it was found that many Puerto Rican children who met *DSM* criteria were (a) not in need of psychiatric treatment (b) were not severely impaired when the Global Assessment of Functioning (GAF) was used, and (c) the seemingly high prevalence of psychiatric morbidity could reflect the higher levels of stress.

All the chapters indicate that child-rearing practices, tolerance of behaviors, cultural differences in help-seeking behaviors, and the expression of the lack of well-being differ from one cultural group to another. Consequently, there is great variation in symptom selection, the remission and exacerbation of symptoms, diagnosis, and prognosis. Thus, the cultural and clinical perspectives need to be balanced in making a *DSM-IV* diagnosis. Indeed, the research on psychopathology indicates the need for a corrective factor to balance the implicit assumption

TABLE 17–4
Items to Include in Clinical Case Reviews

I. Clinical history
   A. Patient identification
   B. History of present illness
   C. Psychiatric history and previous treatment
   D. Social and developmental history
   E. Family history
   F. Course and outcome
   G. Diagnostic formulation (Axes I-V)
II. Cultural formulation
   A. Cultural identity
      1. Cultural reference group(s)
      2. Language
      3. Cultural factors in development
      4. Involvement with culture of origin
      5. Involvement with host culture
   B. Cultural explanations of the illness
      1. Predominant idioms of distress and local illness categories
      2. Meaning and severity of symptoms in relation to cultural norms
      3. Perceived causes and explanatory models
      4. Help-seeking experiences and plans
   C. Cultural factors related to psychosocial environment and levels of functioning
      1. Social stressors
      2. Social supports
      3. Levels of functioning and disability
   D. Cultural elements of the clinician-patient relationship
   E. Overall cultural assessment

that abnormal behavior everywhere is similar in scope and kind (Johnson-Powell, 1996).

Finally and most importantly, transcultural child psychiatry is concerned about the impact of cultural beliefs and practices on the development of psychopathology among children. Such cultural beliefs and practices extend to child-rearing practices, the relationship of the child to the caregiver, and the caregiver's transmission of the cultural values and beliefs. When socialization occurs in a society in which the culture of the child is different from that of the dominant society, the process of socialization and acculturation may be very stressful for children and their families. Also, children in a multicultural environment may respond to the amalgamation of cultural values and behaviors and may exchange or alternate values, beliefs, and behaviors of the country of origin with that of the dominant group. If human social and cognitive development is perceived as the confluence of many interrelated changing systems and subsystems—biological, social, cultural, and historical—clinicians can expect that there will be differences in developmental styles and presentations of psychological stress and dysfunction among children and adolescents that are not currently in the *DSM-IV* as human diversity in this country increases.

References

CANINO, G. (1996). Cultural comments on childhood-onset disorders: I. In J. E. Mezzich, A. Kleinman, H. Fabrega, & D. L. Parron (Eds.), *Culture and psychiatric diagnosis: A DSM-IV perspective*. Washington, DC: American Psychiatric Press.

CANINO, G., & CANINO, I. A. (1992). *Childhood disorders: Supporting paper*. Paper presented to the NIMH Culture and Diagnosis Group.

CANINO, I. A., & SPURLOCK, J. (1994). *Culturally diverse children and adolescents: Assessment, diagnosis and treatment*. New York: Guilford Press.

FOULKS, E. F. (1996). Culture and personality disorders. In J. E. Mezzich, A. Kleinman, H. Fabrega, & D. L. Parron (Eds.), *Culture and psychiatric diagnosis: A DSM-IV perspective*. Washington, DC: American Psychiatric Press.

JOHNSON-POWELL, G. (1996). Cultural and ethnic considerations in the *DSM-IV* diagnosis and classification of childhood-onset disorders. In J. E. Mezzich, A. Kleinman, H. Fabrega, & D. L. Parron (Eds.), *Culture and psychiatric diagnosis: A DSM-IV perspective*. Washington, DC: American Psychiatric Press.

KAZDIN, A. E. (1989). Developmental psychopathology: Current research, issues, and directions. *American Psychologist, 44*(2), 180–187.

OFFORD, D. R., BOYLE, M. H., & SZATMARI, P. (1987). Ontario child health study: II. Six month prevalence of disorder and rates of services utilization. *Archives General Psychiatry, 44*, 832–836.

Index